SOUTH ASIAN ATLANTIC LITERATURE, 1970–2010

EDINBURGH STUDIES IN TRANSATLANTIC LITERATURES
Series Editors: Susan Manning and Andrew Taylor

Modern global culture makes it clear that literary study can no longer operate on nation-based or exceptionalist models. In practice, American literatures have always been understood and defined in relation to the literatures of Europe and Asia. The books in this series work within a broad comparative framework to question place-based identities and monocular visions, in historical contexts from the earliest European settlements to contemporary affairs, and across all literary genres. They explore the multiple ways in which ideas, texts, objects and bodies travel across spatial and temporal borders, generating powerful forms of contrast and affinity. The Edinburgh Studies in Transatlantic Literatures series fosters new paradigms of exchange, circulation and transformation for transatlantic literary studies, expanding the critical and theoretical work of this rapidly developing field.

Titles in the series include:

Ethnicity and Cultural Authority: From Arnold to Du Bois, Daniel G. Williams

Henry James, Oscar Wilde and Aesthetic Culture, Michèle Mendelssohn

American Modernism's Expatriate Scene: The Labour of Translation, Daniel Katz

The Dandy in Irish and American Southern Fiction: Aristocratic Drag, Ellen Crowell

Philanthropy in British and American Fiction: Dickens, Hawthorne, Eliot, and Howells, Frank Christianson

Transatlantic Women's Literature, Heidi Slettedahl Macpherson

Cultural Authority in the Age of Whitman: A Transatlantic Perspective, Günter Leypoldt

Mercenaries in British and American Literature, 1790–1830: Writing, Fighting, and Marrying for Money, Erik Simpson

Spanish America and British Romanticism, 1777–1826: Rewriting Conquest, Rebecca Cole Heinowitz

Transnationalism in Practice: Essays on American Studies, Literature and Religion, Paul Giles

South Asian Atlantic Literature, 1970–2010, Ruth Maxey

Visit the Edinburgh Studies in Transatlantic Literature web site at www.euppublishing.com/series/estl

SOUTH ASIAN ATLANTIC LITERATURE, 1970–2010

◆ ◆ ◆

RUTH MAXEY

EDINBURGH UNIVERSITY PRESS

For my parents, with love and thanks

Edinburgh University Press Ltd
22 George Square, Edinburgh

www.euppublishing.com

Typeset in 11/13 Baskerville MT
by Servis Filmsetting Ltd, Stockport, Cheshire, and
printed and bound in the United States of America

A CIP record for this book is available from the British Library

ISBN 978 0 7486 4188 8 (hardback)

CONTENTS

ACKNOWLEDGEMENTS

Many people have helped me in the years leading up to the completion of this book, which has its origins in my PhD dissertation. I owe a large debt to my two PhD supervisors at University College London (UCL). Kasia Boddy was enthusiastic in getting the project off the ground and was giving of her time, ideas, and books. Hugh Stevens was a tower of strength in the latter stages of the PhD, showing me unfailing kindness and sensitivity, offering invaluable advice at key moments, giving insightful feedback on my work, and providing a listening ear. Above all, he always behaved as if nothing was too much trouble. I am extremely grateful for the constant support he provided.

Melissa Zeiger at Dartmouth College provided crucial early suggestions for how to shape my research, kindly volunteered to read my work, and helped me to improve it. At UCL, Danny Karlin enabled me to study in the department in the first place, where I received funding to attend several international conferences and the opportunity to teach undergraduates. Within the graduate community itself, John Morton was consistently supportive. Susheila Nasta and Ruvani Ranasinha examined my PhD, providing useful and incisive feedback. During my undergraduate studies at Oxford, my tutors, Margaret Kean and the late Julia Briggs, also offered encouragement and inspiration; while Charlotte Brewer, in particular, consistently supported and engaged with me. Indeed, it was her belief that I should pursue academic research which first put the idea in my mind. Even further back, Helen Gillard and Patricia Lancaster had faith in my abilities and were instrumental in my decision to study English literature at degree level.

A number of other people have helped me while I was researching and writing this book. Meena Alexander agreed to be interviewed, gave freely of her time, and was always prepared to explore ideas with me. Amit Chaudhuri and Professor Supriya Chaudhuri were generous with their suggestions and time. Lars Ole Sauerberg published my first article and kindly agreed to act as a referee. More recently, I wish to thank Jackie Jones at Edinburgh University Press – and Susan Manning and Andrew Taylor, the Edinburgh Studies in Transatlantic Literatures series editors – for accepting this book for publication and for being so helpful and positive throughout the writing and submission process. Comments from the Press's two anonymous readers sharpened and improved the book in many ways and I am grateful to them for their time and input.

I could not have completed this study without the sabbatical granted me by the School of American and Canadian Studies at Nottingham University, for which I offer sincere thanks; and I would like to acknowledge the intellectual and emotional support given to me by a number of colleagues and friends in the School, particularly Judie Newman, Helen Oakley, Celeste-Marie Bernier, Stephanie Lewthwaite, and Sinéad Moynihan. And in the years since I began my research, several other friends have offered valuable moral support, including Richard Hogwood, Simon Brumfit, Sharon Parker, Natalie Sheehan, Kirsty Bremner, and Katherine Griffiths. More recently, Sherry Harby has been a great help and reassurance to me throughout the final stages of writing this book.

Finally, I would like to thank my husband and family for their support. My sister, Margaret, has always had faith in me and has offered unfailingly helpful advice – intellectual, professional, and emotional – at every step of the way. I could not have asked for a better sister. My husband, Olly, has given me a huge amount of love and encouragement and it is difficult to find the right words to thank him for all he has done over the years. His generosity has been both emotional and financial; and throughout the writing of this book, he has been unstintingly patient, drawing on boundless reserves of strength, humour, and imagination. Our daughter, Rebecca, has brought us a great deal of happiness and provided a regular, welcome break from the intensity of finishing the book. Last of all, I would like to thank my parents, Robert and Carole, for everything they have done to help bring this book to completion. They consistently provided me with much-needed financial support during my postgraduate research, and they have always given me sound professional and intellectual guidance, making many helpful comments on my work. Above all, they have always shown me great love and without them, I could not have written this book. I therefore dedicate it to them with enormous gratitude.

INTRODUCTION: FRAMING SOUTH ASIAN WRITING IN AMERICA AND BRITAIN, 1970–2010

Historical Background

Britain and the United States have seen major waves of South Asian immigration since 1945. Both countries have, of course, always been nations of migrants. Britain has long had black and South Asian populations, yet[1] – despite this rich history – the numbers of people arriving in the postwar period from South Asia and the Caribbean were unprecedented. This well-known historical process,[2] which followed decolonisation in the migrants' countries of origin, has dramatically altered the UK's demographic configuration. According to the national census in 2001, Britain's 'minority ethnic' population – composed mainly of British Asians[3] and black Britons – increased by 53 per cent between 1991 and 2001, from 3 million to 4.6 million, with some 2.08 million people of South Asian descent registered in Great Britain.[4]

As Dilip Hiro has shown, South Asians generally chose to emigrate to Britain for economic reasons, following the displacement brought about by Partition.[5] They were responding to British demand for labour – doctors, nurses, and factory workers across industry – and they were able to move to the UK because they had British passports. Indeed, conditions were favourable for Indians and Pakistanis to move to Britain until 1962, when the first of a series of increasingly severe laws aimed at reducing immigration was passed.[6] Hiro estimates that the numbers of South Asians in Britain 'swelled from 7,500 in 1960 to 48,000 in 1961. And an almost equal number arrived during the first half of 1962.'[7] From the late 1960s, South Asians from East Africa also began arriving in Britain, and from the early 1970s, Bangladeshis from what had been East Pakistan.[8]

While Britain adopted more draconian immigration laws, the United States relaxed the restrictive legislation which had generally ruled out South Asian emigration there.[9] Indeed, America's mid-twentieth-century increase in new arrivals from across Asia, as well as the Caribbean and Latin America, can be traced directly to its 1965 Immigration Act, which abolished the practice of quotas based on nationality, a system in operation since the 1924 National Origins Act and one designed to prohibit the entry of Asian immigrants.[10] One of the effects of these changes to US legislation has been an increased Asian American presence. Estimated at 10 million in 1997, they are predicted to reach 40 million by 2050, which would amount to 10 per cent of the total US population; and according to the most recent US census of 2010, they are the fastest-growing population in the country.[11] According to the previous US census in 2000, numbers of 'Asian Indians' came to 1.85 million, 'Pakistanis' to 209,273, and 'other Asian', which includes Bangladeshis and Sri Lankans, to 561,485.[12] Such figures are strikingly similar to those of the UK – almost as though an even number of South Asians have emigrated to each country – but they clearly form a far smaller percentage of the US population in 2000 (281.4 million) than British Asians in relation to the UK's demographic statistics in 2001: at 2.08 million, they formed 3½ per cent of the total population of 58.7 million.

As Vijay Prashad has noted, post-1965 South Asian immigrants in the US initially tended to be highly educated, often working as doctors, engineers, and scientists between 1965 and 1977, with some 83 per cent possessing advanced degrees.[13] R. K. Narayan sees such immigrants as materially successful, but 'lonely . . . gnawed by some vague discontent . . . In this individual India has lost an intellectual or expert; but . . . he has lost India too . . . a more serious loss in a final reckoning.'[14] Narayan's negative and somewhat simplistic formula corresponds to a particular socio-economic profile and historical moment. In contrast to the educational and financial privilege which characterises the South Asian Americans he describes, arrivals since the mid-1980s have more often tended to be working-class,[15] a phenomenon which has been explored by film-makers in particular.[16]

The image persists, however, of a 'brain drain' of highly trained South Asians – and particularly Indians – arriving in America as foreign students or professionals and opting to stay, with the success of IT professionals in California's Silicon Valley in the 1990s only reinforcing that stereotype.[17] Perhaps this is because more South Asians continue to choose the United States over Britain for their higher education, to the extent that some British universities have publicly acknowledged that they are being left behind. An article in the Indian newspaper *The Hindu* from February 2006 estimates that in comparison with nearly 80,000 Indian students on

US campuses, there were only 17,000 in Britain.[18] A number of reasons may, of course, account for this. With its greater number of universities and their state-of-the-art facilities, America is perhaps seen as more of a 'market leader' in education and – more saliently in this context – it offers far more scholarships to overseas students.

Above all, however, the United States is a global superpower in ways to which Britain can no longer lay claim. Kirin Narayan addresses this in her novel *Love, Stars, and All That* (1994), set in 1980s America (and discussed in Chapter 1 of this study), when she writes that:

> a map of the world extended in pale pastels . . . It was the world but not the familiar one that Gita knew from geography classes . . . In this, the United States displaced crested England at the centre. Golden and spacious, land of the free, the United States was flanked by two broad oceans. Canada offered salutations, and South America bowed to her feet. Bulky handmaidens, Asia, Africa, and Europe seemed to be bending toward her.[19]

Moreover, in Sandip Roy's short story, 'The smells of home' (1996), Savitri's father tells her that whereas the US is 'the richest country in the world',

> Wordsworth's England is long dead. In your grandfather's time people would go to England for then . . . [it] still had power and glory. Now it is truly a nation of shopkeepers. And most of [them] . . . are Indian anyway.[20]

At the same time, it remains an open question whether South Asians have flourished more – in economic, political, social, religious, and artistic terms – in the US or in the UK. Is it possible to argue, furthermore, that communities in one or the other nation have developed in more diverse and vibrant ways? Other questions persist, too, especially in relation to cultural production: for instance, how to explain the exponential rise of South Asian literary works in the Anglophone world since the 1970s or the greater number of South Asian women writers in America, but of South Asian men writing in Britain. Is it possible to identify a specific South Asian textual aesthetic – in terms of literary form and strategies – or to claim particular affiliations between writers? And why are certain authors more widely read, taught, and researched than others? This Introduction will consider general cultural traffic between South Asians in Britain and America before framing specific literary genealogies and the transatlantic choices made by writers. It will conclude by outlining the scope of this book and its scholarly rationale.

Comparing British Asians and South Asian Americans

Several commentators – generally American rather than British – have situated South Asian migration since the 1960s in transatlantic terms. Meena Alexander states in an interview, for example, that whereas many of the Indians who have come to America have been middle-class, the pattern of immigration in Britain has been more working-class.[21] Sandhya Shukla argues that 'the lack of a colonial past and the accessibility of national languages of inclusion in the United States construct . . . Indian Americans' migrant subjectivities in ways that are distinct from their British counterparts'; in a similar vein, M. K. Chakrabarti has claimed that, unlike the US, Britain is characterised by 'too much colonial complication' to feel 'entirely at ease with its own multiculturalism'.[22]

On the whole, in fact, mainstream Britain tends to come off worse than the United States in these comparisons, whether in specifically historical terms[23] or in relation to the contemporary period, with South Asian American commentators portraying it, rather crudely, as essentially inimical to people of South Asian descent. Writing in the 1990s, Sheila Jasanoff contends that:

> [as] a South Asian woman who has lived, studied and worked in America . . . for 40 years . . . [the] constant ambiguity [of ethnic difference] . . . has always attracted me about life in America. In other places where I have lived as an alien – for example, Britain and Germany – the line of 'belonging', like the lines of race, class and gender, is more rigid and less easy to cross.[24]

Another critic, Susan Koshy, suggests that traditionally the UK has been less welcoming to South Asians than America, because it has 'little ideological space for nonwhite immigrants'.[25] She is nevertheless careful to draw attention to the limits of South Asian inclusion in the United States. Rajini Srikanth has taken this idea further, displaying a markedly pessimistic, post-9/11 attitude to the issue of national belonging for Americans of South Asian descent.[26]

Extrapolating from British Asian and South Asian American literary accounts, Monika Fludernik argues that South Asians are more likely to flourish in America than the UK, where, she claims, 'social unrest is endemic'.[27] This interpretation of South Asian Atlantic politics is problematic, however, since it relies on an outdated contrast between an ahistorical, raceless American Dream – which fails to take into account either the United States' troubled racial past or the complexities of its post-9/11 present – and a bleakly postcolonial and stereotypically racist Britain. On the other hand, Feroza Jussawalla writes that for South Asians in both Britain and America in the late 1990s, 'home' tends to be 'defined for them as their place of origin by their features, appearance, and accent. After twenty-three years in America, people still ask me, "Where are you from?".'[28] Within this transatlantic comparison, the US and the UK fare equally badly while, later in the same essay, Jussawalla contends that modern-day 'Baboos' who historically attempted to '(re)make themselves in the colonisers' image' are still kept in their place with ' "no admission" to the club' in either Britain or America.[29]

Striving for evenhandedness, she cites Farrukh Dhondy's claim in 1988 that

> Britain is a very stratified society. More so than America, I think . . . [and] Indian caste, religion and regionalism . . . [are] almost as stratified as . . . in Britain . . . The difference is . . . in India, nobody is brought up to believe they can move out of it . . . Whereas in Britain everybody believes in the Western dream . . . The class distinctions of Britain have been fluid since the fifties . . . one was ruled by a Conservative Party that has absolutely nothing in common with the Tories of the 20s. They had a grocer's daughter who was virtually the Queen. A miner's son is in charge of the Labour Party. (32–3)

Some twenty years on, the novelist Mohsin Hamid, who is Pakistani-born and has lived in both Britain and the United States, posits some key differences, post-9/11, between what he calls 'the Pakistani American and the Pakistani British experience'. His main contention appears to be that in Britain, people of Pakistani descent are less socially integrated than their US counterparts but feel more able to express their political views.[30]

Within South Asian Atlantic literature since 1970, the vision which emerges is of two countries which are both racist, yet offer the promise of social mobility. This is not to deny the importance of continuing socio-economic differences between South Asians in Britain and the US. South Asian Americans remain highly educated – according to the 2000 census, over 63 per cent of Indian Americans and over 54 per cent of Pakistani Americans have a bachelor's degree or more – and their levels of professional success are attested by similarly high figures: just under 60 per cent of Indian Americans and over 43 per cent of Pakistani Americans work in 'management, professional and related' occupations.[31] Clearly, many are thriving economically, and the same cannot always be said for British Asians.[32] It is, moreover, difficult to dispute the contention among American commentators that Britain has traditionally lacked a recognised immigrant mythology. Yet one could also argue that it is the very complexities and difficulties of being South Asian in Britain which have allowed British Asians to carve out a firm cultural position for themselves: a position which is stronger in some ways than that of South Asian Americans.

Britain's public policy of multiculturalism is often critiqued as outmoded and separatist, yet Koshy has pointed out that, from the 1980s onwards, it empowered black and Asian artists in Britain. She notes that

> public funding of multicultural projects encouraged the growth of a black identity in independent filmmaking, theatre, and literature. Black workshops like Retake and special programming on Channel 4 have been crucial to the emergence of filmmakers like Ahmad Jamal, Pratibha Parmar, and Gurinder Chadha.[33]

One wonders whether this multicultural approach has worked in favour of British Asian artists in ways that America's traditional emphasis on cultural assimilation has not. The postcolonial dynamics associated with Britain, rather than America, may have resulted in further creative tension for British Asians through the need to shout louder because of direct histories of racism and imperialism. And whereas 'Asian' in the American context traditionally means 'East Asian', in Britain, 'the long history of British involvement in the subcontinent and [South Asians'] significant numbers in the minority population have led to the popular conflation of Asian with South Asian identity'.[34] In other words, British Asians are exactly that – Britain's 'Asians' – and, as we have seen, relative to the total population, there are far more of them in Britain than America. For these reasons, British Asians in many ways occupy a more prominent place in the British national consciousness than South Asian Americans do in US culture.

South Asian Cultural Traffic between Britain and America

Some critics have read the move from Britain to the US made by the Indian-born novelist Salman Rushdie in the late 1990s as exemplary of particular cultural flows within the South Asian diaspora.[35] Thus Bruce King argues that

> Rushdie and his main characters moving to New York was [sic] part of a process which was driven by the emergence of the United States as the world's main power and its entrepreneurial capitalism as the source of global liberalisation. Significantly, to establish the fame and international credentials of its

> main characters, part of . . . [Hanif Kureishi's 1990 novel] *Buddha of Suburbia* also takes place in New York.[36]

Several prominent British Asians – the actors Naveen Andrews and Parminder Nagra, for example – are also now based in the United States, while some important South Asian academics (for instance, Homi Bhabha) have made this move too. Such migration arguably confirms America's greater cultural influence over Britain than vice versa, and this can be seen as part of a wider one-way traffic, especially in terms of racial politics.

Since the Civil Rights era, certain American discourses on race and ethnicity have heavily influenced Britain's cultural vocabulary:[37] the ideas behind the Black Power movement and the writings of James Baldwin, Malcolm X, and Angela Davis as models of anti-racist resistance in the UK; the immigrant model of Jewish America for British Asian (and also white British) writers and comedians; and even particular terms such as 'white flight', 'white trash', and 'model minority' which one encounters increasingly in discussions of race and class in the British context. America's pervasive influence on the British Asian writer Hanif Kureishi, for instance, has been discussed by a number of commentators.[38] The American-based critic Kwame Anthony Appiah in fact positions Kureishi's second novel, *The Black Album* (1995), in direct relation to American culture:

> The book's other interest is its vision of the deepening penetration of British life by American culture . . . Kureishi belongs to a generation of English writers who seem to draw their sustenance from this side of the Atlantic. In an emblematic moment, Shahid imagines that an English country house is 'the sort of place an English Gatsby would have chosen' . . . For . . . Kureishi, even Englishness now exists only as a construct of the American imagination. The many literary and musical references are almost all to American works – with the odd gesture to an older Western high canon; even the jejune chronicling of sexual manoeuvres reads like an (admittedly unsuccessful) hommage [sic] to Henry Miller or Philip Roth.[39]

Some commentators have connected America's importance for British Asians with the lack of South Asian role models in the UK at a particular historical moment. In a review of Sarfraz Manzoor's memoir, *Greetings from Bury Park: Race. Religion. Rock 'n'Roll* (2007), the British Pakistani novelist Suhayl Saadi notes, for example, that Manzoor's 1980s teenage obsession with the American musician Bruce Springsteen came from 'the absence of Pakistani working-class heroes with whom he could identify';[40] for 'Pakistani', one might read 'British Pakistani' here. American music continues to resonate for young British people across the racial spectrum and the impact of black American youth culture through musical forms such as rap and hip hop is particularly well recognised.

If one applies this idea of US cultural dominance to British Asians – and, more specifically, to British Asian artists – it will become apparent that the transatlantic cultural traffic which has flowed from American life does not take a South Asian diasporic form. Indeed, one might argue that in terms of popular culture, South Asia itself – in the form of Bollywood cinema – has exerted a far greater influence over British Asians than anything specifically South Asian American. Perhaps this is generational. South Asian American cultural production was, after all, only at a fledgling stage – and thus little known – when younger British Asian writers and artists were coming of age in the 1970s and 1980s. But if the American literary, cinematic, or musical role models available to British Asian artists were not South Asian ones, the reception of 'minority' writing in the United States in the 1970s did create conditions of reception which widened publishing opportunities for later British Asian writers. As Susheila Nasta has argued, 'the enormous commercial popularity of Black Women's writing as a sale-able commodity in the USA . . . encouraged publishers to give space to the retrieval of black and Asian women's histories in Britain, with a view to setting up a similar market in the UK'.[41] Such classic Asian American works as Maxine Hong Kingston's novel *The Woman Warrior* (1976) also belong to this discourse.

It would appear, then, that transatlantic cultural influences have generally operated in one direction – from the US to Britain – and that such influences have not been particularly South Asian. Yet British Asians have, to a certain extent, affected American culture – most specifically in its South Asian forms – through film and literature. In other words, a South Asian transatlanticism can be posited, and this study makes reference to cinema and television because these areas of cultural production have played an important role in the development of British Asian and South Asian American artistic expression. In the British context, they may even be said to explore ideas before literary works do: British Asian literature can appear to lag behind popular culture. At the very least, ideas about Asian Britain often find a wider audience through film and television, as Ruvani Ranasinha has observed.[42] Cinematic works like Stephen Frears's *My Beautiful Laundrette* (1985) or Damien O'Donnell's *East is East* (1999) – scripted by Hanif Kureishi and Ayub Khan-Din respectively (and discussed in Chapter 3) – have arguably been more groundbreaking (and controversial) than any solely literary text.

One could argue that globally, films by and about British Asians have also generated more popular and commercial interest in South Asian diasporic life than any South Asian American cinematic or televisual work has. Kureishi's script for *Laundrette*, for instance, was nominated for British and American Academy Awards and won the 1986 New York Film Critics' Circle Award for Best Screenplay; and although the film cost only £600,000 to make, it earned $15,000,000 worldwide.[43] *East is East* and Gurinder Chadha's *Bend It Like Beckham* (2002) were also international hits. South Asian American films, by contrast, have generally garnered less commercial success. It is revealing in this regard that, in a review of Krutin Patel's low-budget American film *ABCD* (1999), Trevor Johnston places it within a transatlantic framework when he argues that 'this saga of second generation Indians in America sorting out their cultural identity is plain fare compared with our own Hanif Kureishi and *East is East*'.[44]

'Plain fare' does not do justice to the understated complexities of *ABCD*, and British Asian cinema should not be reduced – either in this study or by film critics like Johnston – to *Laundrette* and *East is East* (or *Bend It Like Beckham*, for that matter). But it is intriguing that Johnston's remarks rely on transatlantic comparisons. Such parallels may be simplistic – Johnston does not really prove how *ABCD* might be viewed in relation to *Laundrette* or *East is East* beyond their most obvious thematic similarities – but they do show that the growth in British Asian artistic works has opened up a broader frame of specifically transatlantic diasporic reference. One of the lead actors in *ABCD* has even drawn on this discourse himself. Faran Tahir, who plays Raj in the film, argues that it is

> one of the first [films about South Asian Americans] . . . it's an important story because there's so much stuff that comes out of England about the experience of South Asians there, which is similar but not the same and . . . this [film] addresses the conflicts and the problems that South Asians confront . . . in this set-up, which is quite different.[45]

That similar terms of reference are shared by British Asians has been revealed by Nagra in a recent interview.[46] Such cultural traffic can also be traced in literary terms, as I will demonstrate at greater length in the next part of this discussion.

Literary Genealogies

The idea of South Asian diasporic 'anxieties of influence' has been well rehearsed, particularly as it relates to V. S. Naipaul and Salman Rushdie.[47] Indeed, the intergenerational parallels which come to mind are supported by writers themselves through the use of a familial language to refer to each other. Thus the South Asian American writer Meena Alexander thinks of these literary relationships in 'generational terms'

> because when I first came here [America], I would read the work of older writers: Bharati [Mukherjee] and others. And now I'm very interested in the work of younger South Asian artists . . . I come out of many traditions, and so I use the word 'familial' to think about diaspora, because you feel in a vibrant relationship with a community . . . the diaspora is very important to me emotionally. It's saying, 'You're part of this wave, this group of people, all making art with language. You're not alone'.[48]

Older writers clearly offer a model with which to argue as much as pay homage. In keeping with this paradigm, critics have traced particular lines of descent within South Asian diasporic writing: G. V. Desani, as well as V. S. Naipaul, in relation to Rushdie;[49] Rushdie in connection with Kureishi;[50] Naipaul and Rushdie vis-à-vis the South Asian American writer Bharati Mukherjee;[51] and Kureishi's impact on later British Asian writers.[52] I will now discuss in more detail how these literary genealogies relate to Kureishi, Mukherjee, and a newer generation of South Asian diasporic writers, touching on the issue of transatlantic anxieties of influence, an area which remains under-explored in critical terms.

Amitava Kumar notes that when he asked Kureishi

> how he might be different from a writer like Naipaul . . . he began by talking of the similarities between his father and Naipaul's father. Both men had an interest in education and in writing. Kureishi said, 'They were fastidious men who wanted to be journalists, but they were bitter . . . failed men'. Then he outlined the differences between himself and Naipaul . . . He didn't have Naipaul's interest in India . . . Kureishi said of Naipaul, 'He has a basically conservative sensibility, and I don't mean politically . . . Also, I like women . . . and I've always been interested in sex and relationships between men and women'. Naipaul's books fail, Kureishi said, because Naipaul 'can't write about relationships between men and women, and he can't write about marriage, which seems to be the central institution of the West'.[53]

Despite Kureishi's conscious desire to distance himself from Naipaul and his writerly concerns here, the older author refuses to disappear and in fact emerges twice in Kureishi's family memoir *My Ear at His Heart* (2004): once when Kureishi's cousin Nusrat meets Naipaul in Karachi and later when Kureishi himself visits Naipaul following the death of his father, Rafiushan

Kureishi. In *My Ear*, Kureishi's verdict on Naipaul and his work remains as disparaging, however, as that offered in Kumar's interview:

> there was no Pop or bawdy in Naipaul's work; he lacked [Philip] Roth's sexual fizzle and 60s attitude; he seemed depressed, an out-of-place immigrant wandering through the postwar city unable to find a door he had the nerve to walk through. He was disappointed by everything he saw, determinedly so.[54]

In contrast to Kureishi's dismissals of Naipaul, King has claimed that Naipaul's work has been enabling for a later generation of Indian-born writers including Farrukh Dhondy and Amit Chaudhuri:

> Naipaul . . . showed others . . . how to write significant fiction about the former colonies, people of colour, and hybridity without resorting to the clichés of European writing, and that it was possible to see the interest and problems of local life without nationalist stereotypes.[55]

In stylistic and thematic terms, Mukherjee might be added to this list of writers influenced by Naipaul, at least early on in her career. Returning to issues of writerly self-presentation to a greater extent than Kureishi, she has openly acknowledged Naipaul's impact on her in a series of position pieces. Initially, she sees herself as 'a pale and immature reflection' of him,[56] as she relies on a distinctly Naipaulian vocabulary to discuss exilic status. In later essays, however, she disavows Naipaul's 'state-of-the-art expatriation', claiming that it has ceased to inspire her.[57] Such statements arguably reveal more about the shifting contours of Mukherjee's public self-fashioning than they do about the actual form and content of her work, which has continued to draw on tensions between 'expatriation' and 'immigration'.[58]

As is well known, Rushdie has exerted a major influence on Indian writing in English and on the literature of the South Asian diaspora. In a sense, then, later writers cannot afford to ignore either him or his impact. Kureishi and Mukherjee have openly positioned themselves in relation to Rushdie – much as they have with Naipaul – while suggesting a complex mixture of influence, admiration, and ambivalence. Thus Kureishi has often recalled that it was Rushdie who encouraged him to write the novel which became *Buddha of Suburbia*.[59] Similarly, *Black Album* draws inspiration from Rushdie, or rather from the tumultuous real-life events surrounding the reception of Rushdie's novel *The Satanic Verses* (1988). At the same time, Kureishi has emphasised the differences between Rushdie and himself, telling an interviewer that Rushdie's

> writing is not like my writing in any way . . . We see the world differently . . . It would have been fatal for me to try to write like him. When I read *Midnight's Children* for the first time, I was seduced by it and I thought, This is a great way to write, but he's from Bombay . . . and I'm from the [London] suburbs and I had the sense to realise that I couldn't . . . be like him.[60]

Mukherjee's strategy of both aligning herself with Rushdie, and separating herself from him, shows that (like Kureishi) she feels compelled to engage with him. She claims to 'admire . . . Rushdie enormously' and even devotes an entire essay to a discussion of his work;[61] but, as a whole, this is a complicated debt rather than a straightforward act of literary homage.

One can also view South Asian Atlantic writing within the context of Jewish American literary models. Mukherjee has paid tribute to such older writers as Henry Roth and Bernard Malamud, and her own fiction can be linked in thematic terms and in its bid for vernacular experimentation to the particular American tradition of early twentieth-century immigrant assimilation narrative as practised by such authors as Mary Antin and Anzia Yezierska.[62] We saw earlier that Appiah reads *Black Album* in relation to Philip Roth, and that Kureishi himself invokes Roth as a means of contextualising Naipaul. Kureishi has also compared the reception of *Laundrette* to that of Roth's literary début, *Goodbye Columbus* (1959), and – as he has with Rushdie – often made reference to Roth's professional support and advice early in his career, as has Alexander.[63] Beyond Roth, Kureishi's work demonstrates the influence of a series of other Jewish American writers, a point I have discussed elsewhere.[64]

What about the impact of Kureishi and Mukherjee on later writers? Kureishi's role is in many ways easier to map. Although Ranasinha has shown that Dhondy blazed a trail for later British Asian writers,[65] it is Kureishi who is more often regarded as a cultural pioneer by artists and critics: British Asian, black British, white British, and South Asian American. Sukhdev Sandhu argues that 'if there is one figure who is responsible for dragging Asians in England into the spotlight it is Hanif Kureishi', while Kumar has recalled that 'when I read Kureishi, a whole generation of earlier writers who had written about race suddenly seemed dated – and old'.[66] Vijay Mishra believes that Kureishi's 1980s film scripts gave

> the diaspora not only images of its own self but also images that require high levels of proactive critical engagement in the first place. Moreover, these bodies are now exposed to general public consumption and are no longer

commodities that circulate, like Bombay films, only in the diaspora itself . . . Kureishi's films effectively began this process of engagement.[67]

A number of commentators have argued that when Kureishi appeared on the literary scene, his material – the lives of young British-born Asians, of mixed race or of entirely South Asian descent – was unprecedented. Randeep Ramesh has claimed, for instance, that Kureishi was the first writer to identify what he calls 'the British Asian experience', while Frears, the director of both *Laundrette* and the Kureishi-scripted film *Sammy and Rosie Get Laid* (1987), similarly believes that 'nobody had ever written from that perspective before. It was astonishing because [Kureishi] got it so right. That someone could be . . . so confident about it, make the jokes, be on the inside.'[68] This assumption that *Laundrette* is transparently mimetic of complex realities is problematic,[69] as are the ideas that Kureishi was the first writer to address such themes and that a monolithic 'British Asian experience' exists. But it is difficult to argue with the notion that Kureishi's work was instrumental in redressing the chronic under-representation of British Asians in all forms of cultural production in the 1980s. Indeed, Kureishi has himself recalled that when he was growing up in the 1960s, South Asian people simply did not appear on television; as he has put it, 'Asian people were not seen as part of Britain.'[70]

Kureishi's work has received international, mainstream acclaim: following the plaudits which greeted *Laundrette*, *Buddha of Suburbia* won the Whitbread Prize for best first novel and was translated into thirty languages. One could argue that these successes have altered the way the work of a later generation of British Asian authors has been received. Suhayl Saadi thanks Kureishi in the acknowledgements to his short fiction collection *The Burning Mirror* (2001), while Niven Govinden's novel *Graffiti My Soul* (2006) seems remarkably similar to *Buddha of Suburbia* with its drug-taking, mixed-race, teenaged hero, resident in the home counties, whose father has left his mother for another woman. Govinden is even labelled 'a modern-day Hanif Kureishi' on the book's cover: a mark of Kureishi's ongoing importance in relation to younger writers.[71] This creative impact has been felt transatlantically, too. The South Asian American novelist Jhumpa Lahiri has been quoted as saying that *Buddha of Suburbia* 'opened up something for me: I thought here's something I could do too',[72] and in Chapter 3, I argue that some of Lahiri's recent work owes a debt to *Laundrette*. Another American writer of South Asian descent, Ameena Meer, thanks Kureishi in *Bombay Talkie* (1994), her novel of ethnic return to 1980s India (which I discuss in Chapter 2), for his creative courage and innovation;[73] and she includes a character called Kureishi, along with themes of miscegenation and alternative sexuality (already familiar from Kureishi's early work), and a chapter entitled 'The rainbow sign', which is the name of Kureishi's essay (itself a quotation from James Baldwin's *The Fire Next Time* [1963]) discussing his 'roots' trip to Pakistan in the early 1980s. Both Sandhu and Nasta have discussed Kureishi's 'paternal' status for younger writers,[74] and it is a mark of his cultural importance that this has transcended boundaries of nation, gender, and race.[75]

Like Kureishi, Mukherjee has prolifically explored questions of nation and identity, in this case since the early 1970s, producing seven novels, two collections of short stories, two long works of non-fiction, and numerous essays and articles. Just as Kureishi has done, Mukherjee has claimed that when she began writing, there was an absence of South Asian diasporic models, especially within America; she has argued, furthermore, that American literature was lacking in stories about people like her. Indeed, she has said that the 'urgent' nature of her creative material – Indians in America – compelled her to commit these themes to paper as soon as she began writing seriously.[76] Mukherjee is, in fact, no more the first South Asian American writer than Kureishi is the first chronicler of British Asian life. But, as several critics have noted, she ranks as the first major South Asian American literary voice.[77] One can trace this to Mukherjee's American reception: the breadth of publications in which she has been reviewed, interviewed, and anthologised; the prizes she has been awarded; and the canonical status accorded her through her prominence on university teaching syllabuses and as a subject of academic study.

Mukherjee's views on South Asia and the United States – her Orientalist attitude towards India and her open enthusiasm for assimilation into the American mainstream – have often proved contentious. Kureishi has also courted controversy but, unlike Mukherjee, his screenwriting has made him a popular cultural figure rather than simply a literary one. In contrast to Kureishi, Mukherjee's work, with its particular first-generation concerns, has less obviously influenced a later wave of writers, especially those who are US-born or raised. Indeed, one does not find more recent South Asian American writers acknowledging and thanking Mukherjee as they do Kureishi. Yet they cannot fail to be aware of her achievements; and her work has, like his, paved the way for the current flowering of South Asian literature in the US by helping to create a wider public appetite for it – and for writing by South Asian American women in particular.

It is difficult, for instance, to imagine Lahiri's historic Pulitzer Prize win in 2000 for her literary début, *Interpreter of Maladies*,[78] without thinking back to the literary breakthrough represented by Mukherjee's novel *Jasmine* (1989). However problematic this latter work is, it gained an unprecedentedly wide readership for South Asian American writing and is still widely researched and taught. Just as Naipaul did for her, then, Mukherjee may have energised younger writers by providing them with a paradigm to challenge and reject. Some writers have more consciously recognised this process than others. Alexander, for instance, has recalled that, when she first lived in America, she

> read . . . Mukherjee's work carefully and it was very interesting to me. Through her, there was a particular kind of vision of what it meant to be American and it was useful . . . because she clarified . . . the possibility of living in America and being a writer and having a place in the society. But . . . she has this model of jettisoning the past . . . whereas for me, that doesn't make sense at all; in fact I have, if anything, tried to remember.[79]

Kureishi has rightly observed that 'there are as many versions [of life] in the Asian community as there are in any other community'.[80] But in a body of writing which is still relatively young, certain creative 'versions' have garnered higher levels of attention than others. Beyond Kureishi and Mukherjee, writers like Lahiri in the United States and Monica Ali and Meera Syal in Britain have taken on the mantle of representing South Asianness. As Ranasinha has noted, Syal is 'one of Britain's best-known Asians'.[81] Indeed, she is often perceived by the white mainstream as a kind of official spokesperson for all things British Asian. Thanks to her many accomplishments – as writer, actor, comedian, and media personality – and because of her general visibility, it is often Syal's account of British Asianness which is offered up for wider public consumption. Similarly, Ali's bestselling novel *Brick Lane* (2003) has generated a disproportionate degree of interest at the expense of other works.[82] At the same time, as with Kureishi and Mukherjee, the success enjoyed by these younger authors appears to be acting as an enabling force for newer British Asian and South Asian American writers.

Transatlantic Choices for South Asian Diasporic Writers

Kureishi ultimately rejects America for Britain (or rather London), while Mukherjee overtly discards Britain in favour of the US. In a 1993 interview, she recalls that 'it was especially exciting to go to America because England . . . was associated with all that I had left behind. Because I had gone to school in England as a child I was aware of what it felt like to be a minority, and I knew I didn't want that.'[83] Her stance in some ways recalls that of the African American writer Frederick Douglass, for whom, as Paul

Giles has argued, American national identity is valorised by appropriating and then rejecting an image of Britain.[84] Both writers also make a point of eschewing South Asian countries (Pakistan for Kureishi, India in Mukherjee's case).

Younger British Asian writers generally favour the UK over the US. Like Kureishi, their British birth means that they are invested in the place, however complex that position is, and America is not necessarily given serious consideration. Recent South Asian American authors prefer the United States to Britain but, in contrast to British Asian writing, their work engages with ideas of South Asianness in the two sites more explicitly. Alexander, for one, has discussed her predilection for the United States over Britain on a number of occasions. She suggests, in fact, that the US is more liberating for South Asian writers, arguing that her early poetry was

> written in a very tight form . . . the tightness . . . was hurting me. It was something I'd learned from the British model – the kind of controlled language. Whereas one of the most exhilarating things about coming to America and writing poetry here is that it's much more open about the possibilities of what a poem can be and I . . . find that wonderful as a writer.[85]

Elsewhere Alexander has spoken of the strains imposed on South Asian writers by the British canonical tradition.[86] And speaking about North America more generally, the Sri Lankan Canadian novelist Michael Ondaatje has similarly recalled that

> in Canada you felt you could do anything. I wouldn't have been a writer if I'd stayed in England . . . [Canada] wasn't like England, where you feel, what right do you have to do this because of John Donne and Sir Philip Sidney. England felt repressive in the 50s.[87]

Mukherjee has also positioned her writing in this way, although rather more aggressively.[88] These visions of British literary culture as staid and disempowering are challenged, however, by the vigour of recent British Asian writing, which is in some ways more flexible than South Asian American literature through its greater thematic sweep, formal inventiveness, generic variety, and use of comedy. Such writers as Kureishi, Saadi, Ali, Hari Kunzru, and Nadeem Aslam do not appear to have felt constrained by British linguistic and canonical burdens, although one notes that Alexander, Ondaatje, and Mukherjee belong to an earlier, newly postcolonial generation: each one was born before 1952 (although Kureishi was born not long afterwards, in 1954), each began life in South Asia, and each spent time in Britain before making the move to North America.

On the one hand, the presence of a worldwide South Asian diaspora is taken for granted in a number of literary texts, just as it is in such films as Mira Nair's *Monsoon Wedding* (2002), where relatives from around the world arrive in Delhi for a family wedding,[89] and in Chadha's *Bride and Prejudice* (2004). On the other hand, however, several South Asian American literary works go beyond the assumption of a global diaspora to ask whether life is better for South Asians in Britain or the United States, as I will discuss more fully in Chapter 1. Meanwhile, other writers pay little attention to the choice of America over Britain – or Britain over America – and in a number of these works, the US or UK are, in fact, bypassed altogether. In such cases, when either is referenced – as, for instance, England is by Lahiri when she draws on her own childhood experiences in Croydon – such moments are usually brief.[90] But not all of these authors know both countries, and indeed, emigration to Britain or America does not necessarily entail any implied rejection of the other nation. Thus, for some of the real-life South Asian American figures in S. Mitra Kalita's work of reportage, *Suburban Sahibs* (2003), it is simply a given that the US is the industrial economy *par excellence* and the obvious place to which one would emigrate, especially when family members are already there and significant South Asian settlement has taken place. On this latter point, British Asian communities can be viewed in similar fashion, in both fact and fiction.

To what extent, then, can one talk of South Asian Atlantic literature?[91] As this study will argue, South Asian writers continue to draw strength from transnational – and specifically transatlantic – positions. We have already seen that, where they are invoked, transatlantic cultural flows operate on multiple levels for these writers. By pitting the US against the UK, national concerns can be further interrogated, concerns which are of particular relevance to diasporic peoples. Writers show that for South Asian migrants, it *has* sometimes been a choice between the UK and the US, despite the global reach of the South Asian diaspora. The decision to remain in Britain or America or to move between the two – and the ongoing, explicit sense of a transatlantic community of interests that this creates – thus provides an important discursive space in which to interrogate key thematic questions. When British Asian and South Asian American writers do not engage overtly with transatlantic issues, their works still correspond and speak to one another in a number of suggestive ways through aesthetic and ideological 'parallelisms';[92] and the aim of this study is to explore the discursive possibilities and literary convergences encouraged by this growth in South Asian literature on both sides of the Atlantic.

The Scope of this Study

A number of recent scholarly monographs have mapped literary expressions of changing South Asian migration and settlement in important ways.[93] Yet Koshy's 2002 article, 'South Asians and the complex interstices of whiteness: Negotiating public sentiment in the United States and Britain', represents a rare academic attempt to compare South Asians in Britain and America.[94] Her article concerns South Asian Americans and British Asians in a media and legal, rather than a literary, context and indeed the transatlantic development of South Asian diasporic cultural production generally remains an under-explored area. Sandhya Shukla's *India Abroad: Diasporic Cultures of Postwar America and England* (2003), which includes literature in its discussion; Monika Fludernik's essay 'Imagined communities as imaginary homelands: The South Asian diaspora in fiction' (2003); and Gayatri Gopinath's *Impossible Desires: Queer Diasporas and South Asian Public Cultures* (2005), which ranges across film, fiction, and popular music, are in fact notable exceptions to this rule.[95]

Although critics and reviewers are increasingly reading individual British Asian works alongside South Asian American ones,[96] the growing discipline of transatlantic studies has seldom applied itself to patterns of Asian migration or literary responses to such demographic movement. Literary scholars working within this field – which examines 'a geographic area, a location of material and economic exchange, and a metaphor for the transmission of aesthetic and ideological forms'[97] – have traditionally focused on works produced in the eighteenth, nineteenth, and early twentieth centuries, as Heidi Slettedahl Macpherson has noted.[98] This is not to suggest that current scholarship does not consider more recent literary works. Indeed, within explorations of an Anglophone Atlantic, contemporary British and American texts – produced by white and black (but not Asian) writers – increasingly provide grounds for comparison, as does the phenomenon of present-day literary figures who have left Britain for the US (and, less frequently, vice versa).[99] Despite such a wealth of critical material within transatlantic studies, South Asian diasporic writing as an Atlantic literary phenomenon has been overlooked, while South Asia itself has occupied an understandably central position within studies of this body of writing. Although I acknowledge its centrality here (particularly in Chapter 2), I also seek to offer a more triangulated model, whereby South Asian ancestral space interacts with transatlantic networks and crossings.

An extended consideration of this œuvre in transatlantic terms is necessary in part because of the rapid growth in the primary literature itself, in part as a result of the critical acclaim many writers have received, and in part as a response to rising popular and academic interest in these works. *South Asian Atlantic Literature* therefore addresses this under-researched area by examining a representative range of works – across different genres, particularly prose forms (the novel, short fiction, essays, life-writing), but also referencing works of drama, and key films and television programmes – produced in America and Britain between 1970 and 2010, contending that this is where and when the modern explosion of South Asian immigrant literature has principally occurred. Fiction, in particular, remains the book's chief focus because novels and short stories – rather than poetry or drama – are still the medium most often chosen by writers themselves.

If many of the issues discussed in recent and contemporary South Asian American literature bear a striking resemblance to those explored in British Asian writing, this points to the importance of reading such writing comparatively. Mark Stein has noted that literature increasingly transcends national boundaries both thematically and aesthetically, and in terms of its production and reception; he goes on to posit that unless authors and texts are studied within a comparative framework, writerly affiliations and intertextual connections across culture and ethnicity will remain hidden.[100] In this study, I will consider the preferred formal and aesthetic modes of South Asian Atlantic authors, their use of intertextuality, and the persistence of particular 'anxieties of influence'. By analysing the work of well-known writers,[101] as well as those whose work has yet to receive proper scholarly attention, *South Asian Atlantic Literature* aims to make a useful contribution to several fields of inquiry: contemporary British and American literature; postcolonial literary studies; debates surrounding transnationalism, race, and ethnicity; and transatlantic, diaspora, and Asian American cultural studies.

The book is divided into four main chapters, which are organised thematically. The topics under discussion have been carefully selected as especially reflecting the concerns of transatlantic South Asian writing. In the first chapter, I consider questions of home and nation. Such ideas, a well-recognised feature of postcolonial debates, continue to be crucially important, both politically and culturally, to South Asian writers in Britain and America. Indeed, whether they are first- or second-generation, writers consistently use home to raise provocative questions about changing Western societies and the place of ethnic South Asians within them. If – as some critics have claimed – transnational status is taken for granted in much diasporic writing, how, then, can we account for the enduring significance of national identity for many of these writers? And how can home remain both an issue and not an issue for them? In Chapter 1, I intervene in existing postcolonial scholarship by rethinking the inherent tensions of home as material and ideological space across a range of South Asian Atlantic texts, where the continuing resonances of this idea need to be further analysed and understood.

Chapter 2 addresses themes of travel and return by dealing with what happens when South Asian immigrants go back to the ancestral homeland. What political questions are raised by such 'return-of-the-native' moments, and to what extent is gender a factor? This chapter also interrogates the notion of travel and 'return' for a second generation which has never set foot in the South Asian motherland. Building on the examination of home and nation in Chapter 1, I consider the dialectical importance of these questions within diasporic literary works, where a precarious balance is often struck between how writers critique South Asia and their keen attention to the shortcomings of the adoptive nation. This is complex psychological territory, treated unsentimentally and comically by British Asian artists, whereas South Asian American writers and film-makers often use such themes to reflect with greater seriousness the sacred status of the 'roots search' in American culture. Despite the thematic prevalence of travel and return in recent works from either side of the Atlantic, this rich subject has yet to receive proper scholarly attention in studies of South Asian diasporic literature and film, an imbalance this chapter will seek to redress.

In Chapter 3, I focus on racial mixing. This is another surprisingly under-researched area in discussions of South Asian diasporic literature and cinema. Offering reasons for why so many of these writers explore either interracial relationships or the mixed-race subject (or both), this chapter extends the book's consideration of national and cultural identity by analysing these ideas within a wide selection of texts from Britain and the US. It argues that, beyond autobiographical imperatives, a more radical and utopian project is at work, whereby writers use tropes of miscegenation in their bid to create brave new multiracial nations and rewrite the traditionally racist discourse associated with this issue. Showing that this interest in the progressive possibilities of racial mixing actually belongs to a much longer transatlantic tradition, the chapter also reveals the tensions and controversies surrounding this recurring theme in South Asian Atlantic literature.

Chapter 4 examines the repeated emphasis on food and eating across this body of writing, a topic which – on the basis of titles alone – has ostensibly become a tired means of depicting South Asian diasporic life. The notion that such material has itself become clichéd is, of course, more problematic. Following the book's earlier discussions of national identity, domesticity, and race, this chapter proposes that the central cultural role traditionally played by South Asian foodways makes it difficult for diasporic authors *not* to write about them. Exploring a series of culinary 'parallelisms' which appear throughout transatlantic South Asian literary works, I highlight some important distinctions between the treatment of food in British Asian and South Asian American texts. I contend, moreover, that if South Asian food is regarded as thematically familiar in an artistic context, it remains yet another under-examined aspect of academic work on South Asian diasporic literature as a whole, despite a wider scholarly interest in food. And I ask how food has come to be seen as stereotypical in South Asian cultural production and who perpetuates these putative clichés.

In the Conclusion to this study, I look at the future of British Asian and South Asian American literature. Situating this body of work within the context of genre, prize-giving, and the literary marketplace, I raise questions about how these works are read and received and suggest that, despite an exuberant range of new writing, a few individual works are still being made to appear representative, thereby inviting a disproportionate level of attention. The popularity of certain works at the expense of others can mean that particular, and in many ways familiar, ideas about the South Asian diaspora remain enshrined in British and American national consciousness. Such success arises to some extent, then, from a failure on the part of writers and publishers to move beyond the treatment of apparently familiar themes. At the same time, each mainstream success creates greater interest in – and potentially more nuanced awareness of – the complicated fabric of South Asian diasporic communities.

Returning to my earlier claim that after Kureishi's *Buddha of Suburbia*, British Asian – rather than South Asian American – literature has had a greater international impact, the Conclusion asks whether this situation is now changing, thanks to the growing popularity and critical acclaim enjoyed by a new generation of South Asian writers in the United States. Although many authors in both nations are still published by small, little-known presses, the recent appetite for South Asian cultural productions in both Britain and America appears, if anything, to be energising and encouraging other writers. This in turn is creating increasingly complex literary genealogies which move across class, gender, national, and ethnic boundaries but which also suggest that it is all the more important to understand this writing within a transnational – and transatlantic – frame.

NOTES

1. Fryer, *Staying Power*; Visram, *Ayahs*; and Visram, *Asians*.
2. See Fryer, *Staying Power*, pp. 372–86; and Hiro, *Black British*, pp. 120–5.

3. Such labels as 'British Asian' and 'South Asian American' are inevitably problematic, since they collapse the rich distinctions – ethnic, cultural, religious, linguistic – between different communities. But in a UK context, 'British Asian' arguably has wider currency than other designations (for example, 'South Asian British'), while 'South Asian American' – rather than, say, 'Indian American' – is the umbrella term in widest circulation in its own national setting. These terms – like 'minority', 'second-generation', 'immigrant', 'non-white', 'ethnic' – have been perceived as exclusionary and disempowering because they arise from the need of hegemonic white societies to maintain a centre and a periphery. At the same time, this study is concerned with the specifically *South Asian* nature of this body of writing and retains such markers for that reason. 'South Asian' is often critiqued as an imperfect designation, since it brings together people of Indian, Pakistani, Bangladeshi, Sri Lankan, Nepalese, and Bhutanese descent; see, for instance, Chakraborty, 'Will the real South Asian', p. 125. For want of a better general term, however, I will deploy 'South Asian' throughout this study – and in the transatlantic literary context as defined here, this will generally mean Indian, Pakistani, and Bangladeshi, rather than Sri Lankan.
4. Data on ethnicity were not collected from Northern Ireland. The Chinese community in Britain numbered a much smaller 247,403 people and those categorised as 'other Asian' totalled 247,664. 'Minority ethnic' groups (including a further 677,117 people of 'mixed' ethnicity) amounted to just under 8 per cent of the overall population of 58,789,194. See n.a., 'Ethnicity: Population size'. Information for the most recent UK census (2011) is currently being gathered and in any case falls outside the time period covered by this book.
5. Hiro, *Black British*, p. 121.
6. See Fryer, *Staying Power*, pp. 381–5.
7. Hiro, *Black British*, p. 124.
8. Bangladeshis have a far longer history in Britain than this would suggest; see Adams, *Across Seven Seas*; Visram, *Ayahs*; and Visram, *Asians*.
9. In the early twentieth century, South Asian migration to the United States was mainly confined to small numbers of Punjabi Sikh men who settled in California. See Mazumdar, 'Race', pp. 29–30; and Takaki, *Strangers*, pp. 294–314.
10. Daniels, *Guarding*, pp. 137–9; Steinberg, *Ethnic Myth*, pp. 267–8.
11. Takaki, *Strangers*, p. 493; and see Humes et al., *Overview*, pp. 4–5.
12. See Reeves and Bennett, *We the People*, p. 3. I am relying on this earlier report because a more detailed statistical breakdown of specific Asian groups in the US based on the most recent census data (of 2010) has yet to appear.
13. Prashad, 'How the Hindus', p. 600.
14. Narayan, *Story-Teller's World*, p. 29.
15. See Grewal, 'Indian-American', pp. 97–8.

16. See, for example, Mira Nair's *Mississippi Masala* (1991); Richard Linklater's *SubUrbia* (1996); and Ramin Bahrani's *Man Push Cart* (2005).
17. Mankekar, 'India shopping', pp. 199–200.
18. See Suroor, 'Chris Patten'; and compare Narayan, *Monsoon*, p. 137, where the UK is not even a consideration for ambitious Indians pursuing postgraduate study opportunities in the United States.
19. Narayan, *Love, Stars*, p. 202.
20. Roy, 'Smells', p. 321.
21. Quoted in Bahri and Vasudeva, 'Observing ourselves', p. 38.
22. Shukla, *India Abroad*, p. 167; Chakrabarti, 'Marketplace'.
23. Chatterjee, 'Thoughts', p. 320; and compare Green, *Transatlantic Patterns*, p. 248.
24. Jasanoff, 'To belong', p. 26.
25. Koshy, 'South Asians', p. 40.
26. Srikanth, *World Next Door*, pp. 53–5.
27. Fludernik, 'Imagined communities', p. 283.
28. Jussawalla, 'South Asian diaspora', p. 19.
29. Ibid., p. 21.
30. Quoted in Yaqin, 'Mohsin Hamid', p. 47.
31. Reeves and Bennett, *We the People*, pp. 14, 16.
32. See Modood et al., *Ethnic Minorities*. According to the report's findings, 80 per cent of 'Pakistanis and Bangladeshis . . . live in households with incomes below half the national average', although it also notes that 'African Asians . . . are more likely than whites to earn more than £500 a week . . . and Indian men are well-represented in professional and managerial occupations'; see n.a., 'Landmark'.
33. Koshy, 'South Asians', p. 41.
34. Ibid., p. 39.
35. For discussions of Rushdie as a transatlantic figure, see Giles, *Atlantic Republic*, pp. 331–46; and Sasser, 'Solidarity', pp. 61–80.
36. King, *Internationalisation*, pp. 146–7.
37. Compare Wilson, 'Mixed race', pp. 44–9, 54–6, 59–60.
38. See Moore-Gilbert, *Hanif Kureishi*, pp. 6–8; and Ranasinha, *South Asian*, pp. 229, 231–2; and compare Manzoor, *Greetings*, p. 227.
39. Appiah, 'Identity crisis', p. 42.
40. Saadi, 'Born'; and compare Kunzru, '*White Teeth*'; and Kohli, *Indian Takeaway*, p. 197.
41. Nasta, *Home Truths*, p. 184.
42. Ranasinha, *South Asian*, pp. 65–6.
43. Sandhu, *London Calling*, p. 233; see also Kaleta, *Hanif Kureishi*, pp. 40–1; and Gairola, 'Capitalist', p. 38.
44. Johnston, review of *ABCD*, p. 3.
45. Patel et al., 'Audio commentary'.
46. Thus she notes that 'in England, it feels like there's a lot more [cinematic

and televisual] material to be had . . . There were more British Indians . . . writing their own work and getting it made – instead of other people writing what they thought those experiences were. America still has some catching up to do in that regard'; quoted in Patterson, 'I've had such a blast'; and compare Manzoor, 'I get to sit', where South Asian American actor and comedian Aasif Mandvi sees British television as a 'decade ahead' of the US in its representation of South Asians.

47. I refer, of course, to Harold Bloom's well-known phrase to describe the sometimes agonistic relationship of younger writers to older and more established ones; see Bloom, *Anxiety*. For Naipaul's impact on Rushdie, see, for example, Gorra, *After Empire*, pp. 144–8, 169–72; Nasta, *Home Truths*, pp. 9, 154–8; and Wood, 'Enigmas', pp. 77–92.
48. Cited in Maxey, 'Interview', pp. 29–30.
49. Gorra, *After Empire*, p. 136; Nasta, *Home Truths*, p. 140; Stein, *Black British*, p. 171.
50. Ranasinha, *Hanif Kureishi*, p. 87.
51. Alam, *Bharati Mukherjee*, p. 140.
52. Ranasinha, *South Asian*, p. 270.
53. Kumar, *Bombay*, pp. 158–9.
54. Kureishi, *My Ear*, p. 169.
55. King, *Internationalisation*, p. 59.
56. Blaise and Mukherjee, *Days and Nights*, p. 299.
57. Mukherjee, *Darkness*, p. 2.
58. Compare Maxey, 'Messiness', pp. 194–6.
59. See, for example, Ashraf, 'A conversation'.
60. Ibid.
61. Hancock, 'An interview', pp. 40–1; Mukherjee, 'Prophet', pp. 9–12.
62. The broader influence of Jewish America on South Asian American literature can be gauged by the recurrence of Jewish characters in such novels as Kirin Narayan's *Love, Stars, and All That* (1994); Bapsi Sidhwa's *An American Brat* (1994); and Meena Alexander's *Manhattan Music* (1997).
63. Singer, 'Hanif Kureishi', p. 106; Ali and Rasiah, 'Meena Alexander', pp. 74–5.
64. See Maxey, 'Life in the diaspora', p. 24n.
65. Ranasinha, *South Asian*, pp. 193–4, 196–9, 203, 219–20.
66. Sandhu, *London Calling*, p. 230; Kumar, *Bombay*, p. 155.
67. Mishra, 'Diasporic imaginary', p. 436.
68. Ramesh, 'Mid-life'; Frears quoted in Friedman and Stewart, 'Keeping', p. 233.
69. Compare Ranasinha, *South Asian*, p. 237, where she asks 'how can Frears (or anyone else) confer this authenticity?'
70. Cited in McCabe, 'Hanif Kureishi', p. 40.
71. Govinden, *Graffiti*, front cover. Kureishi's *Buddha of Suburbia* has, moreover, been used as a benchmark in reviews of other contemporary British Asian

writing; see, for instance, the *Mojo* review quoted on the back cover of Manzoor, *Greetings*. In this memoir, Manzoor feels the need to acknowledge the importance of both Rushdie and Kureishi, but goes on to argue that they were not role models for a young British Pakistani boy 'who was not born into wealth and did not have a mixed-race heritage'; ibid., p. 171.

72. Quoted in Jaggi, 'Where East'.
73. Meer, *Bombay Talkie*, n.p.
74. Sandhu, 'Life lines'; Nasta, 'Writing', p. 21; and compare Thomas, *Hanif Kureishi*, p. 2.
75. Stein writes that the black British novelist Diran Adebayo has 'remarked that his writing has been enabled by . . . Hanif Kureishi'; see Stein, *Black British*, p. xv. Zadie Smith has also discussed the personal impact of his writing; see Donadio, 'My beautiful London'.
76. Mukherjee, 'America unbound', n.p.
77. Shukla, *India Abroad*, p. 161; Gabriel, 'Immigrant', p. 85. Mukherjee is pre-dated by such writers as Ved Mehta, A. K. Ramanujan, and Zulfikar Ghose; Kureishi by G. V. Desani, V. S. Naipaul, Anita Desai, Dilip Hiro, and Kamala Markandaya.
78. Lahiri was the first Asian American and the first writer from a South Asian background to win a Pulitzer Prize in the fiction category.
79. Maxey, 'Interview', p. 28.
80. Quoted in McCabe, 'Hanif Kureishi', p. 47.
81. Ranasinha, *South Asian*, p. 247.
82. See Maxey, 'Representative', pp. 217–36.
83. Vignisson, 'Bharati Mukherjee', p. 156.
84. Giles, *Virtual Americas*, p. 16.
85. Quoted in Tabios, *Black Lightning*, p. 207.
86. Cited in Maxey, 'An interview', p. 193.
87. Quoted in Jaggi, 'Soul'.
88. See Mukherjee, 'Love me', p. 189; Vignisson, 'Bharati Mukherjee', p. 156; and Byers-Pevitts, 'Interview', pp. 192–3.
89. In Nair's film, Britain's absence as a point of departure or potential destination for Indian diasporic communities is noticeable. Family members are instead returning from, or planning to take up residence in, America, Australia, and Dubai. For a discussion of the film's transnational politics, see Banerjee, 'Traveling barbies', pp. 448–70. In Nair's *Mississippi Masala*, the Loha family's fifteen years in Britain are effectively erased, both in narrative terms and, at the start of the film, by the extra-diegetic device of a camera moving over a map from Kampala, Uganda, as point of origin to the final destination of Greenwood, Mississippi, with Britain only briefly referenced on the way.
90. See Lahiri, *Interpreter*, pp. 173–4; Lahiri, *Namesake*, p. 212; and Lahiri, *Unaccustomed*, pp. 135–6, 144–7, 159–73.
91. I am, of course, adapting Paul Gilroy's well-known phrase, 'Black Atlantic';

see Gilroy, *Black Atlantic*. At the same time, this study is not intended as another theoretical response to Gilroy's influential work, but rather as a specifically literary study invoking aesthetic currents within a particular transatlantic framework. It is also not the first to reformulate Gilroy's phrase and apply it to South Asian transnational currents; see, for example, Desai, *Beyond Bollywood*, pp. 2–3, 6, 24, 48, 55, where she deploys the term 'Brown Atlantic' as a way of considering South Asian diasporic cinema.

92. Such 'parallelisms' are defined as 'two writers working on similar ideas, divided by a nation and an ocean' in Beer and Bennett, 'Introduction', p. 3.
93. Nelson, *Reworlding*; Innes, *A History*; Nasta, *Home Truths*; Sandhu, *London Calling*; Procter, *Dwelling Places*; Srikanth, *World Next Door*; Stein, *Black British*; Wong and Hassan, *Fiction of South Asians*; Ranasinha, *South Asian*; and Mishra, *Literature*. Such studies generally concern themselves either with Britain – and often 'black' Britain more widely – or America, although surprisingly few scholars have analysed South Asian American literature as a whole; and critics appear more interested in literary history and retrieval than in interpreting the contemporary moment. Mishra's study does consider South Asian diasporic writing in transnational terms, but works with a smaller selection of (more canonical) authors than this book – notably Naipaul and Rushdie – and he devotes space to the Caribbean, Canada, and the Pacific rather than focusing on Britain and America. While ambitious and important, Mishra's study thus offers a different emphasis and argument to mine.
94. Koshy, 'South Asians', pp. 29–50.
95. Shukla, *India Abroad*; Fludernik, 'Imagined communities', pp. 261–85; Gopinath, *Impossible Desires*. Fludernik does little to develop her transatlantic comparisons, while her claim that British Asian writers present the UK more negatively than South Asian American authors depicting the US is a questionable one. Shukla's historical and anthropological investigation is – like Desai's *Beyond Bollywood* – unusual in its status as a book-length, scholarly work which considers South Asians in Britain and America comparatively, but it contains only one chapter on literature, which focuses on a few key writers rather than on South Asian Atlantic writing more widely. The transatlantic focus of Gopinath's impressive study, meanwhile, compares South Asian cultural production in Britain with that of Canada to a greater extent than the US.
96. Two recent works in particular have been read alongside each other: Ali's *Brick Lane* and Lahiri's *Namesake*. For examples of comparative discussions of these novels, see Mishra, 'Enigmas', pp. 42–4; Kral, 'Shaky ground', pp. 65–76; and Dasgupta, 'Locating "home"', p. 80.
97. Manning and Taylor, 'Introduction', p. 5.
98. Macpherson, *Transatlantic*, p. 5. That this has largely been the focus of transatlantic literary studies is reflected in such journals as *Symbiosis: A Journal of Anglo-American Literary Relations*, *Atlantic Studies*, and, to a lesser extent, the more historically and politically orientated *Journal of Transatlantic Studies*.

See also Green, *Transatlantic Patterns*; Massa and Stead, *Forked Tongues?*; Giles, *Transatlantic Insurrections*; Giles, *Virtual Americas*, pp. 22–87; Beer and Bennett, *Special Relationships*; Williams, *Ethnicity*; Katz, *American Modernism*; and Leypoldt, *Cultural Authority*.

99. See, for instance, Brauner, *Post-War Jewish Fiction*; Jones, 'Imaginary black family', pp. 191–202; Varvogli, 'Underwhelmed', pp. 83–95; Giles, *Atlantic Republic*, pp. 343–57; Lea, 'Aesthetics', pp. 3–26; Macpherson, *Transatlantic*; Moynihan, 'Ships in motion', pp. 41–58; and Gunning and Ward, 'Tracing'.
100. Stein, *Black British*, pp. 17 and xv respectively.
101. In my choice of more well-known writers to discuss in the chapters which follow, I have included Naipaul and Rushdie, but deliberately focused on them less than other established authors, since they have received more scholarly attention than, for example, either Kureishi or Mukherjee.

CHAPTER 1

HOME AND NATION IN SOUTH ASIAN ATLANTIC LITERATURE

Introduction

Issues of home and nation are a well-recognised aspect of postcolonial debates,[1] and they continue to be key ideas, both politically and culturally, to South Asian writers in the United States and Britain. Such writers examine home in order to raise provocative questions about changing societies and the place of ethnic South Asians within them. Home thus serves as an important synecdoche for wider social and national concerns, and it is used both to affirm and to call into question the status of Britain and America as sites of permanent settlement. Many writers examining concepts of home and nation are still first- or second-generation. Generally, they came of age in the 1960s and 1970s, when questions of American or British identity – personalised through the idea of home – were particularly pressing, thanks to the US 'ethnic revival',[2] the impact of postcolonial immigration on British society, and the growth of identity politics on both sides of the Atlantic. Thus writers may lack the distance from such issues which might be enjoyed by authors born at a later stage. Some writers even display a kind of proselytising zeal about emigration: part of a broader justification, perhaps, for leaving the ancestral homeland in favour of the US or UK.[3]

Madan Sarup has shown the extent to which the word 'home' is built into the English language.[4] It is polysemic and, for Malashri Lal and Sukrita Paul Kumar, 'a term of reference . . . resonant with indeterminacy'.[5] As Sara Ahmed notes, it is 'where one usually lives . . . where one's family lives or . . . [it is] one's native country'.[6] And indeed, transatlantic South Asian writers deconstruct home in a linguistic and philosophical sense.[7]

For instance, in Chitra Divakaruni's 'The intelligence of wild things' (from her South Asian American short fiction collection, *The Unknown Errors of Our Lives* [2001]), the unnamed narrator reflects on 'home. I turn the sound over on my tongue, trying to figure out the various tenses in which such a word might exist',[8] while *Fault Lines* (1993), the memoir of the South Asian American writer Meena Alexander, distinguishes between its author's floating status as 'a woman cracked by multiple migrations' and her

> *nadu* . . . the Malayalam word for home . . . homeland . . . my mother's home . . . and . . . appa's home . . . together compose my nadu, the dark soil of self. I was taught that what I am is bound up always with a particular ancestral site . . . How tight the bonds are.[9]

Despite this clear sense of ancestral origins, naturalised through the rooted imagery of 'dark soil' and the word for 'homeland' in Alexander's mother tongue, her autobiography is typical of South Asian Atlantic writing in its problematising of such connections and the ways in which it is haunted by a state of 'unhousedness' (129): that is, a sense of psychological homelessness, despite the emotional and imaginative power suggested by the associations of the word 'home'.

South Asian writers in the US return more insistently to the subcontinent, and especially to India, than their British Asian counterparts. Arguably this is because more of them are first-generation, and South Asian houses and homelands thus remain part of living memory. This tendency to draw inspiration from the motherland may also owe something to the American literary traditions which have influenced such writers: especially Asian American literature, which is often concerned with the ancestral homeland;[10] and American immigrant writing more generally, a canon which outstrips anything comparable in the UK and expresses the very different ethno-cultural formation of the United States. For some critics, the continuing emphasis by US-based writers on South Asia is also part of a cultural contingency plan, since Americanness is still largely associated with whiteness and racism continues to impact in multiple ways on Americans of colour. Thus Rajini Srikanth argues that

> Asian Americans . . . never know when their membership in the United States will be called into question . . . The mainstream media's disregard of the abuse and racially motivated attacks suffered by many South Asians in the months following the September 11, 2001, attacks on the World Trade Center and the Pentagon . . . confirm for Asian Americans their perpetual foreignness in the American imagination and consciousness . . . This awareness of one's shaky

> place within the US body politic is reason enough for many Asian Americans to feel justified in retaining economic ties with ancestral homelands . . . preserving memories of past . . . heritages in countries other than the United States.[11]

The recognition of such transnationalism within diasporic communities – and, more specifically, the distinction between 'America as . . . nation [and] . . . places elsewhere as . . . historical, ethnic, or spiritual homeland'[12] – has become a critical commonplace.[13] Indeed many of these texts present transnational identity as a given. In her South Asian American campus novel *Love, Stars, and All That* (1994), for example, Kirin Narayan writes that 'people of that [bourgeois] class and those [independence-era] generations were interconnected across India. Now these ties were spreading across the globe, encircling others as they went.'[14] But later, the novel explicitly highlights issues of home through the half-rhetorical, half-open questions posed by the character Firoze, who asks: 'why is it that some of us go back to live in India and some of us stay on in the US?' (196). His ongoing battle with these questions is underpinned by a parallel struggle with the South Asian diaspora's roots in colonial subjugation and with the cultural syncretism – a source of both confusion and liberation – which has developed as a result of migration. Postcolonial hybridity has directly shaped Firoze's own identity formation and that of any number of fictional figures in transatlantic South Asian literature. The handling of home across this œuvre therefore relies on a tension between its status as a live issue worthy of debate and, at other times, as a matter which demands little or no discussion: a clichéd subject some characters may even wish to avoid. But how can home be, paradoxically, both an issue and *not* an issue within South Asian Atlantic writing? How can we account for the enduring significance of specifically *national* identities to many of these apparently transnational writers? How does the treatment of home overlap and differ in these texts and how do they operate transatlantically? Do writers perpetuate or challenge traditional ideas of home? And are home and nation more important to British Asian or to South Asian American writers? I will return to these questions throughout this chapter.

Critics of South Asian diasporic writing certainly agree on the centrality of home within this body of work,[15] and many of them examine questions of immigration, diaspora, transnationalism, identity, and biculturalism. But there is room for fresh research. Specifically, more attention needs to be paid to the material nature of home.[16] Alison Blunt and Robyn Dowling note that 'home is a *place*, a site in which we live. But, more than this, home is . . . an idea . . . imaginary . . . home is much more than house or household.'[17] Within these works, however, home is often experienced in down-to-earth fashion at the explicitly spatial level of physical environment and quotidian dwelling. As Sanjukta Dasgupta has put it, 'the desire for locating a home in the world and the home as domestic space [in Bengali American women's writing] seem[s] to be intricately enmeshed as cultures, identities, heredity and environment are negotiated'.[18] Life in Britain and the US becomes a series of such material negotiations, whereby alien weather must be survived, and domestic territory claimed. Processes of settlement, reverse colonisation, and postcolonial critique are figured through climate, map-making, horticulture, homeowning, and the rise of regional affiliations. This is a necessarily selective list and while I return to another important material element – food – in Chapter 4, there is no space here to discuss, for instance, education or the external workplace.

Although scholarly work on specific British Asian localities has appeared in recent years,[19] it has rarely been carried out from a literary perspective, while critics of South Asian American writing have seldom discussed US regionalism. In other words, whereas commentators acknowledge the complexity of South Asian feeling towards the new nation, few explore workaday navigations of America or the UK, especially those produced by less canonical writers, such as Manzu Islam and Suhayl Saadi in Britain or Sameer Parekh and Vineeta Vijayaraghavan in the US; and even fewer examine the transatlantic comparisons inscribed by South Asian American and British Asian writers.

Seeking to fill these gaps in existing scholarship, this chapter will explore and rethink the inherent tensions of home as material and ideological space across a range of representative works, set in Britain or the United States rather than South Asia. It will examine texts which interrogate the idea of home in particularly suggestive ways as well as those which make overtly transatlantic comparisons. The chapter will explore such themes as the sojourner-turned-settler, the drive towards property-ownership, and the formation of new regional and national identities. It will consider how authors trace the evolution of particular communities in local and ethnic terms, while discussing such recurring tropes as the relationship between gender and domesticity, and the public and private claiming of territory. This chapter will offer close textual readings in order to illuminate parallels between individual prose works – which include novels, short fiction, and life-writing – while identifying key differences, thus intervening in existing postcolonial scholarship and offering a new contribution to transatlantic literary studies.

Sojourners-Turned-Settlers: The Postwar Moment in Asian Britain

In order to contextualise the idea of home within this body of writing, I will begin by looking briefly at its treatment by an earlier generation of South Asian authors in the UK, who examine the postwar period in which (usually male) migrants came to Britain, rather than the United States. As we saw in the Introduction, this was because the UK represented a more obvious destination for postcolonial South Asians before 1965. Such men started out, in Naila Kabeer's words, 'as "sojourners" rather than "settlers", hoping to return as rich men of high status'.[20] Texts such as Zulfikar Ghose's *Confessions of a Native-Alien* (1965), V. S. Naipaul's *The Mimic Men* (1967), Kamala Markandaya's *The Nowhere Man* (1972), and Abdullah Hussein's *Émigré Journeys* (2000) were all written during – or relate to – a postwar era which Sukhdev Sandhu has described as 'that tough but liberating prelude to mass immigration from the Subcontinent'.[21] The literary drive to frame questions of home through the lives of 'sojourners-turned-settlers' arguably arises from a political desire to chronicle and commemorate this traditionally hidden past: a subculture overlooked in mainstream postwar British fiction. Following a similar counter-historical impulse, Nadeem Aslam's novel *Maps for Lost Lovers* (2004) incorporates forty years of migrant history in the UK, and the evolution of white attitudes to South Asian immigrants, into its account of contemporary British Asian communities.

As Bruce King has noted, the issue of living spaces is particularly important in postwar British Asian works.[22] Indeed, texts discussing this early period of immigration often draw on a wider British tradition of the boarding-house as *topos* in 1950s and 1960s fiction and cinema.[23] Amir, the protagonist of Hussein's novel, *Émigré Journeys*, remembers every last detail of his cramped, clandestine lodgings in mid-twentieth-century Birmingham. His testimonial account of this environment evokes a house which 'resembled a cave' and

> dated back to the time of Queen Victoria . . . Decay had worked itself deep into the walls covered with great big patches where chunks of plaster had fallen off. The damp had made the mortar bulge out in the shape of half-melons . . . Rumour was that the house had been on the council's condemned list for ten years. But it was still on its feet and in use.[24]

Rather like Srinivas's stylised, at times semi-personified, house in Markandaya's novel *The Nowhere Man*,[25] Amir's home has become more than just a place to sleep at night: it has a life of its own, and its degraded physical condition serves as a metaphor for the ways in which his community of 'brothers . . . in trouble' (145) – Pakistani men living in the UK without their loved ones – occupy the margins, suffering ostracism as they seek to find a place within British society, 'unseen and unheard', their 'very existence on . . . earth . . . denied by other men' (2). Despite the existential nihilism Hussein suggests here, his characters survive life in the penumbral house because, at this sojourner stage, they are consumed by their 'ultimate goal': 'to get out of that time and space . . . out of the country, and go home' (106–7).[26] Later, when tragic circumstances force its inhabitants to disperse, the empty house becomes semi-haunted. It thus anticipates that of the murdered couple, Chanda and Jugnu, in *Maps for Lost Lovers*, whose erstwhile dwelling goes 'through a destiny of its own, shut up, abandoned to dust and insects'.[27] Both *Maps* and Meera Syal's British Asian novel *Anita and Me* (1996) make reference to the postwar migrant boarding-house tradition; and in *Maps*, Aslam suggests that, just as migration from Pakistan to Britain is itself ongoing – rather than a discrete historical phenomenon safely located in the past – so the insanitary, crowded situation of the communal immigrant house still exists in present-day Britain. Rather than simply memorialising an increasingly distant past, he deliberately records a subcultural present.

The first-person narrative of Naipaul's novel *The Mimic Men* is preoccupied with postwar questions of home, or rather escape: it is as much about the journeys which propel the bid to find a home as it is about arrival at actual destinations and the decision to remain in one place. Hence, finding an answer to the conundrum of home is the quest which drives the protagonist, Ralph Singh. Indeed, there is a clear slippage between his sense of migrant statelessness and the inability of any built environment to fulfil his needs, whether this is on Isabella, the fictionalised Caribbean island where he grew up, or in Britain, where he makes several attempts to start a new life. Despite his relative privilege, Ralph is never far from domestic squalor in postwar London. Like Sam Selvon – who works such details as leaking roofs, which parsimonious landlords refuse to mend, into his classic novel of early African-Caribbean migration, *The Lonely Londoners* (1956)[28] – Naipaul is unsparing in his attention to the material deficiencies of London living spaces. Thus Ralph refers to his experience of the city as 'anguish' and recalls every claustrophobic detail of postwar domesticity:

> the mean rooms . . . shut door . . . tight window . . . tarnished ceiling . . . over-used curtains . . . rigged shilling-in-the-slot gas and electric meters . . . dreary journeys through terraces of brick, the life reduced to insipidity.[29]

Immigrant negotiations of postwar Britain are inscribed for posterity through the equivocal stance of *Mimic Men* and *Émigré Journeys*, which pays tribute to the pioneering mentality behind South Asian migration, while refusing to forget the gritty realities of adapting to different national and domestic norms. The 'sojourner', rather than 'settler', part of the equation thus remains more important at a stage when domestic settings and Britain-as-nation are navigated and inhabited, rather than claimed. Indeed, where the first generation does believe it has put down roots – as, for example, Srinivas does in *Nowhere Man* – the consequences are dangerous, even fatal.[30] Erstwhile sojourners and their children are presented as laying real claim to British homes only years later.

New Immigrant Homes in the US

As distinct from this British Asian insistence on the downbeat nature of immigrant living conditions, South Asian American writers veer from optimism at the brightness of American modernity, reinscribing the nation's popular status as a 'land of opportunity', to a sense of greater ambivalence at the potential for loneliness and for cultural and political alienation embodied by this vast country. In its explorations of the 'enigma of arrival' (in Naipaul's phrase), South Asian American writing therefore reveals, on the one hand, a palpable excitement at what the US has to offer. This exuberance can be read within the wider context of America's national mythology as the *ne plus ultra* for immigrants, which may also explain why such attitudes are missing from British Asian narratives of arrival. The US is, for the most part, defined positively within these 'coming-to-America' texts, especially by what it is not in relation to South Asian countries. A land of safe, well-made cars in Vineeta Vijayaraghavan's novel *Motherland* (2001),[31] it is also (in its 1980s incarnation) a country, for Gita and Ajay in Narayan's *Love, Stars, and All That*, of:

> working phones . . . Libraries . . . The smooth road . . . No honking, no cows . . . Lines . . . people in the US actually know how to stand in line . . . clean public bathrooms . . . Cable TV . . . Fewer amoebas . . . Automatic tellers . . . Hot showers . . . Ice cream: thirty-one flavours . . . sushi. (229–30)

It is thus a revelation for the first generation to discover what Bapsi Sidhwa calls 'the enchantments of the First World' in her novel *An American Brat* (1994).[32] Her protagonist, Feroza, responds to the ready friendliness and openness of Americans, and repeatedly revels in the freedom she can enjoy as a young Pakistani woman in late 1970s America, rather than within

Lahore's tight-knit Parsi circle. Recalling another South Asian American writer, Bharati Mukherjee, Sidhwa also suggests the sexual liberation the US can offer South Asian immigrant women, as her narrative underlines the erotic frisson between its Pakistani- and US-born characters in a land of 'extraordinary sexual possibilities' (116).

Feroza's uncle, Manek – entirely won over by what he calls 'a free and competitive economy in a true democracy' (124) – praises the 'self-sufficient, industrious, and independent way of American life' (119); and although Sidhwa generally avoids too celebratory a tone, her novel closes with a long paean to America's virtues, which may reflect her own decision to settle there. Certainly this is the option Feroza and Manek choose. America ultimately triumphs in *American Brat*, and Sidhwa's title is revealing in this regard, since it aligns the novel with a long tradition in US culture of reflecting national identity in titular form.[33] Sidhwa could thus be claiming a kind of representative American status for her South Asian diasporic narrative (a less common trend within British Asian cultural production), much as Piyush Dinker Pandya's *American Desi* (2001), Anurag Mehta's *American Chai* (2002), and Varun Khanna's *American Blend* (2006) do in cinematic terms. More than any of these films, however, *American Brat* asks wider national questions (to which I will return shortly) as it reworks classic American immigrant narratives.

In *Unknown Errors of Our Lives*, many of Chitra Divakaruni's newly arrived characters confound the stereotype of immigrants obsessed with the mother country. They have escaped India for a host of reasons, often related to familial or public trauma (especially communal violence), believing that America will offer greater opportunities for privacy, safety, and personal development. In 'The lives of strangers', Leela's parents are Non-Resident Indians or NRIs – although 'Non-Returning Indians' might be more apt[34] – who find other

> people . . . noisy and messy . . . Which was why, early in their lives, they had escaped India to take up research positions in America . . . they never discussed their homeland, a country they seemed to have shed as easily as a lizard drops its tail. (59, 61)

And, as Lilia puts it in Jhumpa Lahiri's short story 'When Mr Pirzada came to dine' (*Interpreter of Maladies* [1999]): '[In America] I would never have to eat rationed food, or obey curfews, or watch riots from my rooftop, or hide neighbours in water tanks to prevent them from being shot, as . . . [my mother] and . . . father had.'[35]

At other times, new immigrant critiques are harsher, particularly where American suburbia is concerned. In 'Blooming season for cacti', Mira is downcast to note that her brother's home in Texas is 'a two-bedroom semidetached exactly like a hundred others' (169). Indeed, India may present harsh and messy situations in *Unknown Errors*, but at least it possesses vitality, unlike the sterility of the US suburbs. In 'Lives of strangers', Leela dreads her return to America, where her 'life waits to claim her, unchanged, impervious, smelling like floor polish' (88), while in 'Unknown errors of our lives', Ruchira is drawn to Biren, precisely because he appears to come from 'a galaxy far, far away from the blandness of auto-malls and AMC cinemas' (217). In Kavita Daswani's novel *For Matrimonial Purposes* (2003), Anju notices, on first arriving in New Jersey, that this is the 'suburban . . . America . . . where big white men . . . drank beer . . . while their blonde wives . . . made potato salad in the kitchen':[36] a combined attack on US suburbia and white American patriarchy.

The homogeneity of US suburbia also induces a profound sense of loneliness. Thus Mrs Dutta in Divakaruni's 'Mrs Dutta writes a letter' perceives America to be 'a country where you might stare out the window for hours and not see one living soul' (*Unknown Errors*, 20). This in turn recalls Ganeshan Kaka in *Love, Stars, and All That*, who claims that America 'is bloody hell, everyone in his box' (194); and R. K. Narayan, who similarly remarks that Indian families in America are 'boxed up in their homes securely behind locked doors'.[37] This is in fact a broader idea within South Asian Atlantic writing – as demonstrated by the self-contained Vasi family, equally 'boxed up' in their 1980s Cardiff home in Nikita Lalwani's British Asian novel *Gifted* (2007) – and it is used to reveal the cultural chasm between living conditions in the subcontinent and adoptive Western homes. Mrs Dutta's experience of the US is thus contrasted with the vibrant sounds of Calcutta, just as it is for another homesick Bengali, Mrs Sen, stranded in New England in Lahiri's story 'Mrs Sen's' (*Interpreter of Maladies*), who 'cannot . . . sleep in so much silence',[38] challenging the idea that slumber relies on noiselessness. In *American Brat*, Feroza's mother, Zareen, finds the lack of noise in residential Denver 'eerie' and misses Lahore's 'mosque stereos [and] . . . the insufferable racket of the rickshaws' (282). In other words, however noisy or crowded South Asian urban settings may be, new arrivals prefer them to America's silence and vast, empty space, both physical and emotional.

These writers do not romanticise South Asian countries, however, since life there is often depicted as tough, deeply sectarian, and relentlessly political. Indeed, their characters seize exciting opportunities to claim the putatively 'virgin' land of America. Yet, for all its purported freedoms, the US is quite often figured through carceral language, as the image of 'boxes', deployed by R. K. and Kirin Narayan, demonstrates. This tension between an abstract freedom and suburban/domestic claustrophobia recalls the bleakness – if not the austerity – of postwar British dwellings. It can also be connected to Rosemary Marangoly George's idea of home as paradoxical haven and prison. She observes that the constituents of home are often binary and oppositional: 'homes are . . . places of violence and nurturing . . . to escape to and . . . escape from . . . Home is the desired place that is fought for and established as the exclusive domain of a few. It is not a neutral place.'[39] The imagery of domestic imprisonment also hints at a more generalised aspect of some South Asian diasporic communities, which, according to Monika Fludernik, are 'represented [in literature] as both a nurturing and . . . strangling home'.[40]

In other words, writers display a clear ambivalence about the United States, constructing an ethnographic critique which highlights the nation's deficiencies in relation to South Asia. Sometimes this takes a relatively mild form: for instance, when Divakaruni draws attention to America's relative lack of history in comparison with India in 'The blooming season for cacti'.[41] Or in Lahiri's novel *The Namesake* (2003), when Ashoke and Ashima, a new immigrant couple, gently reverse outsiders' clichés about India by applying them to late 1960s New England. Thus 'a . . . black cat is permitted to sit as it pleases on the shelves' of a local convenience store in Cambridge, Massachusetts,[42] inverting the idea that it is India rather than the US where animals – cows and monkeys, for instance – roam freely. And it comes as a shock to Ashima, before her move to suburbia, to discover 'dog urine and excrement' on the street and 'roaches in the bathroom' (30) of Cambridge, rather than in the supposedly less sanitary environs of Calcutta,[43] her home town.

A more violent strain of anti-American feeling informs parts of *American Brat*, where Feroza notes the serious poverty of late 1970s New York and perceives that this is

> an alien filth, a compost reeking of vomit and alcoholic belches . . . neglected old age and sickness . . . drugged exhalations and the malodorous ferment of other substances she could not decipher . . . It seemed to her they personified the callous heart of the rich country that allowed such savage neglect to occur. (81)[44]

Meticulously – scientifically even – Sidhwa takes us through every step of Feroza's regionalised American journey, illustrating her feelings of excitement, vulnerability, and isolation. Employing an elegant, drily humorous prose style, which is both compassionate and mocking, Sidhwa offers a wide-ranging ethnographic assessment of the United States, rightly identified by Carmen Faymonville as a 'parodying [of] the dichotomy of the colonialist attitude of the Third World as "uncivilised" and a laughable "civilised" West'.[45] Besides poverty and social inequality, Sidhwa's targets include racial injustice; the American state's non-interference in the lives of its citizens; and the ubiquitous nature of political apathy: namely, America's pre-9/11 inability to see the effects of its foreign policy and the oversimplification, by many Americans, of complex political situations overseas. Starkly contrasted with this luxury of apolitical sensibility is Sidhwa's notion that in South Asia, everyone's daily lives are affected by politics – and sometimes to devastating effect – a point which another Pakistani-born writer, Mohsin Hamid, makes in his more recent, post-9/11 novel, *The Reluctant Fundamentalist* (2007).[46] In *American Brat*, Sidhwa depicts American visitors to Pakistan as selfish and insensitive and, at these politically charged moments, her own voice intervenes powerfully to remark upon the late 1970s international climate she evokes. Although her tone can appear didactic at such points, her anger is generally measured, as she draws attention to events affecting millions of people yet largely ignored by the US and other Western nations.

Reluctant Fundamentalist takes such critique several steps further as it deals with the messy repercussions of 9/11 for South Asians. Subjecting US foreign policy to even greater transnational scrutiny than Sidhwa does, Hamid's novel suggests the impossibility for many South Asian Americans of remaining free from the impact of international events. Significantly, it is during a trip to Chile – with its history of American political intervention – that Changez, Hamid's protagonist, experiences his life-changing disillusionment with the United States. *Reluctant Fundamentalist* might also be classed as 'return-of-the-native' fiction (of the kind discussed in Chapter 2), since Changez narrates his tale of American life from Pakistan. But whereas such works often portray immigrants making temporary return visits and then going back to the material comforts of North America, *Reluctant Fundamentalist* reverses this. As opposed to its 'coming-to-America' precursors, this is arguably the most well-known, recent example of a 'leaving America' narrative,[47] which implies that an external position is best for critiquing the US. Hamid thus challenges popular theoretical notions of transnationalism which celebrate mobility and liminality as utopian possibilities, because his novel implies that such movement is costly: politically, morally, emotionally, and psychologically.[48]

Changez's rejection of the US – in what Hamid has claimed is not an 'anti-American' novel[49] – is particularly stark. After all, he occupies a privileged, 'model minority' position in America as a Princeton graduate in a highly paid job.[50] His securing of the American Dream is therefore not at issue and his decision to leave the US is also not based, as one might expect, on the post-9/11 failure of Americans to accept the Muslim immigrants in their midst. Rather, Changez's response is fuelled by his own morally charged, highly politicised questions about the US. *Reluctant Fundamentalist* may be situated, then, in relation to earlier South Asian American critiques of the adopted nation, but its protagonist is much more questioning of his place in the United States. Perhaps this is because the novel is written in full consciousness of 9/11 and is designed to provoke debate about its aftermath within Muslim-majority countries. In a distinctly un-Hollywood move, America is never allowed to speak in a narrative which deliberately eschews any clear sense of closure, instead offering at the end several frightening possibilities for the reader to decipher and interpret. Thus the novel undercuts popular ideas about border-crossing by raising thorny transnational questions without providing any easy answers. Yet *Reluctant Fundamentalist* is ultimately more about America than it is about Pakistan: despite being a 'leaving America' novel, it never fully escapes its discursive reliance on an imperialist US.[51] As I argued in the Introduction, South Asian American culture is relatively new and, in its ethnographic handling of the United States as home, it demonstrates a sense of ambivalence and flux, of evolving attitudes, and of confusion between surface and depth: that is, the contradiction between the promise of America to new immigrants and its history of racialised exclusion at home and imperialism abroad.

Negotiating an Alien Climate

I will turn now to the notion of navigating a different physical climate, a challenge which appears to be starker for new immigrants in Britain than the US. Indeed, the British weather becomes a pessimistic figure for the difficulties of national belonging, but it is worth noting that this idea is deployed to critique the UK by both British Asian *and* South Asian American writers. In its wintry coldness and darkness, Britain's physical environment is of course a well-documented element of the postcolonial migrant experience,[52] and weather conditions clearly signify the unwelcoming *froideur* of its political, cultural, and social climate, throughout the twentieth century, in relation to non-white newcomers.[53] Such climatic conditions also emphasise the complications of making new homes on British soil. In this section, I will argue that, however familiar a postcolonial strategy this is, the powerful trope of an alien British climate takes on a particular freight of meaning in the hands of South Asian Atlantic writers as they examine questions of home and nation.

In *The Crow Eaters* (1978), Bapsi Sidhwa reveals the Junglewallas' disappointment at the bathetic realities of 'the land of their rulers' by emphasising the pinched and unappealing weather which characterises her cartoonish version of late 1920s London: 'the bitter wind . . . grey, perpetually drizzling sky . . . dull, foggy [atmosphere]'.[54] In *Fault Lines*, Alexander writes of the 'peculiar English weather . . . the threat of rain . . . the ground and air sucked into the innards of an immense wet cheek, light filtered through a porous greyness' (137). In each case, the British weather is used to foreground the nation's alienness, and alienating qualities, for South Asian visitors, themselves 'aliens' in a sense. Later Alexander deploys meteorological imagery to assert the postcolonial subject's sense of superiority towards Britain through a comparative emphasis on India's tropical warmth. Elsewhere she attacks imperialism by pointing to the apparent colourlessness of the UK as opposed to India. Thus in her novel *Nampally Road* (1991), Alexander draws on the figure of Queen Victoria as depicted on an old imperial clock in India, wearing clothing which is 'grey like fog over the Thames':[55] an image which, like *Crow Eaters*, relies on the hoary cliché of London as a Dickensian city perpetually shrouded in fog. This also echoes Rushdie's essay 'The New Empire within Britain' (1982), which critiques British imperial rule by conflating grim weather conditions with a lack of colour[56] and space as the 'pink conquerors' return from India to 'their cold [post-imperial] island . . . [and] the narrow horizons of their pallid, drizzled streets'.[57] Similarly, Sidhwa writes of a colonial British civil servant in India proleptically mourning the return to 'his cold, damp and colourless little country' (*Crow Eaters*, 131). Weather is also used throughout Ameena Meer's novel *Bombay Talkie* (1994) to code different places and specifically to pit a chilly, grey, and parochial Britain against the greater warmth and sensuality of both India and the United States.

Such negative meteorological tropes may, however, also be applied in a North American context. One thinks of the coldness of Canada in Mukherjee's work, which forms part of her wider exposé of 1970s Canadian xenophobia.[58] There is, moreover, an implied connection between the racism of America's Midwest and its freezing winter temperatures in Alexander's *Fault Lines*.[59] Despite this North American coldness – and bitter winters in the northern United States are also a prevalent aspect of the new Bengali immigrant's life in Lahiri's writing[60] – it is worth noting that US weather plays less of a role in South Asian American literature than the British climate does for both UK and US writers. How might one account for this? On the one hand, the meteorological facts – that the United States enjoys consistently hotter and more humid weather conditions than Britain, and suffers from a higher level of weather-related destruction – make America much more analogous to South Asia, for the first generation in particular. On the other hand, despite its own differentiated characteristics, the US weather is much less important than the British climate for such American-based authors as Sidhwa and Alexander. That they choose to highlight the British, rather than American, weather can be connected to their explicitly postcolonial position and to their perception that the US embraces immigrants more readily than the UK. It thus becomes a recognisable feature of their transatlantic critique.

As distinct from this anti-imperialist rejection of Britain by writers resident in the US, British Asian authors illustrate the lived reality of unforgiving UK climatic conditions. Indeed, such weather becomes an important feature of survival in the complicated bid by their characters to secure a British home. In a characteristic gesture, Manzu Islam depicts Bangladeshi Londoners in his short story 'Going home' (from the collection *The Mapmakers of Spitalfields* [1997]) as 'shivering in the howling sub-zero wind';[61] while the drabness of weather conditions in Lalwani's *Gifted* mirrors the emotional privations of the Vasi family. Dreary weather forms the backdrop to key episodes within Lalwani's narrative, illuminating the disappointments of British life for Indians who have resolutely refused to integrate into the wider society, remaining quiet, unobserved expatriates rather than immigrants, in Mukherjee's formulation.[62] Thus Shreene's intense isolation and homesickness for India are captured when she observes 'the wretched shade of grey that seemed to own the sky in this part of the world'.[63] As with the imagery deployed by Sidhwa and Alexander, the message is clear: such weather is categorically not hers and, in a moment of pathetic fallacy, it is rendered alien and inhospitable. Later in the novel, her daughter Rumi's brutal self-harming is played out against a background of coldly uncaring weather: 'it was snowing outside, in a sludgy, soiled, Cardiff sort of a way – a snow that seemed to mix itself with all the different contaminants in the air before falling on to the window-sills or lawns . . . outside' (248). And before Shreene's reunion with Rumi at the end of the novel, Brighton beach is experienced as 'moisture . . . a peculiarly British incense: a soggy odour of wetness dominating the air that Shreene breathed now, as though she was actually sitting inside a big cloud, rather than on a bench by the sea' (267). Despite the Vasis' years of settlement in Britain, its continuingly defamiliarised weather is used both to mirror and to explain their rejection of the nation as home.

In Ardashir Vakil's novel *One Day* (2003), British weather is, once again, 'horrible . . . dark and depressing . . . you never get used to it', its 'grey' pall on a par with 'dirty baths . . . net curtains . . . empty milk bottles':[64] a version of British interiors which recalls Naipaul's 'tarnished ceiling' and 'over-used curtains' in *Mimic Men* and creates a slippage between climatic and domestic gloom. Yet – as distinct from other South Asian Atlantic writers – Vakil treats such grimness with a grudging affection. Through the eyes of Priya, his privileged, Indian-born protagonist, he depicts Britain's physical climate and the domestic hibernation it compels in winter as a source of comfort:

> if you grow to love this place as Priya has, you grow to love its grey moods. Its sulky mulling, ruminative side. The side that obliges you to concentrate on what is indoors, the cushioned wintry state of mind that inspires eating, hours of brooding . . . Man in his cave, hunkered down, water pattering on the slate roof . . . Pelted glass and phosphorescent street lamps illuminating fine spring showers, lights on at 2 p.m., steaming mug of tea, dribbling egg, fat chips. (57)

Vakil's use of soft-sounding verbs here – 'mull', 'hunker', 'dribble' – and his sense that this is essentially mild, gentle weather ('water pattering', 'fine spring showers') result in a warm, cosy, semi-comic tone quite different from the feelings of alienation and displacement implied by other South Asian Atlantic writers.

In Suhayl Saadi's 'Ninety-nine kiss-o-grams', from his short fiction anthology *The Burning Mirror* (2001), the British-born protagonist, Sal, discovers – on a trip to Pakistan, his ancestral homeland (a 'roots journey' which will be discussed further in the next chapter) – that he is pining for Britain's and, more specifically, Scotland's temperate climate, rendered sensuously as 'the cool spaces ae Scola, the feel ae rain on his back'.[65] His own subject position as a second-generation Pakistani Glaswegian is crucial here, since his dead father's struggle as an immigrant in Scotland is tellingly imagined against a merciless backdrop of 'pissin rain' (3). Saadi marks the cultural and emotional distance between father and son through this distinction between their experiences of British rain, which signals Sal's longing for his Scottish homeland as the logical reverse of his father's yearning for *his* birth country.[66]

Through Priya and Sal, if not the characters in 'Going home' or *Gifted* or a range of anti-colonial South Asian American works, we see the figure of the British climate develop into a complex, inherently subjective device as transatlantic South Asian writing has itself evolved in new directions. Like beauty, it seems that weather is in the eye of the beholder. These climatic negotiations are used, then, to effect a reverse ethnography (another aspect of what is in fact a wider South Asian Atlantic perspective); to signal a complete rejection of Britain as possible home; and, conversely, to demonstrate rootedness in the UK and to naturalise British Asian identities.

Claiming Territory: Property-Ownership and Map-Making

If the need to claim territory is challenged through the negotiation of an alien climate, property-ownership is, in contrast, a potent and, for the most part, positive means of staking a claim to American, and particularly British, soil. Indeed, after many years away from South Asia, first-generation characters like Amir in Hussein's *Émigré Journeys* and Dr Azad in Monica Ali's novel *Brick Lane* (2003) have finally come to accept the wisdom of buying a property in Britain. In Aslam's *Maps for Lost Lovers*, Shamas attempts to transform his British house into a version of his Pakistani childhood home as a means of surviving 'the years of exile and banishment' (6). *Émigré Journeys* is, however, more hopeful and less elegaic. Instead Amir derives his sense of self – like some of Kureishi's first-generation patriarchs[67] – from his status as a UK homeowner. Following his initial, sojourner need to secure land in Pakistan – a point to which I will return in Chapter 2 – he comes to cherish the security of his British property, informing Salma, his wife, that 'we possess this now, this land under our feet, these . . . good, strong walls' (54). He makes his point most fanatically when he confronts Martin, the white boyfriend of his daughter, Parvin:

> 'I am a householder . . . This is my house . . . No place for your person here. This . . . is my land'. He was standing in the middle of the room, stamping his foot on the floor and pointing down with his finger as if showing us something on the ground. 'My land . . . freehold land' . . . There was no boast in his voice, only the simple pride of a long labour. (204)

Amir's sense of purpose stems directly from plans or actions connected with home, and most emblematic of all is his successful property-ownership, which signals the firm eventual desire of some immigrants to stay in Britain and marks a resolution of sorts to the dilemmas surrounding return to South Asia. As opposed to the ambivalence towards US suburban homeowning expressed by some South Asian American writers, British Asian property acquisition signals a triumph: over the hand-to-mouth, xenophobic, boarding-house world which greeted the postwar sojourner.

Manzu Islam's trope of maps and map-making – inscribed in his choice of the title *The Mapmakers of Spitalfields* – suggests a collective territorial claim which goes beyond the individualistic need to own a property. This is illustrated by his characters' informal awareness of 'corners, side-walks . . . alleyways' ('Going home', 21) and, in the short story 'The mapmakers of Spitalfields', through Brothero-Man's more formal topographical claims. Situated 'at the very heart of this foreign city', he is empowered by his own skill and freedom in unmapping[68] and remapping his particular district of London:

> bit by bit, he began drawing the secret blueprint of a new city. It wasn't exactly in the likeness of our left-behind cities from the blossoms of memories. Nor did it grow entirely from the soon-to-be-razed foreign cities where we travellers arrived with expectant maps in our dreams . . . Surely a strange new city, always at the crossroads, and between the cities of lost times and cities of times yet to come. (66)[69]

Rumoured to be 'one of the pioneer jumping-ship men' (66) – a reference to the relatively long history of Bangladeshis in London's East End[70] – Brothero-Man's dreamlike city is actually the network of roads around Brick Lane, and the story creates its particular geographical and temporal map through references to specific street-names and historical events, almost inviting the reader to check the accuracy of its co-ordinates. Like a number of other South Asian immigrants, Brothero-Man occupies a paradoxical position: by turns affectionate and vigilant towards his adopted home, he is both central and liminal to it; liminal because he occupies a marginal position in London as a whole – 'the markings of *our* city . . . no more than tiny dots in the sea of their strange city. There were the tall glass-faced skyscrapers of the city of London. Even in the mist and darkness they loomed menacingly over Brick Lane' (78; emphasis in original) – but central through his determined chronicling of his own local community.[71]

Maps are in fact a favoured device across British Asian writing. In Atima Srivastava's British Asian novel *Looking for Maya* (1999), Mira sees her new sexual relationship as 'a different place' with 'no map' and her lover, Amrit, as 'a land . . . that I wanted to live in, make mine', while Hanif Kureishi writes movingly in his family memoir *My Ear at His Heart* (2004) that his dead father 'made all the maps . . . and he's taken them with him'.[72] Aslam's *Maps for Lost Lovers* – which, like *Mapmakers of Spitalfields*, privileges cartography in its title – turns this imagery into a wider political point (again, recalling *Mapmakers*). Deliberately refusing to name his town, Aslam eschews the specific regional pride of other British Asian writers in order, perhaps, to offer a more generalised critique of South Asian communities in the UK. Nonetheless, his migrants lay oral claim to their particular surroundings by renaming local streets in their originary languages, thus reversing British colonial practices: 'numerous . . . places and roads have been given Indian . . . Pakistani and Bangladeshi names to give the map of this English town a semblance of belonging – amassing a claim on the place bit by bit' (156).[73] As Richard Phillips has put it, 'modern maps . . . naturalise the geographies they represent, and normalise the constructions of race, gender, class . . . those geographies inscribe'.[74] The 'maps' in question may be unofficial, but they nevertheless aid local survival through the appropriation of immediate surroundings.

Cartographic imagery also recurs across South Asian American literature, which is filled with maps, both real and imaginary, operating across space and time. Thus in Vijayaraghavan's *Motherland*, Maya, the young protagonist, believes her grandmother has bequeathed her 'maps of my past and future to navigate by . . . I . . . could surpass geography . . . be grafted and take root anywhere . . . anywhere could become home'.[75] Rajiv likens his immigrant mother to a 'mapmaker' in Sameer Parekh's novel *Stealing the Ambassador* (2002); and Lahiri makes important points about Partition and civil war in South Asia through her use of a world map in the story 'When Mr Pirzada came to dine' (*Interpreter*).[76] In 'Sexy' (another story from *Interpreter*), Lahiri deploys maps to suggest white American insularity. It is their absence here which is significant, since the Caucasian character Miranda, who has only 'ever been . . . to the Bahamas once . . . [as] a child' (91), does not own an atlas. Meanwhile the historical importance of cartography is underlined in the story through the image of outdated, imperial-era maps in Boston's Mapparium.[77] Alexander's *Fault Lines* directly invokes the British imperialist project of mapping India;[78] while, as I argued in the Introduction, the hegemonic position of the US on the world map in *Love, Stars, and All That* clearly signals, and even quietly celebrates, the shift from British to American global influence. Like British Asian authors, South Asian American writers foreground such metaphors by incorporating them into their titles, for instance Agha Shahid Ali's poetry collection *A Nostalgist's Map of America* (1991); and Rajini Srikanth and Sunaina Maira's edited poetry and prose collection *Contours of the Heart: South Asians Map North America* (1996).[79] But they do not map their immediate local surroundings in the US in the manner of the British Asian texts discussed above, thus implying a more tentative, less aggressive territorial claim and, by extension, the idea that the need to mark out new soil as South Asian is less urgent in immigrant America than in postcolonial Britain.

At the same time, maps clearly resonate for South Asian writers on both sides of the Atlantic. Why is this? One reason is that they call attention to travel and migration, suggesting the vast distances covered by a pioneering first generation, as well as the colonial voyages which first linked Britain to India and America. In other words, these later South Asian journeys are made, in part, because of Britain's own expansionist endeavours, symbolised so powerfully through maps, which are 'never value-free images', as J. B. Harley has noted.[80] Cartography also offers proof of permanent residential settlement through the post-imperial claiming of space, authenticated and formalised in material terms through maps, even if they are at times unofficial. Harley notes that maps have traditionally served as 'territorial propaganda in the legitimation of national identities' and that they have played an important defensive role.[81] Such ideas are updated here through the exploratory forging of new 'national identities', identities themselves under threat from nativism and xenophobia. In the British context, this process of identity formation encourages new, and often figurative, forms of mapping and the sometimes militaristic need to protect local communities, for instance Bangladeshi immigrant space in east London in 'Mapmakers'.[82] Rather like property-owning, this is also about the need to control territory, no matter how small; as Phillips has put it, 'the authority of maps lies in their ability to circumscribe geography, by enclosing, defining, coding, orienting, [and] structuring . . . space'.[83]

Maps also present 'a set of beliefs about the way the world should be'.[84] In this context, they form a 'blueprint' (Manzu Islam's word in 'Mapmakers'), a model for how local communities in the new nation should be as much as how they actually are. Harley contends that, historically, maps have been subject to 'manipulation by the powerful in society' and that they have constituted 'a socially conservative vocabulary . . . a language of power, not of protest'.[85] Such points are reversed through the way that British Asian authors radically democratise maps, whereby they can be appropriated, subverted, and reinvented by the apparently powerless and used as 'guides' to new possibilities.[86] Cartographic tropes also point to the navigation of a time-space continuum by transatlantic South Asian writers and thus to the idea of interior, psychological, and sometimes altogether imaginary maps.[87] For Phillips

> cartographic and spatial metaphors are both slippery and fluid . . . contested terms, unstable, uncircumscribed, and therefore continually able to open new conceptual spaces, in which new forms of social and political action may be conceived.[88]

Mapping is thus a polysemic metaphor, which continues to be significant for transatlantic South Asian authors because it provides a rich geographical and historical context for ideas of home.

Bids for ownership go beyond the cartographic to take a horticultural form and, with it, an extra symbolic dimension. In *Maps*, Aslam reconfigures English surroundings along tropical lines, creating a densely detailed ecosystem through references to South Asian flora and fauna in a manner which in part recalls Rushdie's celebrated re-imagining of London as Indian in his novel *The Satanic Verses* (1988),[89] and in part reveals, once again, the territorial investment of immigrants in Britain. It also achieves a reverse colonisation, which recalls British imperial attempts to refashion India along its own horticultural lines.[90] This is important in psychological terms: hence, the failure of Kaukab's Pakistani plants to flourish in England signifies her own deracination in contrast to other migrants in the same novel who have 'raised a banana tree successfully' (*Maps*, 96).[91] Similarly in the US, Kamala fails to 're-create a tropical [Indian] garden' in *Motherland* (66–7), a situation which patently reflects her feelings of displacement, and indeed, the need to plant non-native fruit and vegetables in US and UK soil recurs throughout immigrant writing more generally.[92] The harnessing of resources for survival is also at issue here, as we see with family gardens in the US in Meer's *Bombay Talkie*[93] and in the British Asian context within Sarfraz Manzoor's memoir *Greetings from Bury Park: Race. Religion. Rock 'n' Roll* (2007). In Manzoor's case, this space is 'not only a place of beauty but a source of food . . . my mother was able to grow potatoes, onions and mint leaves, which she ground into chutney'.[94] The garden becomes another form of home as it generates nourishment and increases the possibilities for self-sufficiency.

Regionalism in South Asian American Writing

Regional identities within the new nation are important to transatlantic South Asian writers, yet, at first sight, this seems to be more the case for Britain Asian than for South Asian American authors. This may reflect the greater transnationalism of South Asian American writers. Mainly first-generation, their identity formation might be said to derive from a blend of generalised American belonging[95] and South Asian ethnicity and regionalism, so that – along with their fictional characters – they are, for instance, Bengali American, Gujarati American, or Malayali American. Religious affiliation also plays a key role through the identification of characters as Hindu, Parsi, Jain, Christian, Sikh, Muslim, or Jewish. A more particularised American regionalism can nevertheless be detected across this body of writing, which suggests the establishment of roots, the development of loyalty to a particular region of the US, and the making of American homes.

For Meena Alexander, the quintessential immigrant locale of New

York City is key. As Pin-chia Feng has argued in her examination of Alexander's novel *Manhattan Music* (1997):

> the global economic, informational and cultural flows that converge at and are disseminated from the Big Apple makes [sic] it the capital of contemporary transnational passages and . . . ideal background for a discussion of the problematics of diasporic identity.[96]

New York is also where Anju first settles in Daswani's *For Matrimonial Purposes*. It is of strategic importance in Mukherjee's short fiction (*Darkness* [1985], *The Middleman and Other Stories* [1988]) and novels (*Wife* [1975] and *Jasmine* [1989]); and in Lahiri's *Namesake*. Indeed, several commentators have recognised New York's significance for South Asian Americans.[97]

Lahiri draws more often, however, on New England settings, especially Boston, thus reconfiguring a canonical American literary landscape through her juxtaposition of new immigrants with this time-honoured American settler terrain. This, in turn, is a long way from California, which serves as the location for Kirin Narayan's and Chitra Divakaruni's fiction. Divakaruni makes this point explicitly in her short story 'The intelligence of wild things' (*Unknown Errors*), as her unnamed protagonist experiences an uncomfortable 'them and us' moment in Vermont:

> across the deck from me, a group of young men . . . dart sideways glances at me and my Indian clothes. I can tell they haven't seen many of us. I clutch at the boat's railings, shivering, wishing myself back in Sacramento, where no one stares when I walk to the store in my salwaar kameez.[98]

As I noted in the Introduction, California saw some of America's earliest South Asian immigration; and demographically, it is the heart of Asian America. Writers nonetheless present the northeast – New Jersey, rather than Massachusetts or Vermont – as the pre-eminent site for *South* Asian Americans, and this relatively narrow US thus stands in contrast to the diverse South Asian regional heterogeneity of writers' ancestral origins. New Jersey's importance is underscored by its use in S. Mitra Kalita's *Suburban Sahibs* (2003), a work of extended reportage; alongside New York in Alexander's *Manhattan Music*; in Tanuja Desai Hidier's coming-of-age narrative, *Born Confused* (2002); and in Shobhan Bantwal's 'chick lit' novel *The Sari Shop Widow* (2009). This local emphasis is not confined to literature, as shown by such films as Krutin Patel's *ABCD* (1999), Raj Nidimoru and D. K. Krishna's *Flavours* (2003), Danny Leiner's *Harold and Kumar Go to White Castle* (2004), Pandya's *American Desi*, and Mehta's *American Chai*.

As Kalita writes, 'New Jersey has been a central part of Indians' history in America.'[99] Therefore when one learns that the Das family in Lahiri's short story 'Interpreter of maladies' (*Interpreter*) live in New Brunswick, New Jersey, they become a recognisable part of one of the best-established South Asian centres in the United States. But the notion of 'safety in numbers' and the sense in which South Asians have become rooted in New Jersey are unsettled by the state's violent history of white racism towards them, a collective memory discussed in *Fault Lines*; *Manhattan Music*; G. S. Sharat Chandra's short story 'Dot busters' (from his collection *Sari of the Gods* [1998]); and particularly *Suburban Sahibs*.[100] This shameful local history is perhaps less well known than the anti-immigrant narrative of postwar Britain but it, too, reflects the difficulties of immigrants facing the transition from sojourner to settler, and it takes us back to the paradoxical impulse of South Asian American writers both to celebrate and to condemn the US.

Kalita also shows that the sheer concentration of Indians in New Jersey has led to increased political clout at the local level.[101] Indeed, in *Suburban Sahibs*, she meticulously records recent South Asian American history to reveal the robust health of this section of US society. Through her title alone, Kalita also implies that the making of American homes has followed a suburban trajectory for many ethnic South Asians.[102] In contrast to the anti-suburban attitudes considered earlier – and the notion that property-ownership perhaps matters more in British Asian than in South Asian American works – *Suburban Sahibs* suggests that the act of settling an individual plot of land, through the ownership of bricks and mortar, represents just as powerful an investment in the United States as that of the first generation in Britain. The claiming of suburbia – and of both the East and West Coast – explored in South Asian American writing from the 1970s onwards thus suggests a lasting stake in the adopted homeland. No matter how often ancestral places are invoked and even considered to be superior, writers are endlessly energised by the encounter with a domesticated, localised America. Indeed the complexities of the search for home that it invites interrogate, rather than support, their ostensible transnationalism.

The Formation of British Regional Identities

In recent British Asian writing, regionalism plays an even greater role. Perhaps this is because ethnic South Asians have lived in Britain over a longer period and, as I argued in the Introduction, because they constitute a larger percentage of the overall population than do South Asians in the US. In British Asian literature, urban, rather than rural, settings generally offer the best approximation of a home in the UK. As Gail Low has put it, 'migration . . . is intimately bound up with the geographical locations and destinies of cities like London, Manchester, Birmingham, Liverpool, Leicester, Bradford or Leeds'.[103] Beyond London – whose role as a centre of settlement, migrant locale *par excellence*, and 'cultural capital of black Britain' (in James Procter's phrase)[104] is already well rehearsed[105] – such major cities as Birmingham and Glasgow, and the regional loyalties they invite, are crucial in the formation of British Asian identities.[106] Yet, as Seán McLoughlin notes, 'the diverse local configuration of Asian Britain has to a large extent remained unexamined in the [scholarly] literature'.[107]

In Hussein's *Émigré Journeys*, Amir discovers the extent to which Birmingham has worked its way into his consciousness:

> I did not live in a palace back in Birmingham, but . . . I had my comrades around me, the nearness of bodies and souls . . . I . . . longed for the company . . . that I had in Birmingham, where everyone knew everyone else's situation, each one relying on the other. It was a community. (209–10, 213–14)

When he does return to the city, such feelings of nostalgia become even more explicit: 'Birmingham – home from my home, so to speak. As I entered the old city I . . . knew why I had wished to come here: I wanted to regain my pride in the very city where I had once lost it' (221). Although such powerful local allegiances exist among the first generation, as we saw earlier through images of mapping, it is their children who more clearly demonstrate the importance of regional, rather than national, affiliations. In *Burning Mirror*, for instance, Glasgow is an important muse for each of Saadi's Scots Asian characters. He conceives the city on a microcosmic, intra-urban scale and deploys a blend of demotic Scots and Urdu: a linguistic technique which renders his vision all the more distinctive and localised (and, for some readers, opaque perhaps), and which he champions when he attacks the 'idiocy that great thoughts can only be thought in "Standard" English'.[108] Through such strategies, he reveals Glasgow's development as a network of racially diverse neighbourhoods, while critically appraising the Pakistani community itself. Thus in 'The Queens of Govan', the kebab house in which Ruby works is

> in the heart ae Govan which wis gie unusual fur an Asian-run Carry-out. Maist ae those were in the slightly safer territory ae Kinnin Park, where broon faces outnumbered the pink and where the Changezi family held an easy sway wi machetes an hockey-sticks. (23)

The Changezis underscore the prevailing sense throughout *Burning Mirror* of a hierarchy of Pakistani Glaswegian families. Indeed, ten years before Saadi, Farhana Sheikh characterised east London Pakistani communities in her novel *The Red Box* (1991) as similarly divided along economic and class lines. Aslam, too, documents the poorest Muslim, Hindu, and Sikh neighbourhoods of his unnamed, fabular northern English town in *Maps*, rather than 'the rich suburbs' to which 'doctors, lawyers, accountants, engineers' have moved, in an internal migration, 'leaving behind the Pakistanis . . . Bangladeshis, and a few Indians, all of whom work in restaurants, drive taxis and buses, or are unemployed' (46). In contrast to the material success of Glasgow's South Asian businesspeople and racketeers, Saadi's dysfunctional families include one failed Pakistani patriarch after another. In 'Ninety-nine kiss-o-grams' and 'Bandanna', Sal feels contempt towards those members of the first generation who have not advanced materially, but this is really an expression of his own despair towards his mother and father. His need to move away from what he perceives as their constricted world is articulated in spatial terms as his friends and he leave behind such 'pedestrians' (112) on their journey through the 'runnin-board' (112) of Glasgow:

> the Gang turned west, away fae the mosques, towards Maxwell Park . . . To muck up the quiet. To fill it wi gouts ae Bhangra and Baissee. They skatit past the tenement closes, each one a blink in the Gang's eye. The sound of generations carved into each corniced ceiling . . . The black slaves had bled in blue: R 'n' R [sic], hip-hop, reggae, and now the sons of swastika-daubed Paki shop-owners would disembowel the air in syncopation. Together, with night torches, they would fire the swastikas and, in the fractured air, would spin them round in great wheels up and down the streets of Glasgow. And they would feed the skinheads of Ibrox, the white-trash tattoo of Penilee into the great, burning cunt of Mata Kali, where five thousand firewheels spun time . . . It wis aw mixed up . . . Sikh Bhangra, Mussalmaan Qawal, Hindu Raag-Bhajan-Khayals . . . Black Blues, it all swirled together and spurned into a river of Techno-Rave Brummie Beat. (112, 116–17)

If finding a home in Scotland is complicated, then aggressively marking out territory in Glasgow is Sal's challenge. This violent, vibrant passage – in which his gang take ownership of the city through their vivid, particularised vision of it – contrasts with the gently romantic, non-localised quality of Sal's vision of Scotland ('the cool spaces ae Scola, the feel ae rain on his back') when he was in Pakistan in 'Ninety-nine kiss-o-grams' (5). In 'Bandanna', Saadi instead presents a janglingly kinetic, hallucinatory version of Scotland-as-Glasgow which draws eclectically on other ethnic, religious, and regionalised British Asian identities and traditions (the syncretic music represented by 'Sikh Bhangra', 'Hindu Raag-Bhajan-Khayals', 'Techno-Rave Brummie Beat') and reflects the speed and sounds of physical and psychological movement through the city.

The sense of local belonging conferred by Glasgow is also central to Hardeep Singh Kohli's memoir *Indian Takeaway: A Very British Story* (2008). Here he claims that his 'story becomes interesting' when his parents moved from London to Glasgow because 'if we had stayed in London and become another of those Hounslow Indian families, we would have all led fairly unremarkable lives', later noting – humorously and certainly provocatively – that

> being Scottish has improved my life immeasurably. I am funnier, wittier and better looking for it . . . far more likely to invent things and educate the world about the philosophy of economics. That is what it is to be Scottish.[109]

It is arguably true that the story of South Asians in London, with their denser settlement patterns in such areas as Southall, is better known than that of Glaswegian Asians, both Muslim (in Saadi's case) and Sikh (in Kohli's). Kohli's point is also a useful corrective to the London-centrism of, for instance, Kureishi, and Glaswegian identity is clearly a source of pride and a kind of 'unique selling point' for both Kohli and Saadi.[110] But Kohli's polemical statements also reveal that regionalised fault lines and tensions exist within British Asian literature to a greater extent than anything comparable in South Asian American writing. One wonders how readers from west London's Asian communities – of the kind portrayed, for instance, in Gurinder Chadha's 2002 film *Bend It Like Beckham* – would feel about their lives being dismissed as 'unremarkable'.

Similar regional prejudices surface in Lalwani's *Gifted*, where Mahesh Vasi, an academic in Cardiff, congratulates himself on not being

> among the thirty thousand Asians haemorrhaging out of the ugly scar in Uganda's belly that same year [1972], seeping into the dark spaces of Britain . . . the crawling masses who had fallen into the pockets of Leicester and Wembley. (8)

The haematic imagery used here owes much to the bloodshed of Idi Amin's post-independence Uganda and to the notorious 'Rivers of Blood' speech given in 1968 by the British politician Enoch Powell: both explicit points of reference in the same passage. But Mahesh's snobbery towards certain regional locations is also about his sense of intellectual superiority, of individuality and agency (as an immigrant by choice), and thus separateness, in relation to large numbers of what he regards as uneducated South Asian refugees. Thus he imputes passivity to them (they have 'fallen into' the UK) and shudders at their density in particular places such as Leicester and Wembley – which denotes another dismissal of London. His vision of them as 'crawling masses' also reworks the more famous phrase 'huddled masses': a transatlantic reference in that it was first used by Emma Lazarus in her 1866 poem 'The New Colossus' to refer to US immigration.

In Manzoor's *Greetings from Bury Park* and another recent autobiography, Sathnam Sanghera's *The Boy with the Topknot: A Memoir of Love, Secrets and Lies in Wolverhampton* (2008), the traditionally banal, unglamorous English towns of Luton and Wolverhampton – where Manzoor's Pakistani Muslim and Sanghera's Punjabi Sikh families respectively settled in the 1960s and 1970s – are treated in matter-of-fact, yet affectionate, fashion. Manzoor in particular offers a corrective to the unfavourable image of his home town in the national imaginary, revealing early in his memoir the Pakistani appropriation of sections of Luton through details which normalise this ethnic presence: 'with his greying hair, pepper moustache, light-brown kurta pyjama and leather *chupulls*, Sadiq looked like a hundred other men you might see walking along Dunstable Road with bags of halal chicken in their arms' (23). Local places ('Dunstable Road') are mentioned casually, rather than explained, therefore immersing the reader in Pakistani Luton and offering another example of remapping. This forms part of Manzoor's implicit claims to the sheer ordinariness, and Britishness, of his particular story, which is narrated over three generations. His Luton thus recalls Philip Roth's Newark in, for instance, his novel *The Plot Against America* (2004), where to be American is to be Jewish: a sense of national belonging helped by real ethnic settlement. Parallels with Roth's New Jersey are, perhaps, no coincidence in an autobiography which venerates the music of Bruce Springsteen, a well-known son of New Jersey, and in which Manzoor even claims 'I wanted to be a Muslim like Philip Roth was a Jew' (239). Interestingly, Manzoor overlooks the South Asian stake in New Jersey, instead paying homage to the state's white cultural heritage, perhaps because this has had a greater popular impact to date.

After the London bombings of 7 July 2005 (known popularly as '7/7'), Manzoor defends his home town, asking: 'what was it about Luton? When I had been growing up . . . [it] was something of a national joke,[111] but recently it had been inextricably linked with Islamic radicalism . . . When friends asked me whether Luton was as bad as the media portrayed, I would strongly defend its reputation' (262). Such moments suggest that – as much as replacing a sense of national belonging – regional sites (Luton, Glasgow, Birmingham, Wolverhampton) become metonymically British in their provision of a simultaneously local and national home for writers.

Gendered Domesticity

My earlier discussion of postwar British urban dwellings, contemporary US suburban homes, and the wider theme of houseownership should make clear that home as domestic arena can be crucial to migrant identity formation.[112] And if it is a defining element of the masculine pride of some immigrants to own property – whether in South Asia, as I contend in Chapter 2, or in Britain and the US, as we see here – the actual daily maintenance of such homes, and their status as a recreated version of India, Pakistan, or Bangladesh,[113] is regarded as female work by many men and women here.[114] In view of the traditionally patriarchal nature of South Asian societies, it is perhaps unsurprising that domesticity should take this gendered form, although several South Asian Atlantic writers explicitly question the association between women and home. For instance, in Divakaruni's stories – which tackle Indian marital life in America head-on, often as it pertains to housework – many female characters contest their Bengali husbands' vision of domesticity as a female preserve. In 'Intelligence of wild things', we learn, almost in passing, that Sandeep, the unnamed protagonist's husband, is 'like most husbands brought up in India, no help at all' (44); while Shyamoli in 'Mrs Dutta writes a letter' deems her husband, Sagar, unusual in his readiness to help her with housework and is aghast when her mother-in-law tries to take such work off his hands:

> Mother! . . . This is why Indian men are so useless around the house. Here in America we don't believe in men's work and women's work. Don't I work outside all day, just like Sagar? How'll I manage if he doesn't help me at home? (15)

Within British Asian writing, Meera Syal uses her novel *Life Isn't All Ha Ha Hee Hee* (1999) to critique women's domestic arrangements. Thus she exposes the fragility of Chila's perfect suburban home and model housewife status, while drawing attention to the spiritual emptiness of Tania's fashionable urban apartment, bought through her professional success. Neither relationship with the home is presented as satisfactory, although Syal offers no alternative scenarios. *Brick Lane* focuses even more intently on individual, feminised interior spaces,[115] doing so in ostensibly more traditional fashion than Syal, although Ali presents the Bangladeshi immigrant home as both confining and liberating and thus analogous to the paradox which underpins South Asian American literary representations of suburbia. When Ali's characters do experience happiness, it is firmly rooted in the domestic sphere since this is the novel's principal backdrop, with Nazneen's flat serving as its most important example.

After emigrating from India, Mukherjee initially viewed herself as 'permanently stranded in North America',[116] a theme explored throughout her early work, especially *Wife*, which anticipates many of the concerns explored in *Brick Lane* and concludes its study of gendered domesticity in grisly fashion with Dimple murdering her husband, Amit.[117] Like Dimple, Sandhya, the Indian immigrant housewife in Alexander's *Manhattan Music*, negotiates loneliness and depression within the confines of her New York apartment, but instead attempts suicide. In *Maps*, Aslam also depicts immigrant women as 'stranded' (269, 272), this time within a Muslim society which keeps a very close eye on its members. In *Brick Lane*, such surveillance takes several forms. It is spiritual, part of an Islamic eschatology which has shaped believers' consciousness from early life, although the all-seeing, divine gaze which Nazneen senses upon her at all times is reinforced in human form through the community's own watchfulness. Indeed, the threat of public scrutiny means it is almost safer to remain indoors.[118] At the same time, Mrs Azad explicitly conflates gendered domesticity with imprisonment – both inside and outside the home – claiming that 'some women spend ten, twenty years here and . . . sit in the kitchen grinding spices all day and learn only two words of English . . . They go around covered from head to toe, in their little walking prisons.'[119]

Ali suggests that, outside their immediate neighbourhood, first-generation women are invisible. When a white woman does stare at Nazneen,

> *it was the way she might look at a familiar object*, her keys that she had just found, the kitchen table as she wiped the juice her daughter had spilled, a blankness reserved for known quantities like pieces of furniture or brown women in saris who cooked rice and raised their children and obeyed their husbands. (325; emphasis added)

Through a classic racist paradox – that of the simultaneously visible and invisible subject – Ali not only reveals the unconscious dismissal of new immigrant women of colour by some white people, but also captures mainstream British society's association of Nazneen with the domestic: she is objectified in the same way as other household items, her complex subjectivity reduced to a culturalist preconception of her as mother and housewife.[120] Trapped, too, by Bangladeshi cultural expectations, Nazneen often feels a kind of domestic immobility.[121] In a mood rather like the emotional apathy of her friend, Razia – whose damaged state of mind is reflected in the neglected condition of her home[122] – Nazneen ruminates, many years after her arrival in London, upon the sparseness of her immediate surroundings, seeing her life specifically in terms of missed domestic opportunities – that is, the chance to decorate and thus personalise her apartment – because her mode of survival has been to avoid thinking of her future as British.

This idea anticipates *Maps*, where Aslam writes of Mah-Jabin, a second-generation British Pakistani character, that her entry into puberty marks 'a turning point in the appearance of the house: many improvements were made to the interiors *which until then had been seen only as temporary accommodation in a country never thought of as home*' (96; emphasis added). In other words, in a way distinct from Nazneen's attitude in *Brick Lane*, house and homeland are brought together through the family's commitment to their British home, an arena tightly controlled by Kaukab, the matriarch. As Aslam's narrator informs us, for Kaukab, 'everything is here in this house' (65) and 'there is so much outside the house that may not be brought into the house' (93). Such thinking, which designates the family dwelling as a female-controlled realm of tradition – a material extension of Kaukab's psychological and emotional state – also marks another return to George's notion of home as a kind of exclusion zone, reliant on 'closed doors . . . [and] borders'.[123]

These fictionalised forms of gendered domesticity are mirrored in recent examples of British Asian life-writing, across ethnicity and religion, through the figures of the non-Anglophone, largely housebound mothers in *Greetings from Bury Park* and *Boy with the Topknot*. In these texts, both Manzoor and Sanghera create loving, affectionate portraits of their stoical, self-reliant mothers: home-based seamstresses whose earnings have sustained their families. Nazneen makes her living in similar fashion in *Brick Lane*, also remitting money to her sister in Bangladesh, although her apparently confined existence in London is undercut by the irony that it is through this culturally enforced home-working that she is able to embark upon an affair – with Karim, the young middleman whom she encounters in this context – and thus to subvert expectations of wifely obedience.[124] As Gail Low has noted in the context of Sheikh's *Red Box*, 'the . . . home worker's place of residence is both private and public';[125] and in *Brick Lane*, this extends to the forging of new and ostensibly liberating relationships. In *Wife* and *Manhattan Music*, Dimple and Sandhya also engage in extra-marital affairs; just as for Nazneen, Dimple's home provides the site, and alibi, for this adulterous activity. Home as a site of paid work, albeit of an exhausting and repetitive variety, complicates any critique of South Asian diasporic women condemned to a domestic drudgery which is unthinking. As Devon Campbell-Hall has argued of *Brick Lane*:

> the role of the traditionally exploited sewing pieceworker has been unsentimentally transformed into a quiet rebellion against the cultural status quo . . . labour . . . provides the . . . location for . . . transgressive behaviours . . . [and the opportunity] to disengage from the moral and emotional restraints of . . . [the] larger community.[126]

Ali's nuanced representation of Nazneen, Razia, and Mrs Azad in *Brick Lane* can be read alongside the characterisations of first-generation women by such other British Asian women writers as Syal and Sheikh. Their depictions – Syal's bloody-minded Punjabi Hindu mothers in *Life Isn't All* and Sheikh's independent Muslim matriarchs in *Red Box* – sometimes diverge starkly from portrayals by male authors of South Asian migrant women and their attitudes to home. Despite Sanjukta Dasgupta's claim that 'the very basic quest for home, the domestic space, the security of the enclosed space, do not seem to be such an integral part of most migrant male writing',[127] such writers as Hussein and Aslam do address home as a domestic site. Much like Kureishi's less-than-satisfying formulation of older South Asian women,[128] they present a particular model of first-generation women in relation to issues of home: the Pakistani wife and mother with no real desire to be in Britain. In *Émigré Journeys*, Salma is devastated by her enforced migration and only comes to life when discussions turn to stories of 'back home' (95), while Kaukab is depicted in subtle and sometimes harrowing fashion in *Maps*, as she is made to represent a whole community of women broken by the sorrows of exile. Classically gendered ideas of home, in both national and domestic terms, are linked here to the notion of women as the embodiments of cultural tradition. At the same time, *Maps* shows us the divergent attitudes towards home of second-generation British Muslim women and – in a feminist work deeply concerned with social justice – Aslam illustrates their struggle against the traditional gender roles assigned to them.

Domesticity-as-female is a leitmotif in British Asian literature especially, even though South Asian American writing is full of immigrant housewives: Dimple in Mukherjee's appropriately named *Wife*; Aban, Manek's wife in Sidhwa's *American Brat*; Sandhya in *Manhattan Music*; Ashima in Lahiri's *Namesake* and Mrs Sen in her eponymous story; Rajiv's mother in Parekh's *Stealing the Ambassador*, and Prapulla in Chandra's 'Sari of the gods' (from his eponymous collection). On the one hand, these US writers – who include the male voices of Parekh and Chandra – are more interested in anatomising the collision between such women and the outside world; yet *Wife* and *Manhattan Music* do also interrogate the psychological impact of a housebound existence, suggesting that this is a wider trend within South Asian Atlantic women's writing. Across this œuvre, then, home is used to suggest women's feelings of imprisonment and suffocation, while hinting at the growth of a kind of domestic earning-power and even the possibility for sexual experimentation (as we see through Nazneen and Dimple). Male authors – particularly Kureishi and Hussein – do less to problematise connections between South Asian women and home; while Manzoor's and Sanghera's non-fictional accounts of their immigrant mothers are multi-layered, yet fundamentally driven by filial loyalty. Indeed, both writers associate gendered domesticity with childhood security, and food forms a key element of such associations, as I argue in Chapter 4. Although the connection between women and home is a familiar one across cultures,[129] it reveals a rich seam of meaning and possibility within transatlantic South Asian writing.

The US versus Britain in South Asian Atlantic writing

SOUTH ASIAN AMERICAN RESPONSES TO BRITAIN

Just as South Asian American writers deploy the British weather as a vehicle for anti-imperialist critique, so too do they treat Britain itself with suspicion and even derision. Apart from Lahiri's impeccably elegant vision of London in her story 'Only goodness' (from her collection *Unaccustomed Earth* [2008]), where Sudha emigrates and marries a white British man,[130] few of these anti-British narratives are actually set in the UK, yet they attack the nation to sometimes merciless effect through the use of now-familiar tropes: besides bad weather, we have seen that the UK is apparently composed of uniformly colourless, claustrophobically urban settings. Mukherjee in particular presents Britain as no match for the US. Indeed, her acceptance of the United States depends, in a dialectical sense, on her consistent, postcolonially inflected hostility to Britain, which at times becomes the subject of an explicit rejection and at others can be discerned as an absent presence, mentioned fleetingly, if at all.[131] This compares to *The Perfect Man* (2006), a novel by the British Lebanese writer Naeem Murr, in which the child protagonist, Raj Travers, leaves behind post-independence India and then late 1940s Britain, handled briefly and dismissively in the text, for his ultimate destination: the United States. Similarly, in Mira Nair's film *Mississippi Masala* (1991; discussed further in Chapter 3), the Lohas, a Ugandan Asian family, have apparently spent fifteen years in Britain before moving to the US, but – unlike their time in Africa – this period of British residence is completely erased from the narrative. In each case, the text seems to assume an American audience.

For Mukherjee, Britain is, paradoxically, at once unworthy of discussion and crucial to her diasporic self-fashioning. As she herself has put it, 'my love of America is really my rebellion against British colonialism':[132] through its colonial history, Britain simply cannot be avoided. In a 1993 interview, Mukherjee attacks European multiculturalism, arguing that the countries of:

> Western Europe . . . treat their non-European immigrants, even if they have been there for two or three generations, as though they are guest workers. They never . . . accept them as real citizens . . . People who . . . settle in Europe, are encouraged to retain their cultures so that it would not occur to . . . the Turks for instance to think of themselves as Danes and so on. Whereas America, because of its mythology, allows me to think of myself . . . as American . . . in England I would not dare assume I can be an Englishman [sic] unless I was born with a certain kind of name . . . look . . . accent.[133]

Mukherjee is right to draw attention to a fundamentally different American 'mythology'; and, as I argued in the Introduction, the search for a British identity has been complicated by the colonial past for many British Asian writers: perhaps more so than the equivalent quest for South Asian American artists, although one cannot ignore the existence of past and ongoing racial discrimination in the US. At the same time, the cultural capital of British Asians – and Mukherjee's limited experience of life in Britain – make her presentation of the nation as untransformed by its South Asian population outdated, inaccurate, and clichéd.

Mukherjee has also sought to strip the English language of any prior British ownership, claiming to

> have invented my own version of American English . . . Bit by bit, as I've . . . become closer to my material . . . the choice of point of view has become first person . . . the sentences [are] . . . now full of energy and emotion which I would not allow myself because I had been taught by the British education in independent India that that was uncivil . . . My love of America is . . . a liberation from structure.[134]

Freed from the putative staidness and 'structure' of British English, language becomes another means of securing a home for oneself. Rather as Alexander has argued that she uses English 'to make a home . . . sometimes I feel I have no real home except in language'[135] – and Mukherjee and her husband, Clark Blaise, have claimed that '[Salman] Rushdie has made his home in language, in the fecundity and ferocity of his invention'[136] – so Mukherjee herself claims to have constructed a literary, linguistic home on American soil. This US home relies on a fervent anti-imperialism, in which Britain remains a negative intellectual and political force: a body of ideas to be continually overthrown.

Where does this leave South Asian American literary representations of British Asians? In Meer's *Bombay Talkie*, South Asian visitors to 1980s London have difficulty grasping the idea of British Asians in an existential sense. Sitting in a London nightclub, Jimmy, an ageing Bollywood film star, observes that 'a few of the faces look Indian . . . but they're strange, like masks . . . hijras . . . and their voices are the same as the rest of the people around him'.[137] This vision suggests both gender confusion – since the sex of these British Asians is not specified and they are compared, moreover, to eunuchs or 'hijras' – and a kind of aural puzzlement through the implied question: how can Indian-looking people speak like the British and thus, by extension, be British? Jimmy's daughter, Alia, is no less perplexed when, sitting on a London bus, she encounters

> Indian faces mixed in with white English ones . . . There are some Indian girls in short skirts and jackets, just like English girls. They are laughing and telling jokes with harsh British accents. Alia feels sorry for them, having long grey English lives without any hope of the hot Bombay sun burning through the clouds. (203–4)

That these girls are actually locals, rather than simply being '*like* English girls', is not only difficult for this wealthy Indian girl to understand, but is also perceived by her as a palpable disadvantage. And once again the apparent deficiencies of the native climate are integral to this critique of Britain. Although, as I argue in Chapter 2, Sabah, the novel's South Asian American protagonist, encounters local confusion about her own Indianness when she visits the ancestral homeland, *Bombay Talkie* implies that the US is a better place in which to be Indian than Britain. Dull, grey, and limited in comparison with America, Asian Britain – represented entirely through London – is embodied through a single character, Imran, whose unsettling Britishness is once again invoked through accent (he 'sounds like an Angrez' [239]) and is rescued only by his wealth and prospects.

In Daswani's *For Matrimonial Purposes*, Anju rejects Raju, a potential suitor from London, who is presented as deceitful and desperate to appear as white as possible. Like Jimmy and Alia, Anju struggles with the reality of British Asian speech, and her assessment that 'with his brown skin, [his accent] . . . almost didn't fit, it was that extreme' (176) says more about her own prejudices towards British Asians than it does about Raju. In Vijayaraghavan's *Motherland*, Maya, the vulnerable, teenaged American protagonist, is first charmed, then troubled, by her older, British cousin Madhu and her selfish, amoral behaviour. Madhu, yet another possessor of a troublingly British accent, is depicted as badly brought up and eager to assimilate into white British culture: a cautionary figure for Maya, although Madhu is given her say in the novel, particularly on Indian women's rights. Most revealing of all, however, are Vijayaraghavan's lengthier comparisons of South Asians in Britain and America in the late 1980s. Madhu tells Maya that 'all of you who went to the States, you come back here [to India] more than we do, like you're looking to be something more than American. In Britain, we know who we are, and we're not Indian' (102–3). Meanwhile Maya's uncle, Sanjay, claims that 'England [sic] and India still have strong ties, and much to learn from each other . . . America is too young to learn from' (104). Madhu may be regarded as a subversive, even malign, influence but Vijayaraghavan's message is ambiguous, since – despite its absence of an established immigrant 'mythology' – Britain seems to have afforded Madhu a more robust sense of belonging than the United States has offered Maya. Doubts over migration to the US, rather than the UK, underpin the narrative and ultimately, it remains unclear which site Vijayaraghavan favours.

South Asian Americans are also pitted against their British counterparts in Ginu Kamani's transatlantic story 'Just between Indians' (from her short fiction collection *Junglee Girl* [1995]). Here Ranjan and Sahil Patel, Gujarati brothers from London who have been 'raised everywhere',[138] are prospective marriage partners for Daya, an American student. For Subhash, the boys' father, and Rohit, his New York-based brother, Indianness (as the title suggests) – and, more precisely, Gujaratiness – can unite the potential couple beyond any transatlantic differences. Yet Kamani's closed third-person narrator unmistakably views the brothers through Daya's American eyes, emphasising Ranjan's supposedly British diffidence and Sahil's debonair, worldweary, implicitly 'English' charm, while commenting upon their English accents. Indeed, in a way that recalls Meer and anticipates Vijayaraghavan and Daswani, speech is once again an important marker of transatlantic South Asian difference. The story refuses the option of uniting its two Gujarati halves: the match between Ranjan and Daya is a non-starter, while her sexual attraction to Sahil simply results in a one-night stand, and the Patels return to London. It becomes clear in fact that they never had any intention of moving to New York, despite their initial claims, and it is significant that their uncle Rohit's New York home is where their mother killed herself many years before. Although Kamani's story suggests that the erotic adventure between Daya and Sahil has sexually liberated both parties to become involved with other ethnic Indians, 'Just between Indians' depicts an unbridgeable, even doomed, gulf between the British and American sides of the South Asian Atlantic.

In Shobhan Bantwal's *Sari Shop Widow*, the portrayal of Rishi Shah, a biracial, British Gujarati entrepreneur, goes against this trend, since the novel unites him with Anjali Kapadia, its South Asian American protagonist. Rishi is a somewhat unconvincingly depicted 'Indo-Brit', the very choice of word, especially his own use of it,[139] smacking of inauthenticity. His Britishness is continually referenced, despite his early years in India, his international business interests, and his peripatetic existence. As with other South Asian American-inscribed British Asian characters, his ethnic credentials are in question, his accent subjected to scrutiny and mistrust. Beyond the human need to pigeonhole people, especially in an ethnic sense – in the words of the narrative, 'one *Desi* [or South Asian] could always spot another' (32) – there is also a persistent sense here (as in the examples discussed earlier) that, although the South Asian presence in Britain cannot be denied, British Asians themselves represent a contradiction in terms for their American counterparts. As Anjali puts it early in the novel, 'Rishi . . . looks and talks like a Brit, behaves like one' (102): her implication is that he cannot also be Indian, even though she – and other members of her US community – can securely lay claim to *their* Indianness. She seems oblivious to this inconsistency and, despite her own British Asian relatives, Anjali appears to believe that some types of diasporic Indian identity are more acceptable than others.

All of this begs the question of why Bantwal makes Rishi a British Asian, especially in view of her uncertain handling of British culture and the fact that there is no evidence in the novel of any marked awareness on her part of actual British Asian lives. As with Sahil in 'Just between Indians', Rishi's foreign status is perhaps more significant in symbolic terms. His sophisticated, cosmopolitan, non-traditional lifestyle lends him a palpable allure, even as it hints at a sharp divide between the two sides of the South Asian Atlantic, and like Sahil, he is a sexually liberating influence on the female protagonist. Crucially, his Britishness distinguishes him from Gujarati men in the US, who are described as being

> as interesting as plain boiled potatoes. They . . . lacked sophistication . . . Indians in America . . . were a homogenous [sic] bunch . . . essentially decent, honest, hardworking, and obsessively goal-oriented, but the one thing . . . that bored Anjali to tears was their lack of humour. (15)

This sweeping generalisation is clearly open to question, but it paves the way for a transnational ethnic match for Anjali, whose own life is depicted as parochial through her lack of familiarity with life outside the US. The fact that Rishi and she can overcome their rather superficial transatlantic differences – for instance, in the pronunciation of 'schedule' (96) – suggests that, unlike the message of Kamani's story, shared ethnicity (again, Gujarati-ness) can overcome initial misunderstanding. It can also override the inauspicious premise, in a traditional Indian context, of Anjali's widowed status and Rishi's racially mixed provenance. Indeed, his Britishness (further underscored by his white 'half') and the potential move to London it offers promise to free Anjali from the control of her loving, yet 'puritanical . . . [and] conservative' parents (24). *Sari Shop Widow* also highlights the tendency within South Asian Atlantic writing to present the US and Britain as the most viable centres for *desi* settlement outside India.

THE US IN BRITISH ASIAN CULTURAL PRODUCTION

As I argued in the Introduction, the United States exerts a powerful influence on British Asian writing and cinema. It is generally depicted in markedly more favourable terms than Britain is in South Asian American works and indeed, the second generation's sense of place is often addressed in transatlantic terms. Thus in David Attwood's film *Wild West* (1992, scripted by Harwant Bains), young British Asians ultimately choose America over Britain, as west London is exchanged for Nashville. The same trajectory also informs the conclusion to Chadha's later and better-known *Bend It Like Beckham*. These British Asian characters are frozen in transit, however, since their lives in America – and any problems they might face there – remain beyond the scope of the narrative. Interestingly, Naveen Andrews and Parminder Nagra, the respective British Asian stars of these films, have fared well as actors working in the US.

Kureishi's literary works display a pro-Americanism similar to that of such films. In *Black Album*, Chili wishes his father had stood 'in line on Ellis Island' and harbours his own ambitions to 'hit New York'.[140] In this respect, he succeeds Farouk in Kureishi's play *Borderline* (1981), who believes that 'most of England's a miserable place' and plans to emigrate 'to America or Canada eventually'.[141] Charlie, too, welcomes the chance to exchange 'decrepit' 1970s Britain for America in *Buddha of Suburbia*.[142] Such attitudes are undercut by ambivalence, however, since – Charlie aside – these ambitions to settle in the US are rarely fulfilled, rather as we never witness British Asian lives in America in *Wild West* and *Bend It Like Beckham*. This half-hearted transatlanticism, which may reflect Kureishi's own resolution to stay in London, even casts America in an ominous light, for instance when Shahid argues that rising racial inequality in Britain means 'it's gonna be like America. However far we go, we'll always be underneath!' (*Black Album*, 209). Such transatlantic allusions nonetheless reveal the importance to Kureishi and his characters (Jamila in *Buddha*, for instance) of black American models of writing and political resistance.[143]

In *Greetings from Bury Park*, Sarfraz Manzoor directly addresses the choice of Britain over America for ethnic South Asians. His relationship with the US goes through three key stages. Initially, he envisions it as a magical place, and his discovery of the music of Springsteen emblematises his adolescent sense that 'I . . . loved America and hated Luton' (99). But even before this, the United States is the subject of unquestioning veneration:

> I would fantasise that I was an American high-school student . . . the possibility that my . . . experience might differ on account of not being white did not arise . . . All my hopes were encapsulated in the life I imagined was possible in the United States. Why had my father not landed at Ellis Island? . . . It wasn't that I was unaware the United States had its own race problems but even those seemed glamorous . . . I knew more about American black history than I did about the fight for civil rights in Britain. In the absence of British Pakistani role models I borrowed Martin Luther King and Malcolm X . . . I had not read of any discrimination against Pakistanis in America and so the United States remained a place for second chances. Why would they care that I was Pakistani? (128–31)

Rebelling against his father's aversion to America, which represents 'everything he hated about Britain multiplied a hundredfold . . . "Americans are unclean, immoral"' (135), Manzoor resolves to go to the US, a trip he finally makes in 1990, made possible, ironically, by his father's touching generosity.

During this second phase – in which Manzoor actually experiences America – his euphoria is affectionately recalled. It is difficult, incidentally, to imagine a South Asian American experiencing this much excitement about coming to Britain. At the same time, Manzoor recognises that 'I did not look how Americans imagined Brits looked and I was worried that something in my daily behaviour would expose me as not being quite British enough' (142). While in Yuba City, California, Manzoor has his own South Asian Atlantic encounter when he shares a meal with a Pakistani American couple, who inquire about his ancestral village, and he reflects that 'perhaps my father had been right when he had talked about a shared sense of community, it was just that I needed to travel to the United States to witness it first-hand' (147). This moment implies (once again) that South Asian ethnic allegiance can move beyond purely national boundaries.

But Manzoor's transatlantic dream is dealt a huge blow by 9/11: arguably the third stage of his relationship with America. His British Sikh friend, Amolak, reveals that

> 'America isn't ours anymore . . . we always thought . . . if Britain doesn't want us we . . . have America. Not any more . . . now we are going to have to do what we can in this . . . country because you know that the second you . . . land at JFK they are going to haul your arse into jail' . . . The newspaper reports of innocent Asians being detained for questioning and then slung back to Britain confirmed Amolak's grim theory that the United States was no longer our promised land. (235–6)

It is worth noting that the ancestral homeland is never considered part of this contingency plan. Manzoor had in fact already resolved to stay in Britain before 9/11 and its aftermath – for instance, the detention of British Asians at Guantánamo Bay – and his memoir ends by applauding his father's decision to settle in the UK, since 'every opportunity, every job and every chance to pursue my dreams has been offered by this country, not by America, and not by Pakistan' (269). Within this triangulation of South Asia, the US, and the UK, Manzoor's ultimate allegiance to Britain is as much connected to intensely personal family dynamics, especially paternal loyalty, as it is to wider political issues.[144] Despite the primacy of ethnic affiliations, then, South Asian diasporic writers on both sides of the Atlantic are surprisingly keen to maintain the national status quo by vindicating their decisions to remain in America or Britain.

STRATEGIC ANGLOPHOBIA VERSUS STRATEGIC AMERICANOPHILIA

This brings us back to the question, posed at the beginning of this chapter, of why specifically national identities should be so significant to apparently transnational writers. I have argued here and in the Introduction that, although the South Asian diaspora spans the globe,[145] writers explore the notion that their characters could have been either British or American – presented as two quite separate forms of existence – but for different circumstances. Thus British Asian writers effect transatlantic comparisons because, like millions of other immigrants, their characters could logically have gone to the US; hence the image of Ellis Island in *Black Album* and *Greetings from Bury Park*. British Asian artists are tantalised by the prospect of America as a mythic land built on immigration and a country which offers the promise of personal reinvention. They also respond to the international pervasiveness of US culture in a globalised world.

Thanks to old imperial ties, Britain was, on the other hand, a serious destination for early waves of South Asian immigrants. Despite the fact that British rule in India is long gone – and despite the idea that the colonial past has traditionally made Britain a more predetermined, constricted place for South Asians – the UK continues to attract and retain people from the subcontinent. South Asian American writers thus feel the need to engage with it and to explain why they chose not to live there: for instance, Mukherjee, Alexander, and Lahiri all spent time there, albeit briefly, before eventually settling in North America. To adapt Alan Rice's concept of 'strategic Anglophilia' on the part of African American visitors to Britain in the nineteenth and twentieth centuries – 'a very successful tactic for undermining their home country' in the fight against racial injustice[146] – what we witness here are forms of strategic *Americano*philia (harnessed by Kureishi, Manzoor, and several British Asian films) and strategic Anglo*phobia* across a range of South Asian American writing.

Why Anglophobia but Americanophilia? The 'philia' part of the equation suggests a utopian vision of the US, while the 'phobia' part hints at a conversely dystopian Britain. Yet neither reflects reality. As I argued in the Introduction, the US is no more a post-racial, uniformly egalitarian society than the UK is hopelessly atrophied in terms of class and race. In the words of Ann Massa and Alistair Stead:

> the accumulating oft-repeated perceptions that the Americans and the British have had of each other constitute a kind of 'international folklore' . . . that engages in myth-making rather than the strenuous pursuit of something more objectively verifiable.[147]

Instead, such phobias and philias, whereby Britain is used to discuss America and vice versa, serve as powerful instruments with which to validate one's choice of national home. British Asian artists deploy a strategic Americanophilia to question the parameters of South Asian inclusion in the UK. This remains rather superficial because it is never followed through with a full rejection of Britain and often relies on little actual experience of the US. As I argued above, the work of Kureishi and Manzoor ultimately demonstrates their British allegiance, while those films which end by choosing the US fail to take the next step in narrative terms. The Anglophobia which informs South Asian American literature is more sustained and deep-seated, shoring up each creator's patriotic status as an American (and thus reflecting, perhaps, the patriotic pressures exerted by US society) and as an American writer by parallelling India and America through a joint antipathy to British imperialism. This is especially true of Mukherjee. Anglophobia is used to thank America, explicitly and implicitly, for the material, cultural, and heuristic opportunities it has given writers and their characters. Within this Anglophobic discourse, such figures as Madhu in *Motherland* and Raju in *For Matrimonial Purposes* come to perform a more generalised British villainy, rather as Hollywood cinema makes ample use of British 'baddies' and rather as sections of American literature have always relied on forms of Anglophobia.[148] In creating such characters, who exhibit a straightforward, unproblematised form of (post)colonial mimicry, writers like Vijayaraghavan and Daswani may be looking down on British Asians for settling in the country of the ex-colonisers and, in a revealing slippage, for apparently aping white ways.

An element of competition could be at work here through the self-justificatory need of certain writers to prove that South Asians are happier in the United States than in Britain (and vice versa in the case of Kureishi and Manzoor) and that America's global influence has waxed as Britain's has waned. But Vijayaraghavan, Daswani, and Mukherjee at times undercut their strategic Anglophobia by protesting too much. Recalling Faran Tahir's point, discussed in the Introduction, about the historical pre-eminence of British Asian films over South Asian American cinema, South Asian American writers are generally less well known than British Asian ones (Lahiri is a notable exception to this rule). Thus they may feel the need for assertive South Asian Atlantic comparisons in ways that many British Asian authors – statistically part of a much more prominent community in relation to the UK population than their American counterparts vis-à-vis US demographics – do not. Despite the increased visibility of South Asians in the US since the 1970s and 1980s, they barely feature in the British Asian works under discussion in this study. Meanwhile, even in the more favourable South Asian American accounts I have considered, British Asian characters are portrayed as curiosities. This hints at a pervasive mutual ignorance, even though the impulse by artists to frame South Asian lives in transatlantic terms remains strong. For all the transnationalism of their family networks and personal outlook, the daily lives of characters and their creators take place at the domestic level (where 'domestic' may be read as national, local, and material): an old-fashioned message, perhaps, in a globalised era of apparently shrinking distances.[149] Writers use representations of America or Britain – and the rejection of one in favour of the other – in order, then, to support the particular national case they are making and to strengthen their own sense of belonging.

Conclusion

Beyond such overtly transatlantic manoeuvres, home is taken for granted as the thematic foundation for many of these narratives, while actively informing their plotting and characterisation, and their linguistic and rhetorical strategies. Arguably, home is equally important to writers on both sides of the Atlantic, although regional questions appear to preoccupy British Asian writers to a greater extent than South Asian American authors, who show more interest in transatlantic comparisons. Where their treatment of home overlaps most, perhaps, is in its attention to the material conditions of daily living. Blunt and Dowling have considered ideologies of the 'homely and unhomely', while noting that home may act as 'a refuge from work' for men, but not necessarily women.[150] South Asian Atlantic writing explores and problematises such dynamics, highlighting issues like the need to settle land, buy property, and forge a sense of local belonging; the challenges of suburban living; and the home as a site of labour. Some also attempt to contest traditionally gendered ideas of domestic space. This concern with the material aspects of home points to the difficulties of claiming a national home: it is easier to fashion 'homely' domestic surroundings than to achieve a sense of home within a sometimes 'unhomely' nation. Indeed, as Keya Ganguly has argued of South Asian American immigrants, the 'only stability and fixed point of reference is their home'.[151]

That said, we have seen that a number of British Asian and South Asian American writers do 'claim the nation',[152] particularly those who venture bold transatlantic comparisons (sometimes based on little actual knowledge of the US or UK) to bolster their feelings of national belonging and those who assert the representatively British or American nature of their writing. But the continued emphasis within South Asian Atlantic literature on the microcosmic (home-as-house, home-as-immediate locality), to a greater degree than the macrocosmic (home-as-nation), weakens the confidence of these positions. The drive to domesticity is sometimes a retreat – from the harshness of a South Asian past and/or a British or

American present – and it hints at the ongoing experience of putting down roots, sometimes over several generations. It also suggests that the difficulties of this process apply more or less equally to South Asians on both sides of the Atlantic. After all, their presence in decent numbers in the US, but in Britain to an even greater degree, is relatively new in historical terms and represents a story which is still unfolding. Although some writers' handling of these issues (gendered domesticity, for example) remains rather conservative, others continue to deploy home and nation in richly subversive ways as they construct a multi-layered critique of ethnic and cultural assumptions.

NOTES

1. A vast body of scholarly work on home has appeared since the early 1980s. See, for instance, Rushdie, *Imaginary*, pp. 9–21; Martin and Mohanty, 'Feminist politics', pp. 191–212; George, *Politics*; Morley, *Home Territories*; and, for a useful overview of this literature, Blunt and Dowling, *Home*.
2. See Jacobson, *Roots Too*, pp. 3–4.
3. Compare Paranjape, 'Afterword', p. 239.
4. Sarup, 'Home', p. 94.
5. Lal and Kumar, 'Introduction', p. xvi.
6. Ahmed, 'Home and away', p. 340.
7. See Maxey, 'Life in the diaspora', pp. 10, 16, 20.
8. Divakaruni, *Unknown Errors*, p. 50.
9. Alexander, *Fault Lines*, pp. 22–3.
10. Compare Mukherjee, 'Immigrant', p. 29.
11. Srikanth, *World Next Door*, pp. 51–4.
12. Amy Kaplan, quoted in Blunt and Dowling, *Home*, p. 170.
13. For theories of a postnational, borderless world, see Morley, *Home Territories*, pp. 204–5.
14. Narayan, *Love, Stars*, p. 22.
15. See, for example, Jussawalla, 'South Asian diaspora', p. 20; Nasta, *Home Truths*; Procter, *Dwelling Places*; and Lal and Kumar, *Interpreting*.
16. Procter, *Dwelling Places*, does attend to the material aspects of home, but his study differs from mine in that it focuses on black British, as well as British Asian, writing; his selection of South Asian diasporic writers is thus narrower; and his emphasis is not transatlantic. Lisa Lau considers the importance of space within Indian households, but only in the work of women writers and not in the diaspora; see Lau, 'Emotional', pp. 1097–116. Some critiques of Jhumpa Lahiri's short story 'Mrs Sen's' (from her South Asian American collection, *Interpreter of Maladies* [1999]) discuss the recreation of a Bengali ménage in the US, but do so only briefly; see Banerjee, 'No nation woman', pp. 174–5; and compare Dasgupta, 'Locating "home"', p. 83.

17. Blunt and Dowling, *Home*, p. 3, emphasis in original; and compare Chatterjee, 'Thoughts', p. 312, where she observes the 'Bengali . . . distinction between *basha* and *barhi*, "house and home" . . . an emotional distinction between "a mere shelter" and "a place where one belongs"'.
18. Dasgupta, 'Locating "home"', p. 90.
19. See, for example, Procter, *Dwelling Places*, pp. 160–201; and especially McLoughlin, 'Writing', p. 437.
20. Kabeer, *Power to Choose*, p. 198; see also Brah, *Cartographies*, pp. 23–4; and Kureishi, *Dreaming*, pp. 69–70.
21. Sandhu, 'Come hungry', p. 10.
22. King, *Internationalisation*, pp. 15, 44.
23. Compare such novels as John Braine's *Room at the Top* (1957) and Lynne Reid Banks's *The L-Shaped Room* (1960), whose very titles inscribe the idea of dwellings. This era of bleak domesticity is suggested by the phrase 'kitchen sink drama', widely applied to British cinema and theatre of the early 1960s. For a discussion of these issues within 1950s and 1960s black British literature, see Procter, *Dwelling Places*, pp. 21–68.
24. Hussein, *Émigré*, pp. 19, 59.
25. Markandaya, *Nowhere*, pp. 273, 276; see also Rustomji-Kerns, 'Expatriates', pp. 645–54; and Ball, *Imagining London*, pp. 190–1.
26. This obsession with return through the vision of a kind of deferred home will be properly examined in the next chapter.
27. Aslam, *Maps*, p. 359.
28. One might compare this to the lyrics of Lord Kitchener's song, 'My landlady' (1952), included in Ainley and Noblett, *London* [CD]; and see also Procter, *Dwelling Places*, pp. 21, 63n.
29. Naipaul, *Mimic*, p. 58; and compare Sandhu, *London Calling*, p. 205.
30. Srinivas does, however, appear to anticipate later dangers when he initially views his London home as a trap, rather than an achievement: 'what they had done was to shackle themselves to bricks and mortar, and it filled him with misgiving. So long as they were mobile, he liked to believe the way back to India . . . lay open'; Markandaya, *Nowhere*, p. 21.
31. Vijayaraghavan, *Motherland*, p. 15.
32. Sidhwa, *American Brat*, p. 103.
33. This phenomenon ranges from such literary works as Theodore Dreiser's *An American Tragedy* (1925) to Bret Easton Ellis's *American Psycho* (1991) to films which include Paul Schrader's *American Gigolo* (1980) and Sam Mendes's *American Beauty* (1999); for discussions of this trend within American cinema, see Merck, *America First*.
34. Compare George, 'At a slight angle', p. 193n.
35. Lahiri, *Interpreter*, pp. 26–7.
36. Daswani, *For Matrimonial Purposes*, p. 106.
37. Narayan, *Story-Teller's World*, p. 29.
38. Lahiri, *Interpreter*, p. 115.

39. George, *Politics*, p. 9. For a non-literary discussion of this paradox, see Blunt and Dowling, *Home*, p. 214.
40. Fludernik, 'Imagined communities', p. 269; and compare Lau, 'Emotional', p. 1112.
41. Divakaruni, *Unknown Errors*, p. 172; see also Parekh, *Stealing*, pp. 103–4; and Kalita, *Suburban*, p. 127; and compare Tan, *Joy Luck*, p. 250.
42. Lahiri, *Namesake*, p. 29.
43. Throughout this book, I will generally refer to 'Calcutta', 'Bombay', and 'Madras', rather than 'Kolkata', 'Mumbai', and 'Chennai', since this is the nomenclature more often used by writers themselves, often because they are referring to the city in question before it was renamed.
44. See Brians, *Modern*, p. 109; and compare similar observations on New York poverty in Alexander, *Fault Lines*, pp. 161, 176, 182–3.
45. Faymonville, 'South Asian', p. 257.
46. Hamid, *Reluctant Fundamentalist*, pp. 144–5, 149; and see also Ghosh, *Shadow Lines*, p. 204.
47. Hamid has argued that 'a novel of leaving America . . . is as much the immigrant novel of today as a story of going to the United States'; quoted in Yaqin, 'Mohsin Hamid', p. 46.
48 On transnational mobility and cultural hybridity as paradigmatically positive, even utopian, see Rushdie, *Imaginary*, p. 394; and Bhabha, *Location*, pp. 37–8, 112. Such celebrations of hybridity have, of course, been strenuously rejected by many commentators. For a helpful discussion of these debates, see Morley, *Home Territories*, pp. 205–13, 225–42.
49. Quoted in Yaqin, 'Mohsin Hamid', p. 46.
50. By 'model minority', I refer to the well-known notion of law-abiding, family-minded, high-achieving Asian Americans: a problematic term which elides individual differences between Asian Americans, ignores the ongoing difficulties they may face, subtly maintains the implicitly outsider status of Asians in the eyes of mainstream America – foregrounding 'minority' as much as 'model' – while being used sometimes as an invidious means of explaining the lack of 'progression' of other communities of colour.
51. This is supported in literary terms by its use of American and colonial intertexts, including F. Scott Fitzgerald's *The Great Gatsby* (1925) and Joseph Conrad's *Heart of Darkness* (1899). The theme of imperialism is underpinned by references to ancient and medieval empires (Greece, Ottoman Turkey, and – through Changez, whose name recalls 'Genghis' [Khan] – the Mongols) and to places with more recent, US imperial associations such as the Philippines and, as I have already noted, Chile; on the significance of Changez's name, see Shamsie, '*Reluctant Fundamentalist*'.
52. This forms the starting-point for *Lonely Londoners*, for instance; see also Bhabha, *Location*, pp. 169–70; Bryan, 'Homesickness', p. 45; and Candappa, *Picklehead*, pp. 95–6, 179, 285.
53. Compare Claude McKay's description of the English as 'a strangely

unsympathetic people, as coldly chilling as their English fog' and of 1920s London as a 'cold, white city where English culture is great and formidable like an iceberg' in McKay, *A Long Way*, pp. 67, 304; my thanks to Graeme Abernethy for this reference.

54. Sidhwa, *Crow Eaters*, pp. 259–60. Sidhwa draws on a range of other devices to deride Britain in the novel: poverty, dirt (particularly in a lavatorial context), tasteless food (an idea I will revisit in Chapter 4), and the unpleasant corporeality of Caucasians. On this latter point, compare Maxey, 'Who wants', pp. 532–5. Sidhwa's caricatured, colonial-era Britain in *Crow Eaters* forms a marked contrast to her nuanced, layered critique of the US, a country she knows much better, in *American Brat*.
55. Alexander, *Nampally Road*, p. 19.
56. Compare Maxey, 'Who wants', pp. 529–30, 536–7.
57. Rushdie, *Imaginary*, p. 130.
58. See Blaise and Mukherjee, *Days and Nights*, p. 169; Mukherjee, *Middleman*, p. 197; and Mukherjee, *Darkness*, p. 87.
59. Alexander, *Fault Lines*, p. 112.
60. See Lahiri, *Interpreter*, pp. 129, 133; Lahiri, *Namesake*, p. 9; Lahiri, *Unaccustomed*, pp. 62, 224; and compare Meer, *Bombay Talkie*, pp. 19–20. In Lahiri's work, bitingly cold American winters also signal moments of emotional emptiness for the second generation; see Lahiri, *Interpreter*, p. 5; and Lahiri, *Unaccustomed*, pp. 289–90.
61. Islam, *Mapmakers*, p. 16.
62. Mukherjee, *Darkness*, pp. 1–3; Mukherjee, 'Imagining', pp. 71–2, 82.
63. Lalwani, *Gifted*, p. 42.
64. Vakil, *One Day*, pp. 52 and 17 respectively.
65. Saadi, *Burning Mirror*, p. 5. Compare, too, Roy, 'Smells', p. 319, where Savitri, a young Indian woman, prefers to imagine the 'cool . . . fresh' English climate rather than face the reality of 'hot parched Delhi streets and the cruel blue Indian skies'.
66. Compare Upstone, *British Asian*, p. 199.
67. See Maxey, 'Life in the diaspora', pp. 10–11.
68. Compare Phillips, *Mapping*, p. 20: 'post-colonial critics . . . unmap (literally) the geographies of empire, and (metaphorically) the identities, particularly the imperial masculinities, constructed in that geography'.
69. See Nasta, *Home Truths*, p. 197; and Procter, *Dwelling Places*, p. 46, where both critics note the appropriation of local London territory in Selvon's *Lonely Londoners*.
70. See Adams, *Across Seven Seas*.
71. For more on these aspects of the text, see Bromley, *Narratives*, pp. 128–9, 131–2.
72. Srivastava, *Looking for Maya*, pp. 90, 147; Kureishi, *My Ear*, p. 198.
73. Compare Nasta, *Home Truths*, p. 197; Procter, *Dwelling Places*, pp. 53, 55; and Ball, *Imagining London*, pp. 135–6. This tactic provides an important

counterhegemonic reversal of the colonial tradition whereby, in J. B. Harley's words, 'indigenous place-names of minority groups are suppressed on topographical maps in favour of the standard toponymy of the controlling group'; see Harley, 'Maps', p. 289.

74. Phillips, *Mapping*, p. 15.
75. Vijayaraghavan, *Motherland*, p. 232.
76. Parekh, *Stealing*, p. 37; Lahiri, *Interpreter*, p. 26.
77. Lahiri, *Interpreter*, p. 90; and compare Tettenborn, 'Jhumpa Lahiri', pp. 11–12; and Chaudhury, 'Debutante', p. 19, where she describes Lahiri as 'a cartographer charting new worlds'.
78. Alexander, *Fault Lines*, p. 94.
79. Compare *Kartography*, the title of the third novel by the Pakistani writer Kamila Shamsie, published in 2002.
80. Harley, 'Maps', p. 278.
81. Ibid., p. 281.
82. Compare McLoughlin, 'Writing', p. 440.
83. Phillips, *Mapping*, p. 14.
84. Denis Cosgrove, cited in Harley, 'Maps', p. 290.
85. Harley, 'Maps', pp. 278, 294, 301.
86. Goldman, *Paths*, pp. 5–6.
87. Compare Jameson, 'Cognitive mapping', p. 353.
88. Phillips, *Mapping*, p. 14.
89. Rushdie, *Satanic Verses*, pp. 354–5.
90. Compare Procter, 'Nadeem Aslam'; and see also Chatterjee, 'Thoughts', p. 313. A literary example of South Asian plants in a US landscape is offered in Chauhan, 'Home', p. 217.
91. See Bald, 'Images', pp. 421–2, for a discussion of Naipaul's use of plant imagery in a related sense; for British Asian horticultural practices in a non-literary context, see Murphy, 'Back to our roots', pp. 86–7; and within an Indian domestic setting, see Lau, 'Emotional', p. 1111.
92. Thus it plays a psychological role in Maxine Hong Kingston's Chinese American family history *China Men* (1977), and in Timothy Mo's novel *Sour Sweet* (1982), where Chen, a Chinese immigrant in London, successfully raises a mango tree in his British garden; see also Ashley and Wilson, *Growing Good*, n.p., a children's book in which the bicultural heritage of Samuel, a young black British boy, is reflected in unobtrusive fashion through the cultivation of 'beans from St Lucia' and 'old [English] foxgloves, from what was growing here before'.
93. Meer, *Bombay Talkie*, p. 177; and see also Narayan, *Monsoon Diary*, p. 77.
94. Manzoor, *Greetings*, p. 29.
95. Compare Dasgupta, 'Locating "home"', pp. 76–7.
96. Feng, 'Immigrant rhapsody', p. 6.
97. See Vaidyanathan, 'Inside'; and Shukla, *India Abroad*, pp. 80–5, 87–91, 106–18.

98. Divakaruni, *Unknown Errors*, pp. 40–1.
99. Kalita, *Suburban*, p. 13.
100. See also Mazumdar, 'Race', pp. 32–3; Grewal, 'Indian-American', p. 98; and Misir, 'The murder of Navroze Mody', pp. 501–17.
101. For a wider discussion of South Asian political activity in the US, see Prashad, 'How the Hindus', pp. 583–606; and Khagram et al., 'Seen, rich, but unheard?', p. 260.
102. Beyond its alliteration with 'suburban', 'sahib' is an interesting choice. A polite form of address which implies the authority of the person so called through its various meanings (in Urdu, via Persian and Arabic) of 'lord', 'owner', and 'master', its connotations again suggest the right of South Asian immigrants to stake their claim on US land.
103. Low, 'Separate spheres?', p. 23.
104. Procter, *Dwelling Places*, p. 164.
105. See, for example, ibid.; Sandhu, *London Calling*; McLeod, *Postcolonial London*; and Ball, *Imagining London*.
106. Compare Procter, *Dwelling Places*, pp. 160–81, 191–4.
107. McLoughlin, 'Writing', p. 437.
108. Saadi, 'Psychoraag'.
109. Kohli, *Indian Takeaway*, pp. 14, 247–8.
110. On Saadi's assertion of his Scots Asian identity, see Upstone, *British Asian*, pp. 197–9, 201, 204–5.
111. Again one might compare Luton with New Jersey, the latter described by the American novelist Tom Perrotta as 'a national joke [in the 1960s and 1970s] . . . we had that pride that you have when you live in a much-maligned place'; see Maxey, 'New American', p. 277.
112. Compare Ganguly, 'Migrant identities', p. 43; Brah, *Cartographies*, p. 35; Sandhu, *London Calling*, p. 239; and Procter, *Dwelling Places*, p. 61.
113. Compare Dasgupta, 'Locating "home"', pp. 77–8; and Blunt and Dowling, *Home*, p. 212.
114. The perceived female responsibility to sustain a particular ethnic culture within the diasporic home is linked to the well-recognised notion of women as repositories of tradition; see Yuval-Davis, *Gender*, pp. 39, 43–6. For more on the male/female split between house-building and 'home-making', see Blunt and Dowling, *Home*, pp. 4–5.
115. See Hiddleston, 'Shapes', p. 59, where she argues that Ali's 'penetration of interior space' is classically Orientalist.
116. Mukherjee, 'American Dreamer', p. 34.
117. For more on the sources of Dimple's rage, see Koshy, *Sexual Naturalisation*, pp. 145, 153.
118. Compare Mankekar, 'India shopping', pp. 209, 211, for a consideration of this phenomenon in the South Asian American context.
119. Ali, *Brick Lane*, p. 93.
120. For a discussion of such stereotypes, see Brah, *Cartographies*, pp. 13, 68, 74;

Malik, 'Beyond', p. 213; Kabeer, *Power to Choose*, p. 251; and Malek, '*Bhaji*', pp. 123, 125–6.

121. Compare Maxey, 'Representative', p. 223.
122. That domestic interiors should reflect psychological states is of course well understood; see Bachelard, *Poetics*, pp. 18–20.
123. George, *Politics*, p. 18.
124. Compare Campbell-Hall, 'Subversive', pp. 231, 235–6.
125. Low, 'Separate spheres?', p. 29.
126. Campbell-Hall, 'Subversive', pp. 229, 232.
127. Dasgupta, 'Locating "home"', p. 82.
128. See Kureishi, *Dreaming*, pp. 69–70; and compare Maxey, 'Life in the diaspora', pp. 19–20.
129. See Blunt and Dowling, *Home*, pp. 15–16.
130. Usually London is a point of departure for the US in Lahiri's writing, with North America 'the third and final continent', as she puts it in the eponymous story; see Lahiri, *Interpreter*, pp. 173–98. In 'Only goodness', however, Sudha's parents remain Anglophile despite their decision to settle in the US, and they find it easier to accept their daughter's interracial marriage to a white British man than they would have if she had chosen a Euro-American; on Bengali Anglophilia, see Dasgupta, 'Locating "home"', p. 76. Lahiri's own background – like Sudha, she is a British-born Bengali American – has led her to make transatlantic comparisons, especially in interviews with British journalists – for instance, when she notes that 'India was an unknown thing for most Americans [during her 1970s childhood]. I felt that it was basically like the moon to them . . . [but it] has never been as foreign a place to the English . . . because of the . . . colonial past'; quoted in Tayler, 'Change'. At the same time, she does very little to compare the two places in her writing, which includes no British Asian characters.
131. See, for example, Mukherjee, *Holder*, pp. 67, 102, 156, 199; Mukherjee, 'Love me', p. 189. In *Reluctant Fundamentalist*, Hamid never presents settlement in Britain as a viable option for Changez, the protagonist, despite Hamid's own years of living in London and his discussion of the novel's reception in specifically transatlantic terms; see Yaqin, 'Mohsin Hamid', p. 47.
132. Quoted in Byers-Pevitts, 'Interview', p. 193.
133. Vignisson, 'Bharati Mukherjee', pp. 158–9.
134. Byers-Pevitts, 'Interview', pp. 192–3.
135. Gioseffi, 'In the mercy', p. 46; and compare Gunew, 'Mouthwork', p. 100.
136. Blaise and Mukherjee, 'After the Fatwa', p. 31.
137. Meer, *Bombay Talkie*, p. 75, emphasis added.
138. Kamani, *Junglee Girl*, p. 161.
139. Bantwal, *Sari Shop*, p. 161.
140. Kureishi, *Black Album*, p. 54.
141. Kureishi, *Hanif Kureishi: Plays 1*, p. 154.
142. Kureishi, *Buddha*, p. 256.

143. Ibid., pp. 53, 95; and Kureishi, *Dreaming*, pp. 29–31; and compare Ranasinha, *South Asian*, pp. 231–2.
144. For one reviewer, however, both this conclusion, which offers an 'overly schematised narrative of assimilation', and the author's earlier pro-American stance suggest Manzoor's 'publisher's voice' in a post-9/11, post-7/7 climate; see Mukherjee, 'Born in Pakistan'.
145. This global presence includes Canada, the Caribbean, South Africa, the Middle East, Australia, the South Pacific, and South East Asia; see Brown, *Global South Asians*; and Lal et al., *Encyclopedia*.
146. Rice, *Radical Narratives*, p. 187.
147. Massa and Stead, 'Introduction', p. 1.
148. Thus for such nineteenth-century writers as Ralph Waldo Emerson, 'England' is seen as 'an old and exhausted island'; cited in Weisbuch, 'Cultural time', p. 100.
149. Compare Jussawalla, 'South Asian diaspora', p. 20; and Morley, *Home Territories*, pp. 205–13, 225–42.
150. Blunt and Dowling, *Home*, pp. 26, 132, 16 respectively.
151. Ganguly, 'Migrant identities', p. 43.
152. Kim, 'Defining', pp. 103–11.

CHAPTER 2

CLOSE ENCOUNTERS WITH ANCESTRAL SPACE: TRAVEL AND RETURN IN TRANSATLANTIC SOUTH ASIAN WRITING

Introduction

If '"return" is a prevalent theme in post-colonial literature',[1] South Asian Atlantic narratives certainly present India, Pakistan, and Bangladesh as a powerful force for members of the diaspora. Makarand Paranjape has argued that 'diasporas and homelands are locked in peculiar, dialectical relationships';[2] and indeed it is difficult for cultural producers to ignore this relationship, however problematic. As Gargi Bhattacharyya has put it, 'the South Asian diaspora looks to the sub-continent as an anchor for identity formation, however mythical and uncomfortable'.[3] But what happens when ethnic South Asians return to the ancestral homeland, or indeed visit it for the first time? Building on the examination of home and nation in Chapter 1, I will now consider the discursive treatment of travel and return within diasporic literary works: an œuvre in which the precarious balance between writers' critiques of South Asia and the adoptive nation (discussed in the previous chapter) is taken several steps further.

This chapter will begin by briefly addressing return as it is articulated through the notion of a 'deferred home', interrogating writers' use of this trope and asking why it appears more in British Asian than South Asian American writing. I will then analyse at greater length the way in which writers handle 'return of the native' moments: actual first-generation encounters with the originary homeland. In a contemporary review of Bharati Mukherjee's novel *The Tiger's Daughter* (1971), J. R. Frakes noted the 'conventional' nature of '"return of the expatriate" fiction, structured on the familiar pattern of trembling expectation, shock of unrecognition . . . disillusionment, and final sad acceptance of one's alien position between two worlds'.[4] One might take issue with the old-fashioned 'between worlds' nature of this statement, but it is notable that Frakes should detect a potential for cliché here as early as 1972. South Asian American authors in particular have appeared untroubled by such claims, continuing to achieve originality through the richness of their specific, individualised treatments of what going back means.

Next, in discussing what writers do with the return-of-the-native theme, I will ask how US treatments differ from British ones, before assessing the subject of 'ethnic return': namely, when a foreign-born generation seeks to connect with their heritage in the ancestral homeland. Looking first at South Asian American examples before moving on to the British Asian context, I will argue that these 'roots' visits represent a rite of passage as much for 'ethnic' writers and film-makers, creatively and intellectually, as for their fictionalised characters in an emotional and spiritual sense[5] – and that such journeys occupy complex psychological ground. But whereas British Asian artists opt for an unsentimental, sometimes even comical, treatment of these issues, South Asian American writers and film-makers respond in more sombre fashion, perhaps reflecting the sacred status of the roots search in North American culture. Indeed, in the US – a society whose national self-image has been closely linked to the mythology of immigration, following the 'ethnic revival' of the 1960s and 1970s[6] – this tradition remains especially important. For Mukherjee, the 'roots search' is 'that most American of . . . compulsions', while Sunaina Maira has written of

> the American ethnic identity trope of 'the search for roots' – the idea that ethnic identity origins need to be recovered and authenticated. Identity politics in the United States encourages this view of ethnic identity as a search for validating origins, as a claim that must have geographic roots elsewhere.[7]

Popular Irish American roots narratives date back more than half a century to John Ford's classic film *The Quiet Man* (1952);[8] and Stephanie Rains, in her consideration of other Irish American examples of the roots genre, has shown that Alex Haley's Pulitzer Prize-winning, semi-fictionalised family history *Roots* (1976) – which gave rise to the landmark American television series – was responsible for translating 'roots' into a byword for genealogical searching in the American popular consciousness.[9] How, then, do South Asian Atlantic artists handle this wider discourse of 'return'?

Scholars working in various disciplines have increasingly considered the subject of reverse migration, returnees, and the 'ethnic return' experiences of foreign-born generations.[10] They note that studies of diaspora and migration have traditionally overlooked this issue, often treating migration as a unipolar phenomenon.[11] Recent research on ethnic return has examined permanent, second-generation relocation to Japan and Greece, as well as parts of the Caribbean and the South Pacific.[12] There has also been some attention to particular versions of temporary 'roots' visits through academic accounts of 'homeland trips' to Ghana, Scotland, China, and Korea.[13] Such research, while fascinating and valuable, generally overlooks the South Asian context.[14] It also takes a social science approach to this material. In other words, the aesthetic treatment of return – particularly in its literary forms – has largely been ignored;[15] and despite the thematic prevalence of travel and return in recent South Asian Atlantic texts, this rich topic has yet to receive proper attention.[16] This chapter will therefore attempt to redress the existing scholarly imbalance.

Deferred Homes and the Myth of Return

Immigrants ensure psychological survival in the new nation through what might be termed the 'deferred home', particularly within British Asian literature. Thus in Monica Ali's novel *Brick Lane* (2003), Chanu endures the disappointments of life in London by saving up for a house in Dhaka and dreaming of constructing a further home in the Bangladeshi countryside, which will be distinguished, through its 'simple', 'rustic' qualities, from the 'mansions . . . these Sylhetis are building'.[17] And Mohammed Manzoor, the immigrant patriarch in Sarfraz Manzoor's memoir *Greetings from Bury Park: Race. Religion. Rock 'n' Roll* (2007), tells his family, who are permanently resident in 1980s Britain, that

> Pakistan was our true home and Britain merely where we happened to live . . . 'The reason I say to you to speak Urdu and not forget you are Pakistani is that you never know when we might have to leave . . . *That's why I still keep our house in Pakistan* . . . the only country that will never deny you . . . that you can always say is your home'.[18]

This tendency towards a kind of domestic postponement, through the vision of property-ownership in South Asia, allows immigrants like Chanu and Mohammed to maintain their dignity. It also suggests that little has changed since the sojourner mentality of the postwar period, as considered in Chapter 1. Indeed, one might compare this homing instinct to Amir's initial obsession with a return to Pakistan in Abdullah Hussein's novel *Émigré Journeys* (2000). Writing to his wife, Salma, in the 1960s, Amir impresses 'upon her to buy land in the village so that by the time I made my return there were enough acres to my home on which we could live in comfort'.[19]

For some migrants, then, the British experience, from the 1950s right into the twenty-first century, is about saving enough money to fulfil the dream of return: earnings in the here and now are used to buy or maintain a property – or to obtain the land on which to build a dwelling – 'back home'. Sojourners thus reside far from home in order to make a home, with the ontological experience of one's 'true' home constantly deferred. As Sara Ahmed has argued:

> home . . . become[s] a fetish . . . separated from the particular worldly space of living *here*, through the possibility of some memories and the impossibility of others. In such a narrative journey . . . the space which is most like home . . . most comfortable and familiar, is not the space of inhabitance – I am here – but the very space in which one finds the self as almost, but not quite, at home. In such a space, the subject has a destination, an itinerary, indeed a future, but in having such a destination, has not yet arrived.[20]

Within this framework, South Asia becomes a realm of nostalgia. In *Brick Lane*, for instance, Nazneen repeatedly romanticises Bangladesh, which is remembered as vast and dreamlike, despite the nation's relatively small size and high population density. Homesickness and loneliness ensure that the London-based migrants in Manzu Islam's short story 'Going home' (from *The Mapmakers of Spitalfields* [1997]), also envision Bangladesh in an overtly positive way. Islam draws attention to the contradictions necessary to maintain this exilic position when his narrator admits that:

> against our better judgements, and despite what we knew to be the reality, we plunged yet again into talking as if we had grown up in an enchanted garden . . . This was not the end but the beginning of our invariable task: to recreate that fabulous home . . . element by element, paying scrupulous attention to the most minute variations, the infinite odours, and not overlooking even the most transitory of colours, the tactile surfaces of things.[21]

Despite the idea that some migrants do realise their dream of the deferred home – for instance, the Sylhetis whose houses Chanu dismisses as implicitly vulgar – such long-term homing plans are also problematised in British Asian texts. Dr Azad names the phenomenon of endless deferral 'Going Home Syndrome' (*Brick Lane*, 24). He has failed to achieve a permanent return to Bangladesh, following a series of natural and manmade disasters, and *Brick Lane* implies that the project of successfully securing a home in South Asia is unlikely to succeed. Moreover, in Atima Srivastava's novel *Looking for Maya* (1999), Mira's parents return to India to build a house, but soon discover the complexities of this time-consuming process: 'land plots couldn't be abandoned, [and] building work couldn't be left unsupervised in Delhi, which was lawless these days'.[22]

In *Émigré Journeys*, the obsession with securing land in one's birth nation co-exists, paradoxically, with 'hatching plots to get . . . people into this country [Britain], legally or not' (100). Similarly, the Bombay bourgeoisie in *Looking for Maya* spend much of their time 'speculating about Foreign' (namely, the outside world) but 'in London . . . [they] constantly talked of India' (89). This emigrating/homing desire also appears in South Asian American literature. Throughout Mukherjee's early works, for example, fictional migrants will do anything to leave South Asia, but once they have left, can only think about returning to their original starting-point. Salman Rushdie has famously argued that one can never properly return home: that is, to the point from which one set out. Analysing Victor Fleming's classic film *The Wizard of Oz* (1939), he contends that

> the truth is that once we have left our childhood places and started out to make up our lives, armed only with what we have and are, we understand that . . . there is no longer any such place as home: except, of course, for the home we make, or the homes that are made for us, in Oz: which is anywhere, and everywhere, except the place from which we began.[23]

Missing from this discussion is the earlier point that migrants may well see their early home through the sepia tones of nostalgia, as Dorothy does in *Wizard of Oz*: an attitude to home clearly predicated upon belief in an actual return to origins.

The concept of 'return' nevertheless implies a problematic time–space relationship. As Ahmed notes

> migration involves not only a spatial . . . but also a temporal dislocation: 'the past' becomes associated with a home that . . . is impossible to inhabit, and be inhabited by, in the present . . . it is impossible to return to a place that was lived as home, precisely because the home is not exterior to a self, but implicated in it.[24]

Mukherjee reinforces these ideas in her non-fiction, yet she creates fictional expatriates for whom the myth of return is a necessary aspiration: indeed, it is a defining aspect of their existence in the US. The reward of returning to India – to the deferred national home embodied by a future, rather than ancestral, property – is taken for granted by such long-term immigrants as Mrs Chakladar, who claims in the novel *Wife* (1975) that 'we're all planning to go home when our husbands retire. I mean, who would want to die in Kansas City?'[25] In 'Nostalgia', a short story from the collection *Darkness* (1985), Manny, a successful New York-based psychiatrist, holds on to the idea that he can 'always go back to Delhi',[26] in direct proportion to the guilt he feels about neglecting his parents there. But the stressful, demanding work which enables his moneyed American lifestyle has effectively trapped him in the United States, and the story suggests that a return to India will become less likely with each passing year. Analogously, the colonising Englishmen in Mukherjee's historical novel *The Holder of the World* (1993) are 'snared' by the East India Company in southern India; for them, 'there was no going back'.[27] Rushdie's sense that one can never truly return thus becomes a literal reality here.

In Manzu Islam's 'Going home', Zamil plans to establish a community 'conceived on collective principles' (12) back in Bangladesh, its deliberately remote location underscoring further the inaccessible nature of the deferred home. Using sensory, natural details to evoke Bangladesh – the 'sweet smell of jack-fruit . . . the flaming red of cotton-flowers' (12) – Zamil seeks to involve the unnamed narrator in his project. In a symbolic plot twist, however, Zamil dies the next day, implying that living too much in an imaginary home, located in the past and future rather than the present, can be psychologically treacherous, even fatal. When Kalpana tells the narrator that:

> *you came just in the nick of time to take Zamil's place. We mustn't stop here, there's so much to remember and . . . plan, isn't there? . . . The place that Zamil told us about last night, he is surely about to return there now, I can feel it in my bones. One day we must all return there, we can't leave Zamil all alone, can we?* (23; emphasis in original)

she associates a deferred home in Bangladesh with the afterlife. This marks an attempt to reconcile herself to the bitter realisation that, in a bodily sense, Zamil was unable to return home before he died. It is worth noting that Nadeem Aslam uses a similarly eschatological framework in his novel *Maps for Lost Lovers* (2004), where – during a long spell as a self-styled sojourner in Britain – Kaukab deems 'England . . . the equivalent of earthly suffering, the return one day to Pakistan entry into Paradise'.[28]

The reluctant compromise made by migrants with their present circumstances in order to serve future needs signals a difference between home in the literal, quotidian sense of a roof over one's head, as discussed in Chapter 1, and home as an emotional, interior state: the transcendent feeling of security and belonging associated with the ancestral nation.

But beyond the spiritual language of deferred homes deployed in 'Going home' and *Maps* – a form of expression which echoes the soteriological connotations of 'home' in some negro spirituals[29] – the negotiation of a future return to South Asia is often a masculinist, highly materialist endeavour which hinges on control over the building of one's own house in a largely patriarchal society where one's status will not be questioned. *Brick Lane* provides a perfect illustration of this through Chanu, whose carefully preserved memory of cultural recognition and social acceptance, embodied through the image of deferred Bangladeshi homes, compensates for the emasculating effects of professional failure in Britain.

Why, with the exception of Mukherjee, are deferred homes more prevalent in British Asian than in South Asian American writing? One explanation may be that, unlike a largely first-generation cohort of US writers, the 1.5- and second-generation status of such British writers as Ali, Srivastava, and Aslam – the latter two belonging to the so-called '1.5 generation' because they emigrated before reaching adulthood – ensures that attitudes to the originary home are in some sense underdeveloped, even second-hand: inherited, re-imagined, and mediated through parents. But this fails to take into account writers who are first-generation: for instance, Hussein and Islam. Their attention to deferred homes could signal the ongoing sojourner mentality discussed in Chapter 1: ongoing because, as we have seen already, the UK has traditionally provided less space for immigrants in its national imaginary. Indeed, much like the insistence on domesticity charted in Chapter 1, a transnational emphasis on property in South Asia – however unrealistic and fanciful it is to harbour such plans and however much writers themselves question it – undermines the putting down of new national roots in Britain.

Return-of-the-Native Tropes

Rather than offering accounts of successful reverse migration,[30] South Asian Atlantic writers generally examine troubling, temporary return-of-the-native moments, perhaps because this trope offers more room for conflict between characters as well as a legitimate means of critiquing the originary homeland. As Heidi Hansson has observed in the context of nineteenth-century Irish literature, the returnee 'combines an outsider's view with an insider's authority and is therefore often used to express critical ideas'.[31] For Sanjukta Dasgupta, meanwhile,

> the expatriate's sense of feeling 'alien' in the longed-for home, the sense of loss that grows out of the constructions of selective memory and the . . . shock

that the real encounter with the homeland generates, is a riveting study that contemporary literary writing registers and addresses.[32]

Across South Asian American literature, the young Indian woman coming back from the United States to visit her family constitutes a recurrent thematic device.[33] Recalling Balachandra Rajan's novel *Too Long in the West* (1962), these female protagonists – returning to very different parts of the country, for diverse reasons, and at different ages – attempt to come to terms with their 'America-returned' position (to borrow an Indian English phrase). Such novelistic figures include Tara in Mukherjee's *Tiger's Daughter*; Mira in Meena Alexander's *Nampally Road* (1991); Maya in Vineeta Vijayaraghavan's *Motherland* (2001); Priya in Amulya Malladi's *The Mango Season* (2003); and Anju in Kavita Daswani's *For Matrimonial Purposes* (2003). The unnamed first-person narrator of Ginu Kamani's short story 'Ciphers' (*Junglee Girl* [1995]), and Shoba Narayan, recounting her own experiences in her autobiography *Monsoon Diary* (2003), provide further examples, while Shilpi Somaya Gowda's novel *Secret Daughter* (2010) addresses both first- and second-generation 'return' to India.

Return-of-the-native sagas are less common in British Asian literature, possibly for experiential reasons, once again reflecting the reality that fewer British Asian writers were born and raised in South Asia. For Indian-born US writers, on the other hand, there are often compelling autobiographical reasons for exploring such ideas. Their novels usually suggest an India slow to embrace social change and radically different from America in economic terms; and they often take place at a highly charged historical moment. Thus Tara's return to Calcutta in *Tiger's Daughter* is marked by tumultuous political events – the siege of the city by the Communist Naxalites in 1970–1[34] – while Maya's homecoming in *Motherland* takes place immediately after the Indian prime minister, Rajiv Gandhi, was assassinated by Sri Lankan Tamil terrorists in 1989.[35] This latter backdrop is further emphasised by the novel's South Indian setting in which certain Tamil characters may or may not be complicit in the ongoing terrorist campaign. Such tension sharpens Maya's experiences of India, rendering the personal political and vice versa: her troubled emotional situation is, to a certain extent, writ large. That novels set in India are explicitly political reflects the notion that South Asia needs to be understood as a site of political upheaval, as we saw in Chapter 1, although it also runs the risk (inadvertently perhaps) of pitting a 'dangerous' India against a 'safe' US.

In *Tiger's Daughter*, Tara recoils from much of what she sees in Calcutta, 'outraged' because

> there were too many people sprawled in alleys and storefronts and staircases . . . She hated Calcutta because it had given her kids eating yoghurt off dirty sidewalks . . . viruses that stalked the street . . . dogs and cows scrapping in garbage dumps.[36]

Why such poverty leaves Tara feeling 'outraged' is not entirely clear. If her indignation results from a sense of injustice at the extreme social inequality on display in India's cities, so be it. But the fundamental self-absorption of Tara's existential confusion suggests otherwise: she appears to be personally affronted by such squalor, which provides the exterior backdrop to her internal disappointment at the gulf between a romantically remembered India and the reality confronting her. Although Mukherjee has claimed that the 1950s city in which she was raised 'was not the Calcutta of documentary films – not a hell where beggars fought off dying cattle for still-warm garbage',[37] this is precisely the version she reinscribes through the early 1970s Calcutta of the semi-autobiographical *Tiger's Daughter*. Perhaps she deems this permissible because she is Calcutta-born and because she perceives the patrician society of Tara's birth – and, crucially, her own – to be inexorably declining. *Tiger's Daughter* places the blame for this firmly at the feet of the Naxalites and, although this political group did shake to its core the city's socio-economic elite, the world of Tara's (and Mukherjee's) youth has arguably become lost as much through the simple passage of time: a process heightened because that time has been spent outside India.

In *Mango Season*, Malladi's focus on return-of-the-native tropes is so unrelenting that it becomes claustrophobic, as she extracts as much meaning as possible from Priya's reverse culture shock, particularly on the issue of gender politics. As distinct from *Motherland* – where the younger, more impressionable Maya reacts with a certain amount of *naïveté* to the complexities of middle-class Indian society – Priya responds angrily to local mores on her return to the Hyderabad family home after seven years in the United States.[38] The anxiety she feels towards this homecoming manifests itself on several levels. It is physical and sensory, as – much like Tara in *Tiger's Daughter* or Anju in *For Matrimonial Purposes* – she worries about food hygiene and suffers problems with heat, noise, and chaos. It is social and cultural, as she struggles with the constraints placed upon women; with a stifling lack of privacy; and with her community's deep-seated conservatism on matters of marriage and racial difference. Indeed, unmarried at twenty-seven, Priya occupies a socially precarious position. Her discomfort is also emotional, as she experiences guilt about such feelings of impatience and prejudice, while trying to regain her place within the wider family.

By contrast, in Mohsin Hamid's novel *The Reluctant Fundamentalist*

(2007), Changez dismisses such misgivings during a brief return visit to Pakistan from the US, recognising that his initial sense of shame at 'how shabby our house appeared' means that 'I was looking about me with the eyes of a foreigner . . . [an] entitled and unsympathetic American', and then deciding to 'exorcise the unwelcome sensibility by which I had become possessed'.[39] Suitably refamiliarised with the family house – an obvious metonym for his rediscovered connection to the national home (to which he later returns permanently) – Changez takes pride in its 'enduring grandeur' and in the historical value of its artefacts, which include 'Mughal miniatures . . . ancient carpets . . . [and] an excellent library' (142). That his ancestral culture should contain such 'ancient' objects distinguishes it, in Changez's eyes at least, from the relative newness and thus inferiority of an American heritage: an aspect of South Asian American writers' critique of the US discussed briefly in the previous chapter. His restored patriotism may also explain why, as Muneeza Shamsie puts it, 'Changez has very little to say about Pakistan's social iniquities and political oppression.'[40] And gender is significant here. Whereas Changez fails to note the privilege he enjoys as a returning son in a patriarchal society, Priya makes much of the specific difficulties women face during her South Asian homecoming.

Her America-returned status also goes beyond such considerations, however, compelling more generalised behaviour and expectations in others: from the obligatory ritual of present-giving to relatives, which creates its own fictions of South Asian American abundance,[41] to the hypocrisy of parents (and grandparents) who feel pride about the prestige of (grand)children living in America, and then returning to the fold, but intense prejudice about US culture and society itself.[42] Like some other Non-Resident Indians, Priya's loyalties are to her adoptive country – in this case, America – yet India elicits competing impulses which cannot be so easily dismissed, and Malladi uses Priya's return-of-the-native position as a point of departure from which to question home linguistically, metaphorically, and materially. The strain of Priya's return to India expresses itself as an almost out-of-body sensation. Thus in a moment of double consciousness,[43] Priya envisages two distinct selves, separated along temporal and national lines: an American self representing her present and future role as lover and potential wife to Nick, her American fiancé; and an Indian self embodying her older position of daughter and granddaughter.

Grappling with such divided loyalties, she attempts to convince herself that America commands greater loyalty:

> I had never thought about how . . . the cliché 'you can never really go back home' would stand true. This was not home anymore. Home was in San

> Francisco with Nick. Home was Whole Foods grocery store . . . fast food at KFC [Kentucky Fried Chicken] . . . Pier 1 . . . Wal-Mart . . . 7-Eleven and Starbucks. Home was familiar, Hyderabad was a stranger; India was as alien, exasperating, and sometimes exotic to me as it would be to a foreigner. (126)

The text confirms this faith in her US home, presented in ostensibly positive terms[44] – after all, the commodified imagery of 'KFC' and 'Starbucks' is not something everyone would celebrate uncritically – since Priya ultimately returns to San Francisco. Indeed, permanent reverse migration is presented as similarly unviable for Anju in *For Matrimonial Purposes*; Maya in *Motherland*; Gita in Kirin Narayan's novel *Love, Stars, and All That* (1994); Feroza in Bapsi Sidhwa's novel *An American Brat* (1994); and for several of G. S. Sharat Chandra's characters in the short stories collected in *Sari of the Gods* (1998). It is almost as though return to South Asia – and the severing of nostalgic links that this compels through a full-on engagement with current local realities – form a necessary stage in making the transition to a more fully fledged American status. But Priya's obsessive comparisons between India and America actually serve to undercut her putative confidence in her US home. Most importantly, perhaps, it is India, rather than America, which provides the novel's setting. Echoing *Motherland*, Priya's homecoming reinstates the importance, inescapability, and potential dangers of the past as opposed to the apparent normality of an American present.

Within British Asian literature, Prafulla Mohanti's memoir *Through Brown Eyes* (1985) explicitly addresses the complexities of return to India, which are framed through particular difficulties: the hostility of Delhi town planners to his professional ideas and overseas education; the sense of frustration evoked by India's caste system and endemic corruption; and the frightening realities of urban poverty. Rather as Tara recoiled from the degradations suffered by Calcutta's poor, so Mohanti reacts to Bombay's horrifying extremes, asking 'had Bombay changed, or had England changed me?'[45] In contrast to this urban landscape, he idealises his ancestral village, but tellingly does so only when he is in Britain. Indeed, on his return to the village, he discovers how estranged from it he has become as he encounters what he sees as the locals' intrusive curiosity.

Through Brown Eyes never discloses Mohanti's homosexuality and how this might have affected the question of permanent return to India. His autobiography thus recalls the guardedness of an earlier era, even if the issue of sexuality remains pertinent – central even – to his relationship with Britain as home.[46] In view of his direct experiences of British racism, one wonders to what extent his position as a gay man has contributed to his decision to settle in London. Mohanti surely welcomes the more liberal attitudes towards sexuality within a mid-twentieth-century Western metropolis, and the freedom from family pressure to marry and start a family that emigration confers. Instead, he writes that 'there were personal problems which I could not discuss with anybody' (122) and, in an intriguing textual slippage, Indian poverty is cited whenever he feels discomfort over matters of physical intimacy, as though he connects the need to guard his privacy vis-à-vis the reader with an unvoiced shame at withholding his sexuality from his poor, villager parents. His immigrant and sexual status combine to displace Mohanti within both India and Britain, but the UK ultimately represents more of a home for him than India can.

In *Looking for Maya*, Srivastava depicts the straightforward homing desire of Mira's exilic parents, who return to India after more than fifteen years in London. But their apparent happiness at doing so is unsettled not only by the difficulties of making their deferred home a reality, but also by the ambiguity of earlier return visits which punctuate the narrative. For Ravi, Mira's father, going back to India is about proving that he has retained his integrity, spirituality, and essential Indianness. In a way that recalls the attitudes of those British Pakistanis in Farhana Sheikh's novel *The Red Box* (1991) who condemn other members of the community who have sold 'their souls to make money [and] . . . *forgotten who they were*',[47] Ravi is deeply troubled by the idea that Indian friends and family will think he has been 'swallowed up by the West' (141). Mortified that his relatives assume he has forgotten traditional practices, he seeks to inculcate into his daughter the need for cultural sensitivity – 'just because you live abroad . . . doesn't mean you can go to India and throw your money around' (76) – although Mira comments wryly that Ravi's frugality fails to take into account 'a whole generation of Indians who had grown up . . . in his absence . . . [and] never set foot on public transport' (86).

The notion that exile entrenches outdated attitudes to the ancestral homeland[48] also informs *Brick Lane*. When Chanu returns to Bangladesh, he discovers, perhaps predictably, that the experience is anticlimactic, telling his wife, Nazneen, that 'you can't step in the same river twice' (409). Despite the frustrations and miseries of his life in Britain, he was at least surrounded by his family there. But Ali presents Chanu's experiences in Bangladesh at one remove, rather as she does those of Nazneen's sister, Hasina, through letters from Dhaka written in an estranging form of pidgin English.[49] In other words, we do not go to Bangladesh with either of them, perhaps because, as I have argued already, portrayals of the ancestral nation differ according to the writer's own subject position. Thus Manzu Islam, himself a Bangladeshi émigré, offers a richer and more confident depiction of Bangladesh than does the British-raised Ali.

We saw earlier that, through the figure of Zamil in 'Going home', Islam suggests the potentially deadly aspects of becoming obsessed with a return to South Asia. Some writers go further, taking this idea to its logical conclusion. In Aslam's *Maps for Lost Lovers*, an unnamed book-dealer succeeds in returning to Pakistan from Britain, after sending money to 'his nephews for over a decade to buy land and property' (152), only to die shortly after his arrival. In Jhumpa Lahiri's South Asian American novel *The Namesake* (2003), Mr Ghosh expresses regret about his return from Britain to India in the early 1960s mere hours before he is killed in a train accident. *Tiger's Daughter* ends with Tara caught up in a riot which has already killed several of her friends although, rather like the ending of *Reluctant Fundamentalist*, as discussed in Chapter 1, Tara's own fate is not made clear. Mukherjee may even be punishing her for the self-absorption which the novel is unafraid to expose. That she chooses not to spell out what happens next ensures, however, that this conclusion is in some ways more disturbing than a clear, if bloody, finale. It also suggests an ultimately tentative approach to resolving the knotty issues posed by an 'America return', and means that Mukherjee reinforces the problematic aspects of Frakes's critique of the return-of-the-native subgenre by leaving Tara suspended 'between two worlds'.

The fatal consequences of return reverberate most powerfully in Clark Blaise and Bharati Mukherjee's *The Sorrow and the Terror* (1987), a work of investigative reportage. Here Sikh terrorists' obsession with Khalistan, a putative Sikh nation in India, results in the bombing of Air India Flight 182 in June 1985, killing 329 people, almost all from Canada's Hindu community. In this painstaking, non-fictional account of such tragic events, Blaise and Mukherjee reveal that first-generation parents insisted that their Canadian-raised children come to understand India. This results in a

> terrifying irony . . . that besets all the victim-families at one time or another ... These indulgent, doting, fiercely proud parents had wanted the best of both cultures for their children, and now that biculturalism had caused . . . [their] death.[50]

The high proportion of children killed by the bombing is eerily presaged by the Pied Piper imagery of a poem, 'The leader of all', written by one of the young victims, Jyothi Radhakrishnan, ten days before the flight:

Over the bridges, under the walls

Lead me forth, lead me on,
Lead me to where the sorrow is gone

Take me to the promised land
Come, let us go hand in hand. (109)

Rather than the South Asian motherland, Jyothi's 'promised land' becomes a place beyond the quotidian world, as it does for the doomed children led away by the Pied Piper in the traditional story.

How do US treatments differ from British ones? Whereas South Asian American texts tend to chart women's returns – invariably to India, since this reflects the ancestral origins of writers themselves – and to offer a broad canvas, sometimes an entire novel, for this, British Asian writers confine such returns to discrete episodes within their fiction and life-writing[51] and, when writing about first-generation return from a second-generation subject position, they sometimes handle such material uncertainly. South Asian American authors shape what appear to be autobiographical experiences into fiction and, perhaps because they are more often women, they betray a degree of anger (greater than that evinced by British Asian writers) about return to a patriarchal society. Concerned with re-establishing connections and often disappointed by the disjuncture between nostalgia and the harsh realities of South Asia itself, returning 'natives' – both real and fictionalised, from both the US and the UK – feel entitled to condemn the inequalities of the originary homeland in ways that, as we will see in a moment, roots tourists do not. Gender and sexuality are significant here: returning women have less room than men for social manoeuvre in South Asia and less sexual freedom than in the West, while Mohanti's decision not to make a permanent return to India can be linked to his own alternative sexuality, even if this remains outside the text.

Ethnic Return in South Asian American Cultural Production

South Asian Atlantic artists have repeatedly dramatised 'ethnic return' or the encounter on ancestral soil between South Asians and a foreign-born generation, and US works of fiction, autobiography, and cinema, in particular, are powered by such 'roots' visits. They include M. Night Shyamalan's debut feature film, *Praying with Anger* (1992); Ameena Meer's novel *Bombay Talkie* (1994); Zia Jaffrey's work of reportage *The Invisibles: A Tale of the Eunuchs of India* (1996); Jhumpa Lahiri's short story 'Interpreter of maladies' (from her eponymous anthology, 1999); Chitra Divakaruni's short story 'The lives of strangers' (*Unknown Errors of Our Lives*, 2001); Sameer Parekh's novel *Stealing the Ambassador* (2002); and Anita Jain's autobiographical text *Marrying Anita: A Quest for Love in the New India* (2008). Through close readings of *Praying with Anger*, 'Lives of strangers', 'Interpreter of maladies', and *Bombay Talkie* – texts which especially exemplify the problems of second-generation 'return' – I will suggest some reasons why South Asian American writers and film-makers engage with this issue, analysing the function of the roots quest and asking how such diasporic tourism interrogates the idea of transnational mobility as utopian.[52]

In *Praying with Anger*, the year spent by the main character, Dev, as a university exchange student in early 1990s Madras is presented in earnest, ethnographic fashion as a crucial rite of passage. Dev claims that his stay 'feels like a sort of punishment'; and rather as though this were a traditional quest narrative, he faces a series of tests.[53] Discussing what she terms the 'catalysing visit-to-India narrative', Sunaina Maira has argued that second-generation Indian Americans often rely upon the language of a 'culture mission' to frame such visits. This contains

> a ritual dimension . . . The word *mission* evokes the purposefulness of the quest and the importance of the task to be achieved . . . [and] suggests a fervour associated with this journey to India; indeed, *nostalgia as faith* is at work here – a belief in the authenticity of 'Indian culture' as unifying hitherto fragmented lives.[54]

Dev's obstacles include being humiliated by older students, thanks to his cultural ignorance; and forced, albeit only briefly, to experience Indian rural pay and working conditions, after he is robbed of his money while travelling outside Madras. And, again in keeping with ideas of the quest, Dev tries to win the love of Sabitha, a beautiful local woman: a potential means of fusing the diaspora with the ancestral homeland, and a prevalent device within ethnic roots narratives.[55]

Dev's youth is significant, reflecting real-life aspects of Maira's 'visit-to-India narrative', since 'transnational ties and travel often spur a rethinking or new interest in ethnic ancestry for second-generation Indian Americans in late adolescence, when they are old enough to travel to India on their own'.[56] And a roots journey undertaken by a young person may exert a more life-changing impact than one made at a later stage.[57] That Dev is a young man creates a link not only with the quest formula, but also with the coming-of-age elements of the *Bildungsroman* genre, since both rely traditionally on a youthful, male protagonist[58] who often comes, like Dev, from outside the immediate community.

Shyamalan's film also emphasises the gendered aspects of ethnic identity, suggesting that Dev's stay in India can 'make a man' of him and, more precisely, an Indian man. This idea is closely connected to the film's patrilineal, patrimonial elements, since the key emotional event which underpins Dev's visit is his father's recent death. His posthumous need for closeness to his father is a crucial part of what keeps him in India – literally the 'fatherland' here – when things go wrong;[59] and it raises the emotional and dramatic stakes of his roots journey. Shyamalan's narrative turns on the need to locate a paternal home, a theme literally played out when Dev discovers his father's original village dwelling.[60] Dev's filial pilgrimage combines with an early indication of Shyamalan's trademark interest in the supernatural when Dev receives an illusory visitation from his father, ensuring catharsis and a semi-mythical 'atonement with the father'.[61] This highlights the film's use of religious symbols, which encompasses the heuristic potential of penance and pilgrimage, and the importance of prayer as a means of finding one's place in the world (as the film's title suggests), while signalling that ethnic return evokes the notion of 'past lives'.[62]

Beyond the spiritual enlightenment he believes he has gained in India, Dev fulfils his heroic potential when he makes the peace during a local Hindu–Muslim riot, a test of bravery and humanity which apparently proves his integration into the community.[63] Dev's behaviour effectively suggests, however, that only someone from outside the community – an American – can solve India's problems. His national and cultural identity are, in fact, questioned throughout the film when Indians describe him as 'an Indian from America', 'an American', and a 'foreigner'.[64] Similarly, when his would-be relationship with Sabitha fails, the film implies that Dev cannot seriously take the place of a local man. Although the film insists on the intensity of emotion Dev experiences in India – expressed visually through the use of dazzling colours and aurally through its quasi-devotional score – it also vindicates his father's original decision to emigrate by highlighting the country's ongoing economic and social problems: poverty, communalism, and limited opportunities for women. And when Dev returns to the US, he symbolically repeats his father's earlier migration.

Zygmunt Bauman has noted that pilgrimage has always been connected to questions of home and homelessness,[65] and Shyamalan reworks this idea by illustrating that, through a spiritual quest, Dev learns to feel comfortable, on some level at least, in more than one country. Indeed, this option is depicted as preferable for second-generation South Asian Americans. As David Morley has argued, 'identity is not rooted in one single original homeland, but rather depends on . . . [the] ability to inhabit different imaginary geographies simultaneously'.[66] The object of Dev's quest, then, is to assert the Indianness of his identity by establishing spiritual and emotional (rather than professional, political, or economic) ties to his parents' homeland. This quest allows him to 'return' to India in the first place, but then to go back to America, the home which he can reclaim only when, like other quest heroes, he has successfully completed his task.

The denouement of *Praying with Anger* – regarded as 'emotionally immature' by one commentator[67] – is, however, perhaps too neat and celebratory after the bruising impact of Dev's earlier challenges. In short, Shyamalan's auteurist insistence on the ethnic authenticity of Dev's visit[68] – he also wrote and starred in the film – is at odds with his sharp delineation of Dev's frequent faux pas and persistent unease with Indian society. By implying that the ancestral homeland can provide answers to the complexities of ethnic identity politics, Shyamalan reveals his interest in the possibilities of transnational affiliation. He implies that a hyphenated identity represents the best of both worlds, while gesturing towards a kind of US exceptionalism, since only an Indian American can restore calm during the riot. Dev can, moreover, use the spiritual and sentimental education India has given him in his time as a 'returning' son to forge ahead in the more economically advanced United States. Shyamalan's urge to prove the connections between India and its diaspora through Dev's impact on the lives of those around him[69] may also relate to Rajini Srikanth's notion of transnationalism as an 'insurance policy against rejection', since 'Asian Americans . . . never know when their membership in the United States will be called into question'.[70]

The superficially triumphant message of Dev's roots visit contrasts sharply with the scepticism of 'Lives of strangers', where Chitra Divakaruni – Indian-born and raised, but long resident in the United States – imagines how it might feel to experience India for the first time. The immigrant parents of Leela, her protagonist, react with anxiety when she announces her decision to go to India, telling her to avoid crowds, drink boiled water, and keep out of 'the lives of strangers':[71] warnings which recall Lahiri's insistence on the lack of immunity of young South Asian Americans to Indian disease.[72] Like Dev, Leela is struck by India's intensity, expressed through the warm, intimate manner of her relatives. She spends a month in Calcutta, where her Bengali background allows her to assimilate (ostensibly at least) for a time. But Divakaruni's third-person narrator cautions that Leela is experiencing the exhilaration of the unknown, 'a vibrant unreality . . . a Mardi Gras that never ended' (63): a respite from the depression shrouding her American life, thus suggesting the 'therapeutic' possibilities of the motherland.[73]

As in *Praying with Anger*, religion frames and guides Leela's roots trip. Unlike Dev, however, she actually embarks on a pilgrimage – the idea suggested by her relative, Seema – to Shiva's shrine in Amarnath, Kashmir. This forces her to negotiate India's social complexity and sheer physical scale: after an 'interminable train journey' from Calcutta, she must walk for three days 'across treacherous glaciers' (56) in order to reach the shrine. The attempted pilgrimage raises questions of destiny and mortality, as Leela ponders an earlier suicide bid, while, at a broader level, the story asks whether such spiritual journeys in the ancestral homeland can really transform or 'redeem' an American-born generation. Divakaruni's choice of Amarnath is significant in an intertextual sense, since it is the destination for V. S. Naipaul's diasporic pilgrimage in *An Area of Darkness* (1964).[74] But whereas Naipaul successfully reaches Shiva's shrine, Leela never even gets to her destination, thus anticipating the failed transnational links emblematised by this particular roots journey.

India's dangers are embodied here by Mrs Das, a lonely widow and unwanted pilgrim supposedly born under an 'unlucky star' (58). Attempting to dismiss such 'superstition', Leela finds her putatively American pragmatism challenged by Indian belief systems, and by the intensity of the pilgrimage itself. In other words, for all the opportunities Leela's Bengali ancestry has afforded her in Calcutta, it cannot help her to navigate this alien set of rules. The Indianness of Leela's physical appearance is naturalised through epidermal imagery, her ethnic and racial kinship to Mrs Das revealed through 'her fingers . . . brown against the matching brown of Mrs Das's skin' (69). But just as India appears simultaneously knowable and unknowable to the young American visitor, so too can such racialised ties only ever remain fragile,[75] and Leela's fraught, ambiguous position is that of neither a full tourist nor a proper local. Indeed, discomfited by the 'baldness' of Leela's questions, Seema considers that 'a *real Indian* woman would have known to approach the matter delicately, sideways' (87; emphasis added) and Leela is thus exposed as an American whose Indianness runs only skin-deep.[76] But India brings out a need for human connection in Leela, and she believes she can help Mrs Das, who stands in for the traditional Indian social system and embodies the effects of its perceived failings. Leela attributes this idealistic desire to inexplicable forces or 'destiny' (74), which suggests a version of a neo-colonial American 'aid mission', but this quest is as much about proving her own self-worth – by successfully establishing her usefulness in India and therefore her right to belong there – as it is about helping a particular individual.

That this mission fails when Leela abandons Mrs Das is perhaps inevitable. After all, the pessimism of Divakaruni's conclusion is foreshadowed by the precariousness of Leela's status in India and by the symbolic fact that she does not complete the pilgrimage. Above all, perhaps, her failure is presented in moral terms: her final response to Mrs Das is as selfish and cowardly as that of any of the other pilgrims.[77] For all the story's apparent essentialising of India and America – India as spiritual centre, America as site of individualism and disinterested practicality – Divakaruni undercuts such simplistic binaries by revealing the problematic behaviour of the outwardly pious Indian pilgrims and the universal nature of Mrs Das's need for love and respect. Rather like Gish Jen's short story, 'Duncan in China' (1999) – where the eponymous Chinese American protagonist discovers some hard truths about himself during a religious pilgrimage – 'Lives of strangers' reveals the underlying self-interest, and critiques the self-indulgence, of ethnic return by exposing the ease with which American attempts at philanthropy in the ancestral nation are thwarted.

In Lahiri's 'Interpreter of maladies', a South Asian American couple, Raj and Mina Das, visit two religious sites in Orissa: the Sun Temple in Konarak and the Jain 'monastic dwellings' in 'the hills at Udayagiri and Khandagiri'.[78] Although the choice of a religious setting recalls *Praying with Anger* and anticipates 'The lives of strangers', Lahiri's story thematises cultural interaction.[79] Like the other two texts, however, it uses the motherland to explore the degree of Indianness to which Indian Americans can lay claim. Ostensibly at ease in the ancestral homeland – where they regularly visit their respective parents, who have retired to West Bengal – the Dases nevertheless seem displaced by their immediate surroundings, while being strangely oblivious to them. Travelling away from their familiar Bengali base, Raj and Mina are, like Leela, revealingly out of place. Indeed, the idea that they cannot fully transcend their tourist status is underscored by the motif of journeying. Their diasporic vulnerability is represented by their reliance on various objects – guidebook, camera, nail polish, hairbrush – for comfort and support: a consumerist dependence which possibly critiques the materialistic, introspective American society to which they belong.

The Dases' uncertain position may be why Mr Kapasi, their Indian tour guide, struggles to place them, noticing that they 'looked Indian but dressed as foreigners did' (43–4). Indeed, Lahiri contrasts the Dases' American-style clothes, which expose plenty of flesh, with their guide's more decorous attire; and Shyamalan uses similar sartorial markers in *Praying with Anger*. Through Mr Kapasi's perspective, the story establishes the importance of appearances: not only in a cultural sense, but by implying the disparity between how people seem and how they really are. Simon Lewis has argued that 'Lahiri . . . moves beyond Eurocentric or Oriental images of India to those of a contemporary postcolonial nation more concerned with dialogue with its own diaspora than with its former colonisers.'[80] But this 'dialogue' is as unsatisfactory and doomed as that between Leela and Mrs Das.

Several critics have noted that it is Mina's carelessness which leads monkeys towards her unsupervised son, Bobby, whom they then attack.[81] And Mr Kapasi notes that Raj and Mina 'behaved like an older brother and sister, not parents' (49). In this way, they are made to exemplify the absence of family values Lahiri usually associates with mainstream (namely, white) Americans, the demands of travel in India only illuminating such failings more starkly. Animal imagery is also important here for what it reveals about the uncertainties posed by diasporic tourism. Monkeys, in particular, punctuate the story, initially acting as a source of excitement to Raj and his children, but soon coming to represent more ominous possibilities. Raj and Mina's differing reactions to the monkeys illuminate crucial fault lines between them. That neither can handle the monkeys, however, while Mr Kapasi can, shows the extent to which these South Asian Americans are out of their depth – and their normal physical habitat – in India.[82]

Anticipating 'Lives of strangers', Lahiri's use of diasporic tourism captures the ways in which imagined transnational bonds can suddenly spring up between strangers. This point is suggested by the gulf between Mina's romanticised perception of Mr Kapasi's work as an 'interpreter of maladies' and the tragic reality which actually underpins his decision to take on this largely mundane work; and by her sense of an intimate, but fleeting, connection with him which allows her to offload her guilty secret and treat him as a confessor figure, a guru-like repository of Indian wisdom and spirituality.[83] Indeed, the connection between her urge to confess and the story's religious location is arguably deliberate, while its use of a historic monument as backdrop – and sexual misunderstanding as a narrative catalyst – has led several critics to read 'Interpreter' as a rewriting of E. M. Forster's *A Passage to India* (1924).[84] Much like Shyamalan's film and Divakaruni's story, this text actually makes no explicit reference to India's colonial history, suggesting – as I have argued in the two previous chapters – that for some South Asian Americans, Britain is simply not relevant. Indeed, according to Susanna Ghazvinizadeh, the 'British Empire has been replaced . . . by [the] American Empire and Mr and Mrs Das might be considered *third millennium imperial travellers*'.[85] At the same time, India's past remains unavoidable and the employment of pilgrimage and a religious site in Divakaruni's and Lahiri's stories respectively manages to reinscribe the image of an unchanging, pre-industrial India, while

Shyamalan's film is less concerned with Indian modernity, economic or otherwise, than with an emotionally charged diasporic vision of a brightly coloured and only slowly changing ancestral homeland.[86]

Despite Lahiri's own recollection that youthful visits to Calcutta proved that she was 'neither a tourist nor a former resident . . . yet . . . I belonged there in some fundamental way',[87] the Dases are denied any similar sense of belonging. And in contrast to Lahiri's writerly self-presentation and her decision to locate the story in India – thus laying claim to her own authentic Indianness, as Shyamalan does in *Praying with Anger*[88] – her story exposes just how little common heritage there is between these South Asian Americans and the Indians they meet. Indeed, beyond physical similarities, they occupy little shared ground in cultural or linguistic terms[89] and none at all in an emotional or psychological sense. Like Divakaruni, Lahiri thus probes the problematic, catch-all concept of 'Indianness' and reveals that it can become almost void of meaning.

Written with verve, confidence, and a degree of cynicism, Meer's *Bombay Talkie* depicts the roots journey of Sabah, its young protagonist, as traumatic and tragic: a radical departure from the three texts already considered, which only hint at tragedy and seem gentle by comparison. Before her trip (and anticipating Leela in 'Lives of strangers'), Sabah envisages India as a panacea for the problems she has encountered growing up in the United States as the child of Indian Muslim immigrants:

> maybe in India she'd be able to straighten it all out . . . find a happy medium between what her parents wanted her to do (the good Indian girl) and what she wanted to do (the bad American girl). Maybe she'd figure out what it was she really wanted to be.[90]

Even on the aeroplane, however, she regards the trip as 'a terrible mistake' and feels 'overcome with nostalgia for her American youth' (95). This moment is revealing both as a forewarning of the visit's dire denouement – a marital dispute which leads to the fatal burning of Rani, her biracial, American-born friend (I will discuss Meer's handling of miscegenation in the next chapter) – and as a reflection of the greater stability and safety afforded by Sabah's suburban US (past and present) over her experiences of a decadent, urban India.

Here Sabah is a 'conceptual anomaly'[91] to local people in a series of repeatedly emphasised ways: she 'looks so Indian but speaks Hindi like a firungi' (152), has a capacity for cultural 'faux-pas' (153) and little resistance to Indian disease, struggles with the heat, and remains naïve about local prices. Through the turbulent moment of Rani's death, Sabah's inability

– through ignorance, idleness, and physical weakness – to become comfortable in a deeply foreign India has almost become justified. As Christine Vogt-William has argued, Rani serves 'as a projection foil for Sabah . . . showing her the potential of a returned diasporic's transcultural life-style in a metropolitan setting', a doomed potential since 'Rani is punished severely for her attempts to return to her Indian roots'.[92] Suddenly, the antipathy Sabah has felt to the ancestral homeland at some level all along is writ large, since it is a sorrowful place which she must leave as soon as possible. The reader even shares her sense of relief at returning to America, although Meer also problematises the US (if much more briefly) through the 'innocent abroad' figure of Adam, Sabah's privileged Indian cousin, who meets his death in a (stereotypically) heartless New York City.

Meer's novel – which resembles *Praying with Anger* in offering an early and sustained look at a homeland visit – essentialises India, then, but in more violent fashion than Shyamalan's film, 'Lives of strangers', or 'Interpreter'. After all, it portrays a deeply corrupt, hypocritical society, characterised by a particular set of clichés: maharajahs, bride-burning, deep-seated patriarchy, crippling poverty, and sectarian hatred.[93] Meer also exposes the presence of sexual abuse through a brief, shocking scene of pederasty. She has argued that, following her own 'immigrant fantasy of India as . . . nirvana . . . [a] place of social purity and perfection . . . I got there and really had my eyes opened'; and that, after her time as a student there in the late 1980s, she felt moved to 'talk about . . . dowry deaths, social inequities, sexual abuse, communalism, sexuality – especially in the way these things relate to women'.[94] Recalling Hansson's point about the special outsider/insider status of the returning 'native', Meer's recent comments suggest that the implicit authenticity conferred by her own ethnic return produced the right to critique India. The problem, perhaps, is that Sabah's melodramatic experiences in the ancestral homeland – which Brian, a Euro-American character in the novel, refers to as being 'like an Indian movie' (214) – are ultimately so negative that she is left in a state of 'numb coming-to-terms', in the words of one reviewer.[95] Asked by Rob, her white American ex-boyfriend, if she found 'a new identity in India', her wry, understated verdict is simply that 'I gave the old one a coat of fresh paint. And it's already beginning to peel' (262–3).

It is the myopia and selfishness of Raj, Mina, Leela, and arguably Sabah, too, which challenge the redemptive possibilities of diasporic travel suggested so forcefully by *Praying with Anger*. Self-serving and naïve, these characters clash in a troubling and depressing way with native-born Indians – or, in Sabah's case, form local friendships with an inbuilt expiry date – suggesting that spiritual rebirth and emotional catharsis cannot be provided by the ancestral nation. Instead, such stories punish an individualistically American second generation for envisaging India in predominantly solipsistic terms as a site of romance, fantasy, and imaginary nostalgia. After all, their journeys are essentially 'imaginative' because 'there is no premade, packaged cultural identity waiting to be revealed'.[96] They imply that such unrealistic, indulgent attitudes – as Maira notes, a form of 'symbolic ethnicity'[97] – will inevitably be shaken by the failure to connect properly with local people or to see clearly the harsh realities which confront them in India. Clear narrative closure is not provided in any of these texts, despite Shyamalan's best efforts to the contrary. Thus – with the exception of *Bombay Talkie* – we know, at one level, that the Americans in *Praying with Anger*, 'Lives of strangers', and 'Interpreter of maladies' will all return to the US, yet each of the narratives leaves them in India, as if to stress the open-endedness of their situation and, as I argued of Hamid's *Reluctant Fundamentalist* in Chapter 1, to comment upon the US from a long way off.

Roots Journeys in British Asian Literature

Ethnic return has been explored in British Asian cultural production since the 1970s. Examples of this include Farrukh Dhondy's short story 'East End at your feet' (from his eponymous short fiction collection, 1976); Hanif Kureishi's early autobiographical essay 'The rainbow sign' (1986); his short story 'With your tongue down my throat' (1987); and more recently his novel *Something to Tell You* (2008); Shani Grewal's film *Guru in Seven* (1997); sketches from the first series of the BBC comedy show *Goodness Gracious Me* (1998), directed by Nick Wood; Suhayl Saadi's short story 'Ninety-nine kiss-o-grams' (2001); Tariq Mehmood's novel *While There is Light* (2003); Manzoor's *Greetings from Bury Park*; Nikita Lalwani's novel *Gifted* (2007); and Hardeep Singh Kohli's travelogue *Indian Takeaway: A Very British Story* (2008). In contrast to the characteristic earnestness of South Asian American heritage tourism,[98] many of these British works take a more satirical approach to the second generation's ingenuous behaviour and fundamental foreignness in India and, to a larger extent, Pakistan.[99]

Operating on the assumption that the limitations of the roots journey are well understood and that such material has even become clichéd, British Asian writers nevertheless feel the need to engage with it; and 'return' to South Asia, especially Pakistan, is pertinent in this body of writing. Perhaps because this encounter with ancestral culture is often imposed by their parents upon the second generation – to a greater degree than it is upon South Asian Americans – such trips are complicated in multiple ways. For instance, the effects of Partition may mean that one's relatives live in Pakistan, while the ancestral home is actually in modern-day India; and writers, who are themselves generally second-generation, depict life in Pakistan as unfamiliar, unviable, and distinctly troubling.[100] Thus Saadi is eloquent about the perils of 'return', using 'Ninety-nine kiss-o-grams' to explore the failed dream of a deferred home, as Sal tries to locate and sell his dead father's plot of ancestral land. Motivated by a sense of duty, he soon discovers how ill-fated this mission is. Beyond what he perceives to be the chaos of Pakistan, he is assailed by a series of difficult issues surrounding his putative inheritance: the uncertainty of his claim under Pakistani legislation; the potential worthlessness of the 'wasteland' he discovers;[101] an unfavourable exchange rate; and the apparent uselessness of the crumpled deeds which he loses, symbolically, in the uninviting brown terrain of what may or may not be his family's plot. The deeds possessed an enormous emotional weight for his late father, who had 'worn this piece ae paper like a lover as he'd sweatit thru the . . . soor terraces ae Scola on his way tae makin it' (3), and the story ends with Sal scrabbling on the ground, attempting to find them, as he realises that 'he couldnae go hame, empty-handed' (6). One senses, however, that he will be forced to leave without securing the illusory land transaction, whose very ambiguity is a metaphor for this culturally complex, obligatory mission to actualise a parent's deferred home.

Sal starts out with the belief that Pakistan is his 'ane land' (1) but soon rejects what he sees as its unforgiving desolation, and his homesickness is evoked through the vision of a variegated Caledonian landscape, which stands in direct contrast to that of his parents' country. Scotland is characterised by 'aw its shades like the different malts', whereas Pakistan 'wis jis wan, scorched broon' (5).

> Sal looked at the straggly, brown grass so unlike the bright-green mud-grass of Glasgee, and wondered how anyone could have believed that this land would ever be anything other than dry shit . . . This wis his country, the land ae his forefaithers and yet, the stink ae it sickened him tae his gut. That sweet smell ae rotting lemons, of uncollected rubbish, of unrepaired roads. Naa, he thought, and kicked the soil again, this isnae ma country. No ony mair. Mibbee, it nivir wis. (1–2)

Angry and disappointed that this 'real' Pakistan cannot fulfil the patriotic lyricism implied by 'the land ae his forefaithers', Sal refuses to seek out any beauty in Pakistan and gives up on his trip almost as soon as it has begun. Instead he envisages Scotland's chromatic intensity: a move which rebuts the dismissal of Britain as colourless by some US-based writers, a point I discussed in Chapter 1. Embodying a 'diaspora in reverse', in Sara Upstone's phrase,[102] Sal's longing for Scotland is shaped by his second-generation subjectivity, and his misery signals that – like the young South Asian Americans examined above – he is being punished for thinking he can claim ancestral land he barely knows.

Sal's distaste for Pakistan recalls aspects of Kureishi's handling of it[103] and anticipates Aslam's *Maps for Lost Lovers*, where British-born characters refer to the country as 'a great big toilet' (45). For Aslam's second-generation female characters, 'return' to Pakistan is also sinister, as they embark upon arranged marriages in a patriarchal society where they must give up their freedoms and where 'in one . . . province alone, a woman is murdered every thirty-eight hours solely because her virtue is in doubt' (136). Manzoor also expresses disdain for Pakistan in *Greetings from Bury Park*. He dreads the prospect of his first visit at fourteen, regarding the motherland as 'a strange place far away from home' (248); and, once there, the poverty and heat which confront him – and the numerous relatives who 'referred to me as English' (251) – underline Pakistan's essential foreignness, a bitter corrective to Manzoor's secret fantasy that he 'might feel a sense of home' there (251). Despite the adventure of train travel and 'late-night bazaars' (249), he clearly feels grateful towards the father who 'got out' (251) and he may in fact be internalising his father's own impatience with Pakistan, specifically its endemic corruption and what Manzoor *père* sees as locals' lack of drive. But the gender dynamics outlined earlier – that returning men have more room for manoeuvre than women in India and Pakistan – are reversed here, since Manzoor's mother appears 'relaxed, smiling and . . . freer' (250) than she does in Britain.

Forced to undergo another 'return' several years later to attend his brother's wedding, Manzoor devotes the bare minimum of textual space to the trip, as though he wants to get through the memory as quickly as the original experience. Despite his 'sense of being part of something bigger than my direct family' (73), the mandatory nature of the visit – like several of the British Pakistani 'returns' already discussed – makes it a clear antithesis to the voluntary nature of the roots tours we witness in South Asian American texts. That said, Manzoor's youthful sense of relief at flying back to Britain and Sal's homesickness for Scotland mirror the attitudes of Gogol and Sonia as they gratefully return to their US home from India in Lahiri's *Namesake*.[104]

Lalwani's *Gifted* offers an alternative to this model of second-generation British Asian reluctance – and sometimes downright hostility – towards the ancestral homeland, although it is worth noting that India, rather than

Pakistan, is the site of 'return' here. For Rumi Vasi, the young protagonist, India is a source of enormous excitement, providing richly formative experiences, which sustain and strengthen her psychologically. Employed as a framing device, but barely mentioned in contemporary reviews of the novel, the two visits – the first made when she is eight, the second at fifteen – take on a dialectical importance, since the pressures and constraints Rumi faces in her British life (stage-managed by her father to a frightening degree) are highlighted by the converse freedoms, both emotional and imaginative, offered by India. This sense of liberation cannot be disentangled from the changed behaviour of her parents, Mahesh and Shreene: as returning Non-Resident Indians, they themselves feel far more relaxed in India than they do in Britain. In other words, Lalwani challenges the myth that emigration to the West signals greater freedom for immigrants and their children, implying that, for the Vasi family, it has come at a heavy emotional price and that they might have fared better had they stayed in India.[105]

The homeland of Rumi's first 'India trip' offers a physical and emotional warmth that the UK cannot hope to match. Unsurprisingly, Rumi regards it as 'the best time she had experienced in her whole life' and fantasises about moving to India.[106] That the visit is narrated in the present tense reflects the degree to which it breathes new life into Rumi's otherwise drab existence. Lalwani makes use of some familiar Indian 'roots' tropes, particularly of a religious nature, thus recalling the South Asian American narratives discussed earlier. After a Hindu priest's ceremonial palm-reading, Shreene and Rumi embark on a pilgrimage to Mansadevi, 'the place of wishes' (30). The train journey there emphasises divisions between Indians and diasporics, with both mother and daughter shown to be more susceptible to disease than local people. But Rumi is made to feel special in India, where her mathematical gift is recognised. Her relatives accept her unquestioningly and the pilgrimage is treated as a childish adventure, rather than a problem in the manner of Divakaruni's 'Lives of strangers'. Hindu India – a place where the wishes of both adults and children can apparently be granted – is made to seem considerably more magical and mysterious than the Islamic Pakistan of 'Ninety-nine', *Maps*, Manzoor's memoir, or Kureishi's œuvre.

Such fairy-tale elements – which are also present in *Praying with Anger*, 'Lives of strangers', and 'Interpreter of maladies' – result in the idea that a protagonist can make a heuristic quest to a previously unfamiliar place and in the process uncover Indian-based characters and animals which serve an allegorical function, sometimes offer a cautionary dimension, and represent the real importance of myth in Indian culture. Although these characteristics consciously recall Maira's earlier point about the essentially interior, imaginative, and indeed imaginary nature of any roots journey – and the largely mythical nature of secure, stable origins awaiting recovery – most of the South Asian Atlantic texts I am considering in this chapter are actually rather conventional in formal and narrative terms. In other words, they lack the inventiveness and sheer creative zest of, for instance, Jonathan Safran Foer's ethnic return novel *Everything is Illuminated* (2002), whose use of polyphony, detective elements, and a more sustained intertextuality to discuss a journey from America to the Ukraine makes it aesthetically more ambitious than any of these works.[107] Indeed, its imaginative verve reflects Foer's desire to go beyond the potentially predictable nature of roots material in Western culture. At the end of this chapter, I will posit some reasons for the formal conservatism displayed, in contrast, by South Asian American and British Asian writers when examining issues of return.

In *Gifted*, Rumi's second, teenaged trip to India once again allows for escapism, reinvention, and a break from routine. Her 'warm sense of her own instant belonging in a world of brown faces' (156) contests Divakaruni's 'Lives of strangers' by suggesting quite how heady the sensation of epidermal similarity can be. Seen through Indian men's eyes in new ways, Rumi's blossoming womanhood shapes this visit and she, too, views the country differently: as a simultaneously innocent and worldly place and as a site of erotic intrigue. After a male cousin's attempted seduction of her, Rumi's conversations with other relatives reveal 'the love and lust fighting for breath in each pocket of the country of her origin' (171) and, her Hindi improving at the same time, she experiences a more intimate connection to the ancestral nation. Rejecting a 'between worlds' paradigm and recalling the treatment of Indian American identity in *Praying with Anger*, Lalwani allows her protagonist to celebrate the transnational possibilities of being both 'Angrezi' (or British) and Indian (166).

In contrast to two such positive experiences, India fares considerably worse in Dhondy's 'East End at your feet' through a humorously unsentimental exploration of a permanent ethnic returnee. Born and raised in London's East End, Kash is forced to move to Bombay following the sudden death of his father. His white, paternalistic teachers claim that Indians are 'your own people. All this confusion of the East End will disappear', although, for Kash, 'there was no confusion before. My dad was no big shot . . . and the confusion only started when he kicked it.'[108] Anticipating the reactions of such later writers as Mohanti, Dhondy highlights the toughness of Bombay life, as Kash observes the extent of the city's poverty. Noting that 'there isn't any dole here. They just let you die in the street, them loving Indians . . . I've seen it, I tell you' (54), his macho, laconic tone only partially masks his fear, shock, and homesickness for London. As in the British Pakistani narratives considered earlier, 'return' to the ancestral country is enforced, but this time it is for good: no amount of comedy can disguise either its dystopian aspects or the anxiety Kash feels at this apparently irreversible relocation.

As Manzoor does in *Greetings*, Kohli uses life-writing in *Indian Takeaway* to examine his place as a British Asian in the ancestral homeland. Unlike in *Greetings*, however, this is the sole focus of his memoir, which is, more specifically, gastronomically themed travel writing. (I will return to Kohli's consideration of food in Chapter 4.) Although its subtitle – 'a very British story' – foregrounds the text's claims to national UK representativeness, *Indian Takeaway* uses Kohli's tour of India to prove his Scottishness and Punjabiness as well. The book's humorous chapter headings (for instance, 'Of Mysore men' and 'Valley of the dals') are indicative, meanwhile, of the light-heartedness of a quintessentially British Asian approach to roots material. As distinct from Kash or Rumi, Leela or Dev, Kohli has visited India – and, more precisely, the family home in Punjab – on countless occasions. Thus, rather than recounting the shock of the new, this journey overlays many previous ones, resulting in a more layered and palimpsestic, if less dramatic, treatment than those of first-time ethnic return.

The difference for Kohli is that this time he wishes to see much more of India – from Kerala to Kashmir – and to be a 'tourist', who experiences 'the magical and mystical India' his white friends have seen: a journey also framed as a 'quest'.[109] With this comes a fundamental ambivalence, which he is quick to acknowledge:

> I always dislike British Indians who go to India and *act like they're white tourists*, speaking English loudly and slowly. They seem to lack any empathy or . . . humility. I'm worried that I might come over like this. Yet, I realise that I am effectively a tourist; I'm from Glasgow . . . There is no economic imperative to what I am doing . . . I am simply indulging the desire of a westerner . . . travelling India in search of myself. (40, 160–1; emphasis added)

Implicit in this statement is the idea that, unlike 'white tourists' – bedazzled by a 'magical . . . mystical' India and presumably suffering from a similar lack of 'humility' or 'empathy' to those 'British Indians' he critiques here – diasporic Indians should be held to higher standards of behaviour and understanding in the ancestral nation than other (inferior) visitors. Thus, when Kohli attacks Jeremy – a solipsistic Filipino American yoga instructor and latter-day 'colonist' (119) in Mysore, who is handled in a similarly dismissive manner to white tourists – he claims in a somewhat self-justificatory way that, unlike Jeremy:

> I am not a magical, mystical tourist who can choose to leave the country and break my links. My links are lines of heritage. Even in Mysore (a place none of my Punjabi forbears are ever likely to have visited), I feel an innate sense of India and Indianness. (114, 119)

At the same time, Kohli is fully aware of how problematic his own position is through its complicity with the cliché of going to India to 'find' himself. His 'innate . . . Indianness' nevertheless allows him a kind of undercover status at times. His Indian authenticity wins out, for instance, in a flight from Cochin to Kovalam where he is charged 'the Indian price . . . I suspect the . . . airline . . . has mistaken me for . . . a proper Indian rather than a British Indian interloper' (37). But he makes some erroneous claims – for instance, that Punjab is 'the most northerly point in India' (24) and that the language of Kerala is 'Keralan' (37) – and his foreignness and lack of local knowledge are clearly evident, particularly in South India. On the other hand, in his ancestral home – Ferozepure in Punjab – Kohli feels a sense of 'shared history' (277) and easily blends in with the 'tens, maybe hundreds of thousands of other turban-wearing Sikhs' (279). In other words – as we saw when the Dases in 'Interpreter of maladies' and Leela in 'Lives of strangers' ventured outside West Bengal – it is Indian travel outside one's ethnic (and, in Kohli's case, religious) centre which really tests the limits of diasporic belonging. This may also explain why when talking about Hindus, Kohli refers to Indians at a remove – '*their* polytheistic deities' (34; emphasis added) – but employs a collective voice to talk about the family home in Punjab.

Towards the end of the text, he remains simultaneously comfortable and perplexed by his dual identity, asking 'why did I feel the need to apologise for being British when in India, and . . . for being Indian when in Britain?' (155) – a deeply personal, yet familiar, question to many British Asians growing up between the 1960s and the 1980s – but also noting that 'I am a Punjabi Sikh Glaswegian who also feels some empathy with being British . . . a complex blend . . . that changes depending on who I am with, where I am and how I feel on any given day' (193). Such moments are typical of a recursive narrative, where his examinations of his own national and cultural identity can seem rambling, heavy-handed, and repetitive;[110] and it may be that the text could simply have been better edited. But it is these very repetitions which show how few answers his journey through India can give him: the country is so varied, complex, and confusing that the individual visitor, especially from the diaspora, can arrive at a dizzying number of conclusions. As he puts it, 'no one tells you how to feel about your ancestry. There's no manual, no almanac that guides you' (282).

His journey is an attempt, then, to devise his own manual or guide to belonging. The complexities and unanswered, indeed unanswerable, questions it poses might account for the strange blend of intimacy and silence which informs *Indian Takeaway*. Adopting an ostensibly amiable position of familiarity, Kohli addresses the reader as 'you' (51, 159, 176, 269) and 'my friends' (215), asking the audience (presumed to be either non-Sikh and/or non-South Asian) at one point if they are 'still with me?' (280). This companionable tone recalls eighteenth-century English fiction – which is perhaps fitting, given the picaresque nature of the narrative – while underlining a sense of performance: Kohli clearly takes on different roles and, as a self-confessed extrovert, plays to the gallery.[111] The text's performative elements also point to the ways in which it relies on the author's public persona. Thus, while it stresses Kohli's natal family, especially his father, *Indian Takeaway* remains elliptical on the subject of his career and, above all, his wife and children and how they might feel about his voyage of discovery. This latter omission is reflected in the family photographs Kohli chooses to include, which depict only his Glaswegian boyhood, as though he is stuck there in some psychological sense. Like Manzoor in *Greetings* and Sathnam Sanghera in his autobiography *The Boy with the Topknot: A Memoir of Love, Secrets and Lies in Wolverhampton* (2008), Kohli's voice is that of the exceptional, yet self-deprecating, 'I' narrator, which implies that while the reader can identify with his story, it is nonetheless sufficiently unusual to compel wider attention and thus publication. In this rather old-fashioned autobiography, then, Kohli's voice appears to reveal information, while actually remaining rather non-confessional. Like these other British Asian memoirs, however, *Indian Takeaway* is a work of filial tribute. Indeed India appears to bring out Kohli's inner child. Thus, when he admits that a large motivation for touring India is as a 'homage' to his father (234), seen as a pioneering, adventurous figure, he repeats the patrilineal/fatherland connection so central to *Praying with Anger* and the important parent–child dynamics which underpin and explain much second-generation 'return'.

Conclusion

The South Asian Atlantic works discussed in this chapter reach some remarkably similar conclusions to academic studies of ethnic return. To be precise, such scholarly accounts – which do not generally examine the South Asian diasporic context – contend that ethnic returnees enter into such trips with overly romanticised images of the ancestral homeland, which are bound to be destroyed by the tough realities of these often poor, traditional, socially stratified, and culturally homogeneous countries.[112] These works also show that those who have 'stayed behind' do not always welcome – and may even resent – diasporic subjects even as they identify the personal (and especially material) opportunities of such visits;[113] and that both parties (local and diasporic) have contradictory, even mutually exclusive, perceptions of these trips.[114] Finally, such studies argue that return trips ultimately confirm the strength of national and cultural over ethno-racial identity: namely, how British or American rather than, say, Bajan or Korean the returnee is,[115] which can lead to a strengthened bond with other members of the same ethnic community back in the US or UK.[116] Returning to transatlantic South Asian literature, a sense of American or British belonging is enforced by perceived rejection in South Asia (as, for instance, in Manzoor's case), yet local people are mostly depicted as curious, rather than hostile, about diasporic visitors who, in their eyes, do not really belong in India or Pakistan.

The thematic use of travel and return by these artists uncovers a range of oppositions: India versus Pakistan (Bangladesh occupying a relatively minor position), America versus Britain, male versus female, rich versus poor, and first versus second generation. Return-of-the-native narratives are more common in South Asian American than in British Asian literature, and they generally follow America-returned, first-generation women, most often going back to India. That country emerges less positively in such accounts than it does in second-generation US 'roots' texts, where, with the exception of Meer, writers and film-makers are more likely to critique South Asian Americans than Indians. Pakistan, by contrast, emerges more prominently in British Asian writing where male authors, usually recounting ethnic return, reinscribe a stereotypical image of the ancestral homeland as poverty-stricken, corrupt, and misogynist. A degree of pessimism informs the transatlantic treatment of both return-of-the-native and roots visits, but British Asian artists are more likely to deploy comic strategies as a response to the feelings of disappointment and unwelcome surprise that such 'close encounters' with ancestral origins can evoke.

Diasporic inscriptions of the ancestral nation have excited strong reactions in South Asia itself. Addressing the representation of India specifically, Makarand Paranjape has contended, for example, that writers portray

> an India of poverty, violence, urban chaos, rural exploitation, caste conflict, political instability and insurmountable corruption. India automatically

> becomes a 'problem' the solution to which . . . is . . . emigration . . . Considering that most of the contemporary writers . . . left India largely to better their material prospects, such writing becomes self-validating . . . The dirty job of India bashing need no longer be performed by a white man; non-resident Indians will do it equally well, if not better . . . From being . . . insecure, marginalised, denationalised and faceless, such diasporics have suddenly begun to loom large over us [non-diasporic Indians], clouding our own independent access to the world and the world's unhampered assessment of our lives . . . This coup on the part of diasporic writers might be something worth celebrating if there were an accompanying humility, an acknowledgement of the limitations of diasporic representations of the homeland.[117]

This eloquent attack rightly challenges an uncritical acceptance of such diasporic accounts, but it also implies that readers outside India automatically assume the authenticity of these accounts. This is no more true than the idea that a benighted India is the only version of ancestral space available in South Asian Atlantic writing.

Return-of-the-native tropes – and the planned return embodied through the deferred home – are presented as altogether more complex and self-reflexive than Paranjape's critique implies, while the representations of ethnic return by both South Asian American and British Asian creative artists often do exhibit 'an accompanying humility' and a necessary and serious recognition of 'the limitations of diasporic representations of the homeland'. Perhaps this is why foreign-born characters often struggle to negotiate their ancestral country, are sometimes punished for their preconceptions and failure to make a material difference to local lives, and regularly feel a mixture of relief and dread about returning to the United States or Britain. The punitive aspects of these narratives could reflect the unease of South Asian Atlantic artists, both first- and second-generation, in India and Pakistan, as they tacitly acknowledge that their own belonging in South Asia is tenuous at best. Indeed, the often privileged lives of British Asians and South Asian Americans allow them to travel to the motherland, but do not equip them for its challenges, either fresh or remembered; and they can, in any case, turn around and leave. In other words, they lack the toughness of those forced to remain in a harsher South Asian environment. This is especially true of the second generation, who have not suffered the rigours of migration either. Paranjape has also claimed that diasporic writers commodify the motherland;[118] and, beyond autobiographical imperatives, the notion that India and Pakistan 'sell' may, of course, inform the decision by writers and film-makers to deploy South Asian settings.[119]

Despite making ample use of India in her own work, Bharati Mukherjee has provocatively dismissed the handling by second-generation writers of so-called 'third-world material' as

> hokey concoctions composed of family memory and brief visits to ancestral villages. Here they are . . . turning their backs on some of the richest material [namely, the ethnic diversity of the contemporary United States] ever conferred on a writer, for the fugitive attraction of something dead and 'charming'.[120]

By suggesting that multi-ethnic America provides 'some of the richest material', while roots journeys are 'dead', Mukherjee overlooks the idea that India and Pakistan might open up a new frame of reference – and fresh imaginative possibilities and freedoms – for diasporic writers.[121] Not only does South Asia offer an exotic, escapist alternative to Britain or the United States, but it also allows a sense of simultaneous belonging and outsider-ness which results in rich dramatic opportunities. Adventures in any ethnic motherland are likely to throw up surprise, confusion, and puzzlement but India, in particular – with its notable religious, linguistic, and social heterogeneity – proves to be especially bewildering: a dazzling source of intrigue and surprise. South Asian Atlantic writers and film-makers can also draw on its well-known cultural and historical status as a site of religious pilgrimage and popular travel writing. And tropes of return allow artists to investigate, in a particularly urgent fashion, ideas about transnational mobility – and the search for tradition evoked by 'the uncertainties of modern life'[122] – by testing the limits of their protagonists' South Asian and American or British identities. Although such texts reflect, then, what Anders H. Stefansson has called 'the often rather pessimistic accounts of homecoming found in . . . return migration research', they also exhibit the concomitant 'complexity and ambivalence' of such accounts.[123]

Jennifer Bess has argued of Lahiri's stories that they 'embody the author's timely lament over the failure of global living to bridge the gaps between cultures and . . . individuals';[124] and indeed, these narratives relate to an increasingly globalised world, while demonstrating, once again, that questions of national identity and difference continue to be powerful, unsettling, and difficult to resolve.[125] As Mita Banerjee has put it, 'while theorists increasingly herald the obsolescence of things national in the era of globalisation, discourses of popular culture seem to attest to the fact that what is negotiated continues to be national representativeness'.[126] Despite gesturing towards transnationalism, many of these texts foreground such 'national representativeness'. Thus, as we saw in Chapter

1, the global nature of the South Asian diaspora and the importance of ethnic similarity do not cancel out the significance of national identity and the cultural difference it embodies, and this means that 'return' to the ancestral homeland can still embody a major step. But if the limits of Indian or Pakistani inclusion are tested, then so too are the US and the UK critiqued, as I argued about much of the South Asian Atlantic writing considered in the previous chapter. Americanness or Britishness come at the expense of South Asian affiliation; and since the right to belong in South Asia is far from guaranteed, it must be earned through the successful completion of a spiritual and emotional quest.

In the US context, in particular, roots narratives allow artists to re-craft a well-recognised form of Americana: a strategy which – while not derivative exactly – may arise from the desire to draw on existing ethno-cultural traditions. In other words, if national representativeness underpins these transnational journeys, then this claiming of familiar roots terrain is, ironically, as much about artists proving their American authenticity as it is about confirming the strength of their Indian heritage. The 'American' part of 'South Asian American' remains politically and culturally contested territory, after all,[127] and, as Matthew Frye Jacobson has argued in a 1970s Euro-American context: 'the roots trip was as much a national phenomenon as a familial or personal one'.[128] That roots journeys also make their way into British Asian works – whether consciously depicted in this way or not – attests to broader transatlantic currents within popular culture, rather than specifically South Asian 'anxieties of influence', as I argued in the Introduction. What is striking is that creative artists from both sides of the Atlantic choose to narrate a similar tension between local and global for both the first and second generation.

Paranjape's critique converges with Frakes's assessment of diasporic representations of the motherland many years earlier because both spot the potential for cliché and the recycling of particular ideas at work in the 'return' subgenre. This subject, which is not in itself particularly radical, is traditionally underpinned by an assimilationist, coming-to-America/Britain message, which essentialises the ancestral homeland as a rather atrophied place. Perhaps Mukherjee's negative evaluation can be applied to transatlantic South Asian writing after all, although not in the way she intends. To paraphrase her claim, the subject of travel and return is neither 'dead' nor 'charming' – as her own *Tiger's Daughter* richly illustrates – but, as I argued earlier, its treatment remains rather flat, even conservative at times: not only in second-generation 'roots' narratives, but also in those recounting the first generation's experiences. This mirrors in formal ways an uncertainty, even an emotional and intellectual exhaustion, towards the ancestral homeland, as opposed to the US or Britain, and a persistent, arguably old-fashioned, emphasis on national boundaries. Beyond tonal differences, then, these ostensibly transnational narratives are intriguing for the thematic questions and ambiguities they present, but they are not especially oppositional or subversive artistically. With the possible exceptions of *Gifted* and *Indian Takeaway* – and for all their individual interest and illuminating transatlantic overlaps and crossovers – they end up essentialising ancestral space, reinscribing 'the notion of the "impossible homecoming"'[129] and implicitly supporting past and future migration.

NOTES

1. Stein, *Black British*, p. 57.
2. Paranjape, 'Writing across boundaries', p. 231.
3. Quoted in Lau, 'Making', p. 252.
4. Frakes, review of *Tiger's Daughter*, p. 2.
5. In a US context, this subject finds expression throughout Asian American cultural production more widely: witness the use of China 'returns' in Amy Tan's novels *The Joy Luck Club* (1989) and particularly *The Hundred Secret Senses* (1995); Gish Jen's short story 'Duncan in China' (1999); and such films as Peter Wang's *A Great Wall* (1985) and David Ren and Kern Konwiser's *Shanghai Kiss* (2006). Several works of Japanese American life-writing also examine the second generation's exposure to the ancestral nation – see Lydia Minatoya's *Talking to High Monks in the Snow: An Asian American Odyssey* (1991) and David Mura's *Turning Japanese: Memoirs of a Sansei* (1991) – while Andrew X. Pham, who left Vietnam as a boy, records his roots visit in the memoir *Catfish and Mandala: A Vietnamese Odyssey* (1999).
6. See Jacobson, *Roots Too*, pp. 3–4.
7. Mukherjee, *Desirable*, p. 17; Maira, *Desis*, p. 114.
8. The existence of a specific term, 'returned Yank', suggests the degree to which 'return' has informed discussions – and artistic representations – of the Irish diaspora. That the phrase is 'returned *Yank*' reveals not only the primacy of roots searching in US culture, but also the idea that the returnee's claim to the motherland is provisional. 'Plastic Paddy', a derogatory term of UK origin for those outside Ireland whose claims to Irishness are seen as dubious, reflects a characteristically British scepticism towards roots searching; for further discussion of the term, see Hickman, 'Locating', pp. 8–26.
9. Rains, 'Irish roots', pp. 131–2; see also Halter, *Shopping*, pp. 83–4; and Jacobson, *Roots Too*, pp. 31, 42–8, for a consideration of the impact of Haley's text.
10. See Levitt and Waters, *Changing Face*; Harper, *Emigrant Homecomings*;

Markowitz and Stefansson, *Homecomings*; Conway and Potter, *Return Migration*; and Tsuda, *Diasporic Homecomings*.

11. See Stefansson, 'Homecomings to the future', pp. 3, 5–6; Conway and Potter, 'Return of the next generations', p. 7; and Tsuda, 'Introduction', pp. 6, 8.
12. Tsuda, 'When home', pp. 125–45; Christou, 'Emulating', pp. 101–16; Potter and Phillips, 'Bajan-Brit', pp. 79–99; Macpherson and Macpherson, 'It was not', pp. 19–39; Lee, 'Ambivalence', pp. 41–58.
13. See Holsey, 'Transatlantic dreaming', pp. 166–82; Basu, 'Roots tourism', pp. 131–50; Kibria, 'Of blood', pp. 295–311; and Kim, 'Finding our way', pp. 305–24.
14. Levitt, 'Ties that change', pp. 131–4, 137–43, and Maira, *Desis*, pp. 107–17, are exceptions. India does not appear to operate an official version of heritage tourism (as, for example, Ireland, Scotland, and Ghana do) and, despite any number of public traumas, most notably Partition, there is no unifying tragic narrative (such as the Irish potato famine, the Highland Clearances, the Jewish Holocaust, or transatlantic slavery) which is seen to underpin South Asian migration. The voluntary nature of much of that movement out of the Indian subcontinent is arguably reflected in returns to it, as we will see in South Asian Atlantic works charting return of the native and ethnic return visits.
15. See, however, Chu, 'Asian American', pp. 204–21; and Kuortti, *Writing*, pp. 127–46.
16. Critics have analysed Ameena Meer's novel *Bombay Talkie* (1994) and – to a far greater extent – Jhumpa Lahiri's short story 'Interpreter of maladies' (1999), both of which concern South Asian American diasporic tourism; see, for example, Lewis, 'Lahiri's "Interpreter"', pp. 219–21; Ghazvinizadeh, 'E. M. Forster', pp. 1–9; Rajan, 'Ethical responsibility', pp. 129–33; Annesley, *Fictions*, pp. 128–30; and Vogt-William, 'Routes', pp. 309–22. The recurring importance of this subject in South Asian Atlantic writing as a whole, however, has yet to be interpreted – and that is my aim in this chapter.
17. Ali, *Brick Lane*, p. 299.
18. Manzoor, *Greetings*, pp. 240, 254, emphasis added.
19. Hussein, *Émigré*, p. 11.
20. Ahmed, 'Home and away', p. 331, emphasis in original.
21. Islam, *Mapmakers*, pp. 10–11.
22. Srivastava, *Looking for Maya*, p. 10.
23. Rushdie, *Wizard*, p. 57.
24. Ahmed, 'Home and away', p. 343.
25. Mukherjee, *Wife*, p. 184.
26. Mukherjee, *Darkness*, p. 99.
27. Mukherjee, *Holder*, pp. 127, 182.
28. Aslam, *Maps*, p. 96.
29. For instance, the paradisal sense taken on by 'home' in such well-known

spirituals as 'Swing low sweet chariot', which includes the line 'coming for to carry me home'. In a South Asian context, compare the discussion of Anglo-Indians in Haslam, 'Queenie', where he writes that 'given their subservient position within the colonial system, and their father's and forefather's talk of "Home", it is understandable that [Anglo-Indians] . . . would internalise this desire in a way that would have paralleled the hope of their Christian faith for a "promised land"'.

30. In Lahiri's work, the first generation's reverse migration to India is presented, by contrast, as relatively straightforward: especially in the short story, 'Interpreter of maladies' (1999), which I consider later in this chapter; her novel *The Namesake* (2003); and the more recent short story cycle 'Hema and Kaushik' from her collection *Unaccustomed Earth* (2008). See also Rai, 'Indians', which examines return to India from the US on professional grounds. Class privilege and educational background clearly assist such returns, which are often characterised by 'the "soft landing" that many returning Indians seek by living in gated communities', ibid.; and compare Manzoor, 'Brits'.
31. Cited in Moynihan, 'Transnational', pp. 68–9.
32. Dasgupta, 'Locating "home"', p. 78.
33. Exceptions to this gender emphasis are G. S. Chandra's short story 'Bhat's return', from his anthology *Sari of the Gods* (1998), which satirically recounts the visit to India of Bhat and his white American wife, Becky; Mohsin Hamid's novel *The Reluctant Fundamentalist* (2007); and Nagesh Kukunoor's popular Indian film *Hyderabad Blues* (1998).
34. For a historical contextualisation of this Bengali Communist movement, active from 1967 to 1973, see Mitra, 'Luminous', pp. 287–8.
35. Compare Kuortti, *Writing*, 135–6.
36. Mukherjee, *Tiger's Daughter*, pp. 105, 115.
37. Mukherjee, 'Invisible', p. 36.
38. The choice of seven seems deliberate since it is traditionally significant across cultural traditions. Priya travels 'across seven seas to the land of opportunities', a reference to the phrase, 'across seven seas', which is used throughout South Asia to refer to the idea of faraway places; see Malladi, *Mango Season*, p. 126. In *Tiger's Daughter*, Tara also returns after seven years; in each case, the use of the number seven emphasises cultural dislocation and personal transformation in a more symbolic way.
39. Hamid, *Reluctant Fundamentalist*, pp. 140–1.
40. Shamsie, '*Reluctant Fundamentalist*'.
41. Compare Blaise and Mukherjee, *Sorrow and Terror*, pp. 29, 129, where they suggest that for Canada's South Asian communities, short return visits to India are fraught with pressure through the need to prove to those 'back home' that one has triumphed abroad, since it is the ultimate disgrace to return home empty-handed. Such return visits thus carry a heavy emotional, cultural, and material cost, framed by financial abandon (in terms of

present-buying) and cultural conservatism (not forgetting one's Indianness). See also Kalita, *Suburban*, pp. 49, 55, 66, 135; and Kohli, *Indian Takeaway*, p. 63.

42. Compare Mrs Dutta's 'uneasy pride' about the ability of her daughter-in-law, Shyamoli, to 'pass for an American' in Chitra Divakaruni's short story 'Mrs Dutta writes a letter', anthologised in Divakaruni, *Unknown Errors*, p. 3; and the mixture of anxiety and self-importance about Feroza's American life exhibited by her mother and grandmother in Pakistan in Bapsi Sidhwa's novel *An American Brat* (1994).
43. I refer here to W. E. B. DuBois's famous concept of black American 'double consciousness': namely, the experience of 'always looking at one's self through the eyes of others . . . [and] ever feel[ing a] . . . twoness . . . two souls, two thoughts, two unreconciled strivings; two warring ideals in one dark body'; see DuBois, *Souls*, p. 11.
44. Compare Kuortti, *Writing*, p. 141.
45. Mohanti, *Through Brown Eyes*, p. 120.
46. See Nelson, 'Prafulla Mohanti'.
47. Sheikh, *Red Box*, p. 61, emphasis added.
48. Compare Kabeer, *Power to Choose*, pp. 267–8.
49. For further discussion of this, see Maxey, 'Representative', p. 225.
50. Blaise and Mukherjee, *Sorrow and Terror*, p. 117.
51. For a discussion of first-generation return in Hanif Kureishi's writing, see Maxey, 'Life in the diaspora', pp. 13–15, 18–19.
52. See Rushdie, *Imaginary*, p. 394; Bhabha, *Location*, pp. 37–8, 112; and also Morley, *Home Territories*, pp. 205–13, 225–42.
53. Shyamalan, *Praying with Anger*.
54. Maira, *Desis*, pp. 110–11, emphasis in original; and see Halter, *Shopping*, p. 86.
55. Compare its use in Jen's 'Duncan in China', Ren and Konwiser's *Shanghai Kiss*, and several Irish American roots dramas, including Ford's *The Quiet Man* and Eugene Brady's *The Nephew* (1998).
56. Maira, *Desis*, p. 109; and compare Levitt, 'Ties that change', pp. 140–1.
57. See Desforges, 'Checking out', pp. 175–7.
58. Suleiman, *Authoritarian*, p. 65.
59. Compare Chu, 'Asian American', p. 204. In her short story 'A temporary matter' (1999), Lahiri also links an increased second-generation interest in the ancestral nation to paternal death; see Lahiri, *Interpreter*, p. 12. In other ethnic roots narratives, it is the maternal death and ancestral nation as 'motherland' which are more significant – see *The Nephew* and *Shanghai Kiss*; while sometimes the journey to the originary homeland is driven by the protagonist's orphaned status: consider, for example, *The Quiet Man* and Tony Gatlif (dir.), *Exiles* (2004).
60. The discovery or acquisition of a familial property – again, home as house/nation – is another key trope within roots narratives; see, for instance, *The Quiet Man*, *The Nephew*, *Exiles*, and *Shanghai Kiss*. By contrast, in Suhayl

Saadi's British Asian short story 'Ninety-nine kiss-o-grams' (2001), discussed later in this chapter, Sal's roots journey is doomed when he cannot find his family's ancestral land in Pakistan.

61. Campbell, *Hero*, pp. 126–49.
62. See Levitt, 'Ties that change', p. 130.
63. Compare the function of the 'donnybrook' finale in *The Quiet Man*; and see Gibbons, *Quiet Man*, pp. 17, 55, 61.
64. Compare Maira, *Desis*, pp. 115–16; and Purkayastha, *Negotiating Ethnicity*, pp. 72–3.
65. Bauman, 'From pilgrim', pp. 20–1.
66. Morley, *Home Territories*, p. 207.
67. Holden, 'American comes of age'.
68. Maira, *Desis*, pp. 109–10.
69. Compare Campbell, *Hero*, p. 10n: 'rites of passage are intended to touch not only the candidate but also every member of his circle'.
70. Srikanth, *World Next Door*, p. 51.
71. Divakaruni, *Unknown Errors*, p. 61.
72. Lahiri, *Interpreter*, p. 12; and Lahiri, *Namesake*, pp. 36, 81–6; and compare Manzoor, *Greetings*, pp. 247–8.
73. Compare Gibbons, *Quiet Man*, p. 16, where he notes that in *The Quiet Man*, the American roots journey to Ireland is 'motivated by . . . a therapeutic quest to undo the effects of trauma'.
74. Naipaul, *Area*, pp. 154–70; for a critical discussion, see May, 'Memorials', pp. 247–58.
75. Studies of ethnic return in diverse locations note that racial similarity – so reassuring initially to 'visible minorities' with histories of racial exclusion within such white majority societies as the US and UK – does not correspond to cultural belonging and that this point is quickly driven home to the overseas visitor; see Potter and Phillips, 'Bajan-Brit', pp. 83, 87; Kim, 'Finding our way', pp. 305–7, 317; Macpherson and Macpherson, 'It was not', p. 35; and compare Holsey, 'Transatlantic dreaming', pp. 166–7.
76. Compare Jen's 'Duncan in China', where locals tell Duncan, a Chinese American, that 'a Chinese man' would 'figure out' the metaphors used by Chinese people; Jen, *Who's Irish?*, p. 55. As with both Leela and Dev, Duncan's 'foreign' status and helplessness in the ancestral homeland are continually stressed.
77. In discussion of the story, however, Divakaruni accounts for (and arguably excuses) Leela's actions on the grounds that she finally acknowledges 'the genetic memory' of Indian 'superstition'; see Johnson, *Conversations*, p. 65.
78. Lahiri, *Interpreter*, 60.
79. Annesley, *Fictions*, pp. 128–9.
80. Lewis, 'Lahiri's "Interpreter"', p. 219.
81. Brada-Williams, 'Reading Jhumpa Lahiri', p. 457; and Zare, 'Evolving masculinities', p. 106.

82. Compare Ghazvinizadeh, 'E. M. Forster', p. 7.
83. Ibid. p. 6; Rajan, 'Ethical responsibility', p. 130.
84. Lewis, 'Lahiri's "Interpreter"'; Ghazvinizadeh, 'E. M. Forster'; Rajan, 'Ethical responsibility', pp. 131–2.
85. Ghazvinizadeh, 'E. M. Forster', p. 2, emphasis in original.
86. This largely depoliticised, unthreatening vision recalls Ford's technicolour, socially monolithic Ireland in *The Quiet Man*.
87. Quoted in Mandal, 'Oh Calcutta!', p. 19.
88. Some critics have questioned the 'authenticity' of these creative artists, arguing that the representation of India is static and Orientalist in 'The lives of strangers' and 'Interpreter of maladies'; see, for example, Majithia, 'Of foreigners'. For a critique of Lahiri's Indian-based stories more generally, see Narayan, 'India', p. 49; for a counter-position, see Chaudhury, 'Debutante', p. 19; and for Lahiri's own response to such criticisms, see Lahiri, 'My intimate alien', pp. 117–18.
89. These characters literally cannot speak the language – Dev does not understand Tamil, Leela is soon lost in Bengali ('Lives', 57), and Mina fails to comprehend Hindi ('Interpreter', 46). By contrast, the latter story emphasises Mr Kapasi's polyglot work; see Annesley, *Fictions*, p. 130. On the relationship between language and second-generation 'return', see Kibria, 'Of blood', pp. 305–6.
90. Meer, *Bombay Talkie*, p. 35.
91. I refer to Dorinne Kondo's notion of local people's struggle with the 'conceptual anomaly' of a visitor who is racially similar, but culturally other; quoted in Chu, 'Asian American', p. 209.
92. Vogt-William, 'Routes', p. 319.
93. Compare Subramanyam, review of *Bombay Talkie*.
94. Quoted in ibid.
95. Ibid.
96. Maira, *Desis*, p. 111.
97. Gans, 'Symbolic ethnicity', pp. 425–59; and see Maira, *Desis*, pp. 118, 120, 128.
98. It is worth noting that some US works (although none South Asian) have punctured the roots journey's traditionally serious status within American culture: for instance, Jen's 'Duncan in China' and Ren and Konwiser's *Shanghai Kiss*, both of which use humour to defuse the harshness of diasporic experiences in China. See also Tim Van Patten's 'Commendatori' (2000), episode 4 from season 2 of the hit HBO television series *The Sopranos*, where Italian American gangsters in Naples are made to seem comically out of place and out of their depth; and Junot Díaz's 1.5-generation return to the Dominican Republic in Díaz, 'Homecoming'.
99. The fact that, with the exception of *Gifted* and parts of Wood, *Goodness Gracious Me,* these texts are all male-authored may also account for their reliance on comic strategies, since men's confidence is arguably more

connected with the pressure to be funny than that of women, hence the male-dominated world of stand-up comedy in both the US and the UK.

100. For more varied, real-life perspectives, see Dwyer, 'Where are you from?', pp. 192–7.
101. Saadi, *Burning Mirror*, p. 4.
102. Upstone, *British Asian*, p. 199.
103. Maxey, 'Life in the diaspora', pp. 13–16.
104. Compare 'Locating "home"', pp. 79–80.
105. Compare Kohli, *Indian Takeaway*, p. 63.
106. Lalwani, *Gifted*, p. 16.
107. See Varvogli, 'Underwhelmed', pp. 89–90.
108. Dhondy, *East End*, pp. 54–5.
109. Kohli, *Indian Takeaway*, pp. 33, 40, 43, 46, 50; and compare Alibhai-Brown, *Settler's Cookbook*, p. 13, where she refers to roots journeys in India as 'futile quests by people nervous about their own condition'.
110. See also Iyer, 'Words'.
111. Compare Naish, 'Hardeep Singh Kohli'.
112. Potter and Phillips, 'Bajan-Brit', pp. 87–95; Kibria, 'Of blood', p. 311; Kim, 'Finding our way', pp. 314, 319, 321; Macpherson and Macpherson, 'It was not', pp. 25, 27, 33–4.
113. Kibria, 'Of blood', pp. 300, 302–6; Stefansson, 'Homecomings to the future', p. 9; Holsey, 'Transatlantic dreaming', p. 178; Kim, 'Finding our way', pp. 308, 312; Lee, 'Ambivalence', p. 47; Christou, 'Emulating', pp. 101, 111–12. Studies suggest, moreover, that in some contexts, certain diasporic cohorts are favoured over others, depending on the geopolitical significance of their adopted nation; see Tsuda, 'Global inequities', pp. 227–59. Foreign nationality can also be a professional asset; see Potter and Phillips, 'Bajan-Brit', pp. 84–6; and compare Rai, 'Indians'; and Manzoor, 'Brits'. Relevant as it might be to aspects of this book's thesis to posit a preference in South Asia for diasporics from one side of the Atlantic over the other, I have found no textual evidence to support such a claim.
114. Holsey, 'Transatlantic dreaming', pp. 167, 175, 177.
115. Potter and Phillips, 'Bajan-Brit', p. 79; Kibria, 'Of blood', p. 307; Kim, 'Finding our way', pp. 306, 321; and compare Tsuda, 'Introduction', pp. 3–4.
116. Kibria, 'Of blood', pp. 307–8; Chu, 'Asian American', p. 219.
117. Paranjape, 'Afterword', pp. 239–40; and compare George, 'Of fictional cities', pp. 571–4.
118. Paranjape, 'Writing across boundaries', p. 231.
119. Compare Lau, 'Making', p. 240.
120. Mukherjee, 'Immigrant', p. 29.
121. Compare Salgado, 'Writing home', p. 28, where she writes that 'Sri Lanka is . . . the land of my imaginative life, and therefore where I would claim I truly live; I merely reside in England.'

122. Shah, 'Hooray'.
123. Stefansson, 'Homecomings to the future', p. 5.
124. Bess, 'Lahiri's *Interpreter*', p. 125.
125. Compare Annesley, *Fictions*, p. 130.
126. Banerjee, 'Traveling barbies', p. 449; and see also Stefansson, 'Homecomings to the future', p. 3. In a sense, this point about the ongoing importance of national belonging in a globalised age has itself become a critical commonplace.
127. Srikanth, *World Next Door*, pp. 53–5.
128. Jacobson, *Roots Too*, p. 42.
129. Stefansson, 'Homecomings to the future', p. 11.

CHAPTER 3

BRAVE NEW WORLDS? MISCEGENATION IN SOUTH ASIAN ATLANTIC LITERATURE

Introduction

In 1952, Lord Beginner, the Trinidadian calypsonian, claimed that interracial marriages in Britain constituted a growing social movement. His song, 'Mix up matrimony', contends that:

> Mixed marriage is the fashion and the world is saying so
> Lovers choosing partners of every kind they know
> This is freedom from above
> . . . to grab the one they love . . .
>
> The races are blending harmoniously
> White and coloured people are binding neutrally
> It doesn't take no class to see how it come to pass
> Coloured Britons are rising fast.[1]

This commonsense paean to interracial love – which celebrates a British society and a global scenario in which 'mixed marriage' is normal, rather than especially forward-looking or transgressive – suggests that problematic social and political issues are simply not at stake. The logical conclusion of such a position is the idea that mixed-race people[2] (referenced by the phrase 'coloured Britons') are representative of this new national template – and even of a new world order.

In his critique of the same song, Ashley Dawson interprets the text in gendered and colonialist terms,[3] since the proponents of this 'mix up matrimony' are African and Caribbean men marrying white women, a point made unmistakably through Lord Beginner's reference elsewhere in the same song to Seretse Kharma, 'chief of the Bamangwato people in Bechuanaland, who was driven into exile for marrying a white woman'.[4] Dawson reads 'coloured Britons' as black British immigrants, rather than their mixed-race children, and he sees the song as proposing a kind of naïvely felt tribute to Britain as the 'mother country' through its eager desire for assimilation through interracial matrimony.[5] Indeed, the official sanctioning of such marriage, by national, even divine, authority, is implied through the phrase, 'this is freedom from above'.

Dawson's argument raises the important question of whether, in white-dominated societies such as the United States and Britain, interracial relationships have signalled assimilation into the mainstream – a rejection of ancestry, even a form of 'selling out', on the part of the person of colour – or radicalism through the crossing of sometimes rigidly policed racial lines. Although 'race' is often recognised as a social construction, it is clear that human beings rely on such racialised physical markers as skin, hair, and eyes in order to categorise each other and thus to negotiate the world.[6] Such material classifications can be questioned and confused by the biological result of interracial partnerships: the racially mixed subject. In many ways, then, nothing exposes the continuing ideological power of 'race' – as well as the latent, persistent anxieties which underpin it as a concept – more than miscegenation. Does racial mixing therefore signal conservatism by reinscribing the whole premise of racial categories or does it remain a subversive, oppositional move?

Numbers of interracial marriages involving South Asians are still relatively low in Britain,[7] while – according to the US census of 2000 – 293,754 South Asian Americans (out of a total of 2,195,518) are racially mixed.[8] Regardless of the implications of official statistics – which appear to signal that South Asian miscegenation is commoner in the US than in the UK – racial mixing remains a powerful idea in South Asian diasporic cultural production:[9] a liberatory means for the creative artist to imagine new physical and social possibilities in the bid to create brave new multiracial nations. Such artists' reasons for exploring this subject can be autobiographical, too: they mine their own experience of interracial relationships or of being mixed-race. Thus such biracial British Asian writers as Hanif Kureishi and Ayub Khan-Din, and South Asian American literary figures such as Bharati Mukherjee, Meena Alexander, and Jhumpa Lahiri – all mothers of mixed-race children – consistently deploy tropes of miscegenation.

Following Salman Rushdie, Mukherjee has championed the 'mongrelisation' of Western societies,[10] while Kureishi and Khan-Din have turned the mixed-race identity of their characters into a badge of pride, thus rewriting the traditionally racist discourse of 'half-caste' and other derogatory terms associated with racially mixed people. Rejecting the negative 'between worlds' stereotype of the 'tragic' biracial subject – of which the American figure of the 'tragic mulatto' is a particularly well-known variant – such identities instead become a blueprint for new forms of British and American nationhood, in a manner which, in its paradoxical blend of the matter-of-fact and the radical, recalls the utopian vision of 'Mix up matrimony'.

The literary and cinematic presentation of interracial relationships as a social panacea is nonetheless problematic, not least because of the assimilationist principles underwriting such treatments, which are generally reliant on a white party.[11] Indeed, the recurring theme of miscegenation in recent, popular works by or about South Asians has generated controversy, particularly where artists themselves are mixed-race. Thus Yasmin Alibhai-Brown has attributed the success of Monica Ali's novel *Brick Lane* (2003) to its author's membership of 'a new breed of preferred "ethnic" writers . . . mixed-race, au fait with Oxbridge, not too dark or troublingly alien'.[12] Hari Kunzru and Zadie Smith, the latter a novelist of mixed Jamaican and white British parentage, are also included in this apparently elite literary club. Alibhai-Brown nevertheless praises Rushdie, who is Cambridge-educated, and the biracial Kureishi because their work apparently explores 'transgressive ideas'.[13] This shift into a discussion of the kind of material deployed by writers does not, however, disguise the implication behind Alibhai-Brown's remarks: that, in a pigmentocratic sense, lighter-skinned British Asians are more likely to win favour from a white-dominated media establishment and publishing world. If this line of thinking is to be believed, then such industries are reinscribing old British colonial patterns in India whereby, for instance, paler-skinned Parsis and Anglo-Indians – the latter a specific mixed-race community with a long history – were favoured over darker-complexioned Indians, to whom they felt superior, and were rewarded with higher-ranking jobs.[14] I will return to this question of modern-day pigmentocratic dynamics in the conclusion to this chapter.

Daniel Kim has argued that 'a certain sense of racial "belatedness" . . . frames the attempts of Asian American writers to write themselves into a literary landscape largely shaded in black and white'.[15] Ideas about miscegenation in both America and Britain have similarly been 'shaded in black and white', despite the long history of miscegenation in India itself; the presence of distinct interracial Indian communities in America;[16] the growing numbers – and distinct history – of biracial South Asians in both countries; the well-established presence of mixed-race South Asian writers, particularly in Britain; and the enduring interest of transatlantic South Asian artists in racial mixing. And in spite of the increasing volume of Kureishi, Mukherjee, and Lahiri scholarship, and a burgeoning popular and academic interest in different forms of miscegenation in recent years, this subject remains surprisingly under-researched within discussions of South Asian diasporic literature and film.

Attempting to address such scholarly neglect, this chapter will extend the ideas of national and cultural identity considered in Chapters 1 and 2 by analysing the representation of interracial relationships and biracial people within a wide selection of recent South Asian Atlantic texts. It will examine the engagement by artists with the paradoxically utopian and dystopian ideas which traditionally characterise works about miscegenation to argue that this interest in the progressive – and alarming – possibilities of racial mixing belongs to a much longer transatlantic tradition, and that this aligns recent South Asian diasporic writing and cinema with older works by white, black, and East Asian creative artists in both countries.

Before tackling these questions, however, I will briefly establish a broader cultural context for miscegenation in the United States and Britain in order to identify more closely the particular handling of this subject in South Asian diasporic works. I will then analyse the differing treatment of interracial relationships within recent British Asian and South Asian American writing and film, before moving on to the theme of mixed-race identity. The chapter will thus distinguish between the particular social, historical, and ontological questions which relate to the racially mixed subject of South Asian descent and the ways in which writers and, to a lesser extent, film-makers use the separate, yet related, trope of the interracial relationship.

An Overview of Miscegenation in the United States and Britain

It is well documented that historically, interracial relationships and, in particular, people of mixed race were pathologised in Western societies.[17] In the United States, these attitudes found expression through a raft of state laws prohibiting interracial marriage, although only where white people were involved.[18] Although such legislation has never existed in Britain, the two nations overlap in their historical reliance on scientifically racist modes of thought and through the impact and legacy of such 'theories'. These ideas include the claim that biracial children would represent a physically and mentally weaker 'third race';[19] the specific associations of laziness, sexual promiscuity, disease, sterility,[20] poverty, and homelessness with racially mixed people; and the connection between miscegenation and immorality, sometimes expressed in overtly religious terms. Prejudices concerning poverty and homelessness were sometimes fulfilled, since life prospects could indeed be bleaker for mixed-race people in Britain and America between the eighteenth and twentieth centuries.[21] And the popular link between miscegenation and illness, both physical and mental, was sometimes suggested by biracial people themselves. Thus the British-born, mixed-race Chinese North American writer Sui Sin Far (Edith Eaton), who died in 1914 at just forty-nine, argues in her autobiographical essay 'Leaves from the mental portfolio of an Eurasian' (1909) that her biracial status has led to intermittent 'nervous sickness' as the result of racism, social ostracism, sexual harassment, and economic insecurity.[22]

The US has a much longer domestic tradition of miscegenation than Britain: from its well-known history of black–white mixing, particularly in the context of slavery, to Native American *métissage* to *mestizo* Latino peoples to biracial Asian Americans or *hapas*. Arguably, racial mixing remains more commonplace in America than Britain, which has a comparatively short history as a racially diverse, and indeed multiracial, society, and this may be why more academic work has appeared on miscegenation in the US context.[23] At the same time, some British commentators have contended that the UK's rapidly growing number of racially mixed people amounts to a higher proportion of the population than in the US.[24]

But the very fact that in America, specific words – *hapa*, *mestizo*, *métis* – exist for different types of mixed-race people reveals the longevity and complexity of this national history. Indeed, as is well known, the term 'miscegenation' itself originates from the notion of black–white mixing in the United States although, perhaps unsurprisingly, this very issue of language is sensitive and problematic. For one thing, terms such as 'miscegenation', 'racially mixed', and 'multiracial' are polysemic and, as such, ambiguous. Should 'miscegenation' refer to interracial relationships or to those of mixed race or to both? Given its specific black/white American history, how easily can it be applied to different kinds of racial mixing? Some commentators have argued that 'miscegenation' is in any case both pejorative and outdated, part of the pathologising mentality outlined above. The word even begins on an unpromising note through 'mis-', a prefix with implicitly negative connotations.[25] 'Racially mixed' and 'multiracial' are used by commentators to refer to those from several racial backgrounds, yet one also hears such terms being deployed to suggest racial diversity and multiculturalism more generally.

Despite its inherently problematic nature, terminology to discuss this subject has also changed in positive ways with such terms as 'biracial', 'racially mixed', and 'multiracial' largely replacing the animalistic, dehumanising language – for instance, 'half-breed' and 'mongrel' – traditionally applied to the mixed-race subject.[26] 'Half-caste' – another widely used, derogatory, and now discredited term – is particularly relevant to my discussion since it refers originally to specifically Indian forms of miscegenation.[27] Within the American context, 'mulatto', 'quadroon', and 'octoroon', which traditionally referred to black–white miscegenation, are now obsolete; they draw attention to the 'ludicrous mathematics' of miscegenation terminology[28] and indeed, their numerical nature underscores the economic factors behind the usage by white slave-owners of such terms.

Other linguistic shifts have been less straightforwardly positive. Thus whereas 'Anglo-Indian' was still being used in the nineteenth century to mean a white British colonialist in India, with 'Eurasian' applied to a person of mixed white/South Asian (but also East or South-East Asian) heritage, 'Eurasian' has now fallen into disuse while 'Anglo-Indian' currently refers to an Indian from a particular white/South Asian background.[29] Yet 'Anglo-Indian' is still misunderstood and its catachrestic usage is typical of the lexical uncertainties which surround discussions of racial mixing.[30] These difficulties point in turn to language's inherent limits in this regard. As Henry Yule and A. C. Burnell put it, quoting the Imperial Anglo-Indian Association, in their definition of 'Eurasian' in *Hobson-Jobson: The Anglo-Indian Dictionary* (1886): 'no name has yet been found or coined which correctly represents this section. *Eurasian* certainly does not.'[31]

That such problems continue to attend the linguistic aspects of miscegenation is also reflected in the widespread use of a colour-coded vocabulary which draws on gastronomic imagery – for instance, 'café-au-lait', 'mochaccino', 'cinnamon' – to discuss racially mixed people. While not obviously pejorative in the manner of 'half-caste' or 'mulatto', such apparently glamorous language nonetheless risks objectifying mixed-race people because it implicitly exoticises and commodifies them: a 'mochaccino' is, after all, a popular drink available at high street coffee shops on both sides of the Atlantic.[32] In the words of Leila Kamali: 'isn't there something deeply questionable about representing identity through food analogies, let alone grading skin tone as if it were a selection of paint swatches?'[33] The detached nature of such language reveals the continued paradox of fascination and fear in relation to miscegenation, not least when that language is used by those who are not from a racially mixed background themselves.

The term 'mixed-race', popularised from the 1990s onwards by changes to the US and British censuses, is also important.[34] Often used as a marker of self-identification by those who claim more than one racial heritage, it is frequently synonymous with particular racial mixtures: notably black/white, particularly in the UK.[35] Although 'mixed-race' has an ostensibly neutral ring to it, it immediately inscribes a status predicated on race: that is, an explicitly racialised position. Generally employed less than 'mixed-race', 'biracial' arguably has more positive connotations because, like 'bilingual' or 'bicultural', it seems to imply the best of both worlds, the benefits of two traditions, and its quasi-scientific note apparently strips it of the power to hurt. But it is also problematic since, like 'mixed-race', it foregrounds race.[36] And it suggests two halves: a binary mathematical equation rather than a process of mixing in which combinations of genes may produce unpredictable results. Despite their shortcomings, however, such terms are indispensable in discussions of racial mixing – and a vast improvement on both the loaded, overtly racist language previously employed and the apparently benign, but nonetheless paternalistic, terms Kureishi has recalled from his childhood in 1960s Britain.[37]

Whereas in previous eras, biracial people often played down their mixed origins and, if partly Caucasian, even tried to 'pass' as white, this situation has now been reversed, especially in a metropolitan context. Racially mixed people may even constitute a new mainstream in modern British and American cities.[38] Indeed, it has become fashionable to be racially mixed.[39] One positive stereotype to replace the historically negative ones is that multiracial people are more attractive and unusual than those who supposedly belong to only one racial group: a point sometimes perpetuated by the parents of racially mixed children.[40] Positive clichés can, however, be a means of minimising complex realities and of obscuring or justifying the continued existence of more negative stereotypes. As Sander Gilman puts it, 'the most negative stereotype always has an overtly positive counterweight'.[41]

Mixed-race people may play up their alternative racial credentials,[42] precisely because they do evade strict categories. Thanks to the political progress made by the multiracial movement, principally in the US,[43] those of mixed race living in traditionally white or white settler societies can now display pride in, rather than shame about, their non-white origins. Racially mixed people have of course long promoted themselves as the herald of a future which goes beyond strictly national or narrowly racialised identifications. The project of advocating such a future applies to everyone from Sui Sin Far in 'Leaves from the mental portfolio' to the white/black American author Danzy Senna in her debut novel *Caucasia* (1998), to the British-raised Filipina/Austrian musician Myleene Klass.[44] This forms an almost millennialist language whose utopianism is the obverse of the apocalyptic predictions traditionally aimed at the racially mixed subject in other quarters.[45] Such a verdict is motivated by social defiance, self-interest, and the necessity for psychological self-preservation. But the visibility in the US of such racially mixed public figures as President Barack Obama, the Hollywood actress Halle Berry, the singer Mariah Carey, and the golfer Tiger Woods; and in the UK of a proportionately even larger number of well-known biracial sportspeople, actors, and musicians, would seem to endorse this notion of an increasingly multiracial 'future'.[46]

As with Lord Beginner's appeal to a global vision, discussions of miscegenation have both invited, and predicated themselves upon, a discourse of transnationalism. This may be why, as Bruce King has claimed, mixed-race British writers often prefer to write about places outside the UK.[47] Biracial writers – from Sui Sin Far to the British Chinese novelist Timothy Mo – have often led lives characterised by mobility, whether enforced or voluntary. This point is underscored in recent transatlantic literature by or about South Asians, where such biracial protagonists as Jonathan in Kunzru's novel *The Impressionist* (2002), and Raj in Naeem Murr's novel *The Perfect Man* (2006), appear to move quite freely through places and situations thanks to the liminality afforded by their ostensibly indeterminate racial status. And in the context of literature and film, it is perhaps no surprise that critics have frequently read interracial relationships, and the racially mixed children they produce, as national and international allegories.[48] This in turn makes miscegenation a particularly pertinent subject in relation to the transnationalism associated with diasporic communities and may explain why it underpins transatlantic South Asian writing in thematic terms.

Interracial Relationships in British Asian Writing

IMMIGRANT ENCOUNTERS FROM THE POSTWAR TO CONTEMPORARY PERIOD

Miscegenation in British Asian literature follows a discernible historical and generational trajectory, starting with immigrants in the postwar era. The urban Britain of V. S. Naipaul's *The Mimic Men* (1967) and Abdullah Hussein's novel *Émigré Journeys* (2000) is largely dominated by male immigrants whose enforced bachelorhood, combined with the failure of 1950s Britain to welcome them and the imagined impermanence of their new lives, often leads to tawdry, fleeting carnal encounters, sometimes involving sex workers.[49] In *Mimic Men*, Ralph's interracial marriage to Sandra, a white British woman, meets with heavy disapproval from both families; and even the registrar marrying the couple emanates 'controlled reproof'.[50] Unsurprisingly, perhaps, the match does not last – 'a textbook example of the ill-advised mixed marriage' (42) – and it culminates, childless, and following mutual infidelity, in divorce.

Kamala Markandaya's novel *The Nowhere Man* (1972) offers a particularly ambitious examination of postwar interracial relationships in Britain. Thematically, the novel's most important interracial union is that of Srinivas and Mrs Pickering, the white woman with whom he becomes involved following the death of Vasantha, his Indian wife. Srinivas's and Mrs Pickering's unmarried co-habitation, which only gradually becomes sexual, is too radical for their neighbours in 1950s London, who are 'hypocritical about the nature of the relationship . . . pretending it did not exist, shoring up their sense of propriety by delicate references to Mr Srinivas, the landlord, and Mrs Pickering, his tenant'.[51] And in spite of Mrs Pickering's kindness and innate decency, her total absence of prejudice, and the consistently calming effect she has on Srinivas, the novel implies the difficulty of full intimacy between the couple.

Distance is suggested through the withholding of Mrs Pickering's given name while history and politics threaten to expose the cultural chasm between Srinivas and herself. Although they are both opposed to Britain's actions during the 1956 Suez crisis, Srinivas believes that, whereas his reaction 'sprang straight from the blood', Mrs Pickering has come to 'her conclusion by reason and intellect' (99). Later, amidst a tide of rising racial violence in the 1960s, she seems to him to be an 'immune islander' (180): an irrevocable part of postcolonial Britain, which he regards as a parochial, tribal country owing 'debts it had not paid', following 'crimes that had not been atoned for, nor even acknowledged' (177). Unlike Vasantha, Mrs Pickering sometimes appears to Srinivas as a non-Hindu 'stranger' (235) who fails, for instance, to grasp the equality of animals and people: an article of faith for him. Such perceptions are clearly narrated from Srinivas's closed, third-person point of view. Thus they reveal as much about the destructive effects of external forces upon his peace of mind as they do about the strength of his relationship. In such a context, as Ilan Katz has argued, it becomes 'very difficult to separate the personal from the racial elements'.[52]

Émigré Journeys chronicles an unconventional ménage: Mary, the unmarried, pregnant, white lodger, gives birth to a mixed-race (black/white) baby by one man; conducts a live-in relationship with another (Hussain Shah, the putative head of the household); and enters into a marriage of convenience with a third (his nephew, Irshad). Miscegenation may provide social escape for Mary but her marriage to Irshad culminates in the double murder, at each other's hands, of uncle and nephew. Depicted as feckless and untrustworthy, Mary is clearly presented as the catalyst for this tragedy through which Hussein implies that, in the postwar historical moment, relationships between white women and South Asian men can only lead to destruction and disaster.

Fears about the birth of a mixed Pakistani/white child are displaced through Mary's son: a different kind of racially mixed offspring, after all. This fictional aversion towards a biracial South Asian second generation is one way in which British Asian and South Asian American writers negotiate underlying community fears about miscegenation, particularly as felt by older immigrants. In South Asian American texts as different as Chitra Divakaruni's short story 'The unknown errors of our lives', from her eponymous short fiction anthology (2001), and Mukherjee's novel *Jasmine* (1989), it is telling that we never witness the birth of the biracial children expected by pregnant characters. This response to miscegenation may also reflect the conservatism of authors who are themselves first-generation, and indeed, it applies to a range of writers from Naipaul and Hussein in Britain to Divakaruni, Bapsi Sidhwa, and Mohsin Hamid in the United States context. As Shilpa Davé has argued, 'more inter-racial and inter-ethnic marriages . . . occur among second-generation Asian Americans . . . first-generation immigrants tend to marry within their own group'.[53] Challenging this chiefly endogamous attitude, Kureishi's work draws on miscegenation as both straightforward backdrop and key creative inspiration, as I have argued elsewhere.[54] Thus he posits a first generation for whom interracial relationships are common, although sometimes extra-marital and paradigmatically brown–white.[55]

Academic attention has traditionally privileged white reactions to miscegenation in Anglo-dominated societies. By contrast, such texts as Kureishi's screenplay *My Beautiful Laundrette* (1985) and Ayub Khan-Din's play *East is East* (1996) examine South Asian prejudices towards inter-racial relationships. These attitudes often echo white public opinion, which has customarily demonised the Caucasian women involved in such situations.[56] Kureishi's older white women characters, such as Margaret in his first novel, *The Buddha of Suburbia* (1990), and Yvonne in the short story 'We're not Jews' (1997), are depressive and taciturn. They resemble Ella Khan in *East is East* in that each woman is portrayed as working-class and uneducated: not of course negative traits in themselves, but part of a pattern nonetheless where each relatively powerless woman must defend her position against brown or white derision – or both. Yet Khan-Din's portrayal of a woman thought to be based upon his own mother is affectionate and respectful, not least because of Ella's courageous ability to blaze a trail: proud to stand by her decisions, she displays neither Yvonne's public ambivalence about her interracial marriage nor Margaret's snobbery towards South Asian immigrants other than her husband, Haroon.

Beyond Ella or Mrs Pickering in *Nowhere Man* – characterised by her dignity and inner strength, but nevertheless an impoverished and vulnerable figure – other white women in British Asian literature are handled in the more dismissively moralistic fashion of traditional anti-miscegenist discourse. They are sexually promiscuous and irresponsible (Mary in *Émigré Journeys*); poor, drug-using, alcoholic, and socially excluded (Bettina in Kureishi's screenplay *My Son the Fanatic* (1997), and the unnamed white Glaswegian women, or 'gorees', in Suhayl Saadi's Scottish Pakistani short stories 'Ninety-nine kiss-o-grams' and 'Bandanna' [*The Burning Mirror*, 2001]); and, more generally, lost in spiritual and moral terms. Again, this is part of a wider transatlantic trend in which a number of Caucasian women in South Asian American literature are similarly outcast. In Divakaruni's 'The unknown errors of our lives', Biren's ex-girlfriend, Arlene – the woman carrying his biracial child – resembles one of Saadi's white Glaswegian women: skinny, substance-abusing, and expendable.[57] By contrast, across Lahiri's short fiction collections, *Interpreter of Maladies* (1999) and *Unaccustomed Earth* (2008), and in her novel *The Namesake* (2003), white women are – like such older Kureishi characters as Alice in his screenplay *Sammy and Rosie Get Laid* (1987), or Eva in *Buddha of Suburbia* – educated and financially comfortable. It is therefore a danger sign when they are not: in 'Only goodness' (*Unaccustomed Earth*), for instance, Rahul's white girlfriend, Elena – a working-class, single mother – seems to compound his own downward mobility from privileged, 'model minority' status[58] into a drifting, alcoholic existence.

RACIAL MIXING AND THE SECOND GENERATION IN BRITISH ASIAN LITERATURE

The real-life accounts contained within such memoirs as Sarfraz Manzoor's *Greetings from Bury Park: Race. Religion. Rock 'n' Roll* (2007), and Sathnam Sanghera's *The Boy with the Topknot: A Memoir of Love, Secrets and Lies in Wolverhampton* (2008), suggest that to embark on an interracial relationship is seen by the second generation as explosive and potentially disastrous in familial terms. Yet British Asian writers often link sexuality with national belonging through the trope of racial mixing among the second generation. In *Nowhere Man*, after Srinivas and Vasantha learn of the wartime marriage of their son, Laxman, to Pat, an awkward meeting ensues in which Markandaya is careful to disparage neither the 'pale pink' Pat (34) nor Laxman's parents. Instead, the narrative reserves its censure for Laxman, a caricature of the assimilation-obsessed second-generation son. His brutal rejection of his heritage can be explained (if not condoned) by the postwar British climate of racial intolerance and social conformity with which he must contend. Underlining this detachment from his natal family and their Indianness, Vasantha dies without ever meeting Laxman's biracial son, Roy, and shockingly, Srinivas is never introduced to his grandchildren.

Addressing contemporary miscegenation in his short fiction anthology *Burning Mirror*, Saadi generally presents interracial sexual encounters as a troubled means for young British Pakistanis to put down deeper roots in Scotland. Here white women, and the promise of assimilation they seem to offer, are treated as objects of both fantasy and scorn, thus rehearsing the fear/fascination paradox traditionally associated with miscegenation, and recalling Frantz Fanon's classic formulation of black men's bid for acceptance in racist white societies through sexual relationships with white women.[59] In 'Ninety-nine kiss-o-grams', Sal dreams of the eponymous women

> all blond [sic] and bikini'd and stonin in a circle aroon him, and smilin at him wi thur thick, red lips . . . he saw himsel surroondit by them, their wee white breasts pushin intae his broon face, fillin his mooth, his body so that he couldnae breathe fur the whiteness. *So that he could become invisible.*[60]

This second-generation dream of becoming 'invisible' through sexual intimacy with white women – its frenzy conveyed through a suffocating blend of bright colours and heavy textures – is discussed more explicitly later in the same story. Sal has been stung and horrified by his late father's defection into the arms of a 'goree', a defection which leads Sal to reflect that he himself has both 'despised' and envied the British Asian men openly involved with 'mini-skirtit' white women in Glasgow: 'he'd wantit tae . . . huv his ane long-legged, thin-waisted goree tae wave like a white flag at the world' (7). Sal's simultaneous need both to integrate into, and to detach himself from, white society recalls Karim's position in Kureishi's *Buddha*: 'we pursued English roses as we pursued England; by possessing these prizes, this kindness and beauty, we stared defiantly in the eye of the Empire and all its self-regard . . . We became part of England . . . yet proudly stood outside it.'[61] Shifting from England in the 1970s and 1980s to twenty-first-century Scotland, Saadi updates these ambivalent sentiments towards white women, while suggesting that little has changed.

His fictionalised British Asians retain a similar blend of pride, anger, and self-loathing, figured by the image of surrender implied by Sal's 'white flag'.[62] As we saw in the Introduction, it makes sense to read Saadi's stories as responding intertextually to Kureishi's work since he has specifically acknowledged the older writer's influence.[63]

Saadi offers an ultimately pessimistic, decidedly non-utopian vision of interracial relationships, which provide no easy solutions to the complex negotiations of identity and belonging facing young British Asians. He is nevertheless more positive about such relationships when they are confined to white men and British Asian women, perhaps because such a position allows him to contest traditional Western norms of female beauty as white by celebrating the glamour of South Asian women.[64] Yet interracial relationships which concern second-generation women seem no more likely to succeed than those of British Asian men. In Atima Srivastava's novel *Looking for Maya* (1999), Mira's relationship with Luke, her white boyfriend, is a failure, as is that of Parvin with Martin in *Émigré Journeys*. Across British Asian literature, then, interracial alliances are just as inevitable – and potentially just as bleak – for the second generation as they are for postwar South Asian immigrants. Despite the bid by such writers as Kureishi and Khan-Din to create a new, biracial national blueprint, the sometimes difficult realities of racial mixing itself are handled in a cautious, measured way by the majority of British Asian authors. They suggest that, although the social conditions and attitudes governing such relationships have improved since the 1940s, little has changed at the personal level. Interracial unions may be commonplace in these works, but they remain fraught and their chances of survival are no more certain than they were for a postwar, immigrant generation.

Interracial Intimacy in South Asian American Literature

THE FIRST GENERATION

Unlike the largely ambivalent, even critical, attitude of much British Asian literature, a significantly broader range of responses to miscegenation informs South Asian American writing. At one end of the spectrum, Kavita Daswani rules out interracial marriage entirely for Anju, the protagonist of her novel *For Matrimonial Purposes* (2003). Instead, a particular diasporic order is established when Anju marries Rohan, a second-generation Indian American from the same ethnic background (Sindhi) as herself. Although they marry only after falling in love, this denouement suggests the first generation's need to maintain certain forms of South Asian ethnicity on American soil, and thus to secure a stronger sense of home through religious, linguistic, and cultural familiarity. This can be read alongside Divakaruni's message throughout *Unknown Errors* that specific subcontinental cultures (Bengali in Divakaruni's case) need to be protected and preserved, through arranged marriage, in the US.[65]

Kirin Narayan's novel *Love, Stars, and All That* (1994) also rejects miscegenation through the failure of Gita's marriage to Norvin, a white Jewish American academic, and her eventual choice of Firoze, a fellow South Asian American. In Mohsin Hamid's novel *The Reluctant Fundamentalist* (2007), moreover, the relationship between Changez, a young Pakistani in New York, and Erica, a 'beautiful . . . Wasp [sic] princess', never properly succeeds.[66] In such a heavily allegorical work, this failed romantic bond seems reflective of the protagonist's decision to leave America. In other words, the relationship with Erica – whose name some critics have read as a form of 'America'[67] – would have provided a key means of further connection with Changez's adoptive homeland, thus recalling the symbolic function of interracial relationships as international romances. For James Lasdun, this doomed relationship is 'interestingly free of the racial tensions that traditionally afflict such couples in literature',[68] yet in the novel's one sex scene, Changez performs as a dead white man: it is only by pretending to be Chris, Erica's deceased boyfriend, that she will allow him to make love to her. Apparently prostituting his own cultural and emotional ideals in order to gain sexual experience of white America,[69] it is actually Changez's perception of the costs of mainstream American success which is illustrated here, and his role-playing is also entirely appropriate in a novel which is all about performativity.

Hamid's handling of this interracial relationship consistently implies the fear that cultural identity will be lost through miscegenation. This sense of discomfort among writers and their characters about the loss of ancestral heritage through racial mixing is also apparent throughout Divakaruni's *Unknown Errors*.[70] By contrast, some South Asian American authors suggest the sheer ordinariness of interracial love. Meena Alexander's novel *Manhattan Music* (1997) is a case in point, yet in her autobiography *Fault Lines* (1993), anxiety underlies the apparent normality of miscegenation. Here she recalls the painful memory of her own wedding day in India, with 'countless faces staring in through the barred windows at the blonde [sic] foreigner I was marrying' and absent parents who 'wanted nothing to do with the whole business'.[71] Before creating this strangely carceral image – the bride and groom are, after all, trapped behind 'barred windows' – *Fault Lines* also recollects Alexander's teenage encounter with a South Indian–white Canadian marriage in 1960s Khartoum and its absolute strangeness to her, both culturally and physically, at this point. Tiru's white wife, Chloe, is remembered as 'beautiful' and 'pallid . . . I was fascinated by her looks and wondered what it would be like to live in such a body and have a tall dark man like the Tamilian Tiru drawn to her' (101). Alexander observes how out of place Chloe seems in an all-Indian expatriate context and how infantilised the Canadian woman appears, despite – or perhaps because of – her husband's 'immensely proud' attitude towards her (101). Chloe's cultural discomfort, mirrored by her physical alienness, is only exacerbated when the couple go to India, a version of events relayed in surprisingly violent language. Chloe is 'stunned' by India and 'invaded by nightmares' (101); the couple later 'flee' back to Canada (101), where order is apparently restored, but at the cost of future travel to South Asia.

Like Kureishi, Mukherjee deploys interracial relationships as a consistent leitmotif. In her first novel, *The Tiger's Daughter* (1971), the protagonist, Tara, has effectively ruled herself out of a place in Calcutta society by marrying David, a white American man, while Dimple in Mukherjee's second novel, *Wife* (1975), embarks on an affair with Milt, a white Jewish American. The fact that Dimple cannot sustain this marital infidelity symbolises her disastrous inability to assimilate into mainstream America in a traditional, non-transgressive sense. This abortive relationship is a kind of failed miscegenation, which also presages Changez and Erica in *Reluctant Fundamentalist.* In her later work, Mukherjee explores new immigrant paradigms and changing social patterns through the dynamics of 'the reconstituted family' which ensues through migration.[72] Her interracial ménages imply that the all-American – or white – nuclear family has been overtaken by more ethnically diverse arrangements in which adopted Asian American children and nannies from outside America abound. These tropes are brought together in *Jasmine*,[73] where one might read interracial encounters as indicative of Jasmine's successful relationship with American space, both private and public. Thus, for Jasmine, as for a number of Mukherjee's other South Asian immigrant women, racial mixing is a liberating necessity.[74] The process of physical and biological inscription within the US for such characters also relates to Mukherjee's wider intention of writing India into American culture. Anu Aneja therefore writes that 'Jasmine does her best to insert herself into the flesh and blood of America, to the point where her body is literally impregnated by that of the white man.'[75]

Mukherjee's strategy of depicting interracial relationships and biracial South Asian Americans extends to her novel *The Holder of the World* (1993), where miscegenation is used to incorporate modern South Asian migrants into a longer tradition of immigrant America by emphasising India's position in an era of nascent US imperialism.[76] Fakrul Alam has contended that *Holder* represents Mukherjee's most overtly ambitious attempt at American literary revisionism through its reworking of Nathaniel Hawthorne's *The Scarlet Letter* (1850).[77] Mukherjee challenges this earlier text, moreover, by giving a South Asian father to her version of Hawthorne's Pearl. She also reconfigures seventeenth-century captivity narratives through the notion that Hannah's white mother, Rebecca, willingly becomes involved with a Native American. Such multiple interracial couplings are reflected in the modern-day frame narrative where Beigh, the white narrator, is in love with Dev, a South Asian American scientist. Although Mukherjee's version of miscegenation generally assumes white people as the other half of the equation, her response to them is by no means straightforwardly positive, as I have argued elsewhere.[78]

Amulya Malladi's novel *The Mango Season* (2003) offers a psychologically richer, more radical, and paradoxically more old-fashioned, treatment of interracial relationships than that of any of these other writers. Her protagonist, Priya, fears that there will be absolutely no chance of future acceptance when her family discover that her fiancé, Nick, is both 'American and an un-devout Christian to boot'.[79] At the same time, it is simply not an option for her to repay Nick's love with a failure to tell her family about their plans, and she spends the novel weighing up the different forms of love in question in order to decide whether the risk of sacrificing her family is worth taking. This emotional and moral quandary generates the narrative's principal momentum, and it is Malladi's use of a particularly conservative Indian backdrop – the traditional world of a high-caste family in Hyderabad – which lends this scenario its old-fashioned feel. As with Alexander's autobiographical account of her wedding day and of Tiru and Chloe's disastrous visit to South Asia in *Fault Lines*, and the local rejection of Tara's marriage to David in Mukherjee's *Tiger's Daughter*, the fact that the interracial relationship must be negotiated in India, rather than Britain or America, is arguably crucial in raising the stakes.

Through her unapologetic presentation of the love between Priya and Nick, Malladi suggests, like Mukherjee, that interracial relationships can sometimes result in greater liberation for South Asian women in America. Their union is certainly intended to represent freedom from the suffocatingly narrow version of India embodied by Priya's family, whose racism – namely, a sense of superiority towards Caucasians and an even greater disdain for black people – is cast in an ironic light by the novel's dramatic final twist: Nick is African-American. Even though Narayan includes a brown–black couple, Najma and Noah, in *Love, Stars, and All*

That and before that, the director Mira Nair examined such a relationship in her film *Mississippi Masala* (1991), Nick's racial status still comes as a surprise. The 'presumption of Nick's whiteness', as Anita Mannur has put it,[80] perhaps equates to the overuse of 'American' to mean 'white' in South Asian American literature and to the frequent suggestion in Asian American writing generally that interracial relationships usually concern Caucasians.

On the one hand, this reflects social 'reality';[81] on the other, anti-miscegenation laws in the United States – operative across as many as thirty-one states at various points until as late as 1967 – specifically applied to interracial marriage as it affected white people. As Philip Tajitsu Nash has observed, 'nonwhite races were allowed to mix with each other . . . showing that the true intent of anti-miscegenation statutes was to prevent the diluting of the white gene pool with the blood of allegedly inferior races'.[82] In a traditional American context, then, miscegenation involving a white party has been more radical and dangerous in political terms. The emphasis by South Asian American writers on brown–white coupling may therefore be read as a conscious reaction to – or an unintentional reminder of – America's fraught racial past. Yet it also hints at a certain conservatism behind their handling of this subject: that is, racial mixing as a form of assimilation into the social mobility promised by an old-style (read, 'white') American Dream and thus a move which supports, rather than challenges, white hegemony. One might compare this to critiques of South Asian American political self-interest by such commentators as Vijay Prashad,[83] but it is worth remembering that there is still public discomfort in America about brown–white relationships – as Susan Koshy has shown in her analysis of the Louise Woodward/Eappen family affair in 1997[84] – as well as ongoing resistance to such racial mixing in certain quarters of both South Asian America and South Asia itself. And it is revealing that, by and large, British Asian writers draw on the same brown–white template in their treatments of interracial intimacy.

INTERRACIAL ROMANCES FOR A POST-1965 AMERICAN-BORN GENERATION

Certain South Asian American novelists – Lahiri and Sameer Parekh, for example – directly address first-generation fears about the interracial relationships of their children, born in the US following the liberalisation of immigration laws in 1965. In his novel *Stealing the Ambassador* (2002), Parekh addresses the reactionary stance of many Indian American parents towards the prospect of brown–white marriage. Not coincidentally, perhaps, the relationship of Rajiv, the protagonist, with his white girlfriend, Anne, breaks down. Yet it would be reductive to suggest that in transatlantic South Asian literature, a hidebound, judgemental, and humourless first generation always rejects the idea of its children marrying non-South Asians, just as it is clearly a cliché to suggest that an interracial relationship will straightforwardly resolve the second generation's cultural and ontological dilemmas: a strategy persistently favoured in South Asian diasporic cinema and an idea to which I will return in a moment.

Rather as interracial relationships are not confined to the second generation within South Asian Atlantic writing, so an intraracial union is also no guarantee of happiness. Some parents may even welcome the prospect of an exogamous marriage for their offspring. Thus, in Lahiri's *Namesake*, Ashoke and Ashima warn Gogol about 'Bengali men . . . who've married [white] Americans, marriages that have ended in divorce',[85] yet in the same novel Moushumi finds that her plans to marry Graham, a white American, are greeted with less parental disapproval than she had expected. Nevertheless, it is telling that this marriage never actually takes place. Similarly, none of Gogol's relationships with Caucasian women ultimately succeeds. In particular, Maxine's white privilege, unconsidered and uncontested, fails to accommodate his cultural background, thus recalling Eleanor's self-absorbed attitude towards Karim's history in Kureishi's *Buddha:* a novel which provided an important early influence for Lahiri, as I argued in the Introduction to this book.[86] Again like Kureishi, Lahiri suggests the relative scarcity of enduring sexual relationships of any kind: inter- or intra-racial. Gogol's marriage to Moushumi is, after all, short-lived and disastrous.

Unaccustomed Earth, Lahiri's most recent work of fiction, replaces her earlier focus on the limits and perils of interracial relationships with a more matter-of-fact, even optimistic, approach. This recalls the shift from pessimism to acceptance of miscegenation in the work of other Asian American writers, such as the Korean American novelist Chang-rae Lee and the Chinese American author Gish Jen. While one should not rely on easy autobiographical explanations, the subject of racial mixing is of direct relevance to such writers: as with Mukherjee and Alexander, Lee, Jen, and Lahiri have all made interracial marriages and become the parents of biracial children. Several of the stories anthologised in *Unaccustomed Earth* ('Hell-Heaven', 'A choice of accommodations', 'Nobody's business', 'Only goodness', 'Unaccustomed earth') assume the inescapability of such alliances, taking for granted the birth of a new generation of mixed-race children to whom the first generation, now grandparents, respond lovingly.

Overall, then, South Asian writers in the US veer from an outright prohibition on interracial relationships – predicated upon a traditionally pessimistic vision of their difficulties (miscegenation as social 'problem') and a drive towards cultural survival – to a sense of their inevitability and finally to a tentative, sometimes outright, celebration of their possibilities. Their response to this subject is arguably fuller and more complex than that of British Asian writers, perhaps because of the longer and more troubled history of miscegenation in the United States and because of its status as an American social reality and central component within US racial thinking. To tackle the issue of interracial relationships appears to be an equal necessity, however, for South Asian diasporic writers on both sides of the Atlantic.

Racial Mixing in South Asian Diasporic Cinema

The South Asian American director Krutin Patel has contended that his film *ABCD* (1999) is

> a cautionary tale for young Indians in the sense that Nina's decision [to marry her white boyfriend] . . . will come back to haunt her . . . At the end of the film there is [the] potential for happiness . . . It's [about] the repercussions of buying into the American Dream wholesale instead of customising it to your needs.[87]

Patel's notion that marriage to a white person is 'buying into the American Dream wholesale' recalls Fanon's formulations – as well as America's miscegenist history and the question of South Asian American political self-interest – discussed above. Patel does not explain how young South Asian Americans such as Nina and Raj, the film's sister-and-brother protagonists, might actually go about 'customising [the American Dream] . . . to . . . [their] needs', and when he speaks of the 'potential for happiness', his implied optimism is undercut by such words as 'cautionary' and 'haunt'. One might argue, then, that – as with certain literary works – Patel's statement casts interracial couplings, and the quest for a more secure American identity that they seem to imply, in an ultimately negative light.

However ambiguous it may remain in his own mind, however, the ending to Patel's film corresponds to other recent films about the South Asian diaspora from both sides of the Atlantic in that a brown–white relationship provides dramatic resolution. Indeed, whether they save the day – acting as a kind of social, cultural, and narrative panacea – or offer a more ambivalent form of closure, interracial relationships appear to be thematically central. In the UK, such films include Damien O'Donnell's

East is East (1999), his highly successful screen adaptation of Khan-Din's play, which crucially embeds biracial British Asians within the popular consciousness and is in fact one of the few films about South Asian diasporic communities to consider the next stage of an interracial relationship; Jeremy Wooding's *Bollywood Queen* (2002); Gurinder Chadha's commercial hits *Bend It Like Beckham* (2002) and *Bride and Prejudice* (2004); Ken Loach's *Ae Fond Kiss* (2004); Dominic Savage's *Love + Hate* (2005); and Penny Woolcock's *Mischief Night* (2006).[88]

Unlike South Asian diasporic literature, which is often published by small presses and which, as we have seen, is more likely to problematise interracial encounters, films such as *East is East* and *Bend It Like Beckham* have – like Kureishi's *My Beautiful Laundrette* in the 1980s – reached large audiences, generating an appetite for British Asian cultural productions based upon particular representations. One might argue that these mainly white-directed films deploy brown–white couplings to make their ideas and storylines more relevant – and economically viable – to a wider audience, much as Hollywood cinema has traditionally made ubiquitous use of black–white buddy pairings.[89] This question of the box office is significant. In contrast to the commercial success of British Asian films, South Asian American cinema – generally characterised by a greater number of low-key, independent works than mainstream hits – has proved more conservative on interracial matters. This is exemplified by such films as Piyush Dinker Pandya's *American Desi* (2001), Anurag Mehta's *American Chai* (2002), Bala Rajasekharuni's *Green Card Fever* (2003), and Bob Roe's *Dancing in Twilight* (2004; written by Rishi Vij), all of which explicitly favour intra-Indian sexual relationships over interracial ones. Possibly this forms part of a bid to target South Asian diasporic audiences specifically.

Other British Asian and South Asian American films challenge interracial stereotypes by rejecting a heteronormative or brown–white pattern. Homosexual relationships feature in Nisha Ganatra's American movie *Chutney Popcorn* (1999); Harmage Singh Kalirai's British production *Chicken Tikka Masala* (2005); and Pratibha Parmar's Scottish Indian film *Nina's Heavenly Delights* (2006). Since *My Beautiful Laundrette* focused on gay racial mixing well before any of these films, it is again hard to ignore Kureishi's influence on later South Asian diasporic artists in both the US and Britain.[90] As we have seen, Nair's well-known film *Mississippi Masala* depicts a brown–black couple, as do Stephen Frears's 1987 film of *Sammy and Rosie* (through Rani and Vivia's lesbian relationship); Chadha's first UK feature *Bhaji on the Beach* (1994); and *Guru in Seven* (1997), a film by the British Asian director Shani Grewal.

These films make clear that for South Asians, a greater taboo surrounds brown–black sexual relationships than brown–white ones. Indeed, in *Mississippi Masala*, such alliances are acceptable only if they remain platonic or professional. Once the relationship between Mina, the South Asian immigrant protagonist, and Demetrius, her African American lover, is discovered, the Indian community closes ranks, while some of Demetrius's black friends and colleagues are equally censorious. The public scandal of Mina and Demetrius's relationship reveals the claustrophobic nature of contemporary racial divisions within their Mississippi town, while a courtroom scene connected to violent events provoked by their affair recalls the South's history of anti-miscegenist legislation.

The message of Nair's film is that this particular South Asian American community – obsessed with tradition and the past, whether in India or Uganda – must refresh itself through miscegenation. Handsome, morally irreproachable, and deeply respectable, Demetrius partly recalls John Wade Prentice, Sidney Poitier's character in Stanley Kramer's film *Guess Who's Coming to Dinner* (1967); and he represents a much more appealing prospect than any of the South Asian men Mina meets. For all the boldness of its interracial pairing, then, the film rather unsubtly pits the idealistic promise of racial mixing against the apparent inadequacies of intra-ethnic relationships, literally cutting between love scenes concerning Anil and Chanda, an Indian married couple, and Mina and Demetrius to contrast the failed intimacy of a sexless, arranged marriage with the electrical erotic charge made possible through interracial passion.[91]

Crucial in terms of the development of South Asian diasporic cinema, *Mississippi Masala* is now twenty years old. Two much more recent American box office hits, the white-directed 'Harold and Kumar' comedies – Danny Leiner's *Harold and Kumar Go to White Castle* (2004) and Jon Hurwitz and Hayden Schlossberg's *Harold and Kumar Escape from Guantanamo Bay* (2008) – seek to make new points about interracial relationships. Challenging stereotypes of Asian Americans as model minorities – especially through Kumar, the South Asian American 'slacker' protagonist – the films draw, playfully and intertextually, on a range of tropes from earlier film comedies, from Gene Saks's *The Odd Couple* (1968) and Woody Allen's *Annie Hall* (1977) to the 'gross-out' antics of the Farrelly Brothers' work in the 1990s.

In an almost post-ethnic sense, both films take interracial relationships entirely for granted. Whether these relationships are expressed through the sparring intimacy between Kumar and Harold, a Korean American – a new kind of interracial buddy pairing, which is not black–white, but intra-Asian, thus incorporating South Asian Americans into a wider Asian American fold[92] – or through the men's trouble-free sexual encounters with women, presented as exclusively Caucasian or Latina, neither man agonises over the social, cultural, or familial costs of such partnerships. Rather than emphasising the dramatic possibilities of an interracial sexual encounter, we are offered what Sukhdev Sandhu has seen as the 'guiltless' potential that such relationships – and, perhaps more importantly here, an alternative interracial buddy pairing – can offer the second generation.[93] The 'Harold and Kumar' films thus cater to mainstream audiences even as they contest stereotypical expectations.[94] But, as with many films about British Asians, their idealised treatment of miscegenation, through the erasure of any problematic associations it might still possess, may be explained, in part, by the fact that each film is written and directed by a team of white artists.

The Trope of Mixed-Race Identity in British Asian Literature

Beyond the 'Harold and Kumar' series, films by or about diasporic South Asians are more often concerned with the narrative trajectory of what one might call 'the road to marriage': that is, the young protagonist's securing of a 'successful' match, rather than the story of their actual experience of matrimony. This phrase might be adapted for the purposes of this discussion to 'the road to *interracial* marriage' or indeed, 'co-habitation'. As we have seen, the interracial relationship (usually heterosexual), and its temporary survival, rather than its long-term future or the children it might produce, are the object of dramatic attention in such films as *Mississippi Masala*, *ABCD*, *Bend It Like Beckham*, and *Ae Fond Kiss*. Perhaps the social, psychological, and artistic implications of a new mixed-race generation are simply too complex for the kinds of simplistically utopian 'happy endings' such films attempt.

Such thematic strategies also characterise transatlantic South Asian writing, with authors similarly reluctant to address the wider cultural and material consequences of miscegenation. Where racially mixed characters do appear, they tend very often to be children, consigned to incidental roles. In the US, this applies to Dora in Alexander's *Manhattan Music*; the quarter-white, blue-eyed, unnamed sons in Divakaruni's 'The names of stars in Bengali' (*Unknown Errors*); and the babies and toddlers of Lahiri's new biracial generation in *Unaccustomed Earth*. In British Asian works, this point is illustrated through Laxman's son, Roy, and unnamed daughter in Markandaya's *Nowhere Man*; and in Nadeem Aslam's novel *Maps for Lost Lovers* (2004) by Charag's young mixed-race son, who is also nameless, as though, like the examples above, his individual being comes after the role he plays in symbolising the assimilation by his minority parent into the white mainstream. Aslam humorously refers to the lexical uncertainty regarding the boy's racial status through the statement that he is '"half Pakistani and half . . . er . . . er . . . er . . . human" – or so a child on his [white] English mother's side is reported to have described him in baffled groping innocence'.[95] Kaukab, the boy's Pakistani immigrant grandmother, meanwhile sees him as the harbinger of a distant British future in which all trace of her family's South Asian ancestry will have been wiped out. In Ardashir Vakil's novel *One Day* (2003), the racially mixed figure of Whacka may be more fully realised, yet he is still an infant rather than an older child with his own distinct voice.

In view of the long tradition of racially mixed Americans and Britons, and specifically of biracial people in South Asia, one wonders how to account for this depiction of mixed-race characters as children: a move which represents them as a new phenomenon, while quite literally infantilising them. It is also not confined to racially mixed South Asians, since Cynthia Nakashima complains that 'mixed-race people usually appear in Asian American discourse as children . . . certainly not as empowered adults . . . In reality, a lot of us are all grown up.'[96] One reason for this tendency may be that many South Asian diasporic authors draw, perhaps inevitably, on their own individual experience. As we have seen, although not usually of mixed race themselves, they often have biracial children. The subject therefore remains one of compelling personal and social interest to them, yet it is too much of an imaginative leap to follow through the experiential and ontological implications of being, in Amal Treacher's words, 'a different colour from both [one's] . . . parents, who in turn are a different colour from each other'.[97]

Other artistic examples, particularly from American literature, may offer a further explanation. The *métis* son of Fleur Pillager, the Native American protagonist, in Louise Erdrich's novel *Four Souls* (2006), suffers from an unspecified mental disability and is essentially nameless, since he lacks an all-important tribal name; while Mitt, Henry's half-Korean, half-Anglo son in Chang-rae Lee's novel *Native Speaker* (1995), experiences an early, accidental death at the hands of neighbourhood children in a supposedly 'safe', predominantly white, suburb in the northeastern United States. Erdrich and Lee deploy such strategies – namelessness or unusual naming (as Markandaya, Divakaruni, and Aslam do); disability; or early death – to ask whether there is a place in American society for racially mixed children and indeed to underscore the limitations of the interracial alliances that produced them. The burdens borne by both Mitt and Fleur's son are thus a figurative means of suggesting that America – and we may extend this to Britain – is still not ready for racially mixed people. In all of these cases, then, the especial vulnerability of biracial children, rather than adults, powerfully reinforces the traditionally liminal, threatened position of the mixed-race subject.[98] By contrast, however, Caroline Rody reads this device in rather more positive terms, suggesting that in recent Asian American fiction more widely, the racially mixed child is 'the horizon of the book's interethnic vision, the locus of its hopes'.[99]

If, as I am arguing here, biracial South Asian characters remain children because of the difficult existential questions posed by their coming of age – both to authors and to the societies they examine – it is apparently left to writers who are themselves racially mixed to address such questions. Thus Kureishi, Khan-Din, Kunzru, Niven Govinden, Helen Walsh, and Zadie Smith remain among the few British writers to examine the personal costs of being mixed-race.[100] Kureishi has in fact been the principal British chronicler of mixed-race South Asian identity since the mid-1980s, yet existing critical work has focused little on this theme within his work; since I have already considered this subject at length elsewhere,[101] I will not, however, examine it here.

In *East is East*, Khan-Din explicitly considers the difficult territory negotiated by the biracial Khans as the children of George, a Pakistani father, and Ella, their white British mother. Openly critical of 'English' family practices, George refers to his seven children as Ella's when rebuking their apparent godlessness, but reclaims his paternal rights whenever his authority is challenged.[102] And each child has a Muslim name. In debating how to refer to themselves, the Khan children in fact run through various terms from 'half-caste', 'Paki', 'English', and 'Pakistani' to 'Anglo-Indian' and 'Eurasian', with Maneer recalling the idea, discussed above, of language's inbuilt failure to express racial hybridity when he asserts that 'we're not Anglo-Indian, not Eurasian and not English'.[103]

Kunzru's *Impressionist* imagines South Asian miscegenation in an early twentieth-century Indian and British context, offering an ambitious British contribution to literature about Anglo-Indians. The orphaned, transnational protagonist's chameleonic status is most obviously represented by his changing names, so that the reader is never sure how to refer to him and, like Mukherjee's Jasmine, he is usually named by other people. The child of a British colonialist and a privileged Indian woman, he is first 'Pran Nath Razdan', allegedly the scion of a wealthy Agra family, before becoming 'Rukhsana', a teenage, transvestite prostitute; then in Bombay, he is 'Robert' and 'Chandra' to the Reverend Andrew and Mrs Elspeth Macfarlane respectively, as he assists Macfarlane with his experiments in racial 'craniometry' (part of Kunzru's merciless, obsessive satire of scientific racism, which later extends to anthropology, zoology, and botany). He is also 'Pretty Bobby', an errand-runner for brothels in the city's red light district; and finally, in a flagrant piece of identity theft, he is 'Jonathan Bridgeman', a British orphan with links to India, who moves from an English public school to Oxford in the 1920s. Since the protagonist is known as 'Jonathan' more than any other name, I will use it to refer to him here.[104]

Caste-obsessed Indians abhor Jonathan's 'mixed blood', but he is no safer among Anglo-Indians, who look down on 'natives' but are themselves scorned as 'horrid blackie-whites' by the British (46). This racial hierarchy operates according to a strict chromatic taxonomy, whereby to have 'skin the colour of a manila envelope' (47) or 'parchment' (42) ensures only a provisional degree of social status. Anglo-Indians fervently wish to escape the 'clinging swamp of blackness' (48) by steering clear of the sun, which they avoid '*like the plague*, feeling pain with every production of melanin . . . Of course they do not call it that. They have other names. *Dirt, grubbiness*' (47; emphasis added). Their Indian 'half' – 'half-baked bread' (43) and 'half-and-half' (52) are only some of the terms within the rich miscegenist lexicon Jonathan encounters[105] – is as much associated with disease and contamination for them as miscegenation itself appears to be for fastidious 'pure' Indians such as the protagonist's putative father, Amar Nath.

Much of the novel's suspense is generated by its reworking of the racial 'passing' narrative. Unlike Indians or 'blackie-whites', many white people believe Jonathan is 'one of them' (185) and to pass as white becomes a game.[106] But he, too, is fooled by other 'half-and-half' people posing as white when he is drawn to the beautiful socialite Lily Parry, who immediately sees through him and angrily rejects his advances. Members of a secret society in that their racially mixed origins must remain hidden, Lily and Jonathan are epidermally whiter than so-called 'white' people;[107] while, in his urgent need to pass, Kunzru's protagonist is a 'mimic man', whose colonial identity confusion owes a debt to Naipaul's eponymous novel. The sometimes bold, sometimes uncertain stages of his personal reinvention are narrated as an ongoing process through the text's use of the present tense, a device which can almost obscure the fact that the novel is a work of historical fiction. Indeed, this becomes a further piece of imposture in a narrative already consumed by notions of illusion and fraud. The present tense – 'beguilingly cinematic . . . [yet] tiresome', for one reviewer[108] – is also about Jonathan's continuing need both to conceal and to forget his own past. Further exposed to white supremacist attitudes in Britain, he becomes increasingly racist and reminiscent of the 'blackie-whites' who disdained him in India. Although he is largely complicit in British imperialism, it is Jonathan's so-called 'tainted blood' – and the gradually dawning insight into the lives of subject peoples that this finally allows him – which ultimately saves him in the novel's final episode: a doomed British anthropological mission to west Africa.

Khan-Din's second play, *Last Dance at Dum Dum* (1999), updates the Anglo-Indian story by showing elderly members of the community, living quite separately from modern India as they desperately cling to their communal home in 1980s Calcutta. Proudly Indian, they are nonetheless tangled up in a web of prejudices towards both other Indians and the British, who have ignored their rights post-1947, and they feel the need to trade on their former status, however ambiguous that was. Thus Muriel recalls being talent-spotted alongside Merle Oberon, the famous film star of Anglo-Indian origin. Muriel's husband, Bertie, meanwhile highlights the discrimination of Indian doctors towards Anglo-Indians when he recalls that 'one . . . said [dementia] . . . was a problem "inherent in people of mixed blood" ',[109] while Daphne and Elliot bring together old stereotypical associations of mixed-race people with fornication and prostitution, rather as *Impressionist* does.[110] At the same time, the group's elderly status and Muriel's very real mental deterioration symbolise the growing obsolescence of Anglo-Indians (now a large overseas community) in India itself.

To be officially 'Anglo-Indian', one's patrilineal descent must be white British: a reversal of the background of Kureishi, Khan-Din, Kunzru, and Monica Ali, and of the miscegenist patterns generally at work within British Asian writing. Indeed, transatlantic South Asian cultural production challenges the gender dynamic of the white man–woman of colour which has characterised interracial romances in a traditional British and US imperial context,[111] instead suggesting a much more even split. It is perhaps unsurprising, then, that Manzoor has claimed that British Asian writers 'credited with telling typically Asian stories' are often those 'with the Asian name and white partner who . . . [are] more interested in exploring the life of their Asian fathers than their white mother'.[112] This suggests that if contemporary biracial writers wish to pass as anything, it is as ethnic South Asians, and that the 'brown' side of their ancestry is more exciting and glamorous than the 'white'. This status has nevertheless often been predetermined by paternal nomenclature, since 'Hanif Kureishi', 'Ayub Khan-Din', and 'Hari Kunzru' immediately foreground the writer's South Asian ancestry.[113] As with the gender pattern of interracial relationships in a white colonial setting, mixed-race people have also been subject to gender stereotyping, particularly in US culture: as female and, most notably, as the 'tragic mulatta'.[114] Within a British context, Khan-Din, Kunzru, and, above all, Kureishi challenge this assumption through their creation of a cast of biracial British Asian men.

Mixed-Race Lives in South Asian American Writing

Whereas the biracial status of such literary figures as Kureishi, Kunzru, and Ali has almost come to seem synonymous with British Asian writing, there are fewer high-profile, mixed-race authors of South Asian descent in the US. Such racially mixed South Asian American writers as Kirin Narayan,[115] Sara Suleri, and Carmit Delman remain relatively unusual and are less prolific or well recognised than Mukherjee, Alexander, Lahiri, or Divakaruni. Delman has published fewer literary works – and to less commercial and critical acclaim – than these predominantly first-generation, Bengali American women writers, while Suleri and Narayan are better known for their academic work; and in Narayan's one novel, *Love, Stars, and All That*, Gita, the Indian American protagonist, is not biracial.

As with certain British Asian writers – for instance, Saadi in his short story 'The dancers' (2001) – some South Asian American authors write mixed-race adult identity imaginatively: for instance, in such novels as Ameena Meer's *Bombay Talkie* (1994), Indira Ganesan's *Inheritance* (1998), and Shobhan Bantwal's *The Sari Shop Widow* (2009).[116] In *Bombay Talkie*, Rani – the US-raised daughter of an Indian mother and a white American father – moves to India and marries a local man, Hemant, even though she is viewed with suspicion as 'a cheap Anglo-Indian',[117] thus anticipating the anti-miscegenist attitudes, prevalent in both colonial and contemporary India, later evoked by Khan-Din and Kunzru. Rejected by both Hemant and his family, Rani meets a ghastly fate when she is burned to death in a marital fight, and indeed it becomes difficult to disentangle her tragic demise from the apparent problems – social, cultural, and existential – posed by her mixed descent within Indian society. At the same time, as a fashion model, whose picture is on Delhi billboards for all to see, Rani ironically comes to represent a particular version of India: an ideal of Indian beauty, even.

In *Inheritance*, the biracial teenaged protagonist, Sonil, is presented as choosing one side over the other although she has in fact never met her white American father and barely knows Lakshmi, her South Asian mother. Growing up in India and Pi, an invented island north of Sri Lanka, the protagonist claims that 'Sonil [is] . . . a name with no definite roots' and that 'where my mother was a beauty, I was ugly, a changeling child, a half-breed, a mistake . . . I wanted to be . . . boasted of, scolded . . . My identity was lost, and I did not know who I was.'[118] Standard adolescent identity confusion is further complicated here by Sonil's sense of maternal rejection and an overheard language of distaste towards racially mixed people.

Later, Sonil situates the specificities of her mixed heritage by bringing America into the equation – 'I must have appeared strange, half brown, half white, without actually having the cachet of having been to America' (59) – and, more importantly, by referencing Pi's history of miscegenation. Her already uncertain racial status is complicated by her affair with Richard, a white American tourist, who, like her unnamed white father, represents fantasy and escape. Richard forces her to consider the possibility that, through their relationship, she is 'choosing white over brown' (98). If there is a question of choosing one 'side' over another – a somewhat simplistic proposition to begin with, as is Ganesan's discourse of an ontologically 'lost' biracial protagonist – *Inheritance* clearly shows Sonil privileging her matrilineal Indian ancestry.

As I argued in Chapter 1, the Britishness of Rishi Shah in Bantwal's *Sari Shop Widow* initially makes him an object of mistrust for South Asian Americans, a situation potentially exacerbated by his mixed South Asian–white descent. His ethno-cultural appropriateness as a possible marriage partner for Anjali Kapadia, the novel's Gujarati American protagonist, is, however, ensured through his 'purely Gujarati name'[119] and through his rejection of Samantha, a white woman, in favour of an Indian bride: Anjali. Bantwal nevertheless does little to explore Rishi's biracial subjectivity, perhaps because – as I suggested of his British status in Chapter 1 – it is of principally symbolic importance. This background makes him seem appealingly mysterious and complex and allows him to pass as white. He therefore emerges as a more intriguing proposition, for Anjali at any rate, than Gujarati American men: an apparently known quantity in the book's New Jersey context. Rather as I contended earlier of interracial alliances in South Asian Atlantic cinema, Rishi's white lineage seems to offer a Caucasian audience easier entry into the narrative, although Bantwal's characterisation of white people remains superficial through, for instance, the caricatured presentation of Samantha and of Kip, Anjali's ex-boyfriend.

Unlike such writers as Kureishi and Gish Jen, Mukherjee rarely discusses her mixed-race children in her writing or interviews, and rather than examining the life-world of racially mixed characters, she focuses far more on interracial relationships. The deferred birth of Jasmine's mixed-race child beyond the end of the eponymous novel is one case in point.

Yet biracial people do populate Mukherjee's work. Once again, a number are infants or older children: Shawn Patel in the short story 'Saints' (*Darkness* [1985]); Eng, a half-Vietnamese, half-white girl in 'Fathering' (*The Middleman and Other Stories* [1988]); and Hannah's daughter Pearl in *Holder of the World*. The adult status of the biracial protagonists, Ratna in 'The world according to Hsü' (*Darkness*) and Devi in the novel *Leave It to Me* (1997), is therefore exceptional. Like Rani in *Bombay Talkie*, both are used to reinscribe older associations of mixed-race people with ideas of rootlessness: another side to mobility's liberating potential in her work.

Mukherjee suggests that neither Devi nor Ratna, whose 'Indian' side is 'dominant',[120] will easily find a home in either India or North America. Brought up as 'Debby' by Italian American adoptive parents, Devi later discovers that she is actually multiracial, since her biological father is of mixed Asian descent. Claiming that adoption allows her to 'imagine myself into any life',[121] she signals the shifting identities made possible by her mixed descent, and indeed her changes in name anticipate Jonathan's in *Impressionist*. Yet she is also envious of those who 'knew what they were . . . no evasions, no speculations' (66). Mukherjee may celebrate 'mongrelisation' but her treatment of both Ratna and Devi presents a more complex and unsettling picture.

Delman's memoir *Burnt Bread and Chutney* (2002) offers a more extended, subjective account of a mixed South Asian American heritage than either Mukherjee or Ganesan. The narrative traces a very particular biracial background and can be situated in relation to other literary works about the South Asian Jewish diaspora, for instance Shelley Silas's British play *Calcutta Kosher* (2004). Marking the gendered nature of much South Asian American writing, the vanishing traditions of Delman's maternal, Indian Jewish lineage are favoured over those of her Ashkenazi Jewish paternal forebears. The story of European Jewry is, of course, far better known than that of India's Jews. Delman feels a greater sense of physical belonging among ethnic South Asians than among white American Jews, although the ignorance of Indian Americans about India's Jewish history estranges her from them. As she puts it: 'the connection to just India was not enough to stand alone between shy [Indian American] girls. How could I explain to them all I learned in Torah class? They had not even heard of Indian Jews.'[122]

Delman's memoir is an original contribution to the better-known arenas of Jewish and Asian American writing. But rather than aligning it to broader Asian American constituencies, she is more interested in the preservation of her matrilineal heritage and the issue of her own mixed-race Jewishness. Delman is not the first biracial American writer to shore up the claims of non-white Jews to Jewishness.[123] It is nonetheless unusual to find discussions of mixed-race Jewishness in the context of South Asian miscegenation. *Burnt Bread* repeatedly points out that to be seen as 'authentically' Jewish by other Jews in both America and Israel, one must be white. Delman's darker skin clearly challenges this assumption: a status only complicated further, not least in ontological terms, by her part-white descent and by many white American Jews' denial of a specifically Jewish history of racial mixing.

Delman relates her own complex position to that of her parents' interracial marriage, in which 'my father was seen by the Indian side as a prized token of the white people, and my mother, in his circles, could be eyed coolly, because she was not Ivy League-polished and cardigan-clad' (xxii). In Israel, Delman encounters white Israelis who assume that she must be part of the 'large populations of poorer Jewish immigrants from the African and Arab nations' living in deprived areas (162). Explaining that she is 'Indian', she notes that 'to identify myself, I had to clarify what it was that made my skin brown. No matter that I was just as much white' (163). Like Ratna in 'World according to Hsü', but unlike Jonathan in *Impressionist*, her white 'half' – which could become expedient in the face of white racism – seems invisible to those around her, whether Israeli or ethnically South Asian, Gentile or white Jewish American. Delman's privileging of her Indian heritage may also stem from an internalisation of this reaction to her liminal status, which is too complex to be explained easily. Yet this painful, complicated past drives her memoir, since she derives urgency, authority, and creative power from her occupation of a putatively 'outsider' role.

Conclusion

On either side of the Atlantic, miscegenation is a dominant trope within South Asian cultural production, but the theme of interracial relationships is still more prevalent than that of mixed-race identity. Such relationships, among both the first and second generation, are presented as important, inevitable, and often problematic, but they are handled more ambivalently in British Asian than in South Asian American writing. Yet even when South Asian writers in the US offer a celebratory perspective, more troubling issues emerge. Transatlantic South Asian film-makers represent this idea in a more straightforwardly utopian light, perhaps to meet the commercially driven need for a formulaic 'happy ending', while white film-makers like Ken Loach and Damien O'Donnell risk problems of appropriation and inauthenticity when they approach the topic of

South Asian miscegenation. Interracial alliances are nevertheless consistently thematised within cinematic works about the South Asian diaspora – where the individual passion they represent is used, Romeo and Juliet-style, to examine and superficially to resolve thorny social divisions – while in recent television dramas, particularly in the UK, they occur seamlessly and without explicit comment. In both cases, however, such relationships are handled somewhat simplistically because they are devoid of the longer-term problems – what Andrew Anthony has called 'the messy, difficult and tense business of living and loving together'[124] – which might haunt such relationships.

Whereas interracial unions, especially where they concern white people, can suggest conservatism through assimilation into the socio-cultural mainstream, the racially mixed subject remains a more radical and difficult theme in transatlantic South Asian literature. For such writers as Lahiri, Vakil, and Aslam, however, biracial people remain children: a strategy which works to contain the social threat mixed-race characters might pose and minimises the ontological and existential questions they continue to embody, or, in Lewis Gordon's words, 'the unique experience of living the racial realities of more than one group in the course of their innermost private lives'.[125] Other writers – for instance, Mukherjee, Kunzru, and Ganesan – do show mixed-race characters in adulthood, but they reinscribe certain stereotypes, especially the 'tragic mulatto' and the myth of biracial rootlessness.[126] For some of these writers – and various others discussed earlier, such as Markandaya and Alexander – absence of the lived experience of what it means to be mixed-race inevitably comes into play, although such writers are themselves often committed to long-term interracial relationships and have racially mixed children.

That Kunzru's portrayal of Jonathan in *Impressionist* is nonetheless subtle and wide-ranging makes it tempting to attribute his ambitious vision of biracial selfhood to his own mixed descent. Certainly, it appears to be racially mixed South Asian Atlantic writers – for instance, Kureishi, Delman, and Khan-Din – who offer the most sustained and complex accounts of mixed-race lives, drawing on the creative strength afforded by their own position. It is in their work that we witness such tropes as passing, double consciousness,[127] self-naming, the pragmatic forging of situational ethnic affiliations, and the importance of colour itself. Kureishi and Kunzru, in particular, draw attention to the protean physical possibilities of being biracial by creating characters who are simultaneously dark and light, brown and white. This highlights the opportunities for personal reinvention afforded to 'multiracial people . . . [whose] identities might change over a lifetime'.[128] These writers seek to establish a new national model, where to be racially mixed can become the personal and aesthetic ideal, yet this project remains at a fledgling stage and is complicated by a paradox of normality and exceptionalism,[129] because they still present biracial status as a relative rarity and because each character's particular mixed background is different in ethnic terms.

Despite the long history of US miscegenation and, even more pertinently, of Anglo-Indians in the subcontinent, the biracial people examined in these works are conceived as a largely new phenomenon in British and American terms, a discrete incarnation of Mukherjee's 'thing new to US history, someone who had never existed before me and hundreds of thousands like me: an Indo-American'.[130] The biracial writers in question thus chart the difficulties of being what Glenn D'Cruz has called the 'new "Anglo-Indians" . . . the current first generation progeny of "mixed marriages" in multicultural societies . . . who must negotiate two separate cultural traditions in order to define themselves'.[131] This may explain their suggestion of the simultaneous pain and opportunity which arises from being mixed-race. The trajectory for Kureishi's characters and for Kunzru's Jonathan Bridgeman appears to be in one main direction, in fact: towards middle-class whiteness. Kureishi deploys humour to handle the more disturbing, confusing elements of this situation, but even though his treatments are significantly removed from traditional anti-miscegenist stereotypes, they ultimately fail to answer older questions or allay earlier fears.[132]

Returning to Alibhai-Brown's point that biracial British Asian writers seem less 'troublingly alien', one might contend that a largely white readership does indeed identify more with a South Asian writer of mixed parentage. But we have also seen that writers may play up their South Asian rather than their white side, both as a result of nomenclature and perhaps because a 'minority' background sells better. There is both novelty and familiarity to miscegenation as artistic material: while brown–white relationships have become a recognisable, even clichéd, device, the biracial subject remains under-explored, and this will continue until a greater number of racially mixed South Asian writers emerges. In recent British Asian and South Asian American cinema, mixed-race identity takes up even less thematic space – with the notable exception of *East is East.*[133] Despite the sometimes difficult questions about British and American multiculturalism posed by such films as *My Beautiful Laundrette* and *Mississippi Masala*, biracial lives are apparently still too messy and complicated a subject to be tackled in any depth.

Delman aside, it is British Asian writers who have really tackled the implications of being mixed-race. This is perhaps paradoxical in view of

America's richer tradition of racial mixing; and it recalls the contention, made in the Introduction to this book, that British Asian writers and film-makers, rather than their US counterparts, have enjoyed a greater cultural impact, both nationally and internationally. The subject of miscegenation highlights yet again the very different relationships of South Asians to Britain and the United States respectively. But whereas the stronger physical presence of South Asians in the UK extends to a more developed literary treatment of biracial identity, South Asian American writers investigate interracial intimacy in more varied ways.

Miscegenation in transatlantic South Asian literature ultimately draws heavily on the utopian/dystopian paradox which has traditionally characterised discussions of this subject. The utopian strand can be explained by the hope and idealism which underpin two interrelated ideas: love's ability to cross racial boundaries – the interracial relationship's 'privileging [of] personal emotions over social systems'[134] – and the concomitant promise of a racially mixed future, embodied by biracial individuals. A correspondingly dystopian response arises, however, because miscegenation evokes primal fears which can be traced, on the white side, to the impact of European imperialism and post-Enlightenment scientific racism. On the South Asian side, this horror of racial mixing goes further back, since it contravenes caste boundaries for Hindus and, if it involves interreligious alliances, breaks rules for the subcontinent's other faiths: Islam, Sikhism, Jainism, Zoroastrianism, Christianity, and Judaism.[135] The utopian/dystopian dichotomy translates into a kind of superiority/inferiority complex for the biracial subject – who simultaneously embodies cultural loss and gain – which in turn corresponds to the divisive combination of fascination and revulsion which interracial encounters have traditionally attracted. In the case of British Asians and South Asian Americans, fear of miscegenation also relates to community worries over the future maintenance of the diaspora itself.

As Susan Benson has argued, 'in . . . a racially divided society . . . the decision to enter into an interracial union is, inevitably, a political act'.[136] In the hands of these creative artists, moreover, miscegenation is both a subversive and a conservative force: subversive because it charts the courage of individuals prepared to face opposition by crossing racial and cultural lines and to reject the safety of tradition, but conservative because such relationships are almost uniformly heterosexual and because they usually rely on white people as the other half of the equation. As Frank Wu contends, 'if intermarriage and the mixed-race movement are to live up to the optimistic claims that they are the future of race relations, they must hold out a greater promise than that . . . a few individuals are able

. . . to ascend to whiteness'.[137] Several decades after they first appeared, *My Beautiful Laundrette* and *Mississippi Masala* still stand out through their contestation of a heterosexual or brown–white miscegenist orthodoxy. Despite its emphasis on simplistically happy endings, cinema has, however, proved more radical than literature in this regard. Thus the brown–black relationship in Malladi's novel *Mango Season* remains a significant anomaly; and gay interracial relationships are even more rarely explored. Within the American context, relationships between South Asians and Native Americans, Latinos, or East Asians in either literature or film appear virtually non-existent. Writers and film-makers on both sides of the Atlantic have, however, challenged the gender dynamics of the Anglo-American imperialist master narrative of miscegenation by often opting for a man of colour–white woman dyad and by rejecting the traditional feminisation of the racially mixed subject. Such departures ensure that, despite its sometimes contentious nature, miscegenation does not become simply another cliché of South Asian diasporic cultural production.

NOTES

1. Lord Beginner, 'Mix up matrimony', included on Ainley and Noblett, *London* [CD]; and compare the vision of the song 'Melting pot' (1969) by the British pop group Blue Mink, where in 'a hundred years or more', Britain will 'turn out coffee-coloured people by the score'; for further information, see n.a., 'Blue Mink'.
2. I will generally deploy the terms 'mixed-race' and 'biracial' for those people with parents from two different racial groups, and 'multiracial' to refer to those of multiply mixed race (that is, from more than two racial backgrounds). Such terms, which will be discussed in greater detail shortly, are inevitably problematic, since they rely on the notion of immutable racial categories and the possibility of so-called racial 'purity'; compare Sollors, *Neither Black*, p. 3.
3. Dawson, *Mongrel Nation*, p. 43.
4. Noblett, Explanatory notes, n.p.
5. Dawson, *Mongrel Nation*, p. 43.
6. Compare Wilson, 'Mixed race', p. 43.
7. According to the 2001 UK census, 'people from South Asian backgrounds were the least likely of the minority ethnic groups to be married to someone from a different ethnic group. Only 6 per cent of Indians, 4 per cent of Pakistanis, and 3 per cent of Bangladeshis had married someone outside the Asian group'; for more information, see n.a., 'Inter-ethnic marriage'. A 1997 report from the UK's Policy Studies Institute claimed, however, that a fifth of Indian and African Asian men in Britain had a

white partner; cited in Ahmed, 'After Obama', p. 26. In the 1991 British census, only 0.1% of the population were of mixed South Asian–white descent; cited in Phoenix and Owen, 'From miscegenation', p. 81. The 2001 census recorded a mere 189,000 Britons of 'White and [South] Asian' origin out of a total population of 58.7 million, while a further category of 'Other Mixed' is likely to include racially mixed British Asians with no known white history; see Bradford, 'Who are', p. 4. As I noted in the Introduction, information for the most recent UK census (2011) is still being collated and falls outside the time period covered by this book.

8. Barnes and Bennett, 'Asian population', p. 9; these figures – which comprise Indians, Pakistanis, Bangladeshis, Sri Lankans, Nepalese, and Bhutanese – are problematic since, like British census information, they also cover interethnic, as well as interracial, mixing and 'do not add [up] to the total population. This is because the detailed Asian groups are tallies of the number of Asian responses rather than the number of Asian respondents. Respondents reporting several Asian groups are counted several times'; ibid. More specifically, however, Lavina Melwani claims that 'nearly 18 percent of births involving an Asian Indian father or mother in 1993 had an interracial spouse'; see Melwani, 'Beyond black'. Clearly, the UK and US figures I have given are also not strictly comparable, since one refers to marriage and the other to the children of interracial unions, but they do seem to suggest a more dominant trend towards South Asian racial mixing in America than in Britain. For general information on Asian American intermarriage and multiraciality across various censuses, see Wu, *Yellow*, pp. 263–4, 287. As we saw in the Introduction, a more detailed statistical analysis of specific ethnoracial groups in the US based on the most recent census data (of 2010) has not yet been published.
9. Compare Mijares, 'You are an Anglo-Indian?', p. 128, where she writes that 'the historical figure of the Eurasian . . . exerts a fascination on the literary imagination of India's writers in excess of the community's impact on Indian reality, past or present'; and see also Weedon, *Identity and Culture*, p. 123.
10. Rushdie, *Imaginary*, p. 394; Mukherjee, 'Imagining', p. 78.
11. Compare Nesrine Malik's attack on this strategy as a default mechanism in British TV dramas about characters of South Asian descent; Malik, 'TV's shorthand'.
12. Alibhai-Brown, 'Curse'. At the same time, Alibhai-Brown has also done much to champion miscegenation in the British context; see Alibhai-Brown, *Mixed Feelings*. When Sarfraz Manzoor later recapitulates many of the points she raises in the article above, he nonetheless includes Alibhai-Brown in his list of 'atypical' British Asian 'writers credited with telling typically Asian stories'; see Manzoor, 'Why do Asian writers'. The question, however, of what constitutes 'typically Asian' remains an open one.
13. Alibhai-Brown, 'Curse'.

14. See Waris Hussein's film *Sixth Happiness* (1997) for consideration of India's Parsis in this context; and for discussions of the Anglo-Indian superiority complex towards other Indians, see Blunt, *Domicile*, pp. 97, 122, 130, 133, and D'Cruz, *Midnight's Orphans*, pp. 157, 206.
15. Kim, *Writing Manhood*, p. 126.
16. I refer here to the alliances between Punjabi Sikh men and Mexican women in early twentieth-century California; for a detailed study of these communities, see Leonard, *Making Ethnic Choices*.
17. Ifekwunigwe, 'Introduction', pp. 9–10; and Rich, 'Half-caste', pp. 73–9.
18. Koshy, *Sexual Naturalisation*, pp. 1, 3–7. For a discussion of the much freer attitude to miscegenation in colonial America, see Nash, 'Hidden history', pp. 10–15.
19. In literary terms, the idea that the 'half-caste' child is a curse to the white parent is played out in, for instance, W. Somerset Maugham's short story 'The force of circumstance' (1926); see Dolley, *Penguin*, pp. 133, 146, 152, 155, and the early stages of Naeem Murr's novel *The Perfect Man* (2006); see also Lowrie, 'Disruptions', pp. 142–3, 145, 147.
20. The sterility imputed to mixed-race people was also countered by antithetical theories of 'hybrid vigour' and the general 'superiority' attributed to having mixed blood; see Sollors, *Neither Black*, pp. 133–5, 139.
21. Critics have also paid tribute to a range of successful, high-profile historical figures, particularly in the UK, who either were of mixed race or made interracial marriages in this period; see, for instance, Alibhai-Brown, *Mixed Feelings*, pp. 30–1, 36.
22. Sui Sin Far, *Mrs Spring Fragrance*, p. 221. Class and economic factors clearly continue to be important to an understanding of miscegenation. As Andrew Anthony has argued of racial diversity in contemporary Britain: 'it's . . . [working-class] people . . . who live cheek by jowl with new arrivals and adapt to rapid change. They are the ones who really embrace people from other countries and cultures by forming relationships and raising children together'; see Anthony, 'How Britain'. In the American context, compare Gordon, *Her Majesty's Other Children*, p. 69.
23. See, for example, Zack, *American Mixed-Race*; Root, *Multiracial Experience*; Kaup and Rosenthal, *Mixing Race*; and Brennan, *Mixed-Race Literature*.
24. Alibhai-Brown, 'It's a colourful world'; and see also Trevor Phillips's claim that 'almost one in 10 British children now lives in a mixed-race family'; cited in Beckford, 'Trevor Phillips'.
25. Compare Hollinger, 'Amalgamation', p. 1365, where he notes that 'miscegenation' sounds like 'mistaken mixture'.
26. As we have seen, such commentators as Rushdie and Mukherjee have reclaimed 'mongrel' in a positive sense, although see also Sollors, 'Can rabbits', pp. 9–19; and Wu, *Yellow*, p. 285. 'Mulatto' is thought to originate from 'mule'; see Sollors, *Neither Black*, pp. 127–8. In a US historical context, such language relates to the idea that slaves were regarded by their owners

as little more than livestock.

27. See Carton, 'Beyond "Cotton Mary'; and compare Woolcock, *Mischief Night*, where Kimberley rejects 'half-caste' in favour of 'dual heritage', a phrase which suggests historical dignity and taps into the contemporary fashion for tracing one's genealogy.
28. I am grateful to Kiran Patel for this phrase. See also Sollors, *Neither Black*, pp. 113–16, 118–25, for a discussion of the 'calculus of colour' behind the 'scientific racialism' of the Enlightenment; and Ifekwunigwe, '(An)Other', p. 330, where a mixed-race interviewee responds to the phrase 'half-caste' by asking 'Half of what? How can one call oneself half of something?' Compare the use of 'eight-anna', a fraction of an already fractional unit of Indian currency, in Kunzru, *Impressionist*, p. 46, to refer to Anglo-Indians; and see Yule and Burnell, *Hobson-Jobson*, p. 32, where the use of 'anna . . . applied colloquially to persons of mixt parentage' is compared to the 'Scotch expression that a person of deficient intellect "wants twopence in the shilling"', thus signalling a revealing slippage between racially mixed people and mental deficiency. By contrast, Lori Harrison-Kahan argues that 'in replacing "half" with "mixed"', the biracial subject 'prioritises . . . plurality . . . over . . . duality'; see Harrison-Kahan, 'Passing for white', p. 44. Yet the notion of 'halves' persists, as we see, for example, through Junot Díaz's use of 'halfie' in a contemporary American context in his short story, 'How to date a browngirl, blackgirl, whitegirl, or halfie'; Díaz, *Drown*, pp. 111–16.
29. Blunt, who writes that 'Anglo-Indians form one of the largest and oldest communities of mixed descent in the world', cites article 366 (2) of the Indian Constitution for the official definition of an Anglo-Indian: 'a person whose father or any of whose other male progenitors in the male line is or was of European descent but who is domiciled within the territory of India and is or was born within such territory of parents habitually resident therein and not established there for temporary purposes only'; Blunt, *Domicile*, pp. 1, 220. Elsewhere she notes that 'Anglo-Indian' to mean mixed-race was first adopted in the Indian census of 1911; Blunt, 'Geographies', p. 286.
30. 'Anglo-Indian' is also sometimes interchangeable with 'British Asian' in popular British parlance. 'Country-born' is yet another ambiguous term, employed in colonial times to mean both white European and mixed-race subjects born in India, and still used in both senses. Compare the disputed nature of the word 'creole', which can refer both to white colonialists and to people of mixed race in a Caribbean context; see Bost, *Mulattas*, p. 89.
31. Yule and Burnell, *Hobson-Jobson*, p. 344; and compare Carton, 'Beyond "Cotton Mary'; and Houston and Williams, 'Mediating', p. ix.
32. For the use of 'mochaccino', see Jen, *Who's Irish?*, p. 28. The problematic conjunction between food and racialised terminology will be considered further in Chapter 4.
33. Kamali, review of *Brown Eyes*, p. 86.
34. According to Kamal Ahmed, '"mixed-race" hadn't really been invented'

in 1970s Britain; see Ahmed, 'After Obama', p. 26; and see also Mahtani, 'What's in a name?', pp. 471–2, 475, 477.

35. Compare Katz, *Construction*, p. 3; and Mahtani and Moreno, 'Same difference', p. 71.
36. See Mahtani, 'What's in a name?', p. 478; for Ahmed, '"biracial" must be one of [the] worst bureaucratic calumnies against the English language ever invented by people trying to define and not insult'; see Ahmed, 'After Obama', p. 26.
37. Such terms, which recall the 'tragic mulatto' stereotype, include 'caught between two cultures' and 'Britain's children without a home'; Kureishi also cites the verdict of the British politician Duncan Sandys in 1967 that 'the breeding of millions of half-caste children would . . . produce a generation of misfits', to which he responds: 'I wasn't a misfit; I could join the elements of myself together. It was the others, they wanted misfits; they wanted you to embody within yourself their ambivalence'; see Kureishi, *Dreaming*, pp. 69 and 27–8 respectively. Such language, couched in ostensible concern, implies that to be mixed-race is an existential and social crisis of the first order. Compare, too, Benson, *Ambiguous Ethnicity*, p. 10; and Wu, *Yellow*, p. 270, where he astutely observes that 'the very people who ask "won't the children suffer" of a mixed-race marriage are the ones that make it so'.
38. Ifekwunigwe, '(An)Other', pp. 333–5, 339. In endlessly celebrating London as an emblem of British racial syncretism, Kureishi, for instance, suggests that the UK capital is the nation's key site of mixed-race identity.
39. See Senna, 'Mulatto millennium', pp. 12–27; and Wu, *Yellow*, p. 297.
40. Thus the Chinese American writer Maxine Hong Kingston argues: 'Forget territory. Let's make love, mate and mix with exotic peoples, and create the new humane being . . . Hapa children of any combination are the most beautiful'; see Kingston, 'Novel's next step', pp. 38–9; and, more recently, Kingston, *Fifth Book*, p. 263. On Hawaii, the US state whence the term *hapa* originates and one in which 21.4 per cent claimed to be of 'two or more races' in the 2000 census, compare Yamanaka, *Wild Meat*, p. 218, where the *hapa* becomes the aesthetic and social ideal. Kingston and Lois-Ann Yamanaka are both mothers of mixed-race children. For a discussion of this particular positive stereotype about racially mixed people, see Ropp, 'Do multiracial subjects', p. 4; and also Bost, *Mulattas*, pp. 195–8. On the old stereotype of the particular 'beauty' of Anglo-Indian women, see Blunt, *Domicile*, p. 15; and D'Cruz, *Midnight's Orphans*, p. 35.
41. Gilman, *Difference*, p. 18.
42. In an Australian context, it has also become more common in recent years to claim Aboriginal blood; see Shakespeare, *In Tasmania*, p. 180.
43. Wu, *Yellow*, pp. 287–9; and on transatlantic differences in the politicisation of this issue, see Ifekwunigwe, '(An)Other', p. 324.
44. Sui Sin Far, 'Mrs Spring Fragrance', p. 230; Senna, *Caucasia*, pp. 392–3; Klass, 'This much', p. 13.

45. Compare Bost, *Mulattas*, pp. 191–4, and Tony Kushner's play, *Angels in America: A Gay Fantasia on National Themes* (1992), where Belize imagines heaven to be full of 'racial impurity and gender confusion . . . all the deities are creole, mulatto, brown as the mouths of rivers'; Kushner, *Angels*, p. 214.
46. One thinks of such British sports stars as the former athletes Sebastian Coe (of South Asian–white parentage) and Kelly Holmes (of black–white descent); the racing driver Lewis Hamilton (black–white parentage); the former cricketers Mark Ramprakash and Nasser Hussain (both of South Asian–white descent); and most strikingly, the very large proportion of the English football team who are from a black–white background. Thus, through sport alone, Britain might be regarded as Ashley Dawson's 'mongrel nation'. Beyond Coe, Ramprakash, and Hussain, prominent biracial British Asians include the actors Ben Kingsley (born Krishna Bhanji), Jimi Mistry, Indira Verma, Raza Jaffrey, and Chris Bisson; the TV presenter Melanie Sykes; and the comedian Danny Bhoy. Now that census records offer such information, the perception is that numbers of mixed-race people in America and Britain are increasing, a point famously made in the US context by a 1993 issue of *Time* magazine, whose cover featured a computer-generated image of 'Eve', a multiracial woman, and proclaimed – in a gesture of US exceptionalism, which is also ahistorical – 'The new face of America: How immigrants are shaping the world's first multicultural society'. For discussions of the debates provoked by this issue of *Time*, see Bost, *Mulattas*, pp. 1–2; and Santa Ana, 'Affect-identity', pp. 16–19, 27–9.
47. King, *Internationalisation, passim.*
48. Koshy, *Sexual Naturalisation*, pp. 17–20, 23.
49. A relevant intertext here is Sam Selvon's novel *The Lonely Londoners* (1956), which evokes a similar era and milieu; here interracial sexual relationships, however brief, represent a home away from home where white prejudice thankfully plays a lesser role.
50. Naipaul, *Mimic*, p. 51.
51. Markandaya, *Nowhere*, p. 73.
52. Katz, *Construction*, p. 27.
53. Davé, 'No life', p. 54.
54. See Maxey, 'Beige outlaws'.
55. In relation to Kureishi's screenplay *Sammy and Rosie Get Laid* (1987), bell hooks argues that this version of interracial relationships erases women of colour; see hooks, *Yearning*, p. 161.
56. Compare Benson, *Ambiguous Ethnicity*, pp. 4–7, 12; Katz, *Construction*, p. 26; Alibhai-Brown, *Mixed Feelings*, pp. 29–30, 33; and Yu, 'Mixing bodies', p. 451.
57. Compare Woolcock, *Mischief Night*, in which Pakistani British men in Leeds automatically dismiss white women as '*goree* slappers', while making expedient sexual use of them.
58. For a definition of 'model minority', see Chapter 1, n. 50.

59. See Fanon, *Black Skin*, pp. 41–82; and compare Upstone, *British Asian*, p. 196.
60. Saadi, *Burning Mirror*, p. 5; emphasis added.
61. Kureishi, *Buddha*, p. 227.
62. This image recalls the language of exploration and conquest used by Mustafa Sa'eed to discuss his relationships with white British women in London in the interwar period in Tayeb Salih's classic Sudanese novel *Season of Migration to the North* (1969); see Salih, *Season*, pp. 39, 41; see also Kunzru, *Impressionist*, p. 291; and compare Roth, *Portnoy*, p. 235, where the protagonist claims that 'through fucking I will discover America. *Conquer* America . . . Columbus, Captain Smith, Governor Winthrop, General Washington – now Portnoy'; emphasis in original. My thanks to David Gooblar for this last reference.
63. Saadi, *Burning Mirror*, p. vii.
64. See Maxey, 'Who wants', pp. 532, 539.
65. Compare Davé, 'No life', pp. 53–66, which outlines the Gujarati American community's belief in the importance of intra-ethnic marriage within the US.
66. Lasdun, 'Empire'.
67. Hussein, 'A jester'; Halaby, 'Return'.
68. Lasdun, 'Empire'.
69. My thanks to Judie Newman for suggesting this point.
70. Compare Maxey, 'Who wants', pp. 535–6.
71. Alexander, *Fault Lines*, p. 211.
72. Ruppel, 'Re-inventing ourselves', p. 187.
73. Compare Koshy, *Sexual Naturalisation*, p. 137.
74. See ibid., pp. 135, 141, 146, for a discussion of this idea in Mukherjee's work.
75. Aneja, '*Jasmine*', pp. 77–8.
76. See Newman, 'Spaces', for a stimulating historical contextualisation of the novel.
77. See Alam, *Bharati Mukherjee*, p. 11; and Iyer, 'American/Indian'.
78. Maxey, 'Who wants', pp. 532–4.
79. Malladi, *Mango Season*, p. 32.
80. Mannur, *Culinary Fictions*, p. 111.
81. According to Jennifer Lee and Frank D. Bean, the 2000 US census suggests that such mixing is more common statistically; see Lee and Bean, 'Intermarriage', pp. 51, 53.
82. Nash, 'Will the Census', p. 19.
83. Prashad, *Karma*, pp. viii–xi; and compare Wu, *Yellow*, pp. 272–3.
84. Koshy, 'South Asians', p. 45. The racialised elements of the Woodward case anticipate the British media circus which surrounded the Molly Campbell/ Misbah Rana episode nearly a decade later in 2006: a young Scottish-Pakistani teenager of mixed race whose two 'halves' were literally embodied in her two names, Molly/Misbah chose her Pakistani 'half' by emigrating to Pakistan; see Scott-Clark and Levy, 'Why Molly ran'.

85. Lahiri, *Namesake*, p. 117.
86. Beyond the influence of *Buddha* on Lahiri, Rahul's laundromat job in her story 'Only goodness' recalls *Laundrette*: just as Omar's father is ashamed of his son's job, so Rahul's parents recoil from the idea that 'someone they knew would see their son weighing sacks of dirty clothes on a scale'; Lahiri, *Unaccustomed*, p. 151. The notion that Kureishi was washing the community's 'dirty linen' in public was picked up in reviews of Frears, *My Beautiful Laundrette*; see Thomas, *Hanif Kureishi*, pp. 26, 30–2. Lahiri updates this idea, using the laundromat to suggest the exposure of Bengali American secrets.
87. Patel et al., 'Audio commentary'.
88. By contrast, recent British TV drama series have generally approached such relationships in a more understated way: see, for example, Sam Miller, Audrey Cooke, and Nigel Douglas, *This Life* (1996–7); Brian Grant, *Party Animals* (2007); and S. J. Clarkson, Philip John, and Peter Hoar, *Mistresses* (2008–10). As with a number of black–white unions in such programmes, no explicit comment is made on racial differences between South Asian and white characters. One may explain this progressive – yet nevertheless utopian – attitude as owing to the obligation of the BBC and Channel 4, as public broadcasters, to tackle social diversity. My thanks to Liz Evans for suggesting this latter point.
89. For more on the uses of black–white buddy pairings, see Gillan, 'No one knows', pp. 47–8, 50–1; and Nishime, 'I'm Blackanese', pp. 48–51.
90. Compare Desai, *Beyond Bollywood*, p. 59; and for more on queer South Asian Atlantic cinema, see Gopinath, *Impossible Desires*, pp. 1–6, 63–160.
91. See Desai, *Beyond Bollywood*, p. 86.
92. In this context, South Asian Americans are no longer 'a part, yet apart' within a wider Asian American coalition; see Shankar and Srikanth, *A Part, Yet Apart*. On cinematic challenges to traditional interracial buddy tropes, see Nishime, 'I'm Blackanese', pp. 43–60.
93. Sandhu, *London Calling*, p. 257.
94. Compare Hillenbrand, 'Of myths', pp. 69–72.
95. Aslam, *Maps*, p. 10.
96. Nakashima, 'Asian American', p. 112.
97. Treacher, 'Welcome home', p. 99.
98. Compare Pérez-Torres, 'Chicano ethnicity', pp. 169–71.
99. Rody, *Interethnic*, p. 146.
100. There is insufficient space here to consider such novels as Govinden's *Graffiti My Soul* (2006) or Walsh's *Once Upon a Time in England* (2008). Contemporary biracial British Asian authors are pre-dated by the Indo-Irish, British-raised writer Aubrey Menen (1912–89); for a discussion of Menen's work, see Nasta, *Home Truths*, pp. 44–50. In her first novel, *White Teeth* (2000), Zadie Smith – not of South Asian descent herself – tackles British Asian racial mixing as part of a wider treatment of miscegenation; compare Bentley, 'Re-writing Englishness', pp. 496, 500.

101. Maxey, 'Beige outlaws'.
102. George's hypocrisy anticipates Kureishi's discussion of his father's attitudes to white British women, whom he dismisses as 'slutty', despite his own marriage to one; see Kureishi, *My Ear*, p. 115.
103. Khan-Din, *East is East*, pp. 44–5.
104. This is also how Kunzru refers to his protagonist; see Aldama, 'Hari Kunzru', p. 12.
105. Compare Blunt, *Domicile*, p. 130, where she discusses 'British snobbery towards Anglo-Indians' through the term 'Mr Middlerace'.
106. South Asian history also contains examples of people trying to pass as mixed-race in order to secure the benefits sometimes available to members of biracial communities; for this phenomenon in India, see Blunt, *Domicile*, pp. 89–90; and in Sri Lanka, McGilvray, 'Dutch burghers', p. 262.
107. Compare Dyer, *White*, p. 42.
108. Hussein, 'Impressionist'.
109. Khan-Din, *Last Dance*, p. 17.
110. Compare D'Cruz, *Midnight's Orphans*, pp. 33–5, 80. He argues that British colonial literature deploys such Anglo-Indian stereotypes because the mixed-race subject 'transgress[es] the *cordon sanitaire* between coloniser and colonised . . . [colonial] novels . . . represent Anglo-Indians as irredeemably *other* in order to disavow Britain's material connection with India'; ibid., p. 45, emphasis in original. Cynthia Nakashima has traced the connection between sexually 'immoral' behaviour and mixed-race people to the perception that they are themselves the result of 'an immoral union'; cited in Spickard, 'What must I be?', p. 47.
111. Consider the clichéd paradigm of the ill-fated interracial romance between the white man and East Asian woman – a thinly veiled metaphor for the imperial conquest of feminised foreign land – whereby the woman and her equally 'tragic' biracial progeny ('Amerasian', if born to a white American father) are abandoned in their Asian homeland; examples include Onoto Watanna's short story 'A half-caste' (1899) and, more famously, Giacomo Puccini's opera *Madame Butterfly* (1904) and Claude-Michel Schönberg, Richard Maltby, and Alain Boublil's musical *Miss Saigon* (1989); see Koshy, *Sexual Naturalisation*, pp. 13, 29–49. Alternatively, the East Asian woman, orphaned or sold by her family and forced to earn her own living in a *demi-monde* world, is carried off to a better life in the West by her 'white knight'; see Hillenbrand, 'Of myths', pp. 50, 73n. In these scenarios, the US is somehow seen as a superior alternative despite its anti-miscegenation laws and shameful historical record on Asian American rights; for examples of such films, see Joshua Logan's *Sayonara* (1957) and Richard Quine's *The World of Suzie Wong* (1960). Western films addressing the aftermath of the Vietnam War show the white man's compassion through the rescue of his Amerasian offspring; for a critique of such fantasies, see Houston, 'To the coloniser', pp. 69–84. In the British Asian texts under discussion here, the

first-generation subject is generally male and enacts a reverse colonisation by claiming white Britain through miscegenation; compare Fanon, *Black Skin*, pp. 41–82; and Selvon's *Lonely Londoners*. This reverses the patrilineal pattern of official Anglo-Indian descent, although biracial British Asians, especially in the postwar period, act as a reminder of colonial history. It also reflects the gender dynamics suggested by the Policy Studies Institute report cited in n. 7 above and reflects the miscegenist tropes deployed in a series of 'Merchant Ivory' films, for instance James Ivory's *Shakespeare Wallah* (1965), *Bombay Talkie* (1970), and *Heat and Dust* (1983).

112. Manzoor, 'Why do Asian writers'.
113. On the connection between mixed-race identity and naming, see Ang-Lydgate, 'Charting the spaces', p. 179; and Cutter, 'Smuggling', pp. 137–40.
114. Thanks to Sinéad Moynihan for suggesting this point.
115. On Narayan's mixed heritage, see Salgado, 'Interview', pp. 224, 226.
116. An early example of this phenomenon is G. V. Desani's novel *All About H. Hatterr* (1948), where Hatterr's biracial (white–Malay) status arguably affords Desani a powerful position from which to satirise religious charlatanism and the self-importance of British imperialism in India; and see also Murr's *Perfect Man*, where the author – not of South Asian descent himself – creates a mixed Indian–white protagonist, Rajiv (Raj) Travers, taking him on a global journey from India to Britain to a 1950s American South in order to observe all three places, but most of all the US, at a critical distance. Although Murr devotes a certain amount of attention to Raj's mixed blood in the novel, it is generally viewed through the eyes of the other characters, all of whom are white, rather than being considered by Raj himself.
117. Meer, *Bombay Talkie*, p. 163.
118. Ganesan, *Inheritance*, pp. 8, 17.
119. Bantwal, *Sari Shop*, p. 102.
120. Mukherjee, *Darkness*, p. 43.
121. Mukherjee, *Leave It To Me*, p. 28.
122. Delman, *Burnt Bread*, p. 59.
123. See Zack, 'On being'; Azoulay, *Black, Jewish*; and compare Harrison-Kahan, 'Passing for white', pp. 19–48.
124. Anthony, 'How Britain'.
125. Gordon, *Her Majesty's Other Children*, p. 163.
126. Compare Rody, *Interethnic*, pp. 150, 152–4, where she observes this tendency in Asian American literature more widely.
127. See Chapter 2, n. 43, for a brief discussion of this concept.
128. Root, 'Multiracial Asians', p. 35.
129. Compare Jolie Sheffer's idea that mixed-race characters in Asian American literature are at once 'representative and exceptional'; quoted in Rody, *Interethnic*, p. 148.
130. Mukherjee, 'Imagining', p. 82; and compare Nash, 'Hidden history', pp. 15–16, 22.

131. D'Cruz, *Midnight's Orphans*, pp. 173–4.
132. See Maxey, 'Beige outlaws'.
133. In Varun Khanna's film *American Blend* (2006), the presence of Maya, a half-Indian, half-white character, is thus unusual. Yet the narrative avoids proper analysis of her experiences of this mixed status through the notion that she has reached adulthood with no knowledge that she is racially mixed and indeed passing, unwittingly, as white. This is because Jayme, Maya's Caucasian American mother, has kept her daughter's Indian side hidden from her: a secret which is divulged only late on in the film.
134. Janette, 'Out of the melting pot', p. 94.
135. Compare traditional Biblical exegesis in which key passages – for instance, Leviticus 19.19 – have been interpreted as a prohibition on racial mixing. For a classic discussion of these passages, see Douglas, *Purity*, p. 54; on Hindu fears of caste impurity, see ibid., pp. 126–7, 145; and D'Cruz, *Midnight's Orphans*, p. 82.
136. Benson, *Ambiguous Ethnicity*, p. 13.
137. Wu, *Yellow*, pp. 299–300; and compare Koshy, *Sexual Naturalisation*, pp. 157–8.

CHAPTER 4

'MANGOES AND COCONUTS AND GRANDMOTHERS': FOOD IN TRANSATLANTIC SOUTH ASIAN WRITING

Introduction

In Atima Srivastava's British Asian novel *Looking for Maya* (1999), Amrit sneeringly refers to recent South Asian diasporic fiction as 'mangoes and coconuts and grandmothers . . . The Great Immigrant novel'.[1] This verdict has also been applied to recent Indian writing in English. Thus Graham Huggan argues that 'India . . . is more available than ever for consumption; and more prevalent than ever are the gastronomic images through which the nation is to be consumed.'[2] The tropes of food and eating, particularly in a familial setting, undoubtedly inform much current writing by South Asian Atlantic authors; and, on the basis of titles alone, some recent cultural productions do suggest that food has become a tired means of depicting South Asian diasporic life. This food-title fatigue can be traced to a body of work which includes such films as Mira Nair's *Mississippi Masala* (1991) in the United States and Gurinder Chadha's *Bhaji on the Beach* (1993) in the UK,[3] and literary texts which include Carmit Delman's Indian Jewish American autobiography *Burnt Bread and Chutney* (2002), and Nisha Minhas's British Asian novel *Chapatti or Chips?* (1997). These works, none of which is actually about food, belong to a much longer list.[4] What we are witnessing here are, arguably, forms of ' "food pornography": [that is] making a living by exploiting the "exotic" aspects of one's ethnic foodways'.[5] That such material is used exploitatively – or is in itself clichéd, as Amrit implies in *Looking for Maya* – is, however, a more vexed proposition. In this chapter, I will propose that the central cultural role traditionally played by South Asian foodways – and their importance, both public and private, to the development of diasporic communities in Britain and the

US[6] – make it difficult for transatlantic South Asian authors *not* to write about them. This is especially the case in the UK where writers seek to understand why South Asian-inspired foods – the hybrid creation chicken tikka masala, for example – have become national dishes.[7]

How, then, should we account for the importance of food in South Asian diasporic literature? According to Arjun Appadurai, 'South Asian civilisation has invested perhaps more than any other in imbuing food with moral and cosmological meanings.'[8] Beyond this claim, food offers South Asian Atlantic authors the opportunity to explore a number of major themes at the same time: gender roles; family and especially matrilineal connections; regionalism; and cooking as labour, in ways which sometimes become key to socio-economic status. Writers deploy recurrent tropes to examine South Asian diasporic foodways: mealtimes; shopping, especially for 'authentic' ingredients; the cultural and economic importance of restaurants; the binary of South Asian versus 'American' or 'British' food; and the notion of culinary syncretism. Writers also use food to illustrate the tension between preserving one's ancestral heritage and the formation of new cultural and social identities. Indeed, as Rüdiger Kunow has noted, food becomes a major means of affirming one's identity as a South Asian diasporic subject.[9] Mark Stein argues, moreover, that the sheer immediacy of food metaphors means that the reader can engage more actively with the text, since they 'put . . . readers to work . . . [because they] demand that we become involved, getting our hands sticky'.[10]

South Asian foodways may be regarded as thematically familiar, yet traditionally they have been neglected in studies of South Asian Atlantic literature, despite a widespread scholarly interest in food.[11] By comparing a range of representative literary works from both sides of the Atlantic, and devoting particular attention to the under-researched genre of *desi* (or South Asian) food memoir, this chapter will posit transatlantic differences and overlaps as it attempts to shed new light on the important ways in which food is deployed across this œuvre. Exploring the problematic, loaded relationship between originality and stereotype associated with food in a South Asian diasporic context, it will ask how these works deal with – and innovate – the ostensibly familiar discourse of food as marker of ethnic identity.

Cooking as Women's Work?

Amulya Malladi's South Asian American novel *The Mango Season* (2003) appears at first sight to reinscribe stereotypical preoccupations through its choice of title and content: a composite of the 'mangoes' and 'grandmothers' mocked in Amrit's earlier description in *Looking for Maya*. Yet Malladi's narrative avoids this putatively formulaic status through a subtly shifting treatment of food which focuses on regional details, and signals the link, for Indian women, between food and maternal discourse, inherited gender roles, and the ancestral home. Indeed, *Mango Season* indicates that some women actively resist the politics of food preparation and the personal limitations such daily activities can impose. In Chapter 2, we saw that the novel's protagonist, Priya, feels culturally displaced in India after seven years in the US. This sensation is underlined by her ignorance of how best to chop mangoes back in her parents' Hyderabad home: kitchen missteps which are as metaphorical as they are literal. And her awareness that wrongly wielding the 'sharp . . . heavy knife . . . used' for mango-chopping could result in 'missing a few fingers'[12] seems to symbolise the hazards for unmarried Indian women in returning home and attempting to negotiate a safe path through traditional culture. In Priya's case, the knives are, quite literally, out.

In *The Trouble with Asian Men* (2006) – a British play by Sudha Bhuchar, Kristine Landon-Smith, and Louise Wallinger, which brings together real-life interviews conducted with British Asian men – the witty playing-out of the 'chapatti versus naan' debate shows that, within the diaspora, South Asian women are often still expected to do the cooking. According to the play, the debate in question concerns the preference by some busy British Asian women to heat up ready-made, shop-bought naan bread, rather than make chapattis from scratch:[13] arguably, a reaction to the time traditionally involved in preparing home-cooked Indian food.[14] Vicky Bhogal, a British Asian food writer, anticipates such discussions in *Cooking like Mummyji: Real British Asian Cooking*, her 2003 cookbook. Here she recalls her aunt's complaint that 'so many Indian girls . . . don't know how to cook. Nowadays, girls are either . . . busy studying or they . . . have no interest. Gone are the days when they used to stay in the kitchen by their mother's side.'[15] This attitude, recounted in a text whose very title draws on a matrilineal discourse, reflects a diasporic desire to maintain tradition and, as discussed in Chapter 1, it is women who are expected to perform this work of cultural preservation, especially within the home.[16] And for many immigrant women in South Asian Atlantic literature, cooking is simply part of everyday life. Sometimes, it is even a necessary component in their psychological survival. Thus, in the less-than-welcoming 1960s Britain recalled in Meera Syal's novel *Anita and Me* (1996), Meena's mother cooks Punjabi food every day because it is 'soul food . . . the food . . . far-away mothers made . . . seasoned with memory and longing . . . the nearest [Meena's parents] . . . would get for many years, to home';[17] and in Jhumpa Lahiri's

South Asian American short story 'Mrs Sen's' (*Interpreter of Maladies* [1999]), the eponymous protagonist's peace of mind and sense of 'pride . . . [and] self-worth' as a new immigrant in the United States become entirely dependent upon the daily preparation of traditional Bengali fare.[18]

Yet the insistence that, among later generations, it should be women, rather than men, who learn to cook – clearly implied by Bhogal's real-life anecdote and by her own direct appeals to second-generation British Asian women – seems a reactionary one. Seen in this light, Priya's ignorance of culinary methods in *Mango Season* might be regarded less as local and cultural ignorance resulting from her 'America-returned' status, as discussed in Chapter 2, and more as a conscious questioning of – and opposition to – broader gendered traditions and, specifically, to a kind of culinary drudgery. One can read in similar fashion the recollection by the South Asian American writer Meena Alexander of her mother's overriding concern that, as a future wife, Alexander should 'learn how to make good *sambar*':[19] a statement which clearly troubled Alexander as a young girl. It is worth noting, too, that promotion of Chadha's British Asian film *Bend It Like Beckham* (2002) included the strapline, 'who wants to cook aloo gobi when you can bend a ball like Beckham?' This suggests that, for the film's protagonist – a twenty-first-century British Sikh girl – the decision to play football, and thus to assert a more mainstream, gender-neutral identity, must come at the expense of learning to cook traditional Indian food, a dialectic Winnie Chan has intelligently explored.[20] It is surely no coincidence either that, generally speaking, the mother–daughter relationships in which food becomes a *casus belli* are already fraught.

But the connection between food, mothers, daughters, and domesticity is also presented as life-affirming. In Lahiri's novel *The Namesake* (2003), for instance, Sonia Ganguli's desire to learn from her mother, Ashima, how to cook 'the food [she] . . . had complained of eating as a child'[21] marks a touching moment in their growing intimacy. In a non-fictional context, British Asian writers and film-makers have, moreover, celebrated their mothers' cooking. With the exception of Bhogal and Yasmin Alibhai-Brown, it is telling, perhaps, that they are usually men. In other words, they have enjoyed such food without experiencing the pressure of learning to make it. In such recent memoirs as Rohan Candappa's *Picklehead: From Ceylon to Suburbia – A Memoir of Food, Family and Finding Yourself* (2006), Sarfraz Manzoor's *Greetings from Bury Park: Race. Religion. Rock 'n' Roll* (2007), Sathnam Sanghera's *The Boy with the Topknot: A Memoir of Love, Secrets and Lies in Wolverhampton* (2008), and Hardeep Singh Kohli's *Indian Takeaway: A Very British Story* (2008), the writer's mother is presented, in matter-of-fact fashion, as an exceptional home cook. Indeed, it becomes a point of honour to claim one's mother as the finest cook imaginable of Indian cuisine, especially in a particular regionalised form. This also belongs to the political aim of remedying an earlier 'tendency for Asian women's efforts to feed their families to be overlooked by their children and husbands. Their craft went emotionally unrewarded.'[22] I will offer some reasons for why writers now seek to recognise such work a little later in this discussion.

In *Indian Takeaway*, Kohli pays particular tribute to the culinary creativity and ingenuity of his mother, Kuldip, and to her budgetary skills. As I noted in Chapter 2, this text achieves a kind of rhetorical emphasis from its repetitions and, since this is a food narrative, Kuldip's cooking takes on a special significance. As Kohli puts it, 'I am the way I am about food because: My mum is an amazing cook of Indian food.'[23] Touchingly candid about failing to match her apparently formidable skills, he admits that

> I have rarely tasted Punjabi food better than that lovingly prepared by my mum. So good is my mother's food that I have stopped cooking Indian food myself, knowing that I will never come close to her standard. My lamb curry will never have that melt-in-the-mouth consistency, the sauce will never be as well spiced and rich, my potatoes never as floury and soft. My daal will be bereft of that buttery richness, that earthy appeal that warms you from inside. My parathas will never be as flaky and delicious and comforting. (16)

It is worth noting that, like Candappa in *Picklehead*, Kohli has no sister to record – or indeed continue to cook – the type of food made by his mother and described in varying degrees of detail: for instance, a rhapsodic account of Kuldip's mackerel curry, doubling as a makeshift recipe. It is makeshift in that no ingredient amounts or cooking times are included. This fits with the notion that Indian women are instinctive cooks,[24] or as Bhogal's mother puts it: 'we don't use measurements. That's for English people' (*Cooking like Mummyji*, 16).

Kuldip's syncretic British Asian dish, which illustrates 'the story of a work ethic . . . running a family on a limited budget' and the way in which 'Glenryck mackerel fillets in tomato sauce . . . [were] somehow elevated to another place' (82–3), actually enjoys an earlier appearance in *Picklehead.* Noting that mackerel provided 'a flash of iridescent colour . . . in a still drab, grey and sensationally rationed post-war London' and that it 'actually tasted of something', Candappa recalls his mother's 'cheap . . . tinned' version, boasting that 'you won't find [it] in any other recipe book'.[25] It is, moreover,

> completely inauthentic [in a traditional sense] . . . but, in so many other ways . . . as authentic as it gets. Because it gloriously illustrates what immigrants anywhere in the world have to do when they find themselves surrounded by unfamiliar choices and strictly limited options. You take whatever you can get and . . . make it work. And maybe, if you work hard . . . and your kids knuckle down . . . years down the line, you'll discover that tinned fish curry has become a thing of the past. (156)

After Candappa's tribute, there is a touch of déjà vu to Kohli's account. To read them alongside one another also renders Candappa's claim about the unique nature of 'tinned fish curry' invalid, even if individual ingredients in the two recipes differ.[26] And Kohli's straightforward affection for the dish diverges from Candappa's notion that increased financial stability will allow immigrants and their descendents to discard 'tinned fish curry' and the 'limited options' it embodies. In *The Settler's Cookbook: A Memoir of Love, Migration and Food* (2009), Alibhai-Brown is more dismissive still of the 'curried tinned sardines' her mother, another much-admired cook, produced through dire economic necessity, remembering the dish as revolting – 'yuk' – and refusing to include a recipe for it in her otherwise compendious collection.[27] This may also be a matter of taste – tinned mackerel and sardines are not to everyone's liking, after all – but for Candappa and Kohli, the memory of this particular curry is used to celebrate a mother's culinary ingenuity.

Relevant to the idea that different gender dynamics in Kohli's family might have produced a different result – a son less interested in cooking, perhaps – is the author's brief questioning of his mother's designated role as cook. Thus he recalls his father's propensity to bring home 'random produce', in particular a foul-smelling Bombay duck which Kuldip was expected to turn into a meal: 'such was the patriarchal system she'd married into, Mum tugged her metaphorical forelock and put the deep fat fryer on the stove' (81). But this moment of implied critique is actually rather unusual. Indeed, Kohli shares the cultural values embodied by his cherished parents; and by recounting the particular appeal of specific dishes, *Indian Takeaway* becomes his major chance to proclaim his mother's skills publicly and do justice to a lifetime of maternal love as expressed through cooking.

In his short film *A Love Supreme* (2001), Nilesh Patel goes a step further, making his filial tribute to the cooking of his mother, Indumati, the film's sole thematic basis so that the literal focus of the camera is on her hands preparing food.[28] The use of black-and-white photography both aestheticises and de-exoticises what the film synopsis terms 'the making of a humble samosa'.[29] As Sukhdev Sandhu puts it,

> we are forced to attend more closely to a process that we would normally regard as humdrum and prosaic, an aspect of female domestic work that tends to be ignored even by historians of ethnic communities . . . [Indumati's] hands become historical texts that tell hard, complicated stories about female labour, migration, domestic economy.[30]

In the film's final dedication – 'to my Mother, her Mother and your Mother' – Patel assumes that it is mothers, rather than fathers, who cook: a point which draws on traditional gender patterns across cultures. Indeed, the mother who prepares the food, and what she represents, is as important as the food itself. Beyond its perceived deliciousness, that food is part of a whole milieu: one's childhood home and the parental love and protection with which it is associated here, and the sense that as an adult, one is allowed to retreat from day-to-day worries when with one's parents. This may explain why Kohli, for instance, uses emotional language to frame Kuldip's cooking: 'lovingly prepared', 'earthy', 'warms you from inside', 'comforting' (16). Whether it is daughters or sons, however, who assume responsibility for recording and celebrating, learning and therefore perpetuating South Asian culinary skills in the diaspora, these varied tributes across different forms actually spell out the fear that such skills are nearing extinction. Thus, beyond a sense that one cannot match the older generation's culinary skills,[31] love for an ageing mother, now appreciated through the eyes of an adult rather than a child, becomes intricately and intimately bound up with the preparation and consumption of traditional foods.[32]

Women are also shown to take a specific pride in their kitchen expertise which can become an important, even primary, 'vehicle for . . . creative expression' and a marker of 'status'.[33] In Delman's *Burnt Bread*, female relatives display 'a kind of culinary bravado which asked boastfully: Why should I eat that thing that has been made by strangers and machines, when I could cook something so much better myself from scratch?'[34] And in *Mango Season*, Malladi makes clear that Indian women's home-cooked food will always be favoured over that of restaurants, while Kohli notes that, growing up, 'we would never have gone out to eat food that Mum could have made at home' (*Indian Takeaway*, 45). It is revealing, then, that in Chitra Divakaruni's South Asian American short story 'The blooming season for cacti' (from the collection *The Unknown Errors of Our Lives* [2001]), South Asian immigrant men have come to depend upon Indian restaurants in the United States precisely because their wives are absent and because, by implication, they cannot cook. Thus the restaurant in which Mira works principally attracts

> men . . . usually middle-aged, balding, a little down at the heel. H-1 visa holders whose shoulders slump under the hopes of wives and children waiting back in the home country. Who want a down-home meal that doesn't cost too much and like to order the specials.[35]

Often central to the economic survival of immigrants,[36] restaurants are of course a classic means of representing diasporic cultures, as demonstrated in a British context by such novels as Timothy Mo's *Sour Sweet* (1982), Salman Rushdie's *The Satanic Verses* (1988), and Zadie Smith's *White Teeth* (2000). Beyond this, men's reliance on restaurant meals in the US context of Divakaruni's story suggests the need for different kinds of nourishment. As Kunow puts it, 'under exilic conditions . . . food is increasingly consumed as . . . material and emotional sustenance'.[37] And, like Priya's unease in the family kitchen in *Mango Season*, the connection between male immigrants and restaurants is another example of the ways in which transatlantic South Asian writers use food metaphors to signal gendered displacement.[38]

The reality that the food in such restaurants is usually cooked by men – another cross-cultural idea, since chefs the world over are more likely to be male than female – is notable by its absence here. Perhaps this reflects the greater emphasis by these South Asian Atlantic writers on food in the domestic, and thus feminised, sphere, which in turn takes us back to the importance of home as material space in these works, a point I argued in Chapter 1. In *Picklehead*, Candappa offers a different, second-generation perspective on eating out from that experienced by Divakaruni's lonely, fictionalised, immigrant men. It is not until he has left home that the author ventures into 'an Indian restaurant' (269). Once there, he recognises 'very little of what was on the menu . . . I'd grown up with curries that didn't have names' (270–1); similarly, perhaps, Bhogal is 'really confused' by 'Indian' food in restaurants which 'bore no resemblance to anything I ate at home' (*Cooking like Mummyji*, 124). The commonplace British popular cultural experience of 'going for a curry' – where, to an uninformed ethnic outsider, 'Indian' food is served up[39] – is defamiliarised, then, by both Bhogal and Candappa. But *Picklehead* goes on to celebrate the joys of UK restaurant curries because, however inauthentic, they bring together friends and colleagues in a congenial experience which offers 'far more than a pile of poppadoms, a korma and a pint of lager' (301). He is also careful, however, to expose the unpromising, altogether more frightening, context faced by earlier waves of South Asian restaurateurs in Britain, whose eating establishments often formed a mainstream racist, alcohol-fuelled 'front line between certain sections of Asian and white society' (238).

Indian Food and Otherness

DIETARY LAWS AND THE BREAKING OF TABOOS

South Asian Atlantic writers also demonstrate the power of food to contain traditions and guard against Otherness, particularly in the context of Hindu dietary rules: that is, religious laws – subject to wider interpretation, of course – dictating which foods can and cannot be eaten, with a particular emphasis on the avoidance of animal-based products, and how such food should be stored, prepared, and served. In Divakaruni's short story 'Mrs Dutta writes a letter' (*Unknown Errors*), the preparation of Bengali food in America becomes a battleground between Shyamoli and her mother-in-law, Mrs Dutta. According to Appadurai's formulation of what he terms 'gastro-politics', 'disharmony' between Indian female in-laws 'revolves critically around food transactions'.[40] In Divakaruni's fictional scenario, the clash between old-style Bengali values and immigrant compromise is illustrated on one level through Mrs Dutta's insistence on the right way to prepare and store food: 'Surely Shyamoli, a girl from a good Hindu family, doesn't expect her to put contaminated jutha things in with the rest of the food?'[41] On another level, the sharp contours of the gap between generations and in-laws – a gap only intensified by migration – become apparent through the ritual of family mealtimes. The third-person narrator reveals that

> at first Shyamoli had been happy enough to have someone take over the cooking. It's wonderful to come home to a hot dinner, she'd say . . . But recently she's taken to picking at her food, and once or twice from the kitchen Mrs Dutta has caught wisps of words, intensely whispered: cholesterol, all putting on weight, she's spoiling you. (9)

Demonstrating how food can reflect shifting, strained in-law relationships, Divakaruni elucidates the perspectives of both Mrs Dutta and Shyamoli. Combatting her feelings of isolation in the US, the older woman uses food to maintain homeland culture, while making herself useful, even indispensable, to her son's family by cooking for them. On the other hand, Shyamoli – affected by American-inspired medical concerns – senses, through these food-based power struggles, that she is losing influence over her husband and children. The story thus reflects Krishnendu Ray's notion that migrant mealtimes become 'acts on a gastronomic stage on which the American Bengali reenacts larger concerns about ethnicity, patriarchy, and modernity'.[42] By contrast to Mrs Dutta's largely intransigent stance, the visiting Tamil grandmother in Shoba Narayan's South Asian American memoir, *Monsoon Diary: Recipes and Reveries from South India* (2003), goes from denouncing any American food 'she hadn't cooked with her bare hands. This was a foreign land . . . and one never knew if errant cooks had accidentally dumped lard in the supposedly vegetarian items' to an overland trip where, satisfied that she can compare them to particular Indian foods, she consumes a range of ' "outside" food' including yogurt, coffee, doughnuts, fried rice, crisps, and ice cream.[43]

In Anita Desai's South Asian American novel *Fasting, Feasting* (1999), the Pattons' attempts to Americanise Arun, an Indian student in the United States, through food are, however, doomed. Thus Mr Patton's attempts to draw Arun into his family's life through barbecues can never succeed. T. Ravichandran has observed that food becomes a prison for Arun since he never manages to liberate himself from tastes developed during his formative years, no matter how far away from India he ventures.[44] Mrs Patton's food cannot provide sustenance, moreover, in much the same way that America cannot become Arun's home. From Arun's closed third-person perspective, the narrator asks, somewhat plaintively: 'how was [Arun] . . . to tell [her] . . . that these were not the foods that figured in his culture? That his digestive system did not know how to turn them into nourishment?'[45] But such reactions are complicated by Arun's own desire to be as physically strong as Rod, the Pattons' athletic son: a notion apparently rendered impossible by diet and culture, rather than genetics. Striking a note of compassion but also, in a manner reminiscent of V. S. Naipaul, one of ethnographic detachment, Desai writes that

> the idea, in one sense glamorous and flattering, of jogging beside the transcendent Rod, is too fanciful to be entertained. There is no way that a small, underdeveloped and asthmatic boy from the Gangetic plains, nourished on curried vegetables and stewed lentils, could . . . even keep up with this gladiatorial species of northern power. (191)

CONFLICTING ATTITUDES TO VEGETARIANISM

In this sense, to be vegetarian is explicitly associated with the negative properties of being 'small, underdeveloped and asthmatic'. In Ginu Kamani's short story 'Just between Indians' (from the anthology *Junglee Girl* [1995]), it signals a life-denying attitude, moreover, when Daya – a free-spirited, meat-eating, sexually liberated, non-religious Indian American student – dismisses the emotionally repressed, British Asian Patel family as '*uptight vegetarians*'.[46] By contrast, Narayan implies in *Monsoon Diary* that, synonymous with Hinduism, vegetarianism is simply the Indian national standard, while suggesting that vegetarians are more peace-loving than meat-eaters. This discourse is taken significantly further in a much earlier text, Kamala Markandaya's novel *The Nowhere Man* (1972), where the life-long vegetarianism of Srinivas, an ageing Indian immigrant in postwar Britain, is both a passionately moral point and a polysemic metaphor.

Set against an unexciting, predominantly meat-based, 1950s and 1960s British food culture, the rejection of meat by Srinivas serves as a dominant metaphor for a traditional Hindu belief system, amplified by exile. Although he tries to exonerate British 'butchers' shops' by viewing them as 'barbaric necessities of a carnivorous people', his revulsion towards meat consumption is signalled by a re-imagining of Christmas as 'round-the-clock carnage . . . farmyards falling silent, one by one', rather than a communal feast celebrating peace on earth, in the popular expression.[47] Attitudes towards animals become powerfully symbolic later in the novel. Feeling increasingly alienated in an ever more racist Britain, Srinivas effects a devastating, anti-imperial, anti-Christian slippage between memories of animal testing for scientific purposes; the hubristic, wanton destruction of nature in India by (carnivorous) British colonialists; and his bitter recognition of a mainstream British failure to grasp the sacred Hindu tenet that animals and people are equal. Thus,

> the boundaries . . . of a narrow white ethos . . . unable to assimilate the totality of creation, or perhaps finding it inexpedient, introduced puerility in its own image. In the shape of grids which it laid upon natural patterns . . . So then there were areas for compassion, and for indifference, of conservation, and expendability, of animals to cherish and experimental animals, and (extending the same . . . imaginary line . . .) white men and other men, the degree of concern for each being regulated by the grid. (236)

It is consistent, then, that within this bleak context, Srinivas sees himself as being goaded like an animal, while discovering that dead animals have literally been placed on his doorstep. Later he is tarred and feathered 'like . . . a chicken' (252) by Fred – a white tormentor who, in the Western formulation, behaves like 'an animal' – and the death of Srinivas, following Fred's sadistic arson attack, suggests that, like the innocent animals consumed by Britain's uncaring non-vegetarians, he has been sacrificed. And Markandaya's suggestion is that this sacrifice has taken place on an altar of xenophobia and postcolonial hatred.

THE LURE OF MEAT

Significant and even shocking, therefore, in the taboo-breaking contrast they present to Narayan, Srinivas, Arun, and other observant Hindu vegetarians in this body of transatlantic writing, are Daya's sensuous savouring of 'red meat' in Kamani's 'Just between Indians' (172) and Gogol's enthusiastic consumption in early life of 'hot dogs' and 'cold cuts', 'bologna or roast beef' in Lahiri's *Namesake* (65): preferences which recall Geetha Kothari's particular craving for 'bologna, hot dogs, salami' in her autobiographical essay 'If you are what you eat, then what am I?' (1999).[48] Unlike either Narayan or Arun, the figures of Daya, Gogol, and Kothari are all US-raised. Within the context of Kothari's essay, Anita Mannur has argued that the impulse to eat 'American' food signals Kothari's childhood belief that she can 'fuse seamlessly with her friends, and move beyond her racial identity, an external mark of difference – if she eats like them, then she becomes more like them'.[49] This notion that the eating of ethnically other, and indeed traditionally forbidden, foods – particularly meat – will enable assimilation into mainstream America is also played out in Philip Roth's novel *The Plot Against America* (2004). Here Sandy, a Jewish American boy from New Jersey, spends a wartime summer in an agricultural, Gentile community in Tennessee. Most crucially, perhaps, it is his non-kosher consumption of 'bacon, ham, [and] pork chops' on the farm which results in noticeable physical change. Thus his younger brother, Philip, observes that on his return, Sandy is 'some ten pounds heavier than when he'd left . . . his brown hair blondish from working in the fields . . . he'd grown a couple of inches . . . altogether my impression was of my brother in disguise'.[50]

Hindus in South Asian American literature often fail to resist the lure of beef – which can be hard to avoid in any case, given its central importance within American cuisine. But their reactions to this forbidden gastronomic act diverge sharply, an act of consumption which is, in any case, more commonplace than might be expected.[51] Dimple in Bharati Mukherjee's novel *Wife* (1975) initially shrinks in horror from the 'nightmarishly pink roast beef' at a Jewish delicatessen shortly after her arrival in New York.[52] But later, her purchase of this outlawed meat suggests an increasing acculturation. Indeed, it is only a short step from buying 'pinkish red hamburgers . . . dripping blood' to the spiritual contamination of getting 'the pinkish meat . . . under her nails' (175–6) to her physical consumption of it (although she consciously vomits away the abomination) to the sexual treachery of her brief affair with the beef-eating, Jewish American Milt Glasser, with whom, significantly, she bought the beef. In a further, unsettling set of slippages between animal and human flesh, a white American woman, Leni Anspach – as seen through Dimple's estranged gaze – has 'horribly pink' gums (152), and a 'squishy' mouth 'like . . . baby calf liver under plastic wrap' (147). When Dimple eventually murders her husband, she turns butcher herself, stabbing him so that the milk in his breakfast bowl becomes 'a pretty pink' (213).

In Sameer Parekh's South Asian American novel *Stealing the Ambassador* (2002), Vasant and Rajiv, a father and son, strenuously brush their teeth in the bathroom of McDonalds to remove all traces of the meat they have eaten before returning home to face Rajiv's mother. And in Delman's *Burnt Bread*, she recalls her Indian Jewish grandmother's deep-rooted disdain for hot dogs as 'not real food . . . tainted, dirty, unkosher, gristly . . . watered down' (xviii–xix): a last resort which she consumes only on her deathbed, and then unwittingly. By contrast, in *Namesake*, Lahiri suggests no such censure or need for purgation on Gogol's part; and his parents simply understand their children's eating of beef as an unavoidable aspect of a US upbringing. Like differing responses to the new nation itself, the consumption of meat by both immigrants and their children varies in striking ways and, despite the importance of laws forbidding the intake of certain meats in such religions as Judaism and Islam, this situation within South Asian Atlantic writing is viewed largely through the eyes of Hindus, and generally those resident in the United States rather than Britain.

THE SEARCH FOR AUTHENTIC INGREDIENTS

If, in general, South Asian American writers respond more dramatically than British Asian authors to the breaking of dietary taboos, the unavailability of authentic ingredients in the adoptive nation, especially in the 1960s and 1970s, links the UK and America here. Thus in Vineeta Vijayaraghavan's South Asian American novel *Motherland* (2001), Kamala finds it hard to 'duplicate' Indian food in the US because the ingredients available are not 'any substitute';[53] and in the British context, Kohli recalls that KRK, a particular South Asian supermarket in 1970s Glasgow, was

> a lifeline of food and produce . . . the only place you could get spices and lentils, Indian style meat, fish, chicken and mangoes . . . If you couldn't afford an airfare back to the subcontinent all you needed to do was pop down to KRK on Woodlands Road and buy a couple of mangoes and an eight-kilo bag of rice; it was the next best thing. (*Indian Takeaway*, 80)[54]

In Lahiri's work, where, as several critics have acknowledged, food plays a major role,[55] the search for Indian ingredients is particularly important. Sometimes this simply takes the form of a casual reference: in the early 1970s, small-town setting of her short story 'When Mr Pirzada came to dine' (*Interpreter*), for example, where 'chili peppers' can only be 'purchased on monthly trips to Chinatown' and 'mustard oil' cannot be found at the local supermarket.[56] In 'Mrs Sen's', the search for ingredients becomes more pivotal in narrative terms. Indeed, in the words of Asha Choubey, 'food acquires a character' in this story,[57] as Mrs Sen's need to cook Bengali food, in which fresh, whole fish is a staple element, becomes (as I argued earlier) integral to her emotional and psychological wellbeing.[58] But whereas fresh fish can be bought in Calcutta 'in any market, at any hour, from dawn until midnight',[59] it is significantly harder to find in the story's New England milieu – despite its proximity to the Atlantic Ocean – thus questioning the clichéd notion that life in America is materially more convenient for new immigrants. Mrs Sen's increasingly desperate bid to buy fish is what forces her to attempt to drive,[60] the disastrous results of which end her supervision of Eliot, the young white American boy in her care.

In *Namesake*, Ashima's relief about her decision to leave the US for Calcutta is, perhaps significantly, expressed in terms of individual culinary ingredients. The narrator explains that Ashima

> will not have to go to the trouble of making yogurt from half-and-half and sandesh from ricotta cheese. She will not have to make her own croquettes. They will be available to her from restaurants, brought up . . . by servants, bearing a taste that after all these years she has still not quite managed, to her entire satisfaction, to replicate. (277)

At the same time, writers also concede that authentic ingredients are now more easily attainable in both Britain and the United States, a sign of the stronger South Asian presence in both countries.[61] Lahiri's reference to servants, meanwhile – traditionally a part of daily life for the South Asian middle classes – is interesting, because their absence is part of the domestic self-sufficiency that America can teach immigrant characters within these works. Indeed, some characters experience a kind of downward mobility which forces them into new forms of labour, domestic and otherwise. In her novel *An American Brat* (1994), Bapsi Sidhwa describes Manek, a privileged Pakistani studying in Boston, '[who] had never prepared even a cup of tea in Lahore, [but] astonished [his niece] Feroza by the culinary prowess necessity had brought forth'.[62] This challenges, furthermore,

Divakaruni's notion that immigrant men in America depend upon restaurants. That such allusions to domestic staff do not register in the British Asian texts under consideration in this chapter is noteworthy because it suggests the different class dynamics characterising South Asian settlement in Britain: that is, a more working-class pattern of migration, as we saw in the Introduction.

Within South Asian American literature, writers also examine supermarkets, perhaps because they are such an acknowledged bastion of American culture. Prapulla, a new Indian immigrant, in G. S. Sharat Chandra's short story 'Sari of the Gods' (1998) believes US supermarkets are 'sterilised' places where

> you shopped like a robot with a pushcart . . . products lay waiting like cheese in a trap, rather than beseeching you from the stalls of the vendors and merchants in the bazaars and markets of home. The frozen vegetables, the canned fruits . . . the chicken chopped into shapes that were not its own but of the plastic, all bothered her. Besides, everything had a fixed price tag.[63]

By contrast to the eerily personified comestibles of this story, the availability of such whitebread food is embraced by Feroza and Manek in Sidhwa's *American Brat*. Accustomed to the rarity of tinned food in 1970s Pakistan, they perceive its abundance in the US as part of the luxury and excitement the adoptive nation has to offer since, as Sau-ling Wong has argued, for new immigrants, such food 'spells stability of supply'.[64] The South Asian American writer Indira Ganesan even goes so far as to extol the US supermarket experience as 'aisles and aisles of choice . . . freedom . . . quantity' and recalls the joy felt by her Indian immigrant parents at 1960s American convenience food.[65]

Desai's *Fasting, Feasting* offers perhaps the most intense examination of American supermarket culture. As its title implies, the text uses consumption as a leitmotif, defining India and America in parallel and contrast with one other in order to conflate food, home, and parents. In this largely domestic novel of two families, Desai carefully shows that parent–child relationships in both places are distant and dysfunctional, a point expressed through food and particularly through the obsession of the white American matriarch, Mrs Patton, with supermarkets. Her sensation of relaxing 'when . . . [she] enter[s] the Foodmart . . . it is as if she has come home' (208) recalls Don DeLillo's classic treatment of the world of the American supermarket in his novel *White Noise* (1985).[66] It also signals how fundamentally American she is in comparison with an Indian-born figure like Prapulla in 'Sari of the Gods'. There is something semi-religious for

Mrs Patton in the buying – rather than the actual physical ingestion – of food, since the amount she buys is out of all proportion to what her family can actually eat. She fails, moreover, to achieve a closer relationship with Arun through their visits to the supermarket together.

THE PERCEIVED INFERIORITY OF BRITISH AND AMERICAN FOOD

Beyond the search for ingredients necessary to reproduce different South Asian dishes within the diaspora, writers signal the generally superior quality of subcontinental food in relation to American, and particularly British, fare. In Syal's *Anita and Me*, Meena dismisses 1960s British cuisine as 'over-boiled, under-seasoned . . . slop' (26), while the BBC comedy programme *Goodness Gracious Me* (1998; partly written by Syal) mercilessly satirises British food in its well-known 'Going for an English' sketch, where diners at an 'English' restaurant in India request 'the blandest thing on the menu' and then ask the waiter what he has 'that's not totally tasteless'.[67] In Candappa's *Picklehead*, the postwar drabness of the Britain his mother, Beulah, 'found herself in' (152) is epitomised by the inferiority of British fish: 'iced carcasses . . . displayed on marble-cold mortuary slabs . . . all over London . . . [with] no distinguishing taste or smell . . . robbed of all personality' (149). Decades on, the situation has not improved, with 1970s British school dinners remembered as uniformly awful: 'the low-fat spam-fritter-and-chips option' (3), a dessert course of 'blancmange . . . fluorescent pink . . . [which] no one liked' (147), and, intriguingly, a completely inauthentic stab at

> curry . . . [which] looked like a ladle of over-stewed grey school mince. With raisins in it. If there was one thing I had learned from . . . my mother . . . it was that curry never had raisins in it. Curry had chicken or beef or lamb or mutton or fish or prawns in it. It was alive with the heat of chillies, or the tang of ginger, or the sweetness of coconut, the bite of mustard seeds or the sourness of tamarind. It could be light . . . or fierce . . . as you ate it you were surrounded by people . . . telling stories and sharing jokes, and feeling . . . the hot sun of a distant land warm up even the most sullen of 1970s English days. (2–3)

There can be no question here of the gulf between barely edible British fare and the rich subtlety of Beulah's (non-vegetarian) home-cooked curries. It is spelled out for political reasons when, during one of many tributes to the bravery and toughness of his parents – and, by implication, of many other immigrants – in making a new life in Britain, he asks the reader to 'imagine how dull food would be in this country without all the wonderful flavours that immigrants have brought with them' (69).[68] According to Candappa, then, it is newcomers, and particularly South Asian ones, who have radically and singlehandedly transformed British food.

In Sidhwa's first novel, *The Crow Eaters* (1978), members of the racially mixed Anglo-Indian community in 1920s India proudly consume 'English food – Irish stew, roast beef, custard, mint sauce and all that. It's tasteless but we eat it'; while potatoes are disdained as 'mealy . . . [like] cockroaches', and dumplings are dismissed as food that even the servants refuse to eat in colonial Lahore.[69] On the one hand, important regional differences within the British Isles are collapsed here: clearly, 'Irish stew' is not 'English'. On the other hand, the notion that mint sauce or custard, or indeed other traditional British sauces and dishes (especially a host of sweet delicacies), are without doubt stodgy and lacking in either taste or interest is actually a matter of opinion, especially for native-born British Asians. This idea is in fact repeatedly illustrated through Kohli's fondness for hearty British fare – shepherd's pie, toad in the hole, fish and chips – in *Indian Takeaway*. But these different perspectives are also perhaps beside the point. British food, admittedly not world renowned, is characterised by the likes of Sidhwa and Syal – as well as Alibhai-Brown[70] – by what it is not in relation to the spicy flavours demanded by a South Asian palate. The summary dismissal of UK food as 'bland' and 'tasteless' forms a key part of the wider anti-British rhetoric we witnessed in Chapter 1: namely, that the country is perceived to be lacking in important ways, for instance in subcontinental colour or heat. As I argued there – and as Sidhwa demonstrates here – such critiques of the UK, whether focusing on weather, urban landscape, or food, are not, moreover, simply the preserve of South Asian creative artists in Britain but also of writers in the United States.

Yet when it comes to the US, South Asian American writers are also disparaging, noting the homogeneity of a nation obsessed with fast food: for example, through Priya's references to fried chicken ('fast food at KFC') and 'Starbucks' coffee in *Mango Season* (126).[71] Sometimes this reliance on convenience food is implicitly attacked. Thus, in 'Mrs Sen's', Lahiri suggests a stark disparity between Eliot's mother's daily ordering-in of pizzas and Mrs Sen's lengthy, traditional Bengali cooking procedures.[72] Just as Lahiri uses food tropes to question American family values – the pizzas Eliot's mother gives him are clearly a metonym for their perfunctory emotional interaction[73] – so she also uses them to signal that white American children are spoilt, for instance when the young guests at Gogol's birthday parties 'claim they are allergic to milk [and] . . . refuse to eat the crusts of their bread' (*Namesake*, 72). By contrast, when Gogol tries to leave food, his father commands him to 'finish it . . . At your age I ate tin' (55).[74]

If South Asian and mainstream American food traditions are depicted as starkly different, it would nevertheless be a mistake to suggest that they are incommensurate here. Indeed, as Lahiri shows through Ashima's use of 'Rice Krispies' and 'Planters peanuts' to prepare a favourite Indian snack (*Namesake*, 1), there is a middle path of culinary syncretism.[75] Such culinary change and adaptation has, of course, always gone on in a South Asian context, whether at home or in the diaspora, and it calls into question the whole notion of 'authenticity', while signalling the power of food as 'a mark of ethnicity and . . . a means of subverting fixed affiliations'.[76] Returning to the United States, Thanksgiving, the quintessential American national festival, provides one of the best demonstrations of this theme within South Asian American writing. Ashima prepares a 'spiced cranberry chutney' to accompany the turkey (*Namesake*, 271), while Frances, Nick's African American mother in *Mango Season*, offers her own version of Indian food, which involves 'curry powder and turkey' (66). Although curry powder is, by definition, a foreign interpretation of Indianness[77] – and its usage here contrasts with the elaborate, subtly spiced recipes which introduce and punctuate each of the chapters in Malladi's novel – Frances's approximation of the real thing is a bid to make Priya, her future daughter-in-law, feel at home in America. Despite its obvious inauthenticity, it thus becomes a kind of 'third space'[78] which frees Priya from rigid definitions of 'Indian' and 'American'.

In the British Asian context – despite broader prejudices against older culinary traditions in the UK, compounded perhaps by the straitened circumstances of some immigrants and their families and by an intergenerational need to protect ancestral cuisine – a similarly syncretic gastronomic process is also at work. This is formalised through a number of specifically hybrid recipes in Bhogal's book *Cooking like Mummyji*. Initially born of necessity because her immigrant parents were forced 'to make use of the ingredients readily available at the local supermarket' (19), adapted dishes from childhood later inspire affection as she offers instructions on how to make such favourites as a Punjabi version of scrambled eggs, 'eggy bread' (a version of French toast) with garam masala and chilli, and baked beans with spring onion sabji. She also creates her own 'fusion' recipes: pasta with yogurt and chilli drizzle, 'maharajah's mash', Indian hot dogs, and spicy fishcakes and chips. Although such staples as baked beans and fishcakes evidently offer experimental possibilities, Bhogal's relationship to traditional British food, and by extension mainstream society, remains contradictory. Referring in matter-of-fact fashion to 'bland [British] food' (64) – once again, food lacking in Indian spices – she goes on to imply that her 'non-Asian friends' know little about cooking: they have only encountered 'chick peas . . . in a cold salad . . . or hummus' (68) and are content to eat 'reheated pizza' (86). Meanwhile, the food served up to non-South Asian diners at British Indian restaurants would cause 'uproar' were it to be offered in areas of dense South Asian settlement (125). Yet she also mentions her immigrant grandfather who 'loved . . . British food' (153), and, in line with her proudly British Asian stance, she has clearly been shaped as a cook by the experience of adapting and reinterpreting British ingredients and dishes to satisfy South Asian appetites.

Second-Generation Attitudes to Eating

If non-South Asian food is made to appear vapid, the children of immigrants nonetheless often favour it over Indian food, especially in a US context.[79] In Ameena Meer's novel *Bombay Talkie* (1994), Sabah recalls the pleasure of the mainstream foods served up at a friend's home: 'hot dogs and jello and macaroni and cheese . . . I [was] . . . so envious'.[80] And in *Burnt Bread*, Delman reminisces about the joys of family holidays where she could eat 'potato chips . . . ice cream . . . Kentucky Fried Chicken . . . Coca-Cola . . . food [which] was not kosher or spicy' (66). American food – in its populist, whitebread form – becomes associated here with freedom from daily routines and from the responsibilities of family, culture, and religion. In *Namesake*, Gogol's youthful wish to consume popular American food – illustrated earlier through his desire for beef-based products – mirrors a more sustained urge to assimilate into the wider culture.[81] This appetite for conformity leads his parents to take the path of least resistance by letting him

> fill the cart with items that he . . . but not they, consume: individually wrapped slices of cheese, mayonnaise, tuna fish, hot dogs. For Gogol's lunches they stand at the deli to buy cold cuts, and in the mornings Ashima makes sandwiches with bologna or roast beef. At his insistence, she . . . makes him an American dinner once a week as a treat, Shake 'n Bake chicken or Hamburger Helper prepared with ground lamb. (65)

Aamer Hussein has noted that as an adult, Gogol's increasing detachment from the world of his parents is figured in 'culinary terms' with the food he consumes continuing to change as he moves into new social circles.[82] The elegant, European-style food – 'polenta . . . risotto . . . bouillabaisse and osso buco' (137) – he eats with his white American girlfriend, Maxine Ratliff, and her parents reveals both his passive absorption of their affluent New York lifestyle and the underlying differences between Maxine and Gogol. Lahiri may not favour gastronomically based titles or obvious culinary metaphors, but she uses food in consistently suggestive ways throughout her writing: to reflect, quite matter-of-factly, the biculturalism of second-generation Indian Americans like Gogol[83] and to depict the older generation's 'beleaguered, yet determined and inventive, project of keeping Bengali culinary tradition . . . alive in the United States'; to bring the material and sensory elements of a scene to life; to reveal the discomfort and tensions between people who should feel safe with each other; and to illustrate the attempt to express love, often in vain, through cooking.[84] Indeed, she has claimed that 'food . . . has incredible meaning beyond the obvious nutritional aspects. My parents have given up so many basic things coming here [to the US] from the life they once knew . . . food is the one thing that they've really held onto'.[85]

In this affective context, it comes as little surprise, then, that when Maxine finally meets Gogol's parents, his unease about the occasion is signalled through gastronomic cues, from his embarrassment at their tendency not to close 'their mouths fully' when eating to a lunch which is 'too rich for the weather' (148). But the reader cringes, too, as Maxine hands the Gangulis a hamper from Dean and Deluca, the celebrated New York delicatessen, containing 'tinned pâtés . . . jars of cornichons and chutneys that Gogol knows his parents will never open and enjoy' (146). In other words, Maxine's love for a New York-based Euro-American cuisine does not necessarily speak to America's post-1965 immigrants. This episode also illustrates Lahiri's tendency to indicate place through food, so that the broader cultural cosmopolitanism of New York cuisine is pitted against the narrow Bengaliness of the food served at the Gangulis' suburban home. In a sense, however, their alimentary refusal to lose their homeland culture is entirely of a piece with the Ratliffs' behaviour, since both sets of parents impose their values and lifestyle on others through food. This provides perhaps the clearest indication of the lines – drawn equally uncompromisingly – between their separate worlds and foreshadows the eventual breakdown of Gogol's relationship with Maxine. But in his initially eager embrace of the Ratliffs' culinary world – a form of 'successful eating' which arguably 'occurs at the expense of spiritual integrity', to quote Sau-ling Wong, in a slightly different context[86] – Gogol prefers the WASP allure it signifies to what he perceives as the clumsy inability of his parents to assimilate.

Beyond Gogol's need to transform himself culturally, even ontologically, through consumption – that is, the idea, discussed earlier, that eating the foods of a particular cuisine will equal social and national incorporation – is the fact that, for some members of the second generation, mainstream American or British food is what they know and love. Meena's affection for fishfingers and chips in *Anita and Me* reflects the importance of this nursery food for British children from all ethnic backgrounds, as does Kohli's insistence on shepherd's pie and fish and chips in *Indian Takeaway*. The latter dish – claimed as quintessentially British but, as Panikos Panayi has argued, actually a product of immigrant entrepreneurship in the UK[87] – also surfaces in Farrukh Dhondy's short story 'East End at your feet' (1976). Kash, a British Indian teenager forced to move to Bombay following his father's death (as considered in Chapter 2), feels a desperate homesickness for London. This is figured in food-related terms and specifically through the image of fish and chips:

> I get the stink of the drying Bombay Duck and with it I imagine the smell of cod in batter at the local chippy . . . What I wouldn't give for a real fry-up from down Kingsland Road. It's vegetarian food in my grandad's house. All daal and rice and bhendu and enough yogurt to drown an elephant in.[88]

Writers also suggest that forms of gastronomic anxiety haunt the compulsion of many second-generation teenagers to belong to the cultural mainstream. For Rumi, the troubled protagonist of Nikita Lalwani's British Asian novel *Gifted* (2007), the appetite-suppressing mastication of cumin seeds, a reduced and contorted re-interpretation of Indian food culture, becomes a masochistic obsession and a symbol of emotional, as well as physical, hunger. More often, however, this anxiety takes an olfactory form: an idea which emerges particularly in recent British Asian literature.[89] Thus the home – often a sort of inner sanctum in which known cultural and familial rules apply – becomes a culinary space whose pungent aromas embarrassed adolescents long to reject. In Abdullah Hussein's novel *Émigré Journeys* (2000), Parvin, a young British Pakistani girl, perceives her family home as alien to the Britain outside because it smells entirely different. She recalls that, coming home from school:

> I knew that on the other side of my door was a different smell and a separate world . . . [the] smell . . . from the kitchen . . . got into everywhere . . . hung there forever, clinging to the walls and furniture and clothes. It was the smell of onion and garlic being fried in ghee and of . . . turmeric . . . cumin, coriander . . . root ginger and the stinging smell of chilli. Of course once I knew that I bore this smell and that it wasn't the smell of our skin or sweat . . . I said to them at school that our food was not like the half-boiled cattlefeed that they ate, colourless, tasteless and odourless like themselves. We cook our food, I said, it's an art, we put things in it.[90]

Parvin's position suggests a defensive pride which relies, once again, on the dialectical opposition between South Asian food as subtle, sophisticated, and skilfully produced, and the bald dismissal of British food in now familiar terms as 'colourless, tasteless . . . odourless'. But she also implies that the smells of South Asian food – and the ambivalent feelings of pride and shame it can stir up – have an inconvenient tendency to linger.[91] Suggesting that this, too, is a transatlantic phenomenon, the journalist S. Mitra Kalita writes in *Suburban Sahibs* (2003), her non-fictional study of South Asian Americans, about '"IFS" . . . Indian Food Smell . . . [which I] knew existed because my classmates told me so' and she admits to using an air freshener in a bid to expunge the smell before such classmates visited the family home.[92] In Nadeem Aslam's novel *Maps for Lost Lovers* (2004), the Pakistani matriarch, Kaukab, believes that the smell of fenugreek 'refuses to shift' because, unlike Pakistani houses, British dwellings consist of rooms which are 'small and closed up'.[93] She nevertheless takes protective action, keeping her family's coats at a distance from the kitchen so that their clothes will not be considered 'smelly' by white British people (105).

Srivastava's *Looking for Maya* initially resembles these other texts when its British Indian protagonist, Mira, recalls how, in her adolescence, the

> smell of turmeric . . . chillis and garlic . . . clung to my coat and my hair. I used to come home from school and race upstairs to put my coat in the bedroom so it wouldn't reek. When I had made no friends . . . I would silently accuse that smell of garlic, hold it . . . and both my parents responsible by association. (105–6)

But Mira's attitude towards 'IFS' later takes a positive turn when, as an adult, she finds herself 'looking forward to that smell . . . of home. I would cook dahl and lace it with a sizzling tarka, a concoction of seared garlic and chillies, and breathe in the aroma' (106). Significantly, it is only in adulthood – once the horrors of peer pressure have safely passed and indeed, after her parents have gone back to India – that Mira can find this spicy smell reassuring.[94]

The Rise of the Food Memoir

In keeping, perhaps, with a wider transatlantic surge of interest in food since the 1990s – ingredients and their provenance, culinary methods, restaurant culture, cookery programmes, and celebrity chefs[95] – South Asian Atlantic writers have increasingly produced food memoirs. On one level, this can be traced to the wider growth of this subgenre in

Britain and the US, as we see with the success enjoyed by such works as Anthony Bourdain's *Kitchen Confidential: Adventures in the Culinary Underbelly* (2000) and Nigel Slater's *Toast: The Story of a Boy's Hunger* (2003). But it also relates to the pre-eminence of food in the South Asian diaspora as a rich, complex means of cultural expression and economic survival. With 'Indian' restaurants (more likely to be Bangladeshi) such a selling point for diasporic communities, particularly in Britain,[96] writers such as Narayan, Candappa, Kohli, and Alibhai-Brown take their commercial, as much as their literary, cue from a largely captive, non-South Asian audience in love with 'ethnic' food and particularly 'Indian' cuisine. Despite the sense of a publishing bandwagon, critics have claimed the uniqueness of, for instance, Candappa's *Picklehead* and Alibhai-Brown's *Settler's Cookbook. Picklehead* is marketed as 'unique' and 'a book like no other' while reviews of *Settler's Cookbook* hail it as 'path-breaking', 'a story seldom told', and 'a rare contribution'.[97] There is, however, some truth in these assertions. The South Asian diasporic food memoir may not be new, a point perhaps lost on mainstream reviewers, but the distinctive blend of ethnic and historical specificity to be found in individual examples is original. In any case, these South Asian Atlantic texts, which also include Narayan's *Monsoon Diary* and Kohli's *Indian Takeaway*, show a heartfelt, unwavering respect for cooking and eating traditions. This attitude renders them quite separate from the gastronomic superficiality of works which are merely food-titled. In this section, I will ask what purpose is served by such food memoirs, while charting their transatlantic convergences and differences.

Monsoon Diary is a coming-of-age narrative, which – as its title promises – charts in sometimes photographic detail Narayan's childhood and adolescence in Madras, her university years in New England and Tennessee, and her life as a newlywed just outside New York City. Each chapter is framed by one or more recipes, which serve a dual focus: to celebrate the rich history and flavours of Tamil Hindu cooking; and to add an extra layer of knowledge and authenticity to Narayan's linear narrative. Like the other memoirs considered here – *Picklehead* as Indian–Sri Lankan Catholic, *Indian Takeaway* as Punjabi Sikh, and *Settler's Cookbook* as East African Indian Muslim (and, more specifically, Khoja Ismaili) – the particular ethno-religious nature of the author's community, as reflected through food, defines *Monsoon Diary*. For Padma Lakshmi, this regional emphasis is precisely what makes the text a welcome departure from other works on Indian food, since it amounts to 'a loving portrait of a cuisine and culture yet to be celebrated properly'.[98] This sense that South Indian cooking is neglected reflects both India's internal North–South divide and, beyond the subcontinent, the over-representation of certain regional cuisines – particularly, Mughlai dishes – in Indian restaurants. Although the situation is changing, South Indian cooking is still less well-known abroad than a more generalised Northern Indian cuisine. Narayan may even have written *Monsoon Diary* because she sensed this gap, particularly within the food memoir subgenre.[99]

Narayan's text is anecdotal and ethnographic, but not didactic. Indeed, she applies an impressively light touch to her cultural explanations, which are obviously intended for a mainstream American audience. But she can appear defensive, too, recalling, for instance, that

> as I got older, I began to appreciate eating with my hands, which allowed me to savour the warm food through pliant fingers rather than a cold, hard fork or spoon. In fact, Indians believe that hands add flavour to food. When an Indian wants to compliment a person's culinary skills, he doesn't simply say 'She is a good cook'. He says that 'she has good scent in her hands'. (34–5)

This signals, once again, the importance of gender roles in the preparation of South Asian food, since Indian men remark upon Indian women's cooking abilities here. Although Narayan offers no comment at this point on such gender dynamics, they crucially underpin *Monsoon Diary*. As a young tomboy, she is unimpressed by her mother's insistence that a 'new bride' must be adept in the kitchen (72), although she later conforms to these values when she is allowed to study in America only if she can successfully cook a traditional vegetarian feast. What lies behind this fairy-tale-like test is the old-fashioned idea that cooking is proof of feminine worth, which is tightly bound up with moral and cultural purity. In other words, only when Narayan rises to this culinary challenge, having imbibed her mother's cultural teachings after all, can she earn the right to leave India.

In celebrating the artistry and inventiveness of South Indian cuisine, presented as a kind of *ne plus ultra* of vegetarian cooking – a form which, by contrast, has remained unsophisticated in Britain and America until only relatively recently[100] – *Monsoon Diary* reveals the ingenuity and practical thinking behind the creation of different dishes as well as their internal balance of flavours and health benefits. The sheer skill required to produce her ancestral cuisine may also account for Narayan's claim that her grandmother's servant, Maari, made 'rice . . . [with] a grainy yet soft texture that I haven't been able to duplicate with any of the modern gadgets that litter my kitchen these days' (46). Although 'only' talking about cooking rice – on the face of it, a simple enough task – she repeats a common refrain in 'ethnic' food writing here: namely, as we saw earlier, the difficulty in reproducing the apparent perfection of childhood foods. For Narayan, such perfection becomes closely connected to place when she notes that

> I have never eaten a good *idli* in America, although countless Indian restaurants offer them. American *idlis* are hard and lack a tangy sourdough taste. For good *idlis*, you have to go to my hometown. (72–3)

But it is precisely in living outside India that Narayan develops the need to cook traditional food and actually learns how to do so. Paradoxically, cooking only becomes a voyage of personal discovery, and ancestral culture a source of homage, after emigration.[101]

Maari's ability to produce fluffier rice than can Narayan marks an important tension between authenticity and inauthenticity: that is, who can and cannot prepare traditional South Indian food. On the one hand, Narayan invites the reader (presumed to be an American-based ethnic outsider) to make these complex regional recipes in what is as much 'how-to' guide, invitation to join in, and democratisation of a particular tradition of home cooking as personal memoir; and she herself feels free to cook Italian, Greek, Turkish, and Mexican recipes. On the other, Narayan betrays prejudices about white people audacious enough to believe they can make South Indian food. Thus, she recalls an encounter in London with a man who prepares and sells traditional South Indian snacks:

> I am wandering around a weekend open-air market . . . a tiny stall [is] selling – can it be? – *pav-bhaji*. I find myself wandering over, drawn by the smell of cumin, cloves, and cardamom. Behind the counter is a blue-eyed, blond Caucasian. I frown in confusion. A Caucasian making *pav-bhaji*? My chin rises challengingly. His name is Mike Guest, and he hands me a steaming plate. The *pav* is crisp on the outside and buttery soft inside. The *bhaji* vegetables are just right . . . Mike Guest watches with a satisfied smile as I quickly polish off the entire plate. 'I've eaten better,' I say airily to the reincarnated Indian as I pay. 'Can I have another plate to go? For my friend, not for me.' (93)

His 'Caucasian' appearance repeated for rhetorical emphasis, Mike is aptly named because he is indeed a 'guest': a pretender and an impersonator. As a British man, he also belongs outside Narayan's intended US target audience and is thus a safer target for critique. Although she views her own prejudices with honesty and humour, Narayan gestures towards the crucial status of food as a marker of cultural belonging and authenticity and, in the process, reveals the flawed logic of her own apparently inclusive project. The paradoxes of this project – questioned in any case by her

Brahminic privilege in India – may also relate to her simultaneous need, like other 'ethnic' food writers, to guard 'the borders of the . . . community' and challenge 'white assumptions . . . while creating allegiances with . . . American readers'.[102]

Eating in the US signals independent choice and, for Narayan, the process of learning to think for herself. But this sits alongside the enduring status of traditional food as a symbol of 'my lineage . . . identity, and . . . place in the world' (122), simplified even further to '*idlis* and coffee' (74). Indeed, the preparation and consumption of '"pure" South Indian coffee' (73) remains key. Thus, in a return-of-the-native moment, recalling the discussion in Chapter 2, Narayan's prospective husband, Ram, is commended by her family for 'accepting [traditional] coffee . . . Not like these America-returned types who won't touch food or drink in the subcontinent. As if the food here is tainted' (232). The appropriateness of Ram's behaviour duly established, the marriage goes ahead and it becomes a wifely test for Narayan to produce the best traditional food possible as she comes full circle in her perpetuation of familial culture and its gendered values.[103]

Candappa adopts a more humorous approach to the relationship between food and cultural heritage in *Picklehead*: a portmanteau family memoir and, in the sense that it commemorates a vanishing past, a mnemonic site in the style of *Settler's Cookbook* and Delman's *Burnt Bread*.[104] As a title, 'Picklehead' is livelier than the staid-sounding, even cliché-ridden *Indian Takeaway* or *Monsoon Diary*, while some of the memoir's chapter names – 'A pinch of salt', a series of sections offering a 'brief history of curry in Britain', which use the conceit of a 'half' (chapter '8 ½', '9 ½' and so on) – add to its sense of exuberance. Without taking himself too seriously either, Candappa remains explicitly ambivalent about both his British status and his category-defying ethnic identity as a 'South London born and bred', 'Ceylonese-Burmese-Portuguese-Roman Catholic', who exists well beyond the parameters of 'the mythical "Asian community"' (201, 2, 305).[105] Correct, of course, to note the fictional nature of a monolithic 'Asian community', Candappa nonetheless recognises that, in a 1970s context,

> I should have been Hindu, or Sikh, or Muslim. Roman Catholic didn't really fit in with the preconceived ideas of the time . . . I was encountering . . . a dislocation between who I was expected to be and who I actually was. (216–17)

Neither humour nor a life-enhancing pride in his family's culinary history can fully mask the poignant existentialism of his enduring sense that 'whatever I do, wherever I go, a part of me always feels out in the snow with my face pressed up against a window' (71). Even so, Candappa betrays a quintessential Englishness through his popular cultural references, while the complexities of his multiply hyphenated identity galvanise him into celebrating his family's sheer global reach: a cosmopolitan past expressed through a plethora of delicious, sometimes complicated recipes, faithfully reproduced in the memoir.

This celebration relies, however, on a process of excavation. Candappa may recognise the universal importance of food and the ways in which it shores up cultural authenticity and belonging, yet *Picklehead* begins by confessing how far he has moved away from the culture of his early life. That admission of loss is made somewhat guiltily and although he claims to be unsure 'what exactly it was that I had lost' (10), he makes clear that it is food-related. Indeed, his moment of realisation comes when, relying on recipe books to cook 'a proper chicken curry' for his children, he ends up in the 'intangibly unsettling' situation of buying a jar of supermarket korma sauce' (8, 10). More problematising than Narayan's work of remembrance in *Monsoon Diary*, *Picklehead* represents a course of deceptively serious sleuthing, as Candappa searches, through food, for information about his 'family history and history in a far wider sense' (10). This leads him to question how

> over the same period of time that I had drifted away from my culinary heritage, curry had gone from being 'smelly and foreign' to being, according to the late Robin Cook, 'the most popular dish in Britain' . . . And what, if any, was the link between what I had lost and what the country had gained? (11)

This broadening-out of his research lends greater relevance to a specific ancestral history, while his meticulous recording of family recipes suggests that he is educating himself as much as the reader.

Similarly, in Alibhai-Brown's *Settler's Cookbook* – a title which suggests active overtones of reverse colonisation ('settler', as opposed to 'immigrant' or 'exile') and the practicality required to survive ('cookbook' implying a manual) – recipes are both a formula for living and a testimonial, oral way to make sense of, and memorialise, the past. Again, this is not simply about recording personal history. Rather, it is about exploring, in a revisionist sense, the hidden history of a whole community. Thus *Settler's Cookbook* is part of the author's wider political mission to examine South Asian history in East Africa and, to a lesser extent in multicultural Britain, according it its due importance in both places. Alibhai-Brown seeks to do so in a positive, yet objective manner, giving space both to British brutality towards Indian indentured labourers in colonial East Africa and to Ugandan Asians' own persistent anti-black racism. She claims that:

> like many other East African Asians whose forebears left India in the nineteenth century, I search endlessly for . . . the remains of those days. Few maps mark routes of journeys undertaken by these migrants; hardly any books capture their spirit or tell the story. (1)

Although her contention that 'there are no films about our old lives' is not actually true – one thinks, in particular, of Nair's *Mississippi Masala* – her emphasis on the general neglect of this history, though didactic at times, is difficult to dispute.

Deploying food as her leitmotif – since it is the best way, in her words, to 'warm up the past and make it stir again'[106] – Alibhai-Brown therefore uses her memoir to reclaim an epic but vanished and, in her view, deliberately erased past. She describes East African Asians as 'a people who leave no trace' (67); this, then, is her explicit, angry, elegiac attempt to 'leave [a] . . . trace' by remembering her dead parents, lost home(s), and, once again, the soon-to-be-forgotten culinary skills of an earlier generation. It is a response to her British-born children's ambivalence and lack of interest in their ancestry: a bid through food to inculcate this family history into them. And since this is her comprehensive, in many ways definitive, attempt to capture in panoramic terms a whole lost world, Alibhai-Brown's wealth of detail about food extends to her broader community portrait, as she pays homage to a whole cast of characters from her early life.

To a greater extent than *Settler's Cookbook*, *Picklehead* is predicated on the conviction that the cultures of the 'East' – defined here as Burma, Singapore, India, and 'Ceylon' – are superior to those of the 'West' (Britain). Thus Asia's traditions of cooking, eating, hospitality, and general conviviality are apparently finer, its weather hotter and more inviting, and its societies characterised by a higher degree of 'elegance and dignity' (296). The memoir is also shot through with nostalgia for the putatively safer, more innocent world of Candappa's 1970s London childhood, best illustrated by memories of the feasts laid on at 'glorious', culturally hybrid, family Christmases, which combined those

> my mother had grown up with in Burma and India, and the full-on British-style approach . . . a big part of who I am . . . who I aspire to be, can be found round the overladen Christmas tables of my childhood. (66–8)

Behind both beliefs is Candappa's profound respect for his parents, which becomes hard to disentangle from the memoir's emphasis on food. In a series of attitudes which anticipate Kohli's *Indian Takeaway* (beyond the shared memory of tinned fish curry discussed above), Candappa lovingly recalls his parents' achievements, relating a story which, unlike his own, has already unfolded; and which he clearly perceives to be more exciting. As Kohli later does, he also addresses the reader directly, thus drawing him or her into the narrative and suggesting the collective, hospitable, traditional 'Eastern' society he so admires. But much as we saw with Kohli's travelogue in Chapter 2, Candappa appears most comfortable in a filial role, saying remarkably little about his wife and children, who simply appear, albeit comically, as 'Small Child A' and 'Small Child B' (9). Candappa's understated, but loving and sensitive, tribute to his deceased father is particularly moving and it reveals a striking alternative to his light-hearted tone elsewhere in the text. The filial loyalty of both Candappa and Kohli can, however, compromise their objectivity about their parents and, by extension, the problematic aspects of parental culture. *Settler's Cookbook*, as well as such recent family memoirs as Manzoor's *Greetings from Bury Park* and Sanghera's *Boy with the Topknot*, are, by contrast, more critical of parents and communities, even as they venerate the older generation.

In *Indian Takeaway*, Kohli is less interested than Candappa in the historical origins of Indian dishes, but just as concerned with comedy, the particular conditions of a 1970s British childhood, and the need to bear witness to the experiences of one's parents. Food is deployed to commemorate the distinct, yet paradoxically ordinary, twentieth-century history of British Asians, as – rather unusually for these works – Kohli moves beyond the ethno-religious specificities of his own family to reflect a broader spirit of community and solidarity within the diaspora. This is illustrated through the childhood memory of watching Bollywood films at a Glasgow cinema every Sunday in the 1970s and 1980s:

> For six days of the week, cinemas were bastions of British and American film, but on Sunday . . . Bollywood took over. And it felt like every brown person in Glasgow was there . . . There was also food involved. Hot mince and pea samosas were handed round . . . pakoras would be illicitly eaten with spicy chutney. There would be the inevitable spillage and some fruity Punjabi cursing, involving an adult blaming the nearest innocent kid for their own inability to pour cardamom tea from a thermos whilst balancing an onion bhaji on their knee. (8–9)

Through the sensory detail of 'mince and pea samosas', 'pakoras', 'spicy chutney', 'cardamom tea', and the precarious consumption of 'an onion bhaji', Kohli brings this now distant memory to life, while engaging his audience in imaginative terms through what Mannur has termed 'hyperreal eating . . . the practice of simulating eating without physically ingesting food'[107] and playing on a national familiarity with – and enthusiasm for – the Indian snacks which colourfully punctuate this episode.

It is this familiarity, and the idea that 'as a child, the only aspect of being Indian which wider society seemed to celebrate was our food' (44), which drives Kohli's mission to 'return to India what India has so successfully given Britain: food . . . I resolved to take British food to India' (17). The self-indulgent, even doomed nature of this venture – in view of the unpromising reputation enjoyed by British food in India – is not lost on Kohli, however, since he draws attention to its limitations even before he sets off.[108] Yet he does it anyway, preparing everything from toad in the hole in Bangalore to pork belly, mashed potato, and apple sauce in Goa to shepherd's pie in Delhi to a version of fish and chips in Kashmir. Making repeated concessions to the Indian palate, fruitlessly searching for ingredients (its own reversal of immigrants' earlier difficulties in securing authentic produce in Britain and America), and producing, by necessity, a series of distinctly non-British dishes, too, Kohli perseveres with his quest. Perhaps this is because its gimmicky nature provides invaluable textual material and thus the promise of successful book sales. Its comical absurdity elicits the reader's sympathy and interest, moreover, since each cooking episode is so risky and unpredictable. And Kohli's chutzpah is undercut by moments of self-awareness and self-deprecation, and by failures which are as revealing as his successes. After receiving a damning response from an old friend, Bharat Shetty, to his Bangalore toad in the hole, he believes he has learnt nothing about himself. Yet he has discovered the gulf between India and its diaspora when his fusion food (the 'toad' has to be prepared with strips of mutton and the wrong type of fat) makes no impact whatsoever on Bharat.

Cooking provides an organising principle and overarching philosophy but, much like *Monsoon Diary*, Kohli's road and rail trip across India works as a straight paean to the glorious variety of Indian food: idlis, curries, deep-fried plantain, pakoras, samosas, bhajis, dosas, aloo boondi, rajmah chawal, chutneys. It is also a very individual journey in which food becomes the perfect vehicle for an examination of personal and cultural identity and the very question of human existence. Asked by a Goan acquaintance to justify why he is using cooking to 'find' himself in India, Kohli answers that it is 'because I believe in food . . . [it] is the way to people's hearts and souls. Understand someone's food and you understand them' (174). More tellingly, perhaps, he concedes at the end of the travelogue that 'my attempt to bring with me the food of the land of my birth soon became secondary to the search for who I am and how I feel about myself' (284). This recalls the denouement of *Picklehead*, where Candappa asks whether the second generation belongs

> to the world your parents came from . . . Or are you really a product of the world you . . . grew up in? . . . If it is both, then what is the balance between the two worlds? I'm not sure that I've ended up with a definitive answer to any of these questions. But . . . I'm not sure that definitive answers actually exist. (311)

In other words, for both Candappa and Kohli – and, one might add, Alibhai-Brown – it is the exploration through food of such ontological and existential questions, and the energy and tenacity required to do it, which lie at the heart of each memoir.

Uniting these otherwise disparate food memoirs is their emphasis on specific foods and dishes, introduced by their original names, which are then glossed for a presumed non-South Asian readership.[109] Beyond the discussions of tinned fish curry in *Picklehead*, *Indian Takeaway*, and *Settler's Cookbook*, Narayan celebrates *prasadam* in *Monsoon Diary* (21), showing that it spans India's different religious traditions, while Kohli similarly praises *prasad* in hyperbolic terms in the Sikh context. Both Narayan and Candappa write about *rasam* and compare it to 'chicken soup' (*Monsoon Diary*, 36; *Picklehead*, 96). Candappa claims it as 'an age-old Ceylonese recipe' (96), however, and their versions of the dish are distinctly different. Thus the 'toovar dal . . . tomatoes . . . asafetida . . . rasam powder . . . ghee' called for in Narayan's recipe (*Monsoon Diary*, 37) do not appear in Candappa's, which instead includes 'garlic . . . peppercorns . . . onions . . . red chillies . . . [and] curry leaves' (*Picklehead*, 97). The sense of drawing on a particular repertoire of dishes nevertheless brings together these South Asian Atlantic texts across religious lines (Hindu, Sikh, Christian, Muslim); ethno-linguistic differences (Tamil, Punjabi, Sinhalese, Gujarati); and very different histories of migration (to the United States from India and to Britain via northern India, Burma, Sri Lanka, and East Africa). In other words, food provides a unifying language which suggests – despite my arguments to the contrary in Chapter 2 – that a common South Asian identity, and particularly a recognisable Indianness, might exist after all, although this idea is not explored at any great length by writers themselves.

Although I am extrapolating from a small sample of a burgeoning subgenre, it is possible to note distinct transatlantic differences between these food memoirs. Thus Narayan draws on a quintessentially American literary form: namely, the serious, linear immigrant autobiography. In this sense, despite its veneration for ancestral tradition, *Monsoon Diary* recalls such classic coming-to-America works as Jacob Riis's *The Making of an American* (1901) or Mary Antin's *The Promised Land* (1912). By contrast, Candappa and Kohli write from a second-generation, British-born subject position. They deploy humour, especially of a self-deprecating variety, to a far greater extent than Narayan, perhaps because – as I noted in Chapter 2 – the US self-image as a 'nation of immigrants' produces a more solemn response to ethnicity.

Narayan's text is also more ethnographic than *Picklehead*, *Indian Takeaway*, or *Settler's Cookbook*. This may be because she is working within the context of a less recognised tradition for Indian food in the United States[110] than that of her British counterparts. Indeed, Candappa claims, in a moment of anti-American polemic, that 'like so many of the finer cultural things in life, the Americans just didn't get curry' (245), while Indira Ganesan has suggested that, as opposed to the US, 'in England, they might ask for "a curry", at least allowing that there's more than one kind'.[111] The colonial dynamics of Britain's relationship with India have certainly led to a different relationship with South Asian food, albeit in a radically re-imagined, inauthentic form. But the result of such historical differences is that although Kohli, Candappa, and Alibhai-Brown seek to open the reader's eyes to the realities and complexities of South Asian gastronomy, Narayan's tone remains more educative since it relies on less shared knowledge.

Recent British Asian Cookbooks

Just as these recent memoirs blur the line between the genres of recipe book and life-writing, so critics have long read cookbooks as a form of autobiography;[112] and in a chapter devoted to South Asian diasporic food, one cannot ignore the importance of actual cookery manuals. But rather than revisit the already well-documented impact of earlier South Asian Atlantic food writers, particularly Madhur Jaffrey,[113] I will now analyse two more recent recipe books-cum-memoirs: Bhogal's *Cooking like Mummyji* and, more briefly, Simon Daley's *Cooking with My Indian Mother-in-Law: Mastering the Art of Authentic Home Cooking* (2008).

Produced by different publishers and appearing five years apart, both books are nonetheless remarkably similar in a physical and aesthetic sense: that is, in their size, colour (both have dark pink covers), and length. And in each case, the author situates recipes in personal terms, maintains an anecdotal conversation with the reader, and stakes a claim to authenticity. That this claim is crucial is made evident by the fact that it appears, in both cases, in the book's subtitle: 'real British Asian cooking', in Bhogal's case; and the strapline 'mastering the art of authentic home cooking' for Daley. Bhogal may emphasise 'real'-ness – further established through a series of family photographs and reportage-style shots of British Sikh culture – because she has interpreted her mother's traditional cooking from a second-generation vantage point. This suggests a tension between the book's explicit pride in British Asian cuisine, rather than food in India, and a certain discomfort that such culinary knowledge has had to be deliberately and self-consciously acquired. Yet this point of comparison with Narayan, Candappa, and Alibhai-Brown – namely, the learning of traditional recipes only as an adult – may also account for the zeal and determination underpinning the text's culinary purpose. For Daley, authentication is necessary because of his questionable status as an authority: like Mike Guest in *Monsoon Diary*, he is, after all, a white interloper. His uncertain position is, however, rescued and shored up by the presence of Roshan (or Rose) Hirani, his eponymous mother-in-law, as key contributor, and by an enthusiastic endorsement from a top British-based Indian chef, Vivek Singh, who hails the book as 'a faithful record of the *instinctive* cooking that goes on in a *typical* Indian household' (front cover, book dustjacket; emphasis added). Bhogal and Daley also stress authenticity in order to mark out their recipes from the hybridised, inauthentic, watered-down 'Indian' food traditionally on offer in British restaurants.

As regards *Mummyji*, this is perhaps ironic given Bhogal's emphasis on culinary syncretism (as discussed above), but the separation between home and restaurant food is one of the book's defining premises:

> our home food is much simpler than the food you find in Indian restaurants. We use very few spices . . . The main element missing from restaurant food is the female energy. The kitchen is . . . the best place to be in an Indian or British-Asian household. Full of women joking . . . gossiping, confiding . . . The wisdom, love and culture of these women rubs off from their hands into the food to give a special taste. (n.p.)

These ideas correspond to the notion of a woman's hands imparting extra flavour, mentioned in *Monsoon Diary*, and above all to the earlier celebration of mothers-as-cooks in the intimate sphere of one's childhood home rather than the public space of the male-dominated restaurant. This external culinary setting is less authentic, both because it caters mainly for non-South Asians and, implicitly, because men rather than women are doing the cooking.

In Bhogal's explicit homage to matrilineage, then, her otherwise unnamed 'Mummyji' joins the roll call of South Asian mothers who cook superbly, thanks to years of practice – and little choice in the matter. But this paean contains its own irony, similar to that of *Monsoon Diary* and later Daley's cookbook: if it has taken Indian women years to become expert cooks, why should it prove such a simple task to cook their legendary dishes? This also resembles the puzzle of *Picklehead* and *Settler's Cookbook*, as well as *Monsoon Diary*: namely, at what point recipes are actually supposed to be made and at what point they serve a more commemorative function. It is also worth noting that in every work which lauds a mother's cooking, her own voice is absent, mediated instead by children with the time, confidence, literary training, and desire to record her achievements; and this may result from their sense of feeling sufficiently settled in a multicultural society – Britain or the US – to explore issues of cultural history and ethnic pride.

Claiming *Mummyji* as a new type of cookbook, neither written by 'non-Asians' nor containing 'complicated . . . dishes from restaurant kitchens in India' (17), Bhogal argues that it 'is not just a book for other British Asians' (16), although they are clearly a key target audience. Rather it is an attempt to show 'the Western world . . . the secret of real Indian home-cooking': posited as easy to make (despite some recipes which suggest otherwise), offering a 'perfectly balanced meal' which can be cooked 'fresh from scratch without any artificial ingredients . . . healthy . . . [with] much less oil . . . than restaurant food and . . . quite mild' (16). *Mummyji* is, moreover, written with love, verve, and excitement. Thorough and compendious, it is also the product of a writer who is clearly an excellent cook herself. But in several important ways, it is problematic, too. Bhogal's desire to address both British Asians and a 'non-Asian' audience results in an 'autoethnographic cookbook': that is, 'a form which seeks both to represent the group within its own sense of its history and culture and to contradict dominant representations'.[114] But this leads to an awkward mixture of second-person narrative familiarity for potential second-generation women reading the book and moments of ethnographic explanation – for instance, a defence of arranged marriage – as though Bhogal is simply trying to do too much in her first book.[115] Her need to explain Sikh religious ritual also speaks to the difficulty of making her Punjabi heritage synonymous with a broader British constituency of Indian descent, even though – recalling the recurrence of such dishes as *prasad* and *rasam* across the memoirs discussed above – she does note an interethnic, interreligious relevance to many of her dishes.

Her effusive celebration of British Punjabi family life, exemplified by her own close bond to her parents and siblings, also means that – as with Candappa and Kohli – a more measured assessment of diasporic culture is missing. Thus, unlike Sanghera's loving, but clear-eyed, critique of British Sikhs in *Boy with the Topknot*, Bhogal records an array of customs in an unquestioning manner: corporal punishment of children; a reliance on superstition; the arduousness of agrarian life in the Punjab; arranged marriages (but without any attention to their potential difficulties); and the limitations of traditional gender dynamics. Perhaps Sanghera's charged and haunting narrative, which also chronicles the prevalence of Punjabi domestic violence, goes too far in the other direction in ways that would sit very uncomfortably with the ethno-religious pride of British Punjabis like Bhogal, whose love of traditional culture and food, family and British society are, moreover, life-affirming. Neither do I wish to make the crude suggestion that Sanghera's version is 'right' while Bhogal's is 'wrong'. But in comparison with *Boy with the Topknot* – and even *Indian Takeaway*, which chronicles the white racism Kohli so often faced as a boy – *Mummyji* can feel like a relentlessly positive, public relations exercise, even a hagiography of British Sikhs.

In *Cooking with my Indian Mother-in-Law*, Daley gets around Bhogal's dismissal of Indian cookbooks written by 'non-Asians' by celebrating exactly the same matrilineal tradition of home cooking. In his Introduction, Daley fondly recalls his first experience of his mother-in-law's delicious cooking, which marked a kind of parental blessing of his interracial relationship with Rose's daughter, Salima. The book is yet another mnemonic site, containing plenty of visual evidence of Rose at work. Indeed, as did *Mummyji* and Patel's *A Love Supreme*, Salima has photographed her mother's hands making Indian dishes. Vivek Singh's endorsement, quoted above, also attests to the text's memorialising function. Much as Sandhu noted in relation to *A Love Supreme*, he sees the book as a tribute to the 'unsung skills of the home cook' – that is, the culinary work performed by Indian women – and, perhaps even more importantly, as a record of such knowledge now that recipes no longer 'pass orally from one generation to the next' (book dustjacket). That Daley has written his text – more biography and straightforward manual than *Mummyji* – in a less intimate and more objective way can be traced precisely to his status as outsider.

Conclusion

This chapter has shown the extent to which South Asian Atlantic writers rely on foodways to explore questions of identity in national and cultural terms. Once again, some major transatlantic similarities can be discerned through the thematic emphasis by writers on gender roles, specifically the unpaid culinary labour performed by so many immigrant mothers, which is arduous, yet identity-forming and a source of artistic expression;[116] the superiority of Indian cuisine versus 'mainstream' foods in both Britain and America; shopping, the search for ingredients, and the processes of adaptation which inevitably follow; and the navigation of gastronomic taboos, particularly articulated through attitudes to meat-eating.

Fiction and life-writing alike also point to an educative project, which takes several forms. It concerns the need to inform non-South Asians about the ethno-regional and historical differences embodied in subcontinental foodways, and about the important distinction between 'authentic' home cooking and 'inauthentic' restaurant food. It is also an 'autoethnographic' process and, for the second generation especially, an autodidactic one, too. This process arguably achieves a successful negotiation of 'the burden of . . . ethnic food . . . [by] get[ting] over the romanticism to say something more interesting than mere affirmation'.[117] It does so through painstaking research and a deep-seated respect for culinary expertise; through a recognition of family and gender dynamics; and among younger British Asians and South Asian Americans, through an acknowledgement of cultural ignorance about traditional food. This coming-to-terms with one's culinary heritage also follows a particular pattern. Following a period of both conscious and unintentional detachment from the pleasures and limits of parental cooking – in a love-hate relationship which can lead to ethnic shame and a furious desire to assimilate by eating 'mainstream' food – a number of British Asians and South Asian Americans feel a duty to record, and learn to make, the dishes they ate in childhood. This is not confined to women, as Candappa, Kohli, Manzoor, Sanghera, and Patel demonstrate. Indeed, men may feel less ambivalence about food preparation, since sons generally experience less pressure to preserve culinary methods. Nor is the need to engage with such tradition limited to Britain or the US, as demonstrated by Lahiri's second-generation characters and Narayan in *Monsoon Diary*. For the latter, however – and for Alibhai-Brown – that need emerges only after emigrating.

This process of commemoration results in a full embrace of gastronomic tradition and the food text as mnemonic site. Despite the popularity of 'Indian' food abroad, particularly in the UK, such traditions are perceived as endangered and the determination to perpetuate them thus becomes a passionate one. This recalls Elaine Kim's contention that within Asian American literature, writers 'sensitive to the foreboding certainty that the elderly and their life experiences will vanish before they can be understood and appreciated, portray the old with a sense of urgency'.[118] It also suggests that diasporic culture is, in Purnima Mankekar's words, 'reified in terms of loss or fears of loss – something that has to be consciously retained, produced, or disavowed'.[119] But I have argued that this charged engagement can lead to problematic texts where writers are so invested in celebrating and memorialising family through food that their tone becomes defensive, uncritical, fulsome even, resulting in an absence of objectivity.

If food memoirs contain transatlantic differences – namely, a higher degree of familiarity with South Asian food in the British context and thus a more ethnographic tone in South Asian American works – so, too, do fictional works. Although they agree, almost uniformly, on the excellence of South Asian cuisine – its depth and subtlety of flavour reflecting, perhaps, the complexity of subcontinental culture itself – they suggest a greater degree of antipathy towards standard British, than standard American, food. And this attitude of disdain is shared by both British Asian and South Asian American writers. Despite a shared transatlantic embarrassment towards 'Indian Food Smell', then, the young American-born *desi* generation is shown to consume, with more gusto, such US mainstays as hot dogs, bologna, and tuna sandwiches than the equivalent situation for second-generation British Asians. Such behaviour suggests that the consumption of meat (especially beef) occupies an even more central position in US than in UK culture and that American comestibles simply taste better than British food. But this transatlantic distinction also signals the stronger emphasis, illustrated here through eating habits, on immigrant 'integration' in the United States and multicultural 'separatism' in the UK, as I argued in the Introduction to this book. When we consider the treatment of food in South Asian Atlantic literature as a whole, however, such differences can of course be interrogated. After all, a writer like Lahiri handles Indian foodways in the US with subtlety and elegance, sidestepping any need for ethnographic explanation, while Bhogal strays into sometimes unnecessary cultural explication in the British Asian setting of *Mummyji*; and Bhogal, Kohli, and such fictional characters as Kash in 'East End at your feet' show affection for classic British dishes, particularly fish and chips.

On a slightly different note, I will now conclude by returning to the earlier claim that food in South Asian diasporic writing has become a cliché and to the question of who perpetuates this idea. Certainly publishers and critics rely on food imagery, in an unthreatening and sometimes reductive way, to package and discuss these works.[120] One thinks, for instance, of the reception of Monica Ali's novel *Brick Lane* in 2003. Natasha Walter's

Guardian review is entitled 'Citrus scent of inexorable desire', while Suzi Feay's discussion in the *Independent on Sunday* bears the headline, '*Brick Lane* by Monica Ali: It's one raita short of a spicy literary banquet'. Feay concludes with the verdict that the novel is 'bland . . . anglicised fare, perhaps best suited to the sort of person who still orders the "English dishes" in an Indian restaurant – with a sprinkling of garam masala'.[121] Using spice imagery (Feay's 'garam masala' reference) to frame and contain the 'East' is, of course, an age-old feature of Orientalist discourse.[122] But it is worth noting that South Asian commentators have also drawn on food-related rhetoric to discuss *Brick Lane*. Illustrating this point, Sukhdev Sandhu's *London Review of Books* article is called 'Come hungry, leave edgy', and Bobby Ghosh's review in *Time Asia* magazine bears the heading, 'Flavour of the week'. Headlines may be controlled by editors and subeditors, but Sandhu's essay still discusses the current appetite for Bangladeshi food in Spitalfields and Ghosh writes of *Brick Lane* that 'if you've grown up on a diet of Bengali and British-Indian literature, Ali's debut is . . . predictable and lacking in flavour'.[123]

As we saw at the beginning of this chapter, the framing of South Asian writing in unnuanced gastronomic terms is common practice. Thus Ursula Le Guin praises the 'comic sense' of a fellow writer, Manju Kapur, in her novel *The Immigrant* (2009), as 'a kind of gently pervasive and delicious flavour, like that of ginger or coriander used with a light hand'.[124] And Graham Huggan notes, for instance, that John Updike's 1997 review in the *New Yorker* of two novels – Arundhati Roy's *The God of Small Things* (1997) and Ardashir Vakil's *Beach Boy* (1997) –

> merely adds to the gastronomic clichés strewn across Western writing about India, thus completely missing the obvious irony that these clichés are reproduced *for deflating purposes* in several contemporary Indian works, Roy's and Vakil's included among them.[125]

But Huggan also draws attention to the complicity of artists themselves with such supposed clichés. Food-related titles – whether of reviews or of literary works – are part of a marketing machine in which writers play their part. According to Mannur, some South Asian American writers engage in 'a form of cultural self-commodification through which . . . [they] earn a living by capitalising on the so-called exoticism embedded in . . . [their] foodways'.[126] Titles are arguably a shorthand means of achieving such self-Orientalising commodification.

In a Chinese American context, Frank Chin has scathingly dismissed such food-based commodification as

> part cookbook, memories of Mother in the kitchen . . . Mumbo jumbo about spices . . . The secret of Chinatown rice. The hands come down towards the food . . . [which] crawls with culture . . . Food pornography. Black magic.[127]

And the Scottish Pakistani novelist Suhayl Saadi, in an excoriation of the London media and publishing industries, has characterised this commodification as an

> ongoing and disempowering Orientalism. How many more novels about . . . exotic Indian spice-sellers can we stomach? Like vindaloos, they pour endlessly into our system and out the other end, changing nothing in the process . . . We have become bulimic with TV comedy dramas about Asian restaurants . . . and everywhere . . . the odour of curry . . . writers pander to all this because they know . . . that if they don't, the likelihood of publication or production is commensurately less. So let's all jump onto the korma train and dance exotic for the English über-classes![128]

Such broadsides signal the very real relationship between food and ethno-racial stereotyping. But to reject the depiction of 'ethnic' foodways so categorically as exploitative and self-Orientalising – 'mumbo jumbo', 'food pornography', and 'black magic' for Chin, barely digestible 'vindaloos' and the 'korma train' for Saadi – is to overlook the genuine importance of this subject and indeed, in Saadi's case, how key it is to South Asian traditions. It is also to ignore the idea that writers who take creative ownership of their ancestral foodways might ensure that 'food becomes a symbol [proving] . . . the humanity of . . . [their] characters'.[129] The universal centrality of food in any case makes the subject continuingly relevant to any audience.

There is, then, surely a world of difference between a critic or writer who relies on potentially essentialising gastronomic titles and/or material in lazy, commercially motivated fashion and another author's multi-layered treatment of food culture. Thus Nisha Minhas's novel *Chapatti or Chips?* and the film *Chicken Tikka Masala* (2005) by the British Asian director Harmage Singh Kalirai – both unsubtle and shamelessly commercial works, which fail to discuss food[130] – are simply in a different category from many of the texts discussed in this chapter. Or, as Sudheer Apte puts it in a review of Lahiri's *Namesake*, this is not 'another novel employing exotic Indian-American backdrops (breaded chicken cutlets, chickpeas with tamarind sauce) to peddle ordinary storylines'.[131] If the use of food in South Asian Atlantic literature runs the risk of stereotype, then – like other stereotypes – this arises from its status as a kind of 'survival blueprint', in

Timothy Mo's phrase.[132] After all, food has traditionally denoted cultural, economic, psychological, and physical survival in the new nation for South Asian immigrants. Yet to read food simply in terms of survival strategies is to overlook the complexity of its treatment – and the capacity for personal transformation it connotes – in these works. The sheer abundance of food metaphors within both transatlantic South Asian writing and reviews of that writing has resulted in a complex relationship between originality and cliché. Following such critics as Mannur and Jennifer Ann Ho, I would argue, however, that writers generally tread that line carefully and skilfully. By mapping out the multiple and wide-ranging ways in which writers knowingly deploy culinary and gastronomic tropes, this chapter has sought to show that food belongs to an equally developed thematic tradition on both sides of the South Asian Atlantic. This is because, despite historical differences between Britain and the US, it remains a personal, cultural, and creative resource too deep-rooted for artists to ignore.

NOTES

1. Srivastava, *Looking for Maya*, p. 28.
2. Huggan, *Post-Colonial Exotic*, p. 82.
3. On the limitations of Gurinder Chadha's preference for food-related titles and themes, see Chan, 'Curry on the divide', p. 12. For a critique of the use of culinary metaphors in Chadha's US feature, *What's Cooking?* (2000), see Ho, *Consumption*, pp. 137–42; and for a satirical treatment of what I am calling 'food-title fatigue', see Senna, 'Mulatto millennium', p. 15.
4. This list includes everything from the BBC sitcom *Tandoori Nights* (1985–7) to South Asian North American films such as Srinivas Krishna's *Masala* (1992), Nisha Ganatra's *Chutney Popcorn* (1999), and Anurag Mehta's *American Chai* (2002); and much South Asian fiction in English: for example, Carl Muller's *The Jam Fruit Tree* (1993); Kavery Nambisan's *Mango-Coloured Fish* (1998); Kamila Shamsie's *Salt and Saffron* (2000); and David Davidar's *The House of Blue Mangoes* (2002).
5. Wong, *Reading*, pp. 55, 60.
6. Ganguly, *States of Exception*, pp. 123–4.
7. This claim was famously made by the late British politician Robin Cook in a 2001 speech on British national identity; see n.a., 'Robin Cook'. In line with this idea, the UK Ministry of Defence (MoD) now includes curry in its operational ration packs; according to Neil Hind, a spokesperson for Defence Food Services, suppliers to the MoD: 'in many ways it is about . . . a feeling of familiarity . . . many of the guys – as we [British people] all do on a Friday night – go out and have a curry . . . It's very important that we feed them the food that they would normally eat at home. Most soldiers

. . . are curry mad'; quoted in Oliphant and Willox, 'Ruby Murray'. For academic accounts of Britain's long-standing relationship with Indian food, see Chaudhuri, 'Shawls', pp. 231–2, 238–42; Zlotnick, 'Domesticating', pp. 52–3, 58–65; and Panayi, *Spicing*, pp. 27–8. As Hardeep Singh Kohli has noted, historically, the white British embrace of curry has not necessarily signalled a corresponding mainstream acceptance of South Asian immigrants; see Kohli, *Indian Takeaway*, p. 44.

8. Appadurai, 'Gastro-politics', p. 496.
9. Kunow, 'Eating Indian(s)', p. 163.
10. Stein, 'Curry at work', p. 146.
11. Thus Mannur, *Culinary Fictions*, is the first full-length study of food in this context. While valuable, it focuses for the most part on South Asian America, rather than offering proper transatlantic comparisons, and Mannur mainly focuses on different literary texts from those I consider here. Pre-dating this monograph are Chaudhuri, 'Shawls'; Zlotnick, 'Domesticating'; Narayan, *Dislocating*, pp. 161–88; Kunow, 'Eating Indian(s)'; Stein, 'Curry at work'; Roy, 'Reading communities'; and Panayi, 'Immigration', pp. 10, 16–17; as well as articles on individual writers or film-makers, which I have cited here where relevant. On food in East Asian American writing, see Wong, *Reading*, pp. 18–76; Ho, *Consumption*; and Xu, *Eating Identities*.
12. Malladi, *Mango Season*, p. 47.
13. Bhuchar et al., *Trouble with Asian Men*.
14. Some writers suggest, however, that this situation has changed through the enthusiastic adoption of labour-saving devices; see, for instance, Alibhai-Brown, *Settler's Cookbook*, pp. 387–8.
15. Bhogal, *Cooking like Mummyji*, p. 12; and for a South Asian American version of the same idea, see Mankekar, 'India shopping', p. 204.
16. Compare Narayan, *Dislocating*, pp. 175–7, 179; and Kunow, 'Eating Indian(s)', pp. 166–7.
17. Syal, *Anita and Me*, p. 61.
18. Maini, 'Politics', p. 158; and compare Ganguly, *States of Exception*, p. 122.
19. Quoted in Maxey, 'Interview', p. 25.
20. Chan, 'Curry on the divide', pp. 13–17; and compare, too, Syal, *Anita and Me*, pp. 61–2, where, as a young girl, Meena refuses to learn to cook Indian food.
21. Lahiri, *Namesake*, p. 279.
22. Sandhu, '*A Love Supreme*', p. 96; and compare Roy, 'Reading communities', p. 486.
23. Kohli, *Indian Takeaway*, p. 78.
24. Ganguly, *States of Exception*, pp. 128–9.
25. Candappa, *Picklehead*, pp. 154–5.
26. For further erroneous claims of exceptionalism, see Shoba Narayan's contention that readers 'wouldn't find' the recipes in her memoir *Monsoon Diary* (discussed below) 'in other cookbooks'; quoted in Feldman, 'Indian author'.
27. Alibhai-Brown, *Settler's Cookbook*, p. 138.

28. Patel, *A Love Supreme*; see Mannur, *Culinary Fictions*, pp. 138–9; and compare Bhogal, *Cooking like Mummyji*, p. 123.
29. Patel, *A Love Supreme.*
30. Sandhu, '*A Love Supreme*', p. 96.
31. See also Rayner, 'Cooking'; and compare Lee, 'Coming home', p. 168.
32. Compare Döring, 'Subversion', p. 261.
33. Avakian and Haber, 'Feminist food studies', pp. 2, 8.
34. Delman, *Burnt Bread*, p. xix.
35. Divakaruni, *Unknown Errors*, pp. 188–9; compare Narayan, *Dislocating*, p. 182; and Thieme and Raja, 'Introduction', p. xliii.
36. Wong, *Reading*, pp. 56–7.
37. Kunow, 'Eating Indian(s)', p. 157.
38. Compare Ray, *Migrant's Table*, p. 73.
39. See Panayi, 'Immigration', pp. 10–11, where he notes that in Britain's 'Indian restaurants . . . [which] increased from the handful which existed . . . after the . . . Second World War to 8000 by the 1990s . . . the standardisation of the complexity of dishes eaten [in India has resulted in] . . . curries . . . as British as . . . fish and chips'.
40. Appadurai, 'Gastro-politics', p. 500.
41. Divakaruni, *Unknown Errors*, p. 8; and compare Douglas, *Purity*, p. 128.
42. Ray, 'Meals', p. 105.
43. Narayan, *Monsoon Diary*, pp. 264, 269.
44. Ravichandran, 'Entrapments', p. 122.
45. Desai, *Fasting, Feasting*, pp. 184–5.
46. Kamani, *Junglee Girl*, p. 157; emphasis in original.
47. Markandaya, *Nowhere Man*, pp. 71 and 69 respectively.
48. Kothari, 'If you are', p. 6.
49. Mannur, 'Culinary fictions', p. 63.
50. Roth, *Plot Against America*, pp. 100 and 91 respectively.
51. Ray, *Migrant's Table*, pp. 67–8; for a discussion of the British context, see Panayi, *Spicing*, pp. 143, 147–8.
52. Mukherjee, *Wife*, pp. 58–9.
53. Vijayaraghavan, *Motherland*, p. 31.
54. For some historical context on the rise of 'Indian grocery stores' in Britain, see Panayi, *Spicing*, pp. 142–4; and for an anthropological study of 'India shopping' in the US, see Mankekar, 'India shopping', pp. 197–214.
55. See, for instance, Choubey, 'Food metaphor'; Williams, 'Foodways and subjectivity'; Maini, 'Politics'; and Mannur, *Culinary Fictions*, pp. 157–62.
56. Lahiri, *Interpreter*, pp. 30 and 24 respectively.
57. Choubey, 'Food metaphor', n.p.
58. See Ray, 'Meals', pp. 107–8, where he contends that the importance Bengalis attach to fish actually increases when they are in America.
59. Lahiri, *Interpreter*, p. 124.
60. Compare Kunow, 'Eating Indian(s)', p. 168.

61. On the US, see Lahiri, 'Indian takeout'; and Khandelwal, *Becoming American*, pp. 40–1; and on Britain, see Panayi, *Spicing*, p. 144.
62. Sidhwa, *American Brat*, p. 114.
63. Chandra, *Sari*, p. 16.
64. Wong, *Reading*, p. 52.
65. Ganesan, 'Food', pp. 171–2.
66. DeLillo, *White Noise*, pp. 37–8.
67. Wood, *Goodness Gracious Me*. Candappa, *Picklehead*, p. 241, argues that this sketch is 'one of the key moments in the absorption and acceptance of curry . . . [in] Britain'. For historical contextualisations of the stereotypical 'blandness' of British cuisine, see Mennell, *All Manners*, pp. 206, 214, 221–2; and Panayi, *Spicing*, p. 12.
68. See also Panayi, 'Immigration', p. 17, where he claims that 'entrepreneurs from ethnic minority backgrounds established some of the most important symbols of British consumption'.
69. Sidhwa, *Crow Eaters*, pp. 136, 257, 261.
70. Alibhai-Brown, *Settler's Cookbook*, pp. 164–5.
71. Compare Wong, *Reading*, pp. 65–6; and Rogobete, 'Sweet taste', p. 40.
72. Compare Bess, 'Lahiri's *Interpreter*', p. 126, where she observes that Mrs Sen offers Eliot easily prepared American food – peanut butter and crackers – only in a mood of despair at her American life.
73. Within this gendered culinary arena, Lahiri's dichotomy between Mrs Sen as warm Indian caregiver and Eliot's mother as 'cold . . . self-centred' representative of '"Western" womanhood' is, for one critic, rather simplistic; see Kunow, 'Eating Indian(s)', p. 167.
74. Compare Wong, *Reading*, pp. 25, 31, 45.
75. For more on Indian American culinary syncretism, see Ray, 'Meals', p. 106; Ray, *Migrant's Table*, pp. 75–6; and Mannur, *Culinary Fictions*, pp. 196–216.
76. Ho, *Consumption*, p. 145. On the long history of South Asian culinary adaptation, see Thieme and Raja, 'Introduction', p. xx; and Daley, *Cooking*, p. 22.
77. See Narayan, *Dislocating*, pp. 164–5; and Kundu, 'Curry powder', pp. 72–3.
78. Bhabha, *Location*, pp. 36–9; and compare Mannur, *Culinary Fictions*, pp. 214–15.
79. See Ray, *Migrant's Table*, p. 76.
80. Meer, *Bombay Talkie*, p. 178.
81. Compare Mannur, *Culinary Fictions*, pp. 150–7, 178–80.
82. Hussein, 'A passage'; and compare Chan, 'Curry on the divide', pp. 14–15.
83. Compare Ganesan, 'Food', p. 174.
84. Maxey, 'Jhumpa Lahiri'.
85. Mudge, 'Lahiri'.
86. Wong, *Reading*, p. 55.
87. Panayi, *Spicing*, pp. 17–18.
88. Dhondy, *East End*, pp. 53–4; and compare Manzoor, 'Brits', where Ateesh Randev, a British Asian actor trying to succeed in Bollywood, reveals that 'I

get goosebumps just thinking about going home – the first thing I am going to do is have fish and chips and a proper English cup of tea.'

89. Compare Wurgaft, 'Incensed', pp. 58–9; Mannur, 'Culinary', pp. 64–5, on the idea of white perceptions of the smelliness of Indian food in 'Mrs Sen's'; and Chan, 'Curry on the divide', p. 14. Kohli recalls the hypocrisy of a 1970s British 'love affair with Indian food . . . [when] at the same time, you'd get slagged off for smelling of curry'; quoted in Jackson, 'Hardeep Singh Kohli'.
90. Hussein, *Émigré*, p. 96.
91. In her short story 'Hindus', Bharati Mukherjee critiques Indian ghettoisation in New York through the unappealing image of a party where 'the smell of stale turmeric hung like yellow fog from the ceiling'; see Mukherjee, *Darkness*, p. 133; while in 'Nostalgia' (also anthologised in *Darkness*), the need to eat Indian food is made to suggest the destructive emptiness of clinging to an idealised past once in the US.
92. Kalita, *Suburban*, p. 2; and in the British context, compare Rayner, 'Cooking'.
93. Aslam, *Maps*, p. 105.
94. See also Mankekar, 'India shopping', p. 208.
95. Compare Grover, 'Theory', p. 26.
96. Collingham, *Curry*, pp. 215, 218, 220, 223, 226; Panayi, *Spicing*, pp. 172–3; and see also Ray, 'Exotic restaurants', p. 214.
97. Ebury Publishing, press release for *Picklehead*, n.d.; Candappa, *Picklehead*, book-jacket; Alibhai-Brown, *Settler's Cookbook*, n.p.
98. Quoted in Narayan, *Monsoon Diary*, n.p.
99. Narayan has pointed to the dominance of 'North Indian restaurants' in the US; she has also noted that 'the average [New York magazine] editor . . . is not familiar with the nuances within Indian cooking . . . they do not know about Bengali or Assamese cooking'; quoted in Chhabra, 'Shoba beats Jhumpa'.
100. Compare Ganesan, 'Food', pp. 174–5, 178; and Khandelwal, *Becoming American*, p. 38.
101. Compare Roy, 'Reading communities', pp. 481–2; and Mannur, *Culinary Fictions*, p. 27.
102. Avakian and Haber, 'Feminist food studies', p. 20.
103. Compare Mankekar, 'India shopping', p. 203.
104. See also Döring, 'Subversion', pp. 260–1.
105. The author's local origins and use of the phrase 'born and bred' recall Karim in Kureishi, *Buddha*, p. 3, who describes himself as a South London-raised 'Englishman born and bred, almost'.
106. Alibhai-Brown, 'Food and memory'.
107. Mannur, *Culinary Fictions*, p. 82.
108. Kohli is also not the first British Asian to attempt such a mission; see Pandey, '"Bland" British food', which reports on a TV programme, designed to introduce British cuisine to Indians, hosted by Manju Malhi, a British Indian

chef. According to Malhi's website, the 'forty part series . . . "Cooking Isn't Rocket Science" for one of India's leading broadcasters NDTV . . . led to a demand from publishers to come up with a British cookbook for India . . . [while] Manju has been asked to create the concept of a "British" restaurant in Delhi'; see n.a., *Manju Malhi.com*; and n.a., web link for 'Cooking isn't rocket science'.

109. Jacobson, 'No taste', p. 155, notes that 'for Jews, speaking food is as important in reconnecting us to our past as eating it'. Replacing the Yiddish terms – for instance, *gefilte fish*, *kes* – cited by Jacobson with *prasad* or *rasam* suggests a comparable emphasis on 'speaking food' in South Asian Atlantic food writing.
110. See also Ray, 'Exotic restaurants', pp. 213–14.
111. Ganesan, 'Food', p. 177.
112. See Leonardi, 'Recipes for reading'; Goldman, 'I yam'; and Roy, 'Reading communities', pp. 476, 478–83, 488.
113. For discussions of Jaffrey's œuvre, see Roy, 'Reading communities', pp. 476–96; Colquhoun, *Taste*, pp. 363–4; and Mannur, *Culinary Fictions*, pp. 30–5. There is also insufficient space here to cover recent South Asian American cookery writing; for a consideration of this genre, see Mannur, *Culinary Fictions*, pp. 163–71, 196–207.
114. Avakian and Haber, 'Feminist food studies', p. 19.
115. Some commentators might even question the impulse to address fellow British Asians at all. Thus Sarfraz Manzoor contends, somewhat provocatively, that 'nobody who's actually Asian would buy one [an Indian cookbook] unless they are completely estranged from their culture'; quoted in Rayner, 'Cooking'. Anticipating such forms of criticism, perhaps, Bhogal suggests that young British Asian woman can be perfectly comfortable with their cultural heritage, yet unaware of how to cook traditional dishes.
116 Compare Thieme and Raja, 'Introduction', p. xliii.
117. Ray, 'Ethnic succession', p. 124.
118. Kim, 'Defining', p. 105; and compare Bharucha, 'Earth', p. 185; Rayner, 'Cooking'; and Mannur, *Culinary Fictions*, p. 139.
119. Mankekar, 'India shopping', p. 202.
120. See Mannur, *Culinary Fictions*, pp. 14, 110, on the paratextual use of food to sell Asian American fiction. A dependence on food metaphors also surfaces in discussions of both multiculturalism and miscegenation; on the former, see Wagner, 'Boutique multiculturalism', pp. 32–5; on the latter idea, which I broached in Chapter 3, see the reference to 'chocolate milk' in Delman, *Burnt Bread*, pp. 60–1; Singh, 'Writing tough', p. 87, where he draws on the Malay term 'rojak' – a mixed sweet-and-sour salad and recognised image in Singapore for those of mixed race – to refer to his own Sikh–white Scottish background; and for British examples, the 'multiracial lolly' used to refer to Ben and Priya's white British–Indian marriage in Vakil, *One Day*, p. 21; and Hanif Kureishi's screenplay *My Son the Fanatic* (1997), where Farid breaks off

his interracial engagement on the grounds that 'keema' cannot be 'put . . . with strawberries' in Kureishi, *Collected Screenplays*, p. 313.

121. Feay, '*Brick Lane*'; and see also Maxey, 'Representative'.
122. Thieme and Raja, 'Introduction', pp. xxv–xxviii.
123. Ghosh, 'Flavour'.
124. LeGuin, 'A passage'.
125. Huggan, *Post-Colonial Exotic*, p. 60; emphasis in original.
126. Mannur, 'Culinary', p. 59.
127. Quoted in Wong, *Reading*, p. 65.
128. Saadi, 'Psychoraag'.
129. Ho, *Consumption*, p. 19.
130. On Minhas, compare Mannur, *Culinary Fictions*, p. 154. The apparently formulaic title of Kalirai's film may, however, hint at the cultural syncretism it depicts since chicken tikka masala is a famously British Asian food.
131. Apte, '*Namesake*'.
132. Quoted in Jaggi, 'Mixtures'.

CONCLUSION: THE FUTURE OF SOUTH ASIAN ATLANTIC LITERATURE

This study began with the premise that – despite some significant cultural and artistic cross-currents between contemporary South Asian Americans and British Asians – the field of transatlantic literary studies has not paid enough attention to the parallel growth of South Asian writing in Britain and the United States since the early 1970s. *South Asian Atlantic Literature* has sought to fill this scholarly gap by focusing on the dominant, yet in many cases critically neglected, tropes employed by these writers. In so doing, it has presented particular literary texts as belonging to a distinct body of work and as the basis for a sustained comparison, despite some key differences, both formally and in terms of the background of the writers themselves.

In Chapter 1, I examined the thematic and rhetorical importance of home, contending that it is of equal significance to writers on both sides of the Atlantic, although regional questions seem of greater concern to British Asian authors, possibly because more South Asians live in Britain proportionate to the overall population than in the US, and have done so over a longer period. South Asian Atlantic writers consistently return to interior and domestic spaces, specifically exploring their gendered implications and their status as a safe, enduring alternative to the problematic nature of national belonging in both the United States and Britain. While some British Asian writers tend towards a form of strategic Americano*philia* to consider home and nation, however, South Asian American authors are much more likely to employ a transatlantic framework in a critical manner through a strategic Anglo*phobia*; and I argued that such phobias and philias are used to examine, and often validate, the choice of one national home in favour of the other.

In Chapter 2, I analysed the treatment of ethnic return in South Asian Atlantic works by considering literary and cinematic representations of the ancestral homeland. I did so in order to ask how artists highlight – often in strikingly similar ways – questions of gender, intergenerational difference, Pakistan versus India, the US vis-à-vis the UK, economic opportunity, and transnational mobility. Despite a distinctly British, and frequently negative, emphasis on Pakistan and a characteristically American, and more favourable, attention to India, what generally emerges is an analogous critique of the foreign-born generation. And ancestral sites tend, in both cases, to be essentialised, even though writers and film-makers reveal their complexities and harness the rich dramatic possibilities associated with the paradoxical sense of belonging and outsider-ness experienced by transatlantic South Asian visitors. This in turn mirrors some of the tensions lived out by the older immigrant generation, as it sought to find a foothold in postwar Britain or America. Such subtleties notwithstanding, the formal treatment of this subject generally remains rather flat and conventional and I contended that this is because such narratives implicitly support westward migration.

Chapter 3 looked at miscegenation, arguing that within transatlantic South Asian writing such material manages to be both familiar and new, since interracial relationships are an established motif but mixed-race identity remains far less explored in creative terms in both literature and film. I argued that interracial alliances are presented in utopian fashion in South Asian Atlantic cinema in order to provide audiences with a simplistically happy ending, but approached with greater caution in South Asian American and particularly British Asian writing. They also remain overly reliant on a white party and are overwhelmingly heterosexual, although they follow different gender dynamics from colonial miscegenist models by reversing (particularly in the British case) the white man–woman of colour dyad. Despite key differences in the racial history of the United States and Britain, the racially mixed subject embodies a more radical and difficult theme than interracial relationships for South Asian writers on both sides of the Atlantic. This may be why fictionalised biracial characters are either children, thus occupying a marginal narrative position, or adults who perpetuate certain traditional, negative stereotypes. It is the writers who are themselves biracial that offer a fuller, more complex vision of mixed-race lives; and to date more of these writers have been British than American.

In Chapter 4, I discussed the connection between identity and food in South Asian Atlantic literature, illustrating such parallel concerns as the importance of gender roles, the perceived superiority of Indian to 'mainstream' American and British cuisine, 'authentic' versus 'inauthentic'

South Asian food, the possibilities for culinary syncretism experienced by immigrants and their children, and the navigation of gastronomic taboos. These literary works also share a didactic mission aimed at both South Asians and ethno-racial outsiders, although the more ethnographic tone to be found in South Asian American discussions of gastronomy can be attributed to a lesser degree of familiarity with South Asian food in the US than in Britain. I also examined the fraught relationship between originality and cliché which continues to surround this literary emphasis on foodways, contending that there is a crucial difference between complex, heuristic investigations of ancestral food culture and the lazy resort to a stereotypical, superficial culinary language, often for commercial reasons.

What does all of this suggest, then, about the future of South Asian Atlantic literature? No study of this subject would be complete without an attempt to locate it within the context of genre, prize-giving, and the literary marketplace. Transatlantic South Asian writers reconfigure genre in revealing ways – although I would argue that, in formal terms, British Asian writing has been more aesthetically risk-taking. One thinks, for instance, of the linguistic experiments conducted by such authors as Suhayl Saadi or Gautam Malkani in his novel *Londonstani* (2006). Saadi's writing achieves formal inventiveness through its exciting blend of demotic Scots and Urdu, thus using a new linguistic medium to give voice to a marginalised group, to reflect new modes of experience and identity,[1] and to assert difference in defiant fashion. Similarly, in *Londonstani*, Malkani has attempted to capture spoken rhythms in order to do justice to a particular British Asian subculture, recreating the 'authentic . . . *desi* patois', as he has termed it, of young Hindu boys in West London.[2] Pre-dating both Saadi and Malkani, Farrukh Dhondy and Farhana Sheikh made use of British Asian speech patterns, and long before either of them, the London-based Indo-Trinidadian writer Sam Selvon was drawing on Caribbean spoken forms to create a particularised literary language in his novel *The Lonely Londoners* (1956).[3]

Hanif Kureishi and Meera Syal have successfully moved between fiction and screenwriting; and this is a less common trajectory for South Asian American authors. The use of social satire and a kind of reverse ethnography to depict mainstream culture have emerged on both sides of the Atlantic, however, while so-called 'chick lit' by such novelists as Nisha Minhas in the UK and Kavita Daswani in the US has found a market in both countries. Yet – despite the fantastical elements deployed by Chitra Divakaruni in her novel *The Mistress of Spices* (1997), for instance, or the blend of prose and poetry to be found in some of Meena Alexander's writing (*The Shock of Arrival: Reflections on Postcolonial Experience* [1996], for example) or the intertextual ambition of Bharati Mukherjee's fiction – many successful South Asian American novelists and short story writers seem tied to a psychological realist tradition. Thus, although these writers in both the US and Britain share a preoccupation with fiction, and especially the novel, British Asian writers are more likely to reconfigure subgenres within the form.[4] These include, amongst others, the *Künstlerroman* (Kureishi's *The Buddha of Suburbia* [1990] and *The Black Album* [1995] and Atima Srivastava's *Looking for Maya* [1999]); the historical novel (Hari Kunzru's *The Impressionist* [2002]); and in the case of Nadeem Aslam's *Maps for Lost Lovers* (2004), a combination of many genres at once: social critique, thriller, love story, history of immigration, and theological text.

In a sense, these writers are creating new forms within fiction. Mark Stein has classified such works under the label 'the novel of transformation', which

> not only portrays [a] changing Britain but, crucially . . . is also partly responsible for bringing about change. This is accomplished by the symbolic transgression of space . . . depicting racist phenomena . . . redressing the iconography of Britain and . . . the exertion of cultural power.[5]

What writers are doing at the level of form is crucial to this wider project, and their textual hybridity – or mixing of literary subgenres and forms – also mirrors the range of cultural traditions which comprise their own history. While many writers beyond the South Asian Atlantic might be seen as revising earlier genres, the way in which British Asian authors rework existing forms arguably signals a more complex and perhaps more pressing need to position themselves in literary, and indeed national, terms than that demonstrated by South Asian writers in the US. This refers us back to the claim I made in the Introduction that, because of specifically British postcolonial dynamics, South Asian artists in the UK may have felt the need to assert themselves more prominently than their American peers, that the stakes are in some sense higher. I have already noted the significance of demographic statistics in the two countries, and this may result in a smaller, more crowded, and more competitive literary marketplace for South Asian voices in Britain than in the United States.

One of the most striking recent developments in transatlantic South Asian literature has been the surge in life-writing. Following earlier ventures into the genre by such authors as Ved Mehta, Sara Suleri, Abraham Verghese, Mukherjee, and Alexander in the US, the South Asian American writers Carmit Delman, Shoba Narayan (discussed in Chapters 3 and 4 respectively), and Anita Jain have all produced memoirs since 2000; and the British Asian autobiography has gone from being a largely overlooked form – with Prafulla Mohanti's *Through Brown Eyes*, published in 1985 and considered in Chapter 2, for many years a rare example – to one of the most popular and marketable genres available to contemporary writers. Thus autobiographical texts by Kureishi, Sathnam Sanghera, Sarfraz Manzoor, Rohan Candappa, Hardeep Singh Kohli, and Yasmin Alibhai-Brown (all discussed at different points in this book), and by Jasvinder Sanghera, Yasmin Hai, and Imran Ahmad, have all appeared in the past decade, often to a mixture of critical and/or popular acclaim.

How might one account for this trend? In the United States, the autobiography is a quintessentially American genre, appearing in multiple incarnations since the seventeenth century and favoured by new immigrants, as I argued in Chapter 4. Indeed, in its most conservative guise, the US immigrant memoir is a form which endorses cultural assimilation and has in particular served Asian American writers well.[6] Integration into the US mainstream is not in fact what such writers as Alexander or Delman are necessarily trying to achieve; but the sheer volume of American life-writing, especially by writers of colour, provides an august literary lineage, while offering the likelihood of a receptive audience. But the British case initially seems more difficult to explain. Why – when the novel remains the pre-eminent prose form in the UK – would British Asian writers choose to produce memoirs?

One answer may lie in the fact that many of those listed above are journalists (Sathnam Sanghera, Manzoor, Alibhai-Brown, Hai, Kohli) or writers used to publishing non-fiction (Candappa, Jasvinder Sanghera) and thus – critical caveats about the fictional nature of autobiography and the autobiographical nature of fiction aside[7] – they are more comfortable with the factual than the imaginative realm. And the need to shed light on a largely hidden history (that of one's particular South Asian community) and to correct popular misapprehensions and prejudices – to deal in hard data rather than fictional interpretations – clearly informs much contemporary British Asian autobiography. Another possibility is that authors have been encouraged to produce life-writing because of its popular cachet. Weekly UK bestseller lists attest to the commercial impact of celebrity memoirs, a genre which includes recent contributions by such British Asian sportsmen as Monty Panesar, Amir Khan, and Mark Ramprakash. But the drive to write one's personal experiences large and to claim oneself as a new, yet representative, Briton – an ambition which particularly underpins the work of Manzoor, Kohli, and Alibhai-Brown – may reveal a transatlantic debt. After all, this charged work of nation-building and national identity formation through life-writing arguably has deeper roots in the American than in the British literary tradition, and, as I noted earlier in this book, such writers as Kureishi and Manzoor are keenly influenced by US cultural models. For British Asian authors, this cross-current may not be about specifically emulating *South Asian* American writing but it does suggest the possibility of an awareness of US life-writing more generally. That is, after all, a tradition which spans everything from spiritual confessions and guides to self-improvement to slave narratives and presidential autobiography (including, most recently, the bestselling memoirs of Barack Obama). This tendency to publish life-writing also signals a comparable momentum on either side of the Atlantic which is likely to continue for some years to come.

In the Introduction to this book, I touched on the reception of some key fictional works: Mukherjee's novel *Jasmine* (1989) and Jhumpa Lahiri's Pulitzer Prize-winning short fiction collection *Interpreter of Maladies* (1999) in the United States; and Kureishi's *Buddha of Suburbia* and Monica Ali's novel *Brick Lane* (2003) in the UK. This led to the question of why certain South Asian Atlantic works garner prizes and attention at the expense of others, often with the result that a handful of specific texts are made to shoulder what has been called the 'burden of representation'.[8] I have addressed some of these ideas elsewhere, suggesting, for instance, that the splash caused by *Brick Lane* relates to a blend of its pre-publication marketing, fashionable novelty, London focus, and unthreatening version of multiculturalism, while the success of Lahiri's collection can be connected to its particular regional emphasis – the classic literary/settler landscape of New England – and to its 'mixture of old-fashioned literariness and contemporary material', its 'largely unproblematised representation of the American Dream', its debt to canonical short fiction (Anton Chekhov, John Cheever, Raymond Carver), and its skilful, yet often conventional, use of form.[9]

Prizes, press coverage, and sometimes bestseller status have also led to controversy in critical and community circles for Kureishi, Mukherjee, Ali, and indeed Divakaruni – if not Lahiri[10] or, in Britain, Hari Kunzru. This is because the success enjoyed by their work has occurred despite an exuberant range of other new literary works, including the wealth of life-writing cited above; and because its disproportionate impact has sometimes led to the dominance of particular ideas, not always popular with South Asians themselves in Britain and America, about certain ethno-religious constituencies. These ideas, which often sell well, include the patriarchal nature of particular communities; intergenerational strife; identity confusion; the prevalence of arranged marriage; and the need for flight from a benighted, Orientalised South Asian motherland. But it is precisely the appetite for South Asian cultural production generated by the prestige of such authors

– who in any case explore the ideas mentioned above in a critical and nuanced fashion – which serves to energise and encourage other writers, examining different ideas, on both sides of the Atlantic.

Even if many writers are still published by small, little-known presses, the corollary is nevertheless a greater sense of a community of literary interests, especially when writers read each other's work – as suggested by Alexander's notion of belonging to a South Asian diasporic 'wave . . . [a] group of people, all making art with language'[11] – and when students and scholars in both Britain and the US interpret transatlantic works alongside each other. Although some might contest the existence of such an imagined community, especially within the US,[12] it remains the case that for those writers who perceive themselves as belonging to it, this community has the very real impact of creating increasingly complex literary genealogies which move across class, gender, national, and ethnic boundaries. Its presence also suggests the continuing need to understand this writing within a transnational, and specifically a transatlantic, frame. I claimed in the Introduction that British Asian – rather than South Asian American – literature has had a greater international impact, but the popular and critical acclaim enjoyed by such writers as Lahiri, Mukherjee, and Divakaruni in the United States, and the screen adaptations of their work,[13] point to a changing picture. Whether future South Asian writing flourishes more in America or Britain – and particular authors continue to garner all the attention – the sheer scale and variety of South Asian Atlantic literature are set only to increase in the next ten to twenty years. This promises not only more experimentation in terms of form, genre, and content, but also a move away from the burden of representation through a different kind of reception for these works.

NOTES

1. Compare Davis, 'Everyone's story', p. 175.
2. Malkani, reading of *Londonstani*.
3. Nasta, 'Setting up', pp. 82–7.
4. Nasta, 'Homes without walls', p. 97.
5. Stein, *Black British*, p. xvii.
6. See, for example, Ling, 'Race, power', pp. 361–2, 375.
7. Eakin, *Living Autobiographically*, pp. ix–x.
8. Mercer, 'Black art'.
9. Maxey, 'Representative', pp. 220–1, 229–30; Maxey, 'Jhumpa Lahiri'.
10. Although see Maxey, 'Jhumpa Lahiri', for a discussion of the fraught reception of Lahiri's work in India; and compare Paranjape, 'Afterword', and Chakraborty, 'Will the real South Asian', p. 134.

11. Cited in Maxey, 'Interview', p. 30.
12. Thus, one still finds South Asian American writers, new to the literary scene, who claim their history has yet to be represented; see Hidier, 'Tanuja Desai Hidier', where she states that when she wrote her novel *Born Confused* (2002), she could not 'recall . . . [another work] with a South Asian American teen protagonist'. While it may well be true that the story of particular South Asians in the US, according to both age and ethnicity, has yet to reach a wider audience, the assertion of another writer, Kaavya Viswanathan, that 'I've never read a novel with an Indian-American protagonist', quoted in ibid., simply does not tally with the growth of South Asian American literature in the past thirty years. That Viswanathan, herself a transatlantic figure who moved from South India to Scotland to New Jersey, felt the need to plagiarise other South Asian diasporic writers – Salman Rushdie as well as Hidier – in her novel *How Opal Mehta Got Kissed, Got Wild, and Got a Life* (2006) tells its own tale about anxieties of influence.
13. See, for instance, Paul Mayeda Berges's movie of Divakaruni's *Mistress of Spices* (2005) and Mira Nair's film version of Lahiri's novel *The Namesake* (2006).

BIBLIOGRAPHY

All web links accessed 6 May 2011.

n.a., 'Blue Mink Melting Pot lyrics', n.d., http://www.smartlyrics.com/Song578971-Blue-Mink-MeltingPot-lyrics.aspx

n.a., 'Cooking isn't rocket science', NDTV website, n.d., http://goodtimes.ndtv.com/GoodTimesShowPage.aspx?ShowID=6

n.a., 'Ethnicity: Population size – 7.9% from a minority ethnic group' (2001 census), Office for National Statistics website, online article (no longer available).

n.a., 'Inter-ethnic marriage: 2% of marriages are inter-ethnic' (2001 census), Office for National Statistics website, http://www.statistics.gov.uk/cci/nugget.asp?id=1090

n.a. 'Landmark ethnic minorities survey shows mix of poverty and progress', 21 May 1997, Policy Studies Institute website, http://www.psi.org.uk/news/pressrelease.asp?news_item_id=71

n.a., *Manju Malhi.com*, n.d., http://www.manjumalhi.com/about/about-manju.html

n.a., Press release for *Picklehead*, London: Ebury Press, 2 March 2006.

n.a., 'Robin Cook's chicken tikka masala speech', *Guardian*, 19 April 2001, www.guardian.co.uk/world/2001/apr/19/race.britishidentity

Aciman, André (ed.), *Letters of Transit: Reflections on Exile, Identity, Language and Loss* (New York: New York Public Library, 1999).

Adams, Caroline, *Across Seven Seas and Thirteen Rivers: Life Stories of Pioneer Sylhetti Settlers in Britain* (London: Tower Hamlets Arts Project, 1987).

Ahmed, Kamal, 'After Obama, I can be proud of what I really am: black *and* white', *Observer*, 9 November 2008, p. 26.

Ahmed, Sara, 'Home and away: Narratives of migration and estrangement', *International Journal of Cultural Studies* 2.3 (1999), pp. 329–47.

Ainley, Mark, and Richard Noblett, *London is the Place for Me: Trinidadian Calypso in London, 1950–1956* (London: Honest Jon's Records, 2002) [CD]

Alam, Fakrul, *Bharati Mukherjee* (New York: Twayne, 1996).
Aldama, Frederick Luis, 'Hari Kunzru in conversation', *Wasafiri* 45 (Summer 2005), pp. 11–14.
Alexander, Meena, *Nampally Road* (San Francisco: Mercury House, 1991).
Alexander, Meena, *Fault Lines* (New York: Feminist Press at the City University of New York, 2003 [1993]).
Ali, Monica, *Brick Lane* (London: Doubleday, 2003).
Ali, Nasreen, Virinder S. Kalra, and S. Sayyid (eds), *A Postcolonial People: South Asians in Britain* (London: Hurst, 2006).
Ali, Zainab, and Dharini Rasiah, 'Meena Alexander' in King-Kok Cheung (ed.), *Words Matter: Conversations with Asian American Writers* (Honolulu: University of Hawai'i Press, 2000), pp. 69–91.
Alibhai-Brown, Yasmin, *Mixed Feelings: The Complex Lives of Mixed-Race Britons* (London: Women's Press, 2001).
Alibhai-Brown, Yasmin, 'The curse of diversity', *Independent*, 9 July 2003, http://findarticles.com/p/articles/mi_qn4158/is_20030709/ai_n12705162 (web link no longer active).
Alibhai-Brown, Yasmin, 'It's a colourful world in black and white', *Independent*, 21 July 2004, http://www.independent.co.uk/opinion/commentators/yasmin-alibhai-brown/its-a-colourful-world-in-black-and-white-553851.html
Alibhai-Brown, Yasmin, 'Food and memory', *Independent*, 26 February 2009, http://www.alibhai-brown.com/archive/article.php?id=181
Alibhai-Brown, Yasmin, *The Settler's Cookbook: A Memoir of Love, Migration and Food* (London: Portobello, 2009).
Aneja, Anu, '*Jasmine*, the sweet scent of exile', *Pacific Coast Philology* 28.1 (September 1993), pp. 72–80.
Ang-Lydgate, Magdalene, 'Charting the spaces of (un)location: On theorising diaspora' in Heidi Safia Mirza (ed.), *Black British Feminism: A Reader* (London: Routledge, 1997), pp. 168–86.
Annesley, James, *Fictions of Globalisation* (London: Continuum, 2006).
Anthony, Andrew, 'How Britain turned its back on the white working class', *Observer*, 2 March 2008, http://www.guardian.co.uk/commentisfree/2008/mar/02/britishidentity.guardiancolumnists
Appadurai, Arjun, 'Gastro-politics in Hindu South India', *American Ethnologist* 8.3 (August 1981), pp. 494–511.
Appiah, Kwame Anthony, 'Identity crisis: Is the hero of this novel English, Pakistani, Muslim – or all three?', *New York Times*, 17 September 1995, p. 42.
Apte, Sudheer, '*The Namesake*', *MostlyFiction Book Reviews*, 7 September 2003, http://mostlyfiction.com/world/lahiri.htm#namesake
Ashley, Bernard, and Anne Wilson, *Growing Good* (London: Bloomsbury, 1999).
Ashraf, Adnan, 'A conversation with Hanif Kureishi', *Chowk: Ideas and Identities of India Pakistan*, 3 August 1998, online article (no longer available).
Aslam, Nadeem, *Maps for Lost Lovers* (London: Faber, 2004).
Avakian, Arlene Voski, and Barbara Haber, 'Feminist food studies: A brief

history' in Arlene Voski Avakian and Barbara Haber (eds), *From Betty Crocker to Feminist Food Studies: Critical Perspectives on Women and Food* (Amherst: University of Massachusetts Press, 2005), pp. 1–26.

Avakian, Arlene Voski, and Barbara Haber (eds), *From Betty Crocker to Feminist Food Studies: Critical Perspectives on Women and Food* (Amherst: University of Massachusetts Press, 2005).

Azoulay, Katya, *Black, Jewish and Interracial: It Is Not the Colour of Your Skin but the Race of Your Kin and Other Myths of Identity* (Durham, NC: Duke University Press, 1997).

Bachelard, Gaston, *The Poetics of Space*, trans. Maria Jolas (Boston: Beacon Press, 1964).

Bahri, Deepika, and Mary Vasudeva (eds), *Between the Lines: South Asians and Postcoloniality* (Philadelphia: Temple University Press, 1996).

Bahri, Deepika, and Mary Vasudeva, 'Observing ourselves among others: Interview with Meena Alexander' in Deepika Bahri and Mary Vasudeva (eds), *Between the Lines: South Asians and Postcoloniality* (Philadelphia: Temple University Press, 1996), pp. 35–53.

Bald, Suresht Renjen, 'Images of South Asian migrants in literature: Differing perspectives', *New Community* 17.3 (April 1991), pp. 413–31.

Ball, John Clement, *Imagining London: Postcolonial Fiction and the Transnational Metropolis* (Toronto: University of Toronto Press, 2004).

Banerjee, Bidisha, 'No nation woman: The diasporic woman's quest for home' in Sanjukta Dasgupta and Malashri Lal (eds), *The Indian Family in Transition: Reading Literary and Cultural Texts* (New Delhi: Sage, 2007), pp. 168–79.

Banerjee, Mita, '"Traveling barbies" and rolling blackouts: Images of mobility in Mira Nair's *Monsoon Wedding*', *Comparative American Studies* 1.4 (2003), pp. 448–70.

Banwal, Shobhan, *The Sari Shop Widow* (New York: Kensington, 2009).

Barnes, Jessica S., and Claudette E. Bennett, 'The Asian population: 2000', US Census Bureau, February 2002, www.census.gov/prod/2002pubs/c2kbr01-16.pdf

Basu, Paul, 'Roots tourism as return movement: Semantics and the Scottish diaspora' in Marjory Harper (ed.), *Emigrant Homecomings: The Return Movement of Emigrants, 1600-2000* (Manchester: Manchester University Press, 2005), pp. 131–50.

Bauman, Zygmunt, 'From pilgrim to tourist – or a short history of identity' in Stuart Hall and Paul du Gay (eds), *Questions of Cultural Identity* (London: Sage, 1996), pp. 18–36.

Beckford, Martin, 'Trevor Phillips warns that Britain could return to racism as recession bites', *Daily Telegraph*, 19 January 2009, http://www.telegraph.co.uk/finance/financetopics/recession/4290154/Trevor-Phillips-warns-that-Britain-could-return-to-racism-as-recession-bites.html

Beer, Janet, and Bridget Bennett, 'Introduction' in Janet Beer and Bridget Bennett (eds), *Special Relationships: Anglo-American Affinities and Antagonisms 1854–1936* (Manchester: Manchester University Press, 2002), pp. 1–7.

Beer, Janet, and Bridget Bennett (eds), *Special Relationships: Anglo-American*

Affinities and Antagonisms 1854–1936 (Manchester: Manchester University Press, 2002).

Benson, Susan, *Ambiguous Ethnicity: Interracial Families in London* (Cambridge: Cambridge University Press, 1981).

Bentley, Nick, 'Re-writing Englishness: Imagining the nation in Julian Barnes's *England, England* and Zadie Smith's *White Teeth*', *Textual Practice* 21.3 (2007), pp. 483–504.

Bess, Jennifer, 'Lahiri's *Interpreter of Maladies*', *Explicator* 62.2 (2004), pp. 125–8.

Bhabha, Homi, *The Location of Culture* (London: Routledge, 1994).

Bharucha, Nilufer E., 'The earth is not flat: Minority discourse against fundamentalisms', *Journal of Postcolonial Writing* 43.2 (August 2007), pp. 183–90.

Bhogal, Vicky, *Cooking like Mummyji: Real British Asian Cooking* (London: Simon & Schuster, 2003).

Bhuchar, Sudha, Kristine Landon-Smith, and Louise Wallinger, *The Trouble with Asian Men*, dir. Kristine Landon-Smith, Soho Theatre, London, September 2006.

Biggs, Melissa E. (ed.), *In the Vernacular: Interviews at Yale with Sculptors of Culture* (Jefferson, NC: McFarland, 1991).

Blaise, Clark, and Bharati Mukherjee, *The Sorrow and the Terror* (Markham, Ontario: Penguin, 1987).

Blaise, Clark, and Bharati Mukherjee, 'After the Fatwa', *Mother Jones*, April/May 1990, pp. 29–31, 61–5.

Blaise, Clark, and Bharati Mukherjee, *Days and Nights in Calcutta* (St Paul, MN: Hungry Mind Press, 1995 [1977]).

Bloom, Harold, *The Anxiety of Influence: A Theory of Poetry* (New York: Oxford University Press, 1973).

Blunt, Alison, 'Geographies of diaspora and mixed descent: Anglo-Indians in India and Britain', *International Journal of Population Geography* 9 (2003), pp. 281–94.

Blunt, Alison, *Domicile and Diaspora: Anglo-Indian Women and the Spatial Politics of Home* (Malden, MA: Blackwell, 2005).

Blunt, Alison, and Robyn Dowling, *Home* (London: Routledge, 2006).

Blunt, Alison, and Cheryl McEwan (eds), *Postcolonial Geographies* (London: Continuum, 2002).

Bost, Suzanne, *Mulattas and Mestizas: Representing Mixed Identities in the Americas, 1850–2000* (Athens: University of Georgia Press, 2003).

Brada-Williams, Noelle, 'Reading Jhumpa Lahiri's *Interpreter of Maladies* as a short story cycle', *MELUS* 29.3/4 (Fall/Winter 2004), pp. 451–64.

Bradford, Ben, 'Who are the "Mixed" ethnic group?' (London: Office for National Statistics, 2006).

Brah, Avtar, *Cartographies of Diaspora* (London: Routledge, 1996).

Brah, Avtar, and Annie E. Coombes (eds), *Hybridity and Its Discontents: Politics, Science, Culture* (London: Routledge, 2000).

Brauner, David, *Post-War Jewish Fiction: Ambivalence, Self-Explanation and Transatlantic Connections* (Basingstoke: Palgrave, 2001).

Brennan, Jonathan (ed.), *Mixed-Race Literature* (Stanford: Stanford University Press, 2002).

Brians, Paul, *Modern South Asian Literature in English* (Westport, CT: Greenwood, 2003).

Bromley, Roger, *Narratives for a New Belonging: Diasporic Cultural Fictions* (Edinburgh: Edinburgh University Press, 2000).

Brown, Judith M., *Global South Asians: Introducing the Modern Diaspora* (Cambridge: Cambridge University Press, 2006).

Brown, Wesley, and Amy Ling (eds), *Visions of America: Personal Narratives from the Promised Land* (New York: Persea Books, 1993).

Bryan, Beverley, 'Homesickness as a construct of the migrant experience', *Changing English* 12.1 (April 2005), pp. 43–52.

Byers-Pevitts, Beverley, 'An interview with Bharati Mukherjee' in Farhat Iftekharuddin, Mary Rohrberger, and Maurice Lee (eds), *Speaking of the Short Story: Interviews with Contemporary Writers* (Jackson: University of Mississippi Press, 1997), pp. 189–98.

Campbell, Joseph, *The Hero with a Thousand Faces* (London: Paladin, 1988 [1949]).

Campbell-Hall, Devon, 'Subversive migrant labour in Monica Ali's *Brick Lane* and Zadie Smith's *White Teeth*' in C. Vijayasree, Meenakshi Mukherjee, Harish Trivedi, and T. Vijay Kumar, *Nation in Imagination: Essays on Nationalism, Sub-Nationalisms and Narration* (Hyderabad: Orient Longman, 2007), pp. 229–37.

Candappa, Rohan, *Picklehead: From Ceylon to Suburbia – A Memoir of Food, Family and Finding Yourself* (London: Ebury Press, 2006).

Carton, Adrian, 'Beyond "Cotton Mary": Anglo-Indian categories and reclaiming the diverse past', *International Journal of Anglo-Indian Studies* 5.1 (2000), http://home.alphalink.com.au/~agilbert/carton.html

Chakrabarti, M. K., 'Marketplace multiculturalism', *Boston Review*, December 2003/January 2004, http://bostonreview.net/BR28.6/chakrabarti.html

Chakraborty, Mridula Nath, '"Will the real South Asian stand up please?": Transference and the writing of "home" in the psychobab(el) of diaspora' in Malashri Lal and Sukrita Paul Kumar, *Interpreting Homes in South Asian Literature* (Delhi: Dorling Kindersley, 2007), pp. 119–42.

Chan, Winnie, 'Curry on the divide in Rudyard Kipling's *Kim* and Gurinder Chadha's *Bend It Like Beckham*', *Ariel* 36.3–4 (July–October 2005), pp. 1–23.

Chandra, G. S. Sharat, *Sari of the Gods* (Minneapolis: Coffee House Press, 1998).

Chang, Gordon H. (ed.), *Asian Americans and Politics: Perspectives, Experiences, Prospects* (Washington, DC: Woodrow Wilson Center Press, 2001).

Chatterjee, Nonda, 'Thoughts on home . . . ' in Sanjukta Dasgupta and Malashri Lal (eds), *The Indian Family in Transition: Reading Literary and Cultural Texts* (New Delhi: Sage, 2007), pp. 309–21.

Chaudhuri, Nupur, 'Shawls, jewelry, curry, and rice in Victorian Britain' in Nupur Chaudhuri and Margaret Strobel (eds), *Western Women and Imperialism: Complicity and Resistance* (Bloomington: Indiana University Press, 1992), pp. 231–46.

Chaudhuri, Nupur, and Margaret Strobel (eds), *Western Women and Imperialism: Complicity and Resistance* (Bloomington: Indiana University Press, 1992).

Chaudhury, Shoma, 'Debutante of the year', *Biblio: A Review of Books* (July–August 1999), p. 19.

Chauhan, Pradyumna S., '"Home" and the construction of new English fiction' in Malashri Lal and Sukrita Paul Kumar (eds), *Interpreting Homes in South Asian Literature* (Delhi: Dorling Kindersley, 2007), pp. 209–20.

Cheung, King-Kok (ed.), *Words Matter: Conversations with Asian American Writers* (Honolulu: University of Hawai'i Press, 2000).

Chhabra, Aseem, 'Shoba beats Jhumpa in writing sweepstakes', *Rediff.com* (May 2001), http://www.shobanarayan.com/newsevents/articles/rediff.htm (web link no longer available).

Choubey, Asha, 'Food metaphor in Jhumpa Lahiri's *Interpreter of Maladies*', in *The Literature and Culture of the Indian Subcontinent (South Asia) in the Postcolonial Web* (2001), http://www.thecore.nus.edu.sg/post/india/literature/choubey1.html (web link no longer available).

Christou, Anastasia, 'Emulating the homeland – engendering the nation: Agency, belonging, identity and gender in second-generation Greek-American return-migrant life stories' in Dennis Conway and Robert B. Potter (eds), *Return Migration of the Next Generations: 21st Century Transnational Mobility* (Farnham: Ashgate, 2009), pp. 101–16.

Chu, Patricia P., 'Asian American narratives of return: Nisei representations of prewar and wartime Japan' in Rocío G. Davis, Jaume Aurell, and Ana Beatriz Delgado (eds), *Ethnic Life Writing and Histories: Genres, Performance, and Culture* (Berlin: LIT, 2007), pp. 204–21.

Collingham, Lizzie, *Curry: A Tale of Cooks and Conquerors* (London: Vintage, 2005).

Colquhoun, Kate, *Taste: The Story of Britain through its Cookery* (London: Bloomsbury, 2007).

Conway, Dennis, and Robert B. Potter (eds), *Return Migration of the Next Generations: 21st Century Transnational Mobility* (Farnham: Ashgate, 2009).

Conway, Dennis, and Robert B. Potter, 'Return of the next generations: Transnational migration and development in the 21st century' in Dennis Conway and Robert B. Potter (eds), *Return Migration of the Next Generations: 21st Century Transnational Mobility* (Farnham: Ashgate, 2009), pp. 1–16.

Cosgrove, Denis, and Stephen Daniels (eds), *The Iconography of Landscape: Essays on the Symbolic Representation, Design and Use of Past Environments* (Cambridge: Cambridge University Press, 1988).

Crane, Ralph J., and Radhika Mohanram (eds), *Shifting Continents/Colliding Cultures: Diaspora Writing of the Indian Subcontinent* (Amsterdam: Rodopi, 2000).

Cutter, Martha J., 'Smuggling across the borders of race, gender, and sexuality' in Jonathan Brennan (ed.), *Mixed-Race Literature* (Stanford: Stanford University Press, 2002), pp. 137–64.

Daley, Simon, with Roshan Hirani, *Cooking with My Indian Mother-in-Law: Mastering the Art of Authentic Home Cooking* (London: Pavilion, 2008).

Daniels, Roger, *Guarding the Golden Door: American Immigration Policy and Immigrants since 1882* (New York: Hill and Wang, 2004).
Dasgupta, Sanjukta, 'Locating "home" in a liminal space: Longing and belonging in the fiction of "Bengali" American women writers' in Malashri Lal and Sukrita Paul Kumar (eds), *Interpreting Homes in South Asian Literature* (Delhi: Dorling Kindersley, 2007), pp. 75–95.
Dasgupta, Sanjukta, and Malashri Lal (eds), *The Indian Family in Transition: Reading Literary and Cultural Texts* (New Delhi: Sage, 2007).
Daswani, Kavita, *For Matrimonial Purposes* (New York: Plume, 2004 [2003]).
Davé, Shilpa, ' "No life without wife": Gender and modern arranged meetings for Indian Americans', *Catamaran* 5 (2006), pp. 53–66.
Davis, Rocío G., 'Everyone's story: Narrative *you* in Chitra Bannerjee [sic] Divakaruni's "The word love" ' in Rocío G. Davis and Sämi Ludwig (eds), *Asian American Literature in the International Context: Readings on Fiction, Poetry, and Performance* (Hamburg: LIT, 2002), pp. 173–83.
Davis, Rocío G., and Sämi Ludwig (eds), *Asian American Literature in the International Context: Readings on Fiction, Poetry, and Performance* (Hamburg: LIT, 2002).
Davis, Rocío G., Jaume Aurell, and Ana Beatriz Delgado (eds), *Ethnic Life Writing and Histories: Genres, Performance, and Culture* (Berlin: LIT, 2007).
Dawson, Ashley, *Mongrel Nation* (Ann Arbor: University of Michigan Press, 2007).
D'Cruz, Glenn, *Midnight's Orphans: Anglo-Indians in Post/Colonial Literature* (Bern: Peter Lang, 2006).
DeLillo, Don, *White Noise* (London: Picador, 1985).
Delman, Carmit, *Burnt Bread and Chutney: Growing Up Between Cultures – A Memoir of an Indian Jewish Girl* (New York: Ballantine, 2002).
Desai, Anita, *Fasting, Feasting* (London: Chatto and Windus, 1999).
Desai, Jigna, *Beyond Bollywood: The Cultural Politics of South Asian Diasporic Film* (New York: Routledge, 2004).
Desforges, Luke, ' "Checking out the planet": Global representations/local identities and youth travel' in Tracey Skelton and Gill Valentine (eds), *Cool Places: Geographies of Youth Cultures* (London: Routledge, 1998), pp. 175–92.
Dhondy, Farrukh, *East End at Your Feet* (Basingstoke: Macmillan, 1976).
Díaz, Junot, *Drown* (London: Faber, 1996).
Díaz, Junot, 'Homecoming, with turtle', *New Yorker*, 14 June 2004, http://www.newyorker.com/archive/2004/06/14/040614fa_fact1
Divakaruni, Chitra, *The Unknown Errors of Our Lives* (London: Abacus, 2001).
Dixon, Wheeler Winston (ed.), *Re-Viewing British Cinema, 1900-1992: Essays and Interviews* (Albany: State University of New York Press, 1994).
Dolley, Christopher (ed.), *The Penguin Book of English Short Stories* (London: Penguin, 1967).
Donadio, Rachel, 'My beautiful London', *New York Times*, 8 August 2008, http://www.nytimes.com/2008/08/10/magazine/10kureishi-t.html
Döring, Tobias, 'Subversion among the vegetables: Food and the guises of culture in Ravinder Randhawa's fiction' in Beate Neumeier (ed.), *Engendering Realism*

and Postmodernism: Contemporary Women Writers in Britain (Amsterdam: Rodopi, 2001), pp. 249–64.

Döring, Tobias, Markus Heide, and Susanne Mühleisen (eds), *Eating Culture: The Poetics and Politics of Food* (Heidelberg: Winter, 2003).

Douglas, Mary, *Purity and Danger: An Analysis of the Concepts of Pollution and Taboo* (London: Routledge, 1966).

DuBois, W. E. B., *The Souls of Black Folk*, eds and intr. Henry Louis Gates and Terri Hume Oliver (New York: W. W. Norton, 1999 [1903]).

Dwyer, Claire, '"Where are you from?": Young British Muslim women and the making of "home"' in Alison Blunt and Cheryl McEwan (eds), *Postcolonial Geographies* (London: Continuum, 2002), pp. 184–99.

Dyer, Richard, *White* (London: Routledge, 1997).

Eakin, Paul John, *Living Autobiographically: How We Create Identity in Narrative* (Ithaca, NY: Cornell University Press, 2008).

Elliott, Emory (ed.), *The Columbia History of the American Novel* (New York: Columbia University Press, 1991).

Fanon, Frantz, *Black Skin, White Masks*, trans. Charles Lam Markmann (New York: Grove Press, 1967 [1952]).

Faymonville, Carmen, 'South Asian American women writers' cultural dialogue with the mythical West' in Rocío G. Davis and Sämi Ludwig (eds), *Asian American Literature in the International Context: Readings on Fiction, Poetry, and Performance* (Hamburg: LIT Verlag, 2002), pp. 247–61.

Feay, Suzi, '*Brick Lane* by Monica Ali: It's one raita short of a spicy literary feast', *Independent on Sunday*, 1 June 2003, http://www.independent.co.uk/arts-entertainment/books/reviews/brick-lane-by-monica-ali-539638.html

Feldman, Karen, 'Indian author weaves family connection with food', *News Press*, 11 June 2003, p. E.1 [sic].

Feng, Pin-chia, 'Immigrant rhapsody: Geographies of memory in Meena Alexander's *Manhattan Music*' in n.a., *Negotiating the Past: An International Conference on Asian British and Asian American Literatures* (Taipei: Academia Sinica, 2003), pp. 1–13.

Fludernik, Monika (ed.), *Diaspora and Multiculturalism: Common Traditions and New Developments* (Amsterdam: Rodopi, 2003).

Fludernik, Monika, 'Imagined communities as imaginary homelands: The South Asian diaspora in fiction' in Monika Fludernik (ed.), *Diaspora and Multiculturalism: Common Traditions and New Developments* (Amsterdam: Rodopi, 2003), pp. 261–85.

Frakes, J. R., Review of *The Tiger's Daughter*, *Washington Post – Book World*, 9 January 1972, p. BW2 [sic].

Friedman, Lester, and Scott Stewart, 'Keeping his own voice: An interview with Stephen Frears' in Wheeler Winston Dixon (ed.), *Re-Viewing British Cinema, 1900-1992: Essays and Interviews* (Albany: State University of New York Press, 1994), pp. 221–40.

Fryer, Peter, *Staying Power: The History of Black People in Britain* (London: Pluto Press, 1984).

Gabriel, Sharmani Patricia, '"Immigrant" or "post-colonial"? Towards a poetics for reading the nation in Bharati Mukherjee's *The Tiger's Daughter*', *Journal of Commonwealth Literature* 39.1 (2004), pp. 85–103.

Gairola, Rahul K., 'Capitalist houses, queer homes: National belonging and transgressive erotics in *My Beautiful Laundrette*', *South Asian Popular Culture* 7.1 (April 2009), pp. 37–54.

Ganesan, Indira, 'Food and the immigrant' in Claudette Chiawei O'Hearn (ed.), *Half and Half: Writers on Growing Up Biracial and Bicultural* (New York: Pantheon, 1998), pp. 170–80.

Ganesan, Indira, *Inheritance* (New York: Alfred A. Knopf, 1998).

Ganguly, Keya, 'Migrant identities: Personal memory and the construction of selfhood', *Cultural Studies* 6.1 (January 1992), pp. 27–50.

Ganguly, Keya, *States of Exception: Everyday Life and Postcolonial Identity* (Minneapolis: University of Minnesota Press, 2001).

Gans, Herbert J., 'Symbolic ethnicity: The future of ethnic groups and cultures in America' in Werner Sollors (ed.), *Theories of Ethnicity: A Classical Reader* (Basingstoke: Macmillan, 1996), pp. 425–59.

George, Rosemary Marangoly, '"At a slight angle to reality": Reading Indian diaspora literature', *MELUS* 21.3 (Autumn 1996), pp. 179–93.

George, Rosemary Marangoly, *The Politics of Home: Postcolonial Relocations and Twentieth-Century Fiction* (Berkeley: University of California Press, 1996).

George, Rosemary Marangoly, 'Of fictional cities and "diasporic" aesthetics', *Antipode* 35.3 (July 2003), pp. 559–79.

Ghazvinizadeh, Susanna, 'E. M. Forster's *A Passage to India* in Jhumpa Lahiri's short story "Interpreter of maladies"', *Atlantic Literary Review* 6.4 (2005), pp. 1–9.

Ghosh, Amitav, *The Shadow Lines* (New Delhi: Ravi Dayal, 2004 [1988]).

Ghosh, Bobby, 'Flavour of the week', *Time Asia*, 7 July 2003, http://www.time.com/time/magazine/article/0,9171,463124,00.html

Gibbons, Luke, *The Quiet Man* (Cork: Cork University Press, 2002).

Giles, Paul, *Transatlantic Insurrections: British Culture and the Formation of American Literature, 1730–1860* (Philadelphia: University of Pennsylvania Press, 2001).

Giles, Paul, *Virtual Americas: Transnational Fictions and the Transatlantic Imaginary* (Durham, NC: Duke University Press, 2002).

Giles, Paul, *Atlantic Republic: The American Tradition in English Literature* (Oxford: Oxford University Press, 2006).

Gillan, Jennifer, '"No one knows you're black!": *Six Degrees of Separation* and the buddy formula', *Cinema Journal* 40.3 (Spring 2001), pp. 47–68.

Gilman, Sander L., *Difference and Pathology: Stereotypes of Sexuality, Race and Madness* (Ithaca, NY: Cornell University Press, 1985).

Gilroy, Paul, *The Black Atlantic: Modernity and Double Consciousness* (London: Verso, 1993).

Gioseffi, Daniela, 'In the mercy of time – flute music: An interview with Meena Alexander', *World Literature Today* (January–February 2006), pp. 46–9.

Goldman, Anne, '"I yam what I yam": Cooking, culture, and colonialism' in

Sidonie Smith and Julia Watson (eds), *De/Colonising the Subject: The Politics of Gender in Women's Autobiography* (Minneapolis: University of Minnesota Press, 1992), pp. 169–95.

Goldman, Marlene, *Paths of Desire: Images of Exploration and Mapping in Canadian Women's Writing* (Toronto: University of Toronto Press, 1997).

Gopinath, Gayatri, *Impossible Desires: Queer Diasporas and South Asian Public Cultures* (Durham, NC: Duke University Press, 2005).

Gordon, Lewis R., *Her Majesty's Other Children: Sketches of Racism from a Neocolonial Age* (Lanham, MD: Rowman & Littlefield, 1997).

Gorra, Michael, *After Empire: Scott, Naipaul, Rushdie* (Chicago: University of Chicago Press, 1997).

Govinden, Niven, *Graffiti My Soul* (Edinburgh: Canongate, 2006).

Green, Martin, *Transatlantic Patterns: Cultural Comparisons of England with America* (New York: Basic Books, 1977).

Grewal, Gurleen, 'Indian-American literature' in Alpana Sharma Knippling (ed.), *New Immigrant Literatures in the United States: A Sourcebook to Our Multicultural Literary Heritage* (London: Greenwood, 1996), pp. 91–108.

Grover, Jan Zita, 'Theory à la mode', *Women's Review of Books* 19.5 (February 2002), pp. 26–8.

Gunew, Sneja, '"Mouthwork": Food and language as the corporeal home for the unhoused diasporic body in South Asian women's writing' in Malashri Lal and Sukrita Paul Kumar (eds), *Interpreting Homes in South Asian Literature* (Delhi: Dorling Kindersley, 2007), pp. 99–109.

Gunning, Dave, and Abigail Ward (eds), *Atlantic Studies* 6.2 (2009), special issue: 'Tracing black America in black British culture'.

Halaby, Leila, 'Return of the native', *Washington Post*, 22 April 2007, http://www.washingtonpost.com/wp-dyn/content/article/2007/04/19/AR2007041903000.html

Hall, Stuart, and Paul du Gay (eds), *Questions of Cultural Identity* (London: Sage, 1996).

Halter, Marilyn, *Shopping for Identity: The Marketing of Ethnicity* (New York: Schocken, 2000).

Hamid, Mohsin, *The Reluctant Fundamentalist* (London: Penguin, 2008 [2007]).

Hancock, Geoff, 'An interview with Bharati Mukherjee', *Canadian Fiction Magazine* 59 (1987), pp. 30–44.

Harley, J. B., 'Maps, knowledge, and power' in Denis Cosgrove and Stephen Daniels (eds), *The Iconography of Landscape: Essays on the Symbolic Representation, Design and Use of Past Environments* (Cambridge: Cambridge University Press, 1988), pp. 277–312.

Harper, Marjory (ed.), *Emigrant Homecomings: The Return Movement of Emigrants, 1600–2000* (Manchester: Manchester University Press, 2005).

Harrison-Kahan, Lori, 'Passing for white, passing for Jewish: Mixed-race identity in Danzy Senna and Rebecca Walker', *MELUS* 30.1 (Spring 2005), pp. 19–48.

Haslam, Mark, 'Queenie: Smudging the distinctions between black and white',

International Journal of Anglo-Indian Studies 4.1 (1999), http://home.alphalink.com.au/~agilbert/queenie.html

Hickman, Mary J., '"Locating" the Irish diaspora', *Irish Journal of Sociology* 11.2 (2002), pp. 8–26.

Hiddleston, Jane, 'Shapes and shadows: (Un)veiling the immigrant in Monica Ali's *Brick Lane*', *Journal of Commonwealth Literature* 40.1 (2005), pp. 57–72.

Hidier, Tanuja Desai, 'Tanuja Desai Hidier on *Born Confused* and *Opal Mehta*' (2006), http://www.desiclub.com/community/culture/culture_article.cfm?id=265

Higson, Andrew (ed.), *Dissolving Views: Key Writings on British Cinema* (London: Cassell, 1996).

Hillenbrand, Margaret, 'Of myths and men: *Better Luck Tomorrow* and the mainstreaming of Asian American cinema', *Cinema Journal* 47.4 (Summer 2008), pp. 50–75.

Hiro, Dilip, *Black British, White British: A History of Race Relations in Britain* (London: Eyre and Spottiswoode, 1971).

Ho, Jennifer Ann, *Consumption and Identity in Asian American Coming-of-Age Novels* (New York: Routledge, 2005).

Hodes, Martha (ed.), *Sex, Love, Race: Crossing Boundaries in North American History* (New York: New York University Press, 1999).

Holden, Stephen, 'American comes of age amidst India's old ways', *New York Times*, 15 September 1993, http://www.nytimes.com/1993/09/15/movies/reviews-film-american-comes-of-age-amid-india-s-old-ways.html?scp=1&sq=%22Praying+with+Anger%22&st=nyt

Hollinger, David A., 'Amalgamation and hypodescent: The question of ethnoracial mixture in the history of the United States', *American Historical Review* 108.5 (December 2003), pp. 1362–90.

Holsey, Bayo, 'Transatlantic dreaming: Slavery, tourism, and diasporic encounters' in Fran Markowitz and Anders H. Stefansson (eds), *Homecomings: Unsettling Paths of Return* (Lanham, MD: Lexington, 2004), pp. 166–82.

hooks, bell, *Yearning: Race, Gender and Cultural Politics* (Boston: South End Press, 1990).

Houston, Velina Hasu, 'To the coloniser goes the spoils: Amerasian progeny in Vietnam war films and owning up to the gaze', *Amerasia* 23.1 (1997), pp. 69–84.

Houston, Velina Hasu, and Teresa Kay Williams, 'Mediating multiracial zones through text and image', *Amerasia* 23.1 (1997), pp. v–xii.

Huggan, Graham, *The Post-Colonial Exotic: Marketing the Margins* (London: Routledge, 2001).

Humes, Karen R., Nicholas A. Jones, and Roberto R. Ramirez, *Overview of Race and Hispanic Origin: 2010* (Washington, DC: US Census Bureau, 2011).

Hussein, Aamer, '*The Impressionist*, by Hari Kunzru', *Independent*, 23 March 2002, http://www.independent.co.uk/arts-entertainment/books/reviews/the-impressionist-by--hari-kunzru--brthe-house-of-blue-mangoes-by-david-davidar-656071.html

Hussein, Aamer, 'A passage from paneer to pecorino', *Independent*, 9 January 2004, http://findarticles.com/p/articles/mi_qn4158/is_20040109/ai_n9683755 (web link no longer available).
Hussein, Aamer, 'A jester among the jihadis', *Independent*, 23 March 2007, http://www.independent.co.uk/arts-entertainment/books/reviews/the-reluctant-fundamentalist-by-mohsin-hamid-441392.html
Hussein, Abdullah, *Émigré Journeys* (London: Serpent's Tail, 2000).
Ifekwunigwe, Jayne O., '(An)Other English city: Multiethnicities, (post)modern moments and strategic identifications', *Ethnicities* 2.3 (2002), pp. 321–48.
Ifekwunigwe, Jayne O., 'Introduction' in Jayne O. Ifekwunigwe (ed.), *'Mixed-Race' Studies: A Reader* (London: Routledge, 2004), pp. 1–29.
Ifekwunigwe, Jayne O., (ed.), *'Mixed-Race' Studies: A Reader* (London: Routledge, 2004).
Iftekharuddin, Farhat, Mary Rohrberger, and Maurice Lee (eds), *Speaking of the Short Story: Interviews with Contemporary Writers* (Jackson: University of Mississippi Press, 1997).
Inglis, David, and Debra Gimlin (eds), *The Globalisation of Food* (Oxford: Berg, 2009).
Innes, C. L., *A History of Black and Asian Writing in Britain, 1700–2000* (Cambridge: Cambridge University Press, 2002).
Islam, Syed Manzurul (Manzu), *The Mapmakers of Spitalfields* (Leeds: Peepal Tree, 2003 [1997]).
Iyer, Nalini, 'American/Indian: Metaphors of the self in Bharati Mukherjee's *The Holder of the World*', *ARIEL* 27.4 (October 1996), pp. 29–44.
Iyer, Sreedhevi, 'Words: *Indian Takeaway: A Very British Story* by Hardeep Singh Kohli', *M/C Reviews*, 19 January 2009, http://reviews.media-culture.org.au/modules.php?name=News&file=article&sid=3556
Jackson, Tina, 'Hardeep Singh Kohli spices up Indian cooking', *Metro*, 21 August 2008, http://www.metro.co.uk/metrolife/276424-hardeep-singh-kohli-spices-up-indian-cooking
Jacobson, Howard, 'No taste like home', *Psychologies*, September 2010, pp. 155–6.
Jacobson, Matthew Frye, *Roots Too: White Ethnic Revival in Post-Civil Rights America* (Cambridge, MA: Harvard University Press, 2006).
Jaggi, Maya, 'Where East is West', *Guardian*, 29 June 1999, online edition (article no longer available).
Jaggi, Maya, 'The soul of a migrant', *Guardian*, 29 April 2000, http://www.guardian.co.uk/print/0,3858,4012797-103425,00.html
Jaggi, Maya, 'Mixtures like candied napalm: Interview with Timothy Mo', *Guardian*, 7 October 2000, http://books.guardian.co.uk/departments/generalfiction/story/0,6000,378414,00.html
Jameson, Fredric, 'Cognitive mapping' in Cary Nelson and Lawrence Grossberg (eds), *Marxism and the Interpretation of Culture* (Basingstoke: Macmillan, 1988), pp. 347–57.
Janette, Michelle, 'Out of the melting pot and into the *Frontera*: Race, sex, nation,

and home in Velina Hasu Houston's "American Dreams"' in Jonathan Brennan (ed.), *Mixed-Race Literature* (Stanford: Stanford University Press, 2002), pp. 88–105.

Jasanoff, Sheila, 'To belong in America . . . Let us count the ways; forget love', *New York Times*, 26 September 1996, p. 26.

Jen, Gish, *Who's Irish?* (New York: Vintage, 1999).

Johnson, Sarah Anne, *Conversations with American Women Writers* (Hanover, NH: University Press of New England, 2004).

Johnston, Trevor, Review of *ABCD*, in *Time Out Film Guide 2005* (London: Time Out Guides, 2004), p. 3.

Jones, Carole, '"An imaginary black family": Jazz, diaspora, and the construction of Scottish Blackness in Jackie Kay's *Trumpet*', *Symbiosis* 8.2 (October 2004), pp. 191–202.

Jussawalla, Feroza, 'South Asian diaspora writers in Britain: "Home" versus "hybridity"' in Geoffrey Kain (ed.), *Ideas of Home: Literature of Asian Migration* (East Lansing: Michigan State University, 1997), pp. 17–37.

Kabeer, Naila, *The Power to Choose: Bangladeshi Women and Labour Market Decisions in London and Dhaka* (London: Verso, 2000).

Kain, Geoffrey (ed.), *Ideas of Home: Literature of Asian Migration* (East Lansing: Michigan State University, 1997).

Kaleta, Kenneth C., *Hanif Kureishi: Postcolonial Storyteller* (Austin: University of Texas Press, 1998).

Kalita, S. Mitra, *Suburban Sahibs: Three Immigrant Families and Their Passage from India to America* (New Brunswick, NJ: Rutgers University Press, 2003).

Kamali, Leila, Review of *Brown Eyes: A Selection of Creative Expressions by Black and Mixed-Race Women*, *Wasafiri* 50 (Spring 2007), pp. 85–7.

Kamani, Ginu, *Junglee Girl* (San Francisco: Aunt Lute Books, 1995).

Katrak, Ketu, 'Colonialism, Imperialism, and Imagined Homes' in Emory Elliott (ed.), *The Columbia History of the American Novel* (New York: Columbia University Press, 1991), pp. 649–78.

Katz, Daniel, *American Modernism's Expatriate Scene: The Labour of Translation* (Edinburgh: Edinburgh University Press, 2007).

Katz, Ilan, *The Construction of Racial Identity in Children of Mixed Parentage* (London: Jessica Kingsley, 1996).

Kaup, Monika, and Debra J. Rosenthal (eds), *Mixing Race, Mixing Culture: Inter-American Literary Dialogues* (Austin: University of Texas Press, 2002).

Khagram, Sanjeev, Manish Desai, and Jason Varughese, 'Seen, rich, but unheard? The politics of Asian Indians in the United States' in Gordon H. Chang (ed.), *Asian Americans and Politics: Perspectives, Experiences, Prospects* (Washington, DC: Woodrow Wilson Center Press, 2001), pp. 258–84.

Khandelwal, Madhulika S., *Becoming American, Being Indian: An Immigrant Community in New York City* (Ithaca, NY: Cornell University Press, 2002).

Khan-Din, Ayub, *East is East* (London: Nick Hern Books, 1997 [1996]).

Khan-Din, Ayub, *Last Dance at Dum Dum* (London: Nick Hern Books, 1999).

Kibria, Nazli, 'Of blood, belonging, and homeland trips: Transnationalism and identity among second-generation Chinese and Korean Americans' in Peggy Levitt and Mary C. Waters (eds), *The Changing Face of Home: The Transnational Lives of the Second Generation* (New York: Russell Sage, 2002), pp. 295–311.

Kim, Daniel Y., *Writing Manhood in Black and Yellow: Ralph Ellison, Frank Chin, and the Literary Politics of Identity* (Stanford: Stanford University Press, 2005).

Kim, Elaine H., 'Defining Asian American realities through literature', *Cultural Critique* 6 (1987), pp. 103–11.

Kim, Nadia Y., 'Finding our way home: Korean Americans, "homeland" trips, and cultural foreignness' in Takeyuki Tsuda (ed.), *Diasporic Homecomings: Ethnic Return Migration in Comparative Perspective* (Stanford: Stanford University Press, 2009), pp. 305–24.

King, Bruce, *The Internationalisation of English Literature* (Oxford: Oxford University Press, 2004).

Kingston, Maxine Hong, 'The novel's next step', *Mother Jones* (December 1989), pp. 37–41.

Kingston, Maxine Hong, *The Fifth Book of Peace* (London: Secker & Warburg, 2003).

Klass, Myleene, 'This much I know', *Observer Magazine*, 27 July 2008, p. 13.

Knippling, Alpana Sharma (ed.), *New Immigrant Literatures in the United States: A Sourcebook to Our Multicultural Literary Heritage* (London: Greenwood, 1996).

Kohli, Hardeep Singh, *Indian Takeaway: A Very British Story* (Edinburgh: Canongate, 2008).

Koshy, Susan, 'South Asians and the complex interstices of whiteness: Negotiating public sentiment in the United States and Britain' in Samina Najmi and Rajini Srikanth (eds), *White Women in Racialised Spaces: Imaginative Transformation and Ethical Action in Literature* (Albany: State University of New York Press, 2002), pp. 29–50.

Koshy, Susan, *Sexual Naturalisation: Asian Americans and Miscegenation* (Stanford: Stanford University Press, 2004).

Kothari, Geeta, 'If you are what you eat, then what am I?', *Kenyon Review* 21 (Winter 1999), pp. 6–14.

Kral, Françoise, 'Shaky ground and new territorialities in *Brick Lane* by Monica Ali and *The Namesake* by Jhumpa Lahiri', *Journal of Postcolonial Writing* 43.1 (April 2007), pp. 65–76.

Kumar, Amitava, *Bombay–London–New York* (New York: Routledge, 2002).

Kundu, Apurba, 'Curry powder' in Nasreen Ali, Virinder S. Kalra, and S. Sayyid (eds), *A Postcolonial People: South Asians in Britain* (London: Hurst, 2006), pp. 72–3.

Kunow, Rüdiger, 'Eating Indian(s): Food, representation, and the Indian diaspora in the United States' in Tobias Döring, Markus Heide, and Susanne Mühleisen (eds), *Eating Culture: The Poetics and Politics of Food* (Heidelberg: Winter, 2003), pp. 151–75.

Kunzru, Hari, '*White Teeth* (2000)', n.d., http://harikunzru.com/whiter-teeth-2000

Kunzru, Hari, *The Impressionist* (London: Penguin, 2002).

Kuortti, Joel, *Writing Imagined Diasporas: South Asian Women Reshaping North American Identity* (Newcastle: Cambridge Scholars, 2007).

Kureishi, Hanif, *The Buddha of Suburbia* (London: Faber, 1990).

Kureishi, Hanif, *Hanif Kureishi: Plays 1* (London: Faber, 1992).

Kureishi, Hanif, *The Black Album* (London: Faber, 1995).

Kureishi, Hanif, *Collected Screenplays, Vol. 1* (London: Faber, 2002).

Kureishi, Hanif, *Dreaming and Scheming: Reflections on Writing and Politics* (London: Faber, 2002).

Kureishi, Hanif, *My Ear at His Heart: Reading My Father* (London: Faber, 2004).

Kushner, Tony, *Angels in America: A Gay Fantasia on National Themes* (New York: Theatre Communications Group, 2003 [1992]).

Lahiri, Jhumpa, 'Indian takeout', *Food and Wine* (April 2000), http://www.foodandwine.com/articles/indian-takeout

Lahiri, Jhumpa, *Interpreter of Maladies* (London: Flamingo, 2000 [1999]).

Lahiri, Jhumpa, 'My intimate alien', *Outlook* (2000), pp. 116–20.

Lahiri, Jhumpa, *The Namesake* (London: Flamingo, 2004 [2003]).

Lahiri, Jhumpa, *Unaccustomed Earth* (New York: Alfred A. Knopf, 2008).

Lal, Brij V., Peter Reeves, and Rajesh Rai (eds), *The Encyclopedia of the Indian Diaspora* (Singapore: Editions Didier Millet, 2006).

Lal, Malashri, and Sukrita Paul Kumar, 'Introduction' in Malashri Lal and Sukrita Paul Kumar (eds), *Interpreting Homes in South Asian Literature* (Delhi: Dorling Kindersley, 2007), pp. viii–xvii.

Lal, Malashri, and Sukrita Paul Kumar (eds), *Interpreting Homes in South Asian Literature* (Delhi: Dorling Kindersley, 2007).

Lalwani, Nikita, *Gifted* (London: Penguin, 2008 [2007]).

Lasdun, James, 'The empire strikes back', *Guardian*, 3 March 2007, http://www.guardian.co.uk/books/2007/mar/03/featuresreviews.guardianreview20

Lau, Lisa, 'Making the difference: The differing presentations and representations of South Asia in the contemporary fiction of home and diasporic South Asian women writers', *Modern Asian Studies* 39.1 (2005), pp. 237–56.

Lau, Lisa, 'Emotional and domestic territories: The positionality of women as reflected in the landscape of home in contemporary South Asian women's writings', *Modern Asian Studies* 40.4 (2006), pp. 1097–116.

Lauretis, Teresa de (ed.), *Feminist Studies/Critical Studies* (Bloomington: Indiana University Press, 1986).

Lea, Daniel, 'Aesthetics and anaesthetics: Anglo-American writers' responses to September 11', *Symbiosis* 11.2 (October 2007), pp. 3–26.

Leader, Zachary (ed.), *On Modern British Fiction* (Oxford: Oxford University Press, 2002).

Lee, Chang-rae, 'Coming home again', *New Yorker*, 16 October 1995, pp. 164–8.

Lee, Helen, 'The ambivalence of return: Second-generation Tongan returnees' in Dennis Conway and Robert B. Potter (eds), *Return Migration of the Next Generations: 21st Century Transnational Mobility* (Farnham: Ashgate, 2009), pp. 41–58.

Lee, Jennifer, and Frank D. Bean, 'Intermarriage and multiracial identification: The Asian American experience and implications for changing colour lines' in Jennifer Lee and Min Zhou (eds), *Asian American Youth: Culture, Identity, and Ethnicity* (New York: Routledge, 2004), pp. 51–63.

Lee, Jennifer, and Min Zhou (eds), *Asian American Youth: Culture, Identity, and Ethnicity* (New York: Routledge, 2004).

Lee, Maurice A. (ed.), *Writers on Writing: The Art of the Short Story* (Westport, CT: Greenwood, 2005).

LeGuin, Ursula K., 'A passage to Canada', *Guardian*, 18 April 2009, p. 11.

Leonard, Karen Isaksen, *Making Ethnic Choices: California's Punjabi Mexican Americans* (Philadelphia: Temple University Press, 1992).

Leonardi, Susan, 'Recipes for reading: Pasta salad, lobster à la Riseholme, and key lime pie', *PMLA* 104 (1989), pp. 340–7.

Levitt, Peggy, 'The ties that change: Relations to the ancestral home over the life cycle' in Peggy Levitt and Mary C. Waters (eds), *The Changing Face of Home: The Transnational Lives of the Second Generation* (New York: Russell Sage, 2002), pp. 123–44.

Levitt, Peggy, and Mary C. Waters (eds), *The Changing Face of Home: The Transnational Lives of the Second Generation* (New York: Russell Sage, 2002).

Lewis, Simon, 'Lahiri's "Interpreter of maladies"', *Explicator* 59.4 (2001), pp. 219–21.

Leypoldt, Günther, *Cultural Authority in the Age of Whitman: A Transatlantic Perspective* (Edinburgh: Edinburgh University Press, 2009).

Lim, Shirley Geok-lin, John Blair Gamber, Stephen Hong Sohn, and Gina Valentino (eds), *Transnational Asian American Literature: Sites and Transits* (Philadelphia: Temple University Press, 2006).

Ling, Jinqi, 'Race, power, and cultural politics in John Okada's *No-No Boy*', *American Literature* 67.2 (June 1995), pp. 359–81.

Lorente, Beatriz P., Nicola Piper, Shen Hsiu-Hua, and Brenda S.A. Yeoh (eds), *Asian Migrations: Sojourning, Displacement, Homecoming and Other Travels* (Singapore: Asia Research Institute, National University of Singapore, 2005).

Low, Gail, 'Separate spheres?: Representing London through women in some recent black British fiction', *Kunapipi* 21.2 (1999), pp. 23–31.

Lowrie, Claire, 'Disruptions, displacements and homecoming: Exploring colonial attitudes to migration and mobility in Australia and Malaya' in Beatriz P. Lorente, Nicola Piper, Shen Hsiu-hua, and Brenda S.A. Yeoh (eds), *Asian Migrations: Sojourning, Displacement, Homecoming and Other Travels* (Singapore: Asia Research Institute, National University of Singapore, 2005), pp. 128–54.

McCabe, Colin, 'Hanif Kureishi on London', *Critical Quarterly* 41.3 (1999), pp. 37–56.

McGilvray, Dennis B., 'Dutch burghers and Portuguese mechanics: Eurasian ethnicity in Sri Lanka', *Comparative Studies in Society and History* 24.2 (April 1982), pp. 235–63.

McKay, Claude, *A Long Way from Home* (New York: Lee Furman, 1969 [1937]).

McLeod, John, *Postcolonial London: Rewriting the Metropolis* (London: Routledge, 2004).

McLoughlin, Seán, 'Writing British Asian cities', *Contemporary South Asia* 17.4 (December 2009), pp. 437–47.

Macpherson, Cluny, and La'avasa Macpherson, '"It was not quite what I had expected": Some Samoan returnees' experiences of Samoa' in Dennis Conway and Robert B. Potter (eds), *Return Migration of the Next Generations: 21st Century Transnational Mobility* (Farnham: Ashgate, 2009), pp. 19–39.

Macpherson, Heidi Slettedahl, *Transatlantic Women's Literature* (Edinburgh: Edinburgh University Press, 2008).

Mahtani, Minelle, 'What's in a name? Exploring the employment of "mixed race" as an identification', *Ethnicities* 2.4 (2002), pp. 469–90.

Mahtani, Minelle, and April Moreno, 'Same difference: Towards a more unified discourse in "mixed race" theory' in David Parker and Miri Song (eds), *Rethinking 'Mixed Race'* (London: Pluto Press, 2001), pp. 65–75.

Maini, Irma, 'The politics of home and food in Jhumpa Lahiri's *Interpreter of Maladies*' in Sanjukta Dasgupta and Malashri Lal (eds), *The Indian Family in Transition: Reading Literary and Cultural Texts* (New Delhi: Sage, 2007), pp. 157–63.

Maira, Sunaina, *Desis in the House: Indian American Youth Culture in New York City* (Philadelphia: Temple University Press, 2002).

Maira, Sunaina, and Rajini Srikanth (eds), *Contours of the Heart: South Asians Map North America* (New York: Asian American Writers' Workshop, 1996).

Majithia, Sheetal, 'Of foreigners and fetishes: A reading of recent South Asian American fiction', *SAMAR* 14 (2001), www.samarmagazine.org/archive/article.php?id=59

Malek, Bilkis, '*Bhaji on the Beach*: South Asian femininity at "home" on the "English" seaside' in David Rogers and John McLeod (eds), *The Revision of Englishness* (Manchester: Manchester University Press, 2004), pp. 121–37.

Malik, Nesrine, 'TV's shorthand for misogyny', *Guardian*, 12 May 2009, http://www.guardian.co.uk/commentisfree/2009/may/12/tv-writers-race-misogyny

Malik, Sarita, 'Beyond "the cinema of duty"? The pleasures of hybridity: Black British film of the 1980s and 1990s' in Andrew Higson (ed.), *Dissolving Views: Key Writings on British Cinema* (London: Cassell, 1996), pp. 202–15.

Malkani, Gautam, Reading of *Londonstani* at London Review Bookshop, London, 8 June 2006.

Malladi, Amulya, *The Mango Season* (London: Piatkus, 2003).

Mandal, Somdatta, 'Oh Calcutta! The new Bengal movement in diasporic Indian English fiction', *Anthropologist* 2 (2007), pp. 9–23.

Mankekar, Purnima, '"India shopping": Indian grocery stores and transnational configurations of belonging' in James L. Watson and Melissa L. Caldwell (eds), *The Cultural Politics of Food and Eating: A Reader* (Malden, MA: Blackwell, 2005), pp. 197–214.

Manning, Susan, and Andrew Taylor, 'Introduction: What is transatlantic literary

studies?' in Susan Manning and Andrew Taylor (eds), *Transatlantic Literary Studies: A Reader* (Edinburgh: Edinburgh University Press, 2007), pp. 1–13.
Manning, Susan, and Andrew Taylor (eds), *Transatlantic Literary Studies: A Reader* (Edinburgh: Edinburgh University Press, 2007).
Mannur, Anita, 'Culinary fictions: Immigrant foodways and race in Indian American literature' in Kent A. Ono (ed.), *Asian American Studies after Critical Mass* (Malden, MA: Blackwell, 2005), pp. 56–70.
Mannur, Anita, *Culinary Fictions: Food in South Asian Diasporic Culture* (Philadelphia: Temple University Press, 2010).
Manzoor, Sarfraz, 'Why do Asian writers have to be "authentic" to succeed?', *Observer*, 30 April 2006, http://www.guardian.co.uk/books/2006/apr/30/1
Manzoor, Sarfraz, *Greetings from Bury Park: Race. Religion. Rock 'n' Roll* (London: Bloomsbury, 2007).
Manzoor, Sarfraz, 'Brits in Bollywood', *Guardian*, 29 May 2008, http://www.guardian.co.uk/film/2008/may/29/india
Manzoor, Sarfraz, 'I get to sit on the fence between cultures', *Guardian*, 8 June 2009, http://www.guardian.co.uk/media/2009/jun/08/aasif-mandvi-tv-daily-show-usa
Markandaya, Kamala, *The Nowhere Man* (New York: John Day, 1972).
Markowitz, Fran, and Anders H. Stefansson (eds), *Homecomings: Unsettling Paths of Return* (Lanham, MD: Lexington, 2004).
Martin, Biddy, and Chandra Talpade Mohanty, 'Feminist politics: What's home got to do with it?' in Teresa de Lauretis (ed.), *Feminist Studies/Critical Studies* (Bloomington: Indiana University Press, 1986), pp. 191–212.
Massa, Ann, and Alistair Stead (eds), *Forked Tongues? Comparing Twentieth-Century British and American Literature* (Harlow: Macmillan, 1994).
Massa, Ann, and Alistair Stead, 'Introduction' in Ann Massa and Alistair Stead (eds), *Forked Tongues? Comparing Twentieth-Century British and American Literature* (Harlow: Macmillan, 1994), pp. 1–14.
Maugham, W. Somerset, 'The force of circumstance' [1926] in Christopher Dolley (ed.), *The Penguin Book of English Short Stories* (London: Penguin, 1967), pp. 129–56.
Maxey, Ruth, '"The messiness of rebirth as an immigrant": Bharati Mukherjee's changing language of migration', *South Asian Review* 26.2 (December 2005), pp. 63–82.
Maxey, Ruth, 'Interview: Meena Alexander', *MELUS* 31.2 (Summer 2006), pp. 21–39.
Maxey, Ruth, '"Life in the diaspora is often held in a strange suspension": First-generation self-fashioning in Hanif Kureishi's narratives of home and return', *Journal of Commonwealth Literature* 41.3 (September 2006), pp. 5–25.
Maxey, Ruth, '"Who wants pale, thin, pink flesh?": Bharati Mukherjee, whiteness, and South Asian American writing', *Textual Practice* 20.3 (September 2006), pp. 529–47.

Maxey, Ruth, 'An interview with Meena Alexander', *Kenyon Review* 28.1 (Winter 2006), pp. 187–94.

Maxey, Ruth, 'Jhumpa Lahiri', *Literary Encyclopedia*, 26 November 2008, www.litencyc.com

Maxey, Ruth, "'Representative' of British Asian fiction? The critical reception of Monica Ali's *Brick Lane*" in Neil Murphy and Wai-chew Sim (eds), *British Asian Fiction: Framing the Contemporary* (Youngstown, NY: Cambria Press, 2008), pp. 217–36.

Maxey, Ruth, 'New American moralities', *Gulf Coast: A Journal of Literature and Fine Arts* 22.2 (Summer/Fall 2010), pp. 272–80.

Maxey, Ruth, "'Beige outlaws': Hanif Kureishi, miscegenation and diasporic experience' in Jonathan P. A. Sell (ed.), *Metaphor and Diaspora in Contemporary Writing* (Basingstoke: Palgrave Macmillan, forthcoming).

May, Brian, 'Memorials to modernity: Postcolonial pilgrimage in Naipaul and Rushdie', *ELH: English Literary History* 68 (May 2001), pp. 241–65.

Mazumdar, Sucheta, 'Race and racism: South Asians in the United States' in Gail M. Nomura, Russell Endo, Stephen H. Sumida, and Russell C. Leong (eds), *Frontiers of Asian American Studies: Writing, Research, and Commentary* (Pullman: Washington State University Press, 1989), pp. 25–38.

Meer, Ameena, *Bombay Talkie* (London: Serpent's Tail, 1994).

Melwani, Lavina, 'Beyond black, white or brown', *Little India*, April 1996, http://www.littleindia.com/archive/april96/color1.htm

Mennell, Stephen, *All Manners of Food: Eating and Taste in England and France from the Middle Ages to the Present* (Urbana: University of Illinois Press, 1996).

Mercer, Kobena, 'Black art and the burden of representation', *Third Text* 10 (Spring 1990), pp. 61–78.

Merck, Mandy (ed.), *America First: Naming the Nation in US Film* (London: Routledge, 2007).

Mijares, Loretta, '"You are an Anglo-Indian?": Eurasians and hybridity and cosmopolitanism in Salman Rushdie's *Midnight's Children*', *Journal of Commonwealth Literature* 38.2 (2003), pp. 125–45.

Mirza, Heidi Safia (ed.), *Black British Feminism: A Reader* (London: Routledge, 1997).

Mishra, Pankaj, 'Enigmas of arrival', *New York Review of Books*, 18 December 2003, pp. 42–4.

Mishra, Vijay, 'The diasporic imaginary: Theorising the Indian diaspora', *Textual Practice* 10.3 (September 1996), pp. 421–47.

Mishra, Vijay, *The Literature of the Indian Diaspora: Theorising the Diasporic Imaginary* (London: Routledge, 2007).

Misir, Deborah N., 'The murder of Navroze Mody: Race, violence, and the search for order' in Min Zhou and James V. Gatewood (eds), *Contemporary Asian America: A Multidisciplinary Reader* (New York: New York University Press, 2000), pp. 501–17.

Mitra, Indrani, '"Luminous Brahmin children must be saved": Imperialist ideologies, "postcolonial" histories in Bharati Mukherjee's *The Tiger's Daughter*' in Deepika Bahri and Mary Vasudeva (eds), *Between the Lines: South Asians and Postcoloniality* (Philadelphia: Temple University Press, 1996), pp. 284–97.

Modood, Tariq, Richard Berthoud, James Nazroo, Satnam Virdee, Jane Lakey, and Sharon Beishon, *Ethnic Minorities in Britain: Diversity and Disadvantage* (London: Policy Studies Institute, 1997).

Mohanti, Prafulla, *Through Brown Eyes* (New Delhi: Penguin, 1989 [1985]).

Moore-Gilbert, Bart, *Hanif Kureishi* (Manchester: Manchester University Press, 2001).

Morley, David, *Home Territories: Media, Mobility and Identity* (London: Routledge, 2000).

Moynihan, Sinéad, 'Ships in motion: Crossing the black and green Atlantics in Joseph O'Connor's *Star of the Sea*', *Symbiosis* 12.1 (April 2008), pp. 41–58.

Moynihan, Sinéad, 'Transnational "tragic mulatto": Phil Lynnott [sic], *The Nephew* and mixed race Irishness', *Internationalist Review of Irish Culture* 1 (2009), pp. 60–77.

Mudge, Alden, 'Lahiri probes the immigrant identity in her first novel', *BookPage* (September 2003), www.bookpage.com/0309bp/jhumpa_lahiri.html (web link no longer available).

Mukherjee, Bharati, *The Tiger's Daughter* (Boston: Houghton Mifflin, 1971).

Mukherjee, Bharati, *Wife* (New York: Ballantine, 1975).

Mukherjee, Bharati, 'An invisible woman', *Saturday Night* (March 1981), pp. 36–40.

Mukherjee, Bharati, *Darkness* (Markham, Ontario: Penguin, 1985).

Mukherjee, Bharati, 'Immigrant writing: Give us your maximalists!', *New York Times Book Review*, 28 August 1988, pp. 1, 28–9.

Mukherjee, Bharati, 'Prophet and loss: Salman Rushdie's migration of souls', *Village Voice Literary Supplement* (March 1989), pp. 9–12.

Mukherjee, Bharati, *Jasmine* (London: Virago, 1989).

Mukherjee, Bharati, *The Middleman and Other Stories* (London: Virago, 1989 [1988]).

Mukherjee, Bharati, *The Holder of the World* (New York: Ballantine, 1993).

Mukherjee, Bharati, 'Love me or leave me' in Wesley Brown and Amy Ling (eds), *Visions of America: Personal Narratives from the Promised Land* (New York: Persea Books, 1993), pp. 187–94.

Mukherjee, Bharati, 'American Dreamer', *Mother Jones* (January/February 1997), pp. 32–5.

Mukherjee, Bharati, *Leave It To Me* (New York: Alfred A. Knopf, 1997).

Mukherjee, Bharati, 'Imagining homelands' in André Aciman (ed.), *Letters of Transit: Reflections on Exile, Identity, Language and Loss* (New York: New York Public Library, 1999), pp. 65–86.

Mukherjee, Bharati, *Desirable Daughters* (New York: Hyperion, 2002).

Mukherjee, Bharati, 'America unbound', keynote lecture delivered to the British Association of American Studies conference, Manchester, 15 April 2004.

Mukherjee, Neel, 'Born in Pakistan, bred in Luton', *Daily Telegraph*, 21 June 2007, http://www.telegraph.co.uk/culture/books/3665973/Born-in-Pakistan-bred-in-Luton.html#

Murphy, Dominic, 'Back to our roots', *Guardian Weekend Magazine*, 29 October 2005, pp. 86–7.
Murphy, Neil, and Wai-chew Sim (eds), *British Asian Fiction: Framing the Contemporary* (Youngstown, NY: Cambria Press, 2008).
Naipaul, V. S., *An Area of Darkness* (New Delhi: Penguin, 1968 [1964]).
Naipaul, V. S., *The Mimic Men* (London: Picador, 2002 [1967]).
Nair, Mira, *Mississippi Masala* (film). New York: Cinecom Pictures, 1991.
Naish, John, 'Hardeep Singh Kohli goes in search of identity', *The Times*, 6 September 2008, http://www.timesonline.co.uk/tol/life_and_style/food_and_drink/article4681954.ece
Najmi, Samina, and Rajini Srikanth (eds), *White Women in Racialised Spaces: Imaginative Transformation and Ethical Action in Literature* (Albany: State University of New York Press, 2002).
Nakashima, Cynthia L., 'Asian American studies through (somewhat) Asian eyes: Integrating "mixed-race" into the Asian American discourse' in Kent A. Ono (ed.), *Asian American Studies after Critical Mass* (Malden, MA: Blackwell, 2005), pp. 111–20.
Narayan, Kirin, *Love, Stars, and All That* (New York: Washington Square Press, 1994).
Narayan, R. K., *A Story-Teller's World: Stories, Essays, Sketches* (New Delhi: Penguin, 1990).
Narayan, Shoba, *Monsoon Diary: Reveries and Recipes from South India* (London: Bantam, 2003).
Narayan, Shyamala A., 'India' [Annual survey of Indian literature], *Journal of Commonwealth Literature* 35.3 (2000), pp. 45–72.
Narayan, Uma, *Dislocating Cultures: Identities, Traditions, and Third World Feminism* (New York: Routledge, 1997).
Nash, Gary B., 'The hidden history of *mestizo* America' in Martha Hodes (ed.), *Sex, Love, Race: Crossing Boundaries in North American History* (New York: New York University Press, 1999), pp. 10–34.
Nash, Philip Tajitsu, 'Will the Census go multiracial?', *Amerasia* 23.1 (1997), pp. 17–27.
Nasta, Susheila, 'Setting up home in a city of words: Sam Selvon's London novels', *Kunapipi* 17.1 (1995), pp. 78–95.
Nasta, Susheila, 'Homes without walls: New voices in South Asian writing in Britain' in Ralph J. Crane and Radhika Mohanram (eds), *Shifting Continents/Colliding Cultures: Diaspora Writing of the Indian Subcontinent* (Amsterdam: Rodopi, 2000), pp. 83–101.
Nasta, Susheila, *Home Truths: Fictions of the South Asian Diaspora in Britain* (Basingstoke: Palgrave, 2002).
Nasta, Susheila, 'Writing a life: Hanif Kureishi and Blake Morrison in conversation', *Wasafiri* 21.2 (July 2006), pp. 19–26.
Negra, Diane (ed.), *The Irish in Us: Irishness, Performativity, and Popular Culture* (Durham, NC: Duke University Press, 2006).

Nelson, Cary, and Lawrence Grossberg (eds), *Marxism and the Interpretation of Culture* (Basingstoke: Macmillan, 1988).

Nelson, Emmanuel S., 'Prafulla Mohanti', in *GLBTQ: An Encyclopedia of Gay, Lesbian, Bisexual, Transgender, and Queer Culture*, n.d., http://www.glbtq.com/literature/south_asian_lit,2.html

Nelson, Emmanuel S. (ed.), *Reworlding: The Literature of the Indian Diaspora* (Westport, CT: Greenwood, 1992).

Neumeier, Beate (ed.), *Engendering Realism and Postmodernism: Contemporary Women Writers in Britain* (Amsterdam: Rodopi, 2001).

Newman, Judie, 'Spaces in-between: Hester Prynne as the Salem Bibi in Bharati Mukherjee's *The Holder of the World*' in Monika Reif-Hülser (ed.), *Borderlands: Negotiating Boundaries in Post-Colonial Writing* (Amsterdam: Rodopi, 1999), pp. 69–87.

Nishime, LeiLani, '"I'm Blackanese": Buddy-cop films, *Rush Hour*, and Asian American and African American cross-racial identification' in Eleanor Ty and Donald C. Goellnicht (eds), *Asian North American Identities: Beyond the Hyphen* (Bloomington: Indiana University Press, 2004), pp. 43–60.

Noblett, Richard, Explanatory notes in Mark Ainley and Richard Noblett, *London is the Place for Me: Trinidadian Calypso in London, 1950–1956* (London: Honest Jon's Records, 2002), n.p.

Nomura, Gail M., Russell Endo, Stephen H. Sumida, and Russell C. Leong (eds), *Frontiers of Asian American Studies: Writing, Research, and Commentary* (Pullman: Washington State University Press, 1989).

Nyman, Jopi, and Pere Gallardo (eds), *Mapping Appetite: Essays on Food, Fiction and Culture* (Newcastle: Cambridge Scholars, 2007).

O'Hearn, Claudette Chiawei (ed.), *Half and Half: Writers on Growing Up Biracial and Bicultural* (New York: Pantheon, 1998).

Oliphant, Catriona, and Ian Willox, 'Ruby Murray: The secret story of curry' (radio programme), BBC Radio 4, 9 April 2010.

Ono, Kent A. (ed.), *Asian American Studies after Critical Mass* (Malden, MA: Blackwell, 2005).

Panayi, Panikos, 'Immigration and food in 20th-century Britain: Exchange and ethnicity', *Journal for the Study of British Cultures* 13.1 (2006), pp. 7–20.

Panayi, Panikos, *Spicing Up Britain: The Multicultural History of British Food* (London: Reaktion, 2008).

Pandey, Geeta, '"Bland" British food goes Indian', *BBC News Online*, 14 June 2007, http://news.bbc.co.uk/go/pr/fr/-/1/hi/world/south_asia/6747981.stm

Paranjape, Makarand, 'Afterword: What about those who stayed back home? Interrogating the privileging of diasporic writing' in Ralph J. Crane and Radhika Mohanram (eds), *Shifting Continents/Colliding Cultures: Diaspora Writing of the Indian Subcontinent* (Amsterdam: Rodopi, 2000), pp. 225–45.

Paranjape, Makarand, 'Writing across boundaries: South Asian diasporas and homelands' in Monika Fludernik (ed.), *Diaspora and Multiculturalism: Common Traditions and New Developments* (Amsterdam: Rodopi, 2003), pp. 231–59.

Parekh, Sameer, *Stealing the Ambassador* (New York: Simon & Schuster, 2002).
Parker, David, and Miri Song (eds), *Rethinking 'Mixed Race'* (London: Pluto Press, 2001).
Patel, Krutin, Faran Tahir, and Aasif Mandvi, 'Audio commentary', DVD of *ABCD* (n.p.: Wellspring Media, 2004).
Patel, Nilesh, *A Love Supreme* (film). London: Production company unknown, 2001.
Patterson, John, 'I've had such a blast', *Guardian*, 9 March 2009, http://www.guardian.co.uk/culture/2009/mar/09/parminder-nagra
Pérez-Torres, Rafael, 'Chicano ethnicity, cultural hybridity, and the *mestizo* voice' in Monika Kaup and Debra J. Rosenthal (eds), *Mixing Race, Mixing Culture: Inter-American Literary Dialogues* (Austin: University of Texas Press, 2002), pp. 163–84.
Phillips, Richard, *Mapping Men and Empire: A Geography of Adventure* (London: Routledge, 1997).
Phoenix, Ann, and Charlie Owen, 'From miscegenation to hybridity: Mixed relationships and mixed parentage in profile' in Avtar Brah and Annie E. Coombes (eds), *Hybridity and Its Discontents: Politics, Science, Culture* (London: Routledge, 2000), pp. 72–95.
Potter, Robert B., and Joan Phillips, 'Bajan-Brit second-generation return migration: " . . . Where am I supposed to be – in *mid-air*?!"' in Dennis Conway and Robert B. Potter (eds), *Return Migration of the Next Generations: 21st Century Transnational Mobility* (Farnham: Ashgate, 2009), pp. 79–99.
Prashad, Vijay, *The Karma of Brown Folk* (Minneapolis: University of Minnesota Press, 2000).
Prashad, Vijay, 'How the Hindus became Jews: American racism after 9/11', *South Atlantic Quarterly* 104.3 (Summer 2005), pp. 583–606.
Procter, James, *Dwelling Places: Postwar Black British Writing* (Manchester: Manchester University Press, 2003).
Procter, James, 'Nadeem Aslam', *British Council: Contemporary Writers*, 2008, http://www.contemporarywriters.com/authors/?p=auth519d19600c41d29afotixlc2ab2b
Purkayastha, Bandana, *Negotiating Ethnicity: Second-Generation South Asian Americans Traverse a Transnational World* (New Brunswick, NJ: Rutgers University Press, 2005).
Rai, Saritha, 'Indians find they can go home again', *New York Times*, 26 December 2005, http://www.nytimes.com/2005/12/26/business/worldbusiness/26recruit.html
Rains, Stephanie, 'Irish roots: Genealogy and the performance of Irishness', in Diane Negra (ed.), *The Irish in Us: Irishness, Performativity, and Popular Culture* (Durham, NC: Duke University Press, 2006), pp. 130–60.
Rajan, Gita, 'Ethical responsibility in intersubjective spaces: Reading Jhumpa Lahiri's *Interpreter of Maladies* and "A Temporary Matter"' in Shirley Geok-lin Lim, John Blair Gamber, Stephen Hong Sohn, and Gina Valentino (eds), *Transnational Asian American Literature: Sites and Transits* (Philadelphia: Temple University Press, 2006), pp. 123–41.

Ramesh, Randeep, 'Mid-life Kureishi', *Independent on Sunday*, 3 May 1998, http://www.independent.co.uk/life-style/interview-hanif-kureishi--midlife-kureishi-1161701.html

Ranasinha, Ruvani, *Hanif Kureishi* (Plymouth: Northcote House, 2002).

Ranasinha, Ruvani, *South Asian Writers in Twentieth-Century Britain* (Oxford: Clarendon Press, 2007).

Ravichandran, T., 'Entrapments at home and abroad in Anita Desai's *Fasting, Feasting*', *Indian Journal of English Studies* 40 (2002–3), pp. 115–24.

Ray, Krishnendu, 'Meals, migration, and modernity: Domestic cooking and Bengali ethnicity in the United States', *Amerasia Journal* 24.1 (1998), pp. 105–27.

Ray, Krishnendu, *The Migrant's Table: Meals and Memories in Bengali-American Households* (Philadelphia: Temple University Press, 2004).

Ray, Krishnendu, 'Ethnic succession: A review essay', *Food, Culture and Society* 8.1 (Spring 2005), pp. 124–31.

Ray, Krishnendu, 'Exotic restaurants and expatriate home cooking: Indian food in Manhattan' in David Inglis and Debra Gimlin (eds), *The Globalisation of Food* (Oxford: Berg, 2009), pp. 213–26.

Rayner, Jay, 'Cooking with mother', *Observer*, 27 May 2007, http://www.guardian.co.uk/lifeandstyle/2007/may/27/foodanddrink.features16?INTCMP=SRCH

Reeves, Terrance J., and Claudette E. Bennett, *We the People: Asians in the United States* (Washington, DC: US Census Bureau, 2004).

Reif-Hülser, Monika (ed.), *Borderlands: Negotiating Boundaries in Post-Colonial Writing* (Amsterdam: Rodopi, 1999).

Rice, Alan, *Radical Narratives of the Black Atlantic* (London: Continuum, 2003).

Rich, Paul, 'The "half-caste" pathology' in Jayne O. Ifekwunigwe (ed.), *'Mixed-Race' Studies: A Reader* (London: Routledge, 2004), pp. 73–9.

Robertson, George, Melinda Mash, Lisa Tickner, Jon Bird, Barry Curtis, and Tim Putnam (eds), *Travellers' Tales: Narratives of Home and Displacement* (London: Routledge, 1994).

Rody, Caroline, *The Interethnic Imagination: Roots and Passages in Contemporary Asian American Fiction* (Oxford: Oxford University Press, 2009).

Rogers, David, and John McLeod (eds), *The Revision of Englishness* (Manchester: Manchester University Press, 2004).

Rogobete, Daniela, 'Sweet taste of India: Food metaphors in contemporary Indian fiction in English' in Jopi Nyman and Pere Gallardo (eds), *Mapping Appetite: Essays on Food, Fiction and Culture* (Newcastle: Cambridge Scholars, 2007), pp. 28–51.

Root, Maria P. P. (ed.), *The Multiracial Experience: Racial Borders as the New Frontier* (Thousand Oaks, CA: Sage, 1996).

Root, Maria P. P., 'Multiracial Asians: Models of ethnic identity', *Amerasia* 23.1 (1997), pp. 29–41.

Ropp, Steven Masami, 'Do multiracial subjects really challenge race? Mixed-race Asians in the United States and the Caribbean', *Amerasia* 23.1 (1997), pp. 1–16.

Roth, Philip, *Portnoy's Complaint* (London: Vintage, 1999 [1969]).

Roth, Philip, *The Plot Against America* (London: Vintage, 2005 [2004]).
Roy, Parama, 'Reading communities and culinary communities: The gastropoetics of the South Asian diaspora', *positions: east asia cultures critique* 10.2 (Fall 2002), pp. 471–502.
Roy, Sandip, 'The smells of home', in Sunaina Maira and Rajini Srikanth (eds), *Contours of the Heart: South Asians Map North America* (New York: Asian American Writers' Workshop, 1996), pp. 319–25.
Ruppel, F. Timothy, '"Re-inventing ourselves a million times": Narrative, desire, identity, and Bharati Mukherjee's *Jasmine*', *College Literature* 22.1 (1995), pp. 181–92.
Rushdie, Salman, *Imaginary Homelands: Essays and Criticism 1981–1991* (London: Granta, 1991).
Rushdie, Salman, *The Wizard of Oz* (London: British Film Institute, 1992).
Rushdie, Salman, *The Satanic Verses* (London: Vintage, 1998 [1988]).
Rustomji-Kerns, Roshni, 'Expatriates, immigrants and literature: Three South Asian women writers', *Massachusetts Review* 29.4 (1988), pp. 655–65.
Saadi, Suhayl, *The Burning Mirror* (Edinburgh: Polygon, 2001).
Saadi, Suhayl, 'Psychoraag: The gods of the door', *Spike Magazine*, February 2006, http://spikemagazine.com/0206-suhayl-saadi-censorship-in-the-uk.php
Saadi, Suhayl, 'Born in the UK', *New Statesman*, 21 May 2007, http://www.newstatesman.com/200705210050
Salgado, Minoli, 'An interview with Kirin Narayan' in Farhat Iftekharuddin, Mary Rohrberger, and Maurice Lee (eds), *Speaking of the Short Story: Interviews with Contemporary Writers* (Jackson: University of Mississippi Press, 1997), pp. 219–227.
Salgado, Minoli, 'Writing home' in Maurice A. Lee (ed.), *Writers on Writing: The Art of the Short Story* (Westport, CT: Greenwood, 2005), pp. 27–31.
Salih, Tayeb, *Season of Migration to the North*, trans. Denys Johnson-Davies (London: Penguin, 1969).
Sandhu, Sukhdev, 'Come hungry, leave edgy', *London Review of Books*, 9 October 2003, pp. 10–13.
Sandhu, Sukhdev, *London Calling: How Black and Asian Writers Examined a City* (London: HarperCollins, 2003).
Sandhu, Sukhdev, 'Life lines', *Daily Telegraph*, 28 August 2004, http://www.telegraph.co.uk/arts/main.jhtml;jsessionid=3OXLVM1QTIAVVQFIQMFSFGGAVCBQ0IV0?xml=/arts/2004/08/28/bokur28.xml&page=2 (web link no longer available).
Sandhu, Sukhdev, '*A Love Supreme* and *Dim Sum*', *Gastronomica* 4.1 (Winter 2004), pp. 96–7.
Santa Ana, Jeffrey J., 'Affect-identity: The emotions of assimilation, multiraciality, and Asian American subjectivity' in Eleanor Ty and Donald C. Goellnicht (eds), *Asian North American Identities: Beyond the Hyphen* (Bloomington: Indiana University Press, 2004), pp. 15–42.
Sarup, Madan, 'Home and identity' in George Robertson, Melinda Mash, Lisa Tickner, Jon Bird, Barry Curtis, and Tim Putnam (eds), *Travellers'*

Tales: Narratives of Home and Displacement (London: Routledge, 1994), pp. 93–104.

Sasser, Kim, 'Solidarity through difference: Rushdie's anti-example in *The Jaguar Smile*', *Symbiosis* 13.1 (April 2009), pp. 61–80.

Schulze-Engler, Frank, and Sissy Helff (eds), *Transcultural English Studies: Theories, Fictions, Realities* (Amsterdam: Rodopi, 2009).

Scott-Clark, Cathy, and Adrian Levy, 'Why Molly ran', *Guardian*, 23 June 2007, http://www.guardian.co.uk/world/2007/jun/23/pakistan.familyandrelationships

Sell, Jonathan P. A. (ed.), *Metaphor and Diaspora in Contemporary Writing* (Basingstoke: Palgrave Macmillan, forthcoming).

Senna, Danzy, *Caucasia* (New York: Riverhead, 1998).

Senna, Danzy, 'The mulatto millennium' in Claudette Chiawei O'Hearn (ed.), *Half and Half: Writers on Growing Up Biracial and Bicultural* (New York: Pantheon, 1998), pp. 12–27.

Shah, Deepa, 'Hooray for Bollywood', *Observer*, 24 March 2002, www.guardian.co.uk/film/2002/mar/24/bollywood.features/print

Shakespeare, Nicholas, *In Tasmania: Adventures at the End of the World* (London: Vintage, 2005).

Shamsie, Muneeza, '*The Reluctant Fundamentalist*', *Literary Encyclopedia*, 21 May 2009, www.litencyc.com

Shankar, Lavina Dhingra, and Rajini Srikanth (eds), *A Part, Yet Apart: South Asians in Asian America* (Philadelphia: Temple University Press, 1998).

Sheikh, Farhana, *The Red Box* (London: Women's Press, 1991).

Shukla, Sandhya, *India Abroad: Diasporic Cultures of Postwar America and England* (Princeton, NJ: Princeton University Press, 2003).

Shyamalan, M. Night, *Praying with Anger* (film). n.p.: Crescent Moon Pictures, 1992.

Sidhwa, Bapsi, *The Crow Eaters* (Glasgow: Fontana, 1982 [1978]).

Sidhwa, Bapsi, *An American Brat* (Minneapolis: Milkweed, 2006 [1994]).

Singer, Elyse, 'Hanif Kureishi: A Londoner, but not a Brit' in Melissa E. Biggs (ed.), *In the Vernacular: Interviews at Yale with Sculptors of Culture* (Jefferson, NC: McFarland, 1991), pp. 103–9.

Singh, Kirpal, 'Writing tough – staying honest: Challenges for a writer in Singapore' in Maurice A. Lee (ed.), *Writers on Writing: The Art of the Short Story* (Westport, CT: Greenwood, 2005), pp. 85–90.

Skelton, Tracey, and Gill Valentine (eds), *Cool Places: Geographies of Youth Cultures* (London: Routledge, 1998).

Smith, Sidonie, and Julia Watson (eds), *De/Colonising the Subject: The Politics of Gender in Women's Autobiography* (Minneapolis: University of Minnesota Press, 1992).

Sollors, Werner (ed.), *Theories of Ethnicity: A Classical Reader* (Basingstoke: Macmillan, 1996).

Sollors, Werner, *Neither Black nor White yet Both: Thematic Explorations of Interracial Literature* (New York: Oxford University Press, 1997).

Sollors, Werner, 'Can rabbits have interracial sex?' in Monika Kaup and Debra

J. Rosenthal (eds), *Mixing Race, Mixing Culture: Inter-American Literary Dialogues* (Austin: University of Texas Press, 2002), pp. 3–22.

Spickard, Paul R., 'What must I be? Asian Americans and the question of multi-ethnic identity', *Amerasia* 23.1 (1997), pp. 43–60.

Srikanth, Rajini, *The World Next Door: South Asian American Literature and the Idea of America* (Philadelphia: Temple University Press, 2004).

Srivastava, Atima, *Looking for Maya* (London: Quartet, 1999).

Stefansson, Anders H., 'Homecomings to the future: From diasporic mythographies to social projects of return' in Fran Markowitz and Anders H. Stefansson (eds), *Homecomings: Unsettling Paths of Return* (Lanham, MD: Lexington, 2004), pp. 2–20.

Stein, Mark, 'Curry at work: Nibbling at the jewel in the crown' in Tobias Döring, Markus Heide, and Susanne Mühleisen (eds), *Eating Culture: The Poetics and Politics of Food* (Heidelberg: Winter, 2003), pp. 133–49.

Stein, Mark, *Black British Literature: Novels of Transformation* (Columbus: Ohio State University Press, 2004).

Steinberg, Stephen, *The Ethnic Myth: Race, Ethnicity, and Class in America* (Boston: Beacon Press, 2001).

Subramanyam, Arundhati, Review of *Bombay Talkie*, *Sawnet: The South Asian Women's NETwork*, 16 February 2009, http://www.sawnet.org/books/reviews.php?Bombay+Talkie

Sui Sin Far, *Mrs Spring Fragrance and Other Writings*, eds and intr. Amy Ling and Annette White-Parks (Urbana: University of Illinois Press, 1995).

Suleiman, Susan Rubin, *Authoritarian Fictions: The Ideological Novel as a Literary Genre* (New York: Columbia University Press, 1983).

Suroor, Hasan, 'Chris Patten coming to woo students to Oxford', *Hindu*, 15 February 2006, http://www.hindu.com/2006/02/15/stories/2006021503611300.htm

Syal, Meera, *Anita and Me* (London: Flamingo, 1997 [1996]).

Tabios, Eileen, *Black Lightning: Poetry-in-Progress* (New York: Asian American Writers Workshop, 1998).

Takaki, Ronald, *Strangers from Another Shore: A History of Asian Americans* (Boston: Little, Brown, 1989).

Tan, Amy, *The Joy Luck Club* (London: Vintage, 1998 [1989]).

Tayler, Christopher, 'Change and loss', *Guardian*, 21 June 2008, http://www.guardian.co.uk/books/2008/jun/21/saturdayreviewsfeatures.guardianreview5

Tettenborn, Eva, 'Jhumpa Lahiri's *Interpreter of Maladies*: Colonial fantasies in "Sexy"', *Notes on Contemporary Literature* 32.4 (2002), pp. 11–12.

Thieme, John, and Ira Raja, 'Introduction' in John Thieme and Ira Raja (eds), *The Table is Laid: The Oxford Anthology of South Asian Food Writing* (Oxford: Oxford University Press, 2007), pp. xvii–lv.

Thieme, John, and Ira Raja (eds), *The Table is Laid: The Oxford Anthology of South Asian Food Writing* (Oxford: Oxford University Press, 2007).

Thomas, Susie, *Hanif Kureishi: A Reader's Guide to Essential Criticism* (Basingstoke: Palgrave, 2005).

Treacher, Amal, 'Welcome home: Between two cultures and two colours' in Avtar Brah and Annie E. Coombes (eds), *Hybridity and Its Discontents: Politics, Science, Culture* (London: Routledge, 2000), pp. 96–107.

Tsuda, Takeyuki, 'When home is not the homeland: The case of Japanese Brazilian ethnic return migration' in Fran Markowitz and Anders H. Stefansson (eds), *Homecomings: Unsettling Paths of Return* (Lanham, MD: Lexington, 2004), pp. 125–45.

Tsuda, Takeyuki (ed.), *Diasporic Homecomings: Ethnic Return Migration in Comparative Perspective* (Stanford: Stanford University Press, 2009).

Tsuda, Takeyuki, 'Global inequities and diasporic return: Japanese American and Brazilian encounters with the ethnic homeland' in Takeyuki Tsuda (ed.), *Diasporic Homecomings: Ethnic Return Migration in Comparative Perspective* (Stanford: Stanford University Press, 2009), pp. 227–59.

Tsuda, Takeyuki, 'Introduction' in Takeyuki Tsuda (ed.), *Diasporic Homecomings: Ethnic Return Migration in Comparative Perspective* (Stanford: Stanford University Press, 2009), pp. 1–18.

Ty, Eleanor, and Donald C. Goellnicht (eds), *Asian North American Identities: Beyond the Hyphen* (Bloomington: Indiana University Press, 2004).

Upstone, Sara, *British Asian Fiction: Twenty-First-Century Voices* (Manchester: Manchester University Press, 2010).

Vaidyanathan, Siva, 'Inside a "model minority": The complicated identity of South Asians', *Chronicle of Higher Education*, 23 June 2000, http://chronicle.com/free/v46/i42/42b00401.htm

Vakil, Ardashir, *One Day* (London: Penguin, 2003).

Varvogli, Aliki, '"Underwhelmed to the maximum": American travellers in Dave Eggers's *You Shall Know Our Velocity* and Jonathan Safran Foer's *Everything is Illuminated*', *Atlantic Studies* 3.1 (April 2006), pp. 83–95.

Vignisson, Runar, 'Bharati Mukherjee: An interview', *SPAN: Journal of the South Pacific Association for Commonwealth Literature and Language Studies* 34–5 (November 1992–May 1993), pp. 153–68.

Vijayaraghavan, Vineeta, *Motherland* (New York: Soho Press, 2001).

Vijayasree, C., Meenakshi Mukherjee, Harish Trivedi, and T. Vijay Kumar (eds), *Nation in Imagination: Essays on Nationalism, Sub-Nationalisms and Narration* (Hyderabad: Orient Longman, 2007).

Visram, Rozina, *Ayahs, Lascars and Princes: Indians in Britain 1700–1947* (London: Pluto Press, 1986).

Visram, Rozina, *Asians in Britain: 400 Years of History* (London: Pluto Press, 2002).

Vogt-William, Christine, 'Routes to the roots: Transcultural ramifications in *Bombay Talkie*' in Frank Schulze-Engler and Sissy Helff (eds), *Transcultural English Studies: Theories, Fictions, Realities* (Amsterdam: Rodopi, 2009), pp. 309–22.

Wagner, Tamara S., 'Boutique multiculturalism and the consumption of repulsion: Re-disseminating food fictions in Malaysian and Singaporean diasporic novels', *Journal of Commonwealth Literature* 42.1 (2007), pp. 31–46.

Watson, James L., and Melissa L. Caldwell (eds), *The Cultural Politics of Food and Eating: A Reader* (Malden, MA: Blackwell, 2005).

Weedon, Chris, *Identity and Culture: Narratives of Difference and Belonging* (Maidenhead: Open University Press, 2004).

Weisbuch, Robert, 'Cultural time in England and America' in Susan Manning and Andrew Taylor (eds), *Transatlantic Literary Studies: A Reader* (Edinburgh: Edinburgh University Press, 2007), pp. 97–104.

Williams, Daniel, *Ethnicity and Cultural Authority: From Arnold to DuBois* (Edinburgh: Edinburgh University Press, 2006).

Williams, Laura Anh, 'Foodways and subjectivity in Jhumpa Lahiri's *Interpreter of Maladies*', *MELUS* 32.4 (Winter 2007), pp. 69–79.

Wilson, Anne, '"Mixed race" children in British society: Some theoretical considerations', *British Journal of Sociology* 35.1 (March 1984), pp. 42–61.

Wong, Mitali P., and Zia Hassan, *The Fiction of South Asians in North America and the Caribbean: A Critical Study of English-Language Works since 1950* (Jefferson, NC: McFarland, 2004).

Wong, Sau-ling Cynthia, *Reading Asian American Literature: From Necessity to Extravagance* (Princeton, NJ: Princeton University Press, 1993).

Wood, Michael, 'Enigmas and homelands' in Zachary Leader (ed.), *On Modern British Fiction* (Oxford: Oxford University Press, 2002), pp. 77–92.

Wood, Nick, *Goodness Gracious Me* (TV comedy series). London: BBC, 1998.

Woolcock, Penny, *Mischief Night* (film). London: Company Pictures, 2006.

Wu, Frank H., *Yellow: Race in America Beyond Black and White* (New York: Basic Books, 2002).

Wurgaft, Benjamin Aldes, 'Incensed: Food smells and ethnic tension', *Gastronomica* 6.2 (Spring 2006), pp. 57–60.

Xu, Wenying, *Eating Identities: Reading Food in Asian American Literature* (Honolulu: University of Hawai'i Press, 2008).

Yamanaka, Lois-Ann, *Wild Meat and the Bully Burgers* (London: Minerva, 1996).

Yaqin, Amina, 'Mohsin Hamid in conversation', *Wasafiri* 54 (Summer 2008), pp. 44–9.

Yu, Henry, 'Mixing bodies and cultures: The meaning of America's fascination with sex between "Orientals" and "whites"' in Martha Hodes (ed.), *Sex, Love, Race: Crossing Boundaries in North American History* (New York: New York University Press, 1999), pp. 444–63.

Yule, Henry, and A. C. Burnell, *Hobson-Jobson: The Anglo-Indian Dictionary* (Ware: Wordsworth, 1996 [1886]).

Yuval-Davis, Nira, *Gender and Nation* (London: Sage, 1997).

Zack, Naomi (ed.), *American Mixed-Race: The Culture of Microdiversity* (Lanham, MD: Rowman and Littlefield, 1995).

Zack, Naomi, 'On being and not-being black and Jewish' in Maria P.P. Root (ed.), *The Multiracial Experience: Racial Borders as the New Frontier* (Thousand Oaks, CA: Sage, 1996), pp. 140–51.

Zare, Bonnie, 'Evolving masculinities in recent stories by South Asian American women', *Journal of Commonwealth Literature* 42.3 (2007), pp. 99–111.
Zhou, Min, and James V. Gatewood (eds), *Contemporary Asian America: A Multidisciplinary Reader* (New York: New York University Press, 2000).
Zlotnick, Susan, 'Domesticating imperialism: Curry and cookbooks in Victorian England', *Frontiers: A Journal of Women Studies* 16.2/3 (1996), pp. 51–68.

INDEX